REPUBLICA ARGENTINA
DIRECCION
NACIONAL DE MIGRACIONES
13 NOV 2000

IMMIGRATION
30 NOV 2000
FALKLAND ISLANDS

ARTMENT OF IMMIGRATION
PERMITTED TO ENTER
AUSTRALIA
24 APR 1996
on
For stay of 12 Month
SYDNEY AIRPORT 54

IMMIGRATION DIVISION BANGKOK THAILAND
A
72
DEPARTED
EXIT
- 6 FEB 1998
SIGNED

IMMIGRATION & ETHNIC AFFAIRS
.... Person
30 OCT 1999
DEPARTED
AUSTRALIA
SYDNEY 32

T R A V E L E R ' S
ARGENTINA
C O M P A N I O N

中华人民共和国
广东省公安厅

上陸許可
ADMITTED
15. FEB. 1996
Status: 4-1-   4
Duration: 90 days
NARITA(N)
Immigration Inspector
日本国

ADMITTED
20 OCT. 1998
Status: 4-1-16
Duration   180 da
Port: HANEDA
Signature

№ 011278

THE UNITED STATES
OF AMERICA
NONIMMIGRANT VISA
ISSUED AT
...SED
Air Port

U.S. IMMIGRATION
170 HHW 1710
JUL 20 1998

HONG KONG
(1038)
- 7 JUN 1997
IMMIGRATION
OFFICER

The 2001–2002 Traveler's Companions
ARGENTINA • AUSTRALIA • BALI • CALIFORNIA • CANADA • CHILE • CHINA •
COSTA RICA • CUBA • EASTERN CANADA • ECUADOR • FLORIDA • HAWAII •
HONG KONG • INDIA • INDONESIA • IRELAND • JAPAN • KENYA •
MALAYSIA & SINGAPORE • MEDITERRANEAN FRANCE • MEXICO • NEPAL •
NEW ENGLAND • NEW ZEALAND • NORTHERN ITALY • PERU • PHILIPPINES •
PORTUGAL • RUSSIA • SOUTH AFRICA • SOUTHERN ENGLAND • SPAIN • THAILAND •
TURKEY • VENEZUELA • VIETNAM, LAOS AND CAMBODIA • WESTERN CANADA

Traveler's ARGENTINA Companion

First published 2001
The Globe Pequot Press
246 Goose Lane, PO Box 480
Guilford, CT 06437 USA
www.globe-pequot.com

© 2001 by The Globe Pequot Press, Guilford CT, USA

ISBN: 0-7627-0354-7

Distributed in the European Union by
World Leisure Marketing Ltd, Unit 11
Newmarket Court, Newmarket Drive,
Derby, DE24 8NW, United Kingdom
www.map-guides.com

Created, edited and produced by
Allan Amsel Publishing, 53, rue Beaudouin
27700 Les Andelys, France.
E-mail: Allan.Amsel@wanadoo.fr
Editor in Chief: Allan Amsel
Editor: Anne Trager
Original design concept: Hon Bing-wah
Picture editor and designer: David Henry

Printed by Samwha Printing Co. Ltd., Seoul, South Korea

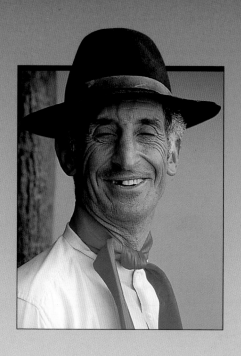

TRAVELER'S
ARGENTINA
COMPANION

by Joe Yogerst and Maribeth Mellin

photographed by Robert Holmes

The Globe Pequot Press

GUILFORD
CONNECTICUT

Contents

TRAVELER'S ARGENTINA COMPANION

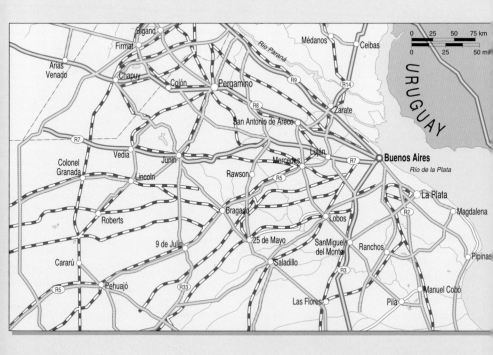

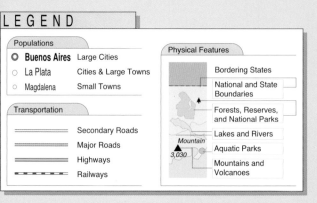

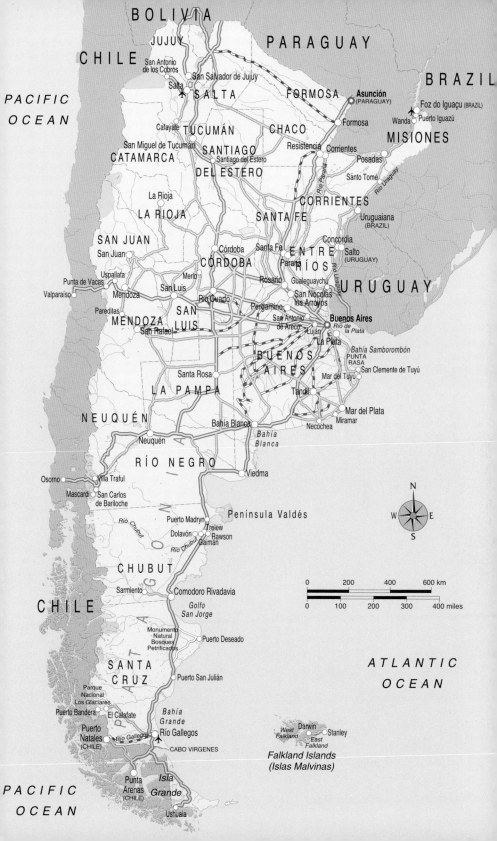

TOP SPOTS

Ascend the Andes

THE ROAD SEEMS TO CLIMB INTO THE CLOUDS, a rough gravel track that zigzags across the face of a rust-colored slope. The sort of route that isn't for the faint of heart or anyone with even the slightest vertigo — the drop off the edge is several thousand meters. But what a view! All around are jagged, snow-covered peaks, the very highest of the High Andes, the tallest mountains in the western hemisphere. A panorama of stone, ice and deep blue sky usually reserved for condors and the most intrepid climbers.

Like an old mule, our truck groans with every bump in the road. Half an hour later we reach the crest of La Cumbre Pass. We are met by a bronze statue of Cristo Redentor (Christ the Redeemer) erected in 1902 to mark the end of a border dispute between Chile and Argentina. There was no road then, only a llama and donkey path. But it saw plenty of movement. The Conquistadors came this way when they pioneered the western Pampas from the Pacific Coast. Three hundred years later, General San Martín marched his vaunted Army of the Andes in the opposite direction to liberate Chile from the Spanish. Charles Darwin also clambered up and over La Cumbre Pass during a detour from his voyage around the world on HMS *Beagle*.

The Pan-American Highway was chiseled through the pass in 1929; for more than half a century this was the only means of driving between Buenos Aires and Santiago without diverting nearly a thousand miles north or south. The old road became obsolete almost overnight when the 1,350-m (4,500-ft) Redentor Tunnel opened in 1980. Nowadays the only way to reach La Cumbre and Cristo Redentor is from the Argentine side, via the serpentine road we'd just climbed.

Perched at 4,000 m (13,000 ft) and pounded by constant wind, the pass is a high-altitude desert, a bleak and stony place devoid of all but the most meager vegetation. But it's hard to beat the view: a vast tableau of stone and ice wrapped in wispy clouds. The kind of vista that literally takes your breath away.

The wind finally drives me into the ruins of an old hotel on the Chilean side of the border. Snow has tumbled in through the open windows and the walls are black with soot from campfires stoked by long-gone trekkers and climbers. Eventually I amble back to the Argentine side, where I take refuge in a stone-walled café. The proprietor sports a bushy mustache, his skin shriveled like an Inca mummy after so many years in the Andes. He smiles, and offers me hot coffee with a touch of cognac. "Perfect for the cold," he assures me. And also perfect for calming jittery nerves on the roller-coaster drive back down the pass.

OPPOSITE: Cerro Aconcagua, South America's highest mountain. ABOVE: The rugged terrain near Uspallata is a dead-ringer for the Himalayas.

Gallop with Gauchos

"THE GAUCHO MADE OUR COUNTRY," says Juan Camilo Echamendi. "They fought the revolution against the Spanish and they went everywhere, to every corner of the land, working with cattle. They were the real pioneers of Argentina. Without the gaucho you have nothing!" Having made his point, the old cowboy takes another swig and slams his glass on the counter, a beacon to the bartender that he wants another shot of whisky.

Similar scenes are being played out up and down the old wooden bar at Bessonart, a combination general store and saloon in San Antonio de Areco, about two hours west of Buenos Aires. Nearly everyone who ventures to Argentina comes with romantic visions of gauchos riding across the open plains, branding bulls and felling steers with one quick swing of their trusty *bola*. But in the age of big-business agriculture — helicopter roundups and 16-wheeler transport — San Antonio is one of the few places in Argentina where traditional gaucho life endures.

Blame it on author Ricardo Güiraldes, the beloved bard of gaucho culture, who rode and wrote at Estancia La Porteña on the outskirts of San Antonio. His most renowned book — a 1926 classic of Argentine literature called *Don Segundo Sombra* — romanticized the life and times of the Argentine cowboy in much the same way that Zane Grey's books idealized the individualism of the American West.

Modern-day San Antonio strives to keep the memory of Güiraldes and gaucho ways alive through numerous means. There is a fine museum dedicated to cowpoke culture and workshops that produce some of the finest silver and leather equestrian gear in all of Argentina. The town's annual festival, the Día de la Tradición in November, is firmly dedicated to riding, roping and other gaucho skills. Many of the local *estancias* (including the lovely La Porteña) welcome visitors for overnight stays and rides across the Pampas.

And then there's Bessonart, a place where old ways and means flourish every night around 7 PM — when the gauchos start to wet their whistles and talk about the old times. Old men clad in berets and boots, red or black scarves tied around their necks, silver buckles supporting baggy pants, the trademark gaucho knife lodged in their waistbands. Many of them are bowlegged from so many years in the saddle. But they're quick with a smile, even for a stranger.

Get Wet at Iguazú

"YOU WANNA GET WET?" the boatman asks in Spanish as we cast off from a rocky landing near Iguazú Falls. I casually nod my head, figuring a little spray will drift our way. The boatman seems to read my mind. "I mean *really* wet?" he stresses. I give him a reluctant thumbs up (how wet is really wet?) and reach for the nearest safety line as we speed toward the liquid labyrinth.

Even from a distance, the Cataratas del Iguazú are mighty impressive — a raging wall of water that plummets 80 m (230 ft) down the sheer face of a basalt plateau, creating a plume of spray that towers several hundred feet above the jungle and dozens of rainbows that arch over the Río Iguazú gorge. Emerald-green islands divide the spectacle into 275 separate falls that span a distance of four kilometers (two and a half miles) between Argentina and Brazil.

The name Iguazú means "big water" in the language of the local Guaraní Indians. But you don't realize just how big until you are face-to-face with the giant, cowering in the bow of a little rubber boat. *Bang! Bang! Bang!* Our Zodiac slaps into waves generated by San Martín Fall, one of the largest and most violent of Iguazú's cataracts. As the boatmen edges closer and closer to the towering cascade, the relentless mist drenches my entire body. By the time we reach the bottom of the falls, the thunder of crashing water makes it impossible to talk in anything other than shouts.

Then it's time to get *really* wet. The boatman revs the engine and we head right into the falls. Completely immersed, water slaps my face at a hundred miles an hour, the sort of force generated by a hurricane. The boat bucks up and down, and then spins around. I gasp for breath and hang on for dear life as the Zodiac drifts back into calm water. What a rush!

Tour operators on both sides of the border organize Zodiac trips to the bottom of the falls. On the Argentine side, Iguazú Jungle Explorer ((3757) 421600 FAX (3757) 420311 offers "soak trips" beneath San Martín. On the Brazilian, Ilha do Sol Turismo ((45) 574-4244 offers an exhilarating one-hour trip called the "Macuco Safari" that takes you right up to the base of Devil's Throat.

ABOVE: Corrientes province gauchos dressed in their Sunday best. RIGHT: The most turbulent part of Iguazú is the famed Garganta del Diablo (Devil's Throat).

Conga till Dawn

THE ANNUAL BRAZILIAN BASH MIGHT BE MORE FAMOUS, but the cities of northern Argentina know how to put on a pretty good party when Carnival time rolls around.

Corrientes and Salta take on a festive air before Lent, with major streets blocked off and grandstands erected for "Corso" parades that extend from just after sunset until the middle of the night. There are literally thousands of participants: sinuous samba bands, strolling mariachis, tango troupes, baton twirlers and beauty queens, incredibly gaudy floats pulled by trucks and tractors, and thousands of male and female dancers clad in the most outrageous costumes.

Name your fantasy and you're bound to find it somewhere at Carnival. Inca warriors clad in great feather headdresses. Shimmering silver American cowboy outfits. Huge blue-and-orange insects that look as if they've just stepped down from a movie screen. Arabian Nights belly dancers in slinky black frocks with gold trim. An entire barnyard full of six-meter (20-ft) chickens being chased by a gray wolf.

The sidelines are just as crazy. Kids roam up and down the Corso route spraying spectators with shaving-cream from aerosol cans. Vendors barbecue super *panchos*, *empanadas* and even thick steaks at makeshift stalls behind the grandstands. The music is so loud your ears are ringing by parade end. The fun spills over onto adjoining streets and plazas, a party that rages until dawn.

The Carnival parades in Salta and Corrientes take place on Friday, Saturday and Sunday nights on the two weekends before Lent, starting around 9 PM and running until two or three in the morning. Admission prices range from US$1 general admission in Salta to US$200 for special VIP boxes in Corrientes that include all-you-can-down champagne and caviar.

Closer to Brazil, Corrientes Carnival is supposed to be the more risqué of the two, with lots of scantly clad female dancers and a sensuous interpretation of traditional samba songs. The Salta version is much more Andes based, dominated by indigenous dance troupes from the northwest desert and nearby Bolivia and Salta.

Salta's annual Carnival reaches fever pitch with a parade through the city center.

Follow in Evita's Footsteps

EVA MARIE DUARTE PERÓN IS AN UNLIKELY ICON. Many Argentines are bewildered by the world's fascination with the most famous woman in the country's history. Others worship the former First Lady with a fervor more commonly associated with religious personages. Andrew Lloyd Weber certainly contributed to the mystique with his hit musical; Madonna did her part in the movie. But none of the legends could exist without the very human, flawed, and determined character known to all as Evita.

Her tomb in the La Recoleta cemetery is one of the most popular tourist attractions in Buenos Aires. Evita tours are an essential element in the well-rounded Buenos Aires itinerary. Tourists who know absolutely nothing about Argentina's history immerse themselves in one short, significant era that forever changed the political and social fabric of the country.

Eva Duarte was an illegitimate child born in 1919 in rural Buenos Aires Province. She moved to the capital city at the age of 15 and embarked upon a mediocre career as an actress who gained access to high society by hitching herself to more famous stars. She met Juan Domingo Perón in 1944 during a fundraising event, became the First Lady when Perón was elected president in 1946, and died in 1952 at the age of 33. In less than a decade she became the champion of the *descamisados* (shirtless ones), the scourge of the upper classes, and an international celebrity. She championed the causes of workers and the disadvantaged with an unceasing ferocity, and served as a standard bearer for the majority long ignored by the elite.

Her death from uterine cancer at such a young age served to inflame the passion of her followers. She haunted her enemies long after her death. Her corpse traveled about like an aimless wanderer for years before coming to rest at La Recoleta. In life and in death, Evita lent her name and personality to the most bizarre, noble, and ignoble aspects of the Argentine character.

If you have fallen under Evita's spell, read *Santa Evita*, the eloquent novel by Tomás Eloy Martínez, before visiting Buenos Aires, then sign up for an Evita tour. The typical circuit begins at Luna Park, the concert hall where Eva first met Perón. Next comes the Casa Rosada, where the most famous scenes in the movie and play take place. The president and first lady often addressed their followers from the Casa Rosada's balcony, as have dozens of leaders for the past century. Today, it's hard for the average traveler to look at the Casa Rosada (or Evita's tomb) without humming "Don't Cry for me Argentina."

Tour buses cruise past the CGT building, where the Eva Perón Foundation was headquartered during her reign. The foundation was the cornerstone of her charitable works; the needy stood in line for hours and days to appeal to her beneficence, asking for assistance with housing, health care, and financial problems. After her death, Evita's body was kept in this building for many months under the supervision of Doctor Pedro Ara, a famous Spanish embalmer. Evita's portrait appears on a tiled mosaic on one wall of the building, next to an eternal flame.

The most fascinating stop in the Evita tour is at the Instituto Nacional Juan D. Perón, which is housed in the building where Evita died. Visitors are shown film clips from the 1940s: finally, the true Eva Perón comes to light. She looks regal, beautiful and happy in newsreels from her European tour in 1948, when world leaders alternately courted and rejected her (depending on their post World War II proclivities). The only official monument to Evita stands near the institute in front of the National Library. The sculpture was dedicated by President Carlos Menem in 1999, more than 60 years after Evita's death.

La Recoleta is the final stop on the Evita circuit. Some guides point out the neighborhood apartment building where Eva and Juan lived apart or together (depending upon the rumor) before their marriage. The tour ends at the cemetery, where Evita's body finally came to rest 18 years after her death. Tomas Eloy Martínez fashioned his novel around the peregrinations of Evita's corpse. The story of paranoid generals, love-smitten embalmers, and devious plots is like something out of surrealistic fiction, yet much of it is true. The military leaders who forced Juan Perón out of power in 1955 were afraid of Evita and intimidated by her influence over national and international opinion. They commissioned at least one replica of the corpse, moved both around the city, and finally shipped them off to Europe. Her corpse became a symbol of the national conflict between the haves and have-nots.

"It's too big a body now, bigger than the country," says a conspirator in *Santa Evita*. "That body is like loaded dice now." Those in power feared the masses would revere the corpse and turn Evita into a saint. Their fears have come true.

Tackle the Tango

YOU CAN'T ESCAPE TANGO'S SAD, SENSUOUS REFRAIN while traveling in Argentina. The music is everywhere, drifting in the background from televisions, radios and stereo speakers set on sidewalks. Dancers strike dignified, aloof poses on street corners and stages, then slink into a series of steps and swoops that defy one's normal sense of rhythm. You can't simply jump on stage and join in the fun, whirling about with the beat. It takes discipline to tango correctly.

Tango teachers are in great demand these days as the dance continues to captivate the country's collective consciousness. Classes are held in hotel basements and trendy bars throughout Argentina. The best one I've ever seen took place in the dusty, dimly lit ballroom at the Confitería Ideal in Buenos Aires. It was about 2 PM, and the downstairs café was deserted. But I heard the distinctive mournful notes from a bandoneón upstairs, and followed the sound to a ghostly ballroom that looked like it belonged in black-and-white film.

The characters were completely out of place, however. They were wearing T-shirts and sneakers, sundresses and sandals, jeans and walking shoes. Their faces were set in a concentration that forebode frivolity. Half the dancers were tourists; the others were attending their regular class. Everyone seemed utterly determined to step properly. A few couples broke into giggles.

The tango is as sexy as the lambada and as formal as a Viennese waltz. The dance originated in the 1880s, with music and moves strung together by a mix of immigrants. Experts cite Italian, Spanish, Cuban, and German influences, all overlaid with gaucho dance steps and lyrics. Men frequently danced the tango together, perfecting intricate footwork that implied sensuality while prohibiting intimacy. The elite looked down upon the dance as a vulgar amusement for the lower immigrant classes until the tango caught on in Europe, becoming all the rage in Paris in the early 1900s.

Enter Carlos Gardel, the Frank Sinatra of tango. Born in France in 1890, Gardel was the personification of tango themes. His mother emigrated to Argentina in 1892, just as the tango was taking hold in immigrant neighborhoods. By the 1920s, the handsome crooner with slicked back dark hair and impassioned eyes personified the music of the displaced; his songs spoke of the melancholy and nostalgia of thousands who yearned for

their homes in the Old Country. Songwriters composed mournful lyrics echoing the pain of unrequited love. Tango orchestras grew to include violins, pianos, and guitars. Like the famed flappers of the Prohibition Era in the United States, fashionable Argentines dressed to the nines in stiletto heels, skin tight frocks, and tuxedos and flocked to dance halls.

Gardel was killed in a plane crash in 1935 at the age of 44 and became a national hero. Recordings of his music made in the 1930s are still among the most popular renditions of tango classics, played on all-tango radio and television stations throughout the country. Tango fell in and out of fashion in its homeland, but the world would not let it go.

The people of Argentina are currently immersed in a surge of national pride and have embraced the tango as a symbol of their identity. Tango dancers draw crowds wherever they appear, be it the seaside plaza in Mar del Plata or the underground crypts in Córdoba. Professional dancers are incorporating jazz and ballet steps into tango routines, while amateurs are learning the basic steps in schools and community halls.

Anyone who spends time in Buenos Aires should attend a few tango shows. The most professional, tourist-oriented performances are held in clubs in San Telmo; you can easily spend US$50 on a ticket for a major tango

Youngsters tango under the sun by the Casino Central in Mar del Plata.

show. But budget travelers needn't miss out on the tango experience. Amateur and professional dancers drop by Confitería Ideal, Café Tortoni, and other popular hangouts late at night and in the wee hours of the morning to practice new steps. Dancers perform almost daily at the Recoleta Cultural Center, the Plaza Dorrego in San Telmo, and the Calle Museo Caminito in La Boca. If you're lucky, an empathetic dancer will hold out his or her arms and draw you into the mood and music. You'll probably feel like a clumsy oaf at first. But nothing compares with the sensation of getting through a whole song without stumbling. It takes skill to conquer the tango.

Cruise the Wild Seas

I SAILED TOWARD CAPE HORN LIKE THE EXPLORERS OF OLD, battered by the fierce South Atlantic Ocean. Waves crashed over the bow of the Clipper Adventurer; freezing winds battered the brave souls shivering on deck keeping watch for the Wandering Albatross.

Half the passengers were confined to their cabins, enduring the near-death sensations of seasickness. Nearly everyone dipped into the bowl of anti-nausea pills at the cruise director's desk. The doctor, a kindly German gentleman who spent his free time in the ship's well-stocked library, was busy administering shots and sympathy. The kitchen crew had it easy.

After three dark and stormy days and nights, the sun broke through gray clouds and the ship steamed forth on a steady, calm course. Pallid invalids emerged from their cabins and sipped ginger ale and mint tea. A seasoned wag on the crew added the following quote to the list of the day's activities: "Some of us are over the seasick stage and no longer want to die."

These words from the log of the Nimrod, captained by Ernest Shackleton in 1902, echo the sentiments of nearly everyone who has journeyed through the South Atlantic. Sailors, whalers, explorers, and adventurers have feared this lonely expanse of unpredictable ocean for centuries. But winds and waves haven't held humans at bay. European explorers in the fifteenth century willingly subjected themselves to the Atlantic's mercy to reach the shores of the New World. Settlers and traders endured months of misery at sea to build new homes and markets from South America to Hawaii. Whalers from Great Britain and New England followed the migrations of their prey during the great whale-oil boom of the nineteenth century. Explorers sailed onward to the great white continent of Antarctica, losing their lives in the race for fame and immortality.

Freighters and commercial fishing boats still battle the South Atlantic on a regular basis. During the spring, they're accompanied by sightseers in cushy cruise ships. Several lines offer cruises along the coast of Brazil and Argentina while repositioning ships for Antarctic itineraries. After checking out the Amazon and Iguazú Falls, passengers spend a night or two in Buenos Aires, then head to more serious latitudes.

White-bellied killer whales, slow-moving right whales, grouchy elephant seals, and hungry sea lions all gravitate to the Península Valdés, which juts into the Atlantic off Patagonia. Cruise passengers have the great fortune to approach the peninsula from the open water, following seaborne mammals into two protected gulfs. In September and October, right whales float in the gulfs to give birth. Massive bull elephant seals lumber to shore to breed at Punta Norte; Magellanic penguins burrow in nests at Punta Tombo. The best months for sighting wildlife at Península Valdés are from September to November, which coincides nicely with transitional cruises. Unless the seas are temperamental, cruise ships typically spend a night or two at

OPPOSITE: Glitter and gloves are part of the formal tango costume worn by performers in San Telmo. ABOVE: Kayakers are dwarfed by Perito Moreno Glacier.

Valdés. Passengers spend hours boating in small Zodiacs and hiking through nature preserves, studying whales, penguins, and seals under the tutelage of experienced naturalist guides.

The Clipper *Adventurer* and other ships spend another couple of days traveling about the Islas Malvinas (Falkland Islands), the most controversial outpost in the South Atlantic. It's hard to imagine anyone fighting over possession of these remote rocks, yet Argentina and Great Britain did just that in 1982. The Brits won, though you'd hardly guess so while traveling through Argentina.

"Las Malvinas son Argentinas" (The Malvinas Islands are Argentine) is a popular pronouncement among many Argentines. Tourists wishing to visit the islands usually do so from Great Britain or Chile, though there may be flights from Argentina soon. The easiest way to get there is via cruise ship, and the experience is worth any measure of discomfort or seasickness. Penguins love this cluster of some 400 islands and protruding rocks 480 km (300 miles) east of Argentina. So do more than 2,000 islanders who believe they live in Paradise.

Our ship sailed on to Tierra del Fuego, while most passengers flew to Santiago, Chile. A new crew and slew of guests flew to Ushuaia to embark on a three-week Antarctic journey. My South Atlantic experience paled in comparison to theirs — the White Continent is a land of extremes.

Various itineraries for exploring the South Atlantic are offered by several cruise lines. See SPECIAL INTERESTS, page 43 in YOUR CHOICE.

Ponder the Penguin

LEWIS CARROLL SHOULD HAVE WRITTEN ABOUT PENGUINS. They're perfect Wonderland characters. Silly, pompous, sleek, and clumsy, penguins are utterly captivating. No wonder they star in so many wildlife shows.

Argentina is blessed with an abundance of penguin colonies. Península Valdés, Tierra del Fuego, and Patagonia all harbor several penguin species, each as individualistic as human beings. All colonies have some things in common, however. The stench of hundreds of penguins brooding over their eggs is unmistakable and overwhelming, as is the sound of a thousand birds chattering. They squeak, bleat, yawn, and cluck and they preen themselves and each other, always keeping one eye on their nests. Each species presents a different spectacle.

The Magellanic penguins, who burrow their nests in tufted hillocks at Península

Valdés and Río Gallegos, are shy characters with distinctive white stripes around their eyes and necks. They're as playful as any other penguin when strutting about the beach — nicknamed "jackasses," they can be as comical as a cartoon character. But they become reclusive when guarding their eggs under mounds of sand, dirt and grass.

King penguins are far bolder, strolling about among their fluffy brown chicks. With their brazen orange crowns and beaks, the kings stand taller than their peers; some are over one meter (three feet) tall. They cradle their eggs on their feet while regally peering about and preening. Smaller gentoos hang out around kings, and also have bright orange markings.

Rockhoppers are true comedians. Bright yellow plumes stick out from above their eyes like wayward brows. They bop about as if

awkwardly playing with pogo sticks, and check out strangers with avid curiosity. Macaroni penguins were named for their resemblance to seventeenth century English dandies; their feathery gold plumes look like ostentatious accessories.

All penguins are far more dignified in water than on land, though their approach to and from the sea is often wildly amusing. Some slide gracefully from rocky perches into calm bays; others prefer belly-flops. Once in the water, however, they glide about as if soaring through the sky. Penguins are, after all, wingless birds and can propel their bodies like streaking plump bullets through salty seas.

If you're determined to see several penguin species you'll have to follow a rather involved itinerary. It's relatively easy to reach the Magellanic colonies on the Península Valdés.

Tour companies run trips to Punta Tombo from the Welsh town of Trelew during the breeding season. Viewing is better if you drive to the penguin colonies on your own and stay as long as you wish. Travel to the Reserva Cabo Virgenes penguin rookeries in Patagonia is more complicated. You're best off driving from Río Gallegos to the colonies, where some 30,000 Magellanic penguins dig their nests. Reserve overnight lodging at nearby *estancias* in advance, as rooms are scarce. King penguins can sometimes be spotted during boat tours out of Ushuaia to Isla Martillo. A trip to Antarctica or the Falkland Islands is akin to hitting the penguin jackpot. Lucky cruise-ship passengers spot several species during their journeys.

Sightseeing boats cruise the chilly waters at Parque Nacional Los Glaciares.

YOUR CHOICE

The Great Outdoors

From snow-covered mountains and cotton-candy blue glaciers to lush rainforest and red-rock deserts, Argentina is endowed with a little bit of everything that South America has to offer in terms of scenery. The country presents ideal terrain for long-distance backpackers, hardcore climbers and anyone else who likes to get off the beaten path; a wealth of places where you can "drop out" for a week, a month or an entire year.

Many of the country's foremost natural attractions are protected within the boundaries of national parks and provincial preserves. The federal government oversees 31 national parks, from vast tracts of pristine wilderness to tiny little slivers of countryside that protect a single species or habitat.

Only three of the parks are immensely popular. **Parque Nacional del Iguazú** in the northeast draws millions of people each year to see the roaring thunder of Iguazú Falls.

Away from the falls, the park protects a huge expanse of subtropical rainforest. **Parque Nacional Los Glaciares** in southern Patagonia boasts some of the most awesome scenery in the entire Andes, including Argentina's most famous glaciers, largest freshwater lakes and toughest granite peaks. **Parque Nacional Nahuel Huapi** in the Lake District is a haven for all sorts of outdoor recreation including climbing, trekking, kayaking, rafting, fishing, scuba diving, parasailing, mountain biking and skiing.

Others parks remain little explored, their range is truly amazing. **Parque Nacional Tierra del Fuego** embraces a chilly subantarctic landscape of glaciers, mountains and Southern beech forest along the shores of Beagle Channel. At the opposite end of the country, tucked up near the Bolivian border, is **Monumento Natural Laguna de los Pozuelos**, a treeless high-mountain landscape where water birds gather on their long migration across the continent. **Parque Nacional El Palmar** in the Espinal region of Entre Ríos Province protects the fragile habitat of the Yatay palm, while **Parque Nacional Chaco** near Roque Sáenz Peña harbors endangered animals such as tapir, jaguar, maned wolf and cayman, indigenous to the Gran Chaco region. El Palmar lies about 360 km (223 miles) north of Buenos Aires via Ruta 14; Chaco is about 140 km (86 miles) west of Corrientes off Ruta 16.

Argentina's most renowned provincial park is the **Reserva Faunística Península Valdés** near Puerto Madryn in northern Patagonia, an anvil-shaped peninsula that juts into the South Atlantic. Local beaches bustle with hundred of thousands of sea creatures including elephant

---

OPPOSITE: The towering Fitzroy Range in Parque Nacional Los Glaciares. ABOVE: *Cardón* cactus and other desert plants flourish in the Quebrada de Cafayate.

Sporting Spree

From soccer bad boy Diego Maradona to tennis champion turned *Playboy* centerfold Gabriela Sabatini to five-time world grand prix auto racing champion Juan Fangio, Argentina has produced a long list of international stars in a wide variety of sports.

With World Cup victories in 1978 and 1986 and a runners-up trophy in 1990, **soccer** is the undisputed king of Argentine sport. According to legend, British sailors who used to kick a ball around empty lots adjacent to the Buenos Aires docks introduced soccer around the end of the nineteenth century. Local kids — especially Italian immigrants — quickly picked up the sport and became world masters. The country's most famous team is Boca Junior, based in a rough and tough harborside district called La Boca, where Diego Maradona and many other soccer stars grew up.

Much like in Europe, Argentine soccer can get a little rough — not on the field, mind you, but in the stands, where boisterous fans sometimes run rampant over rival fans. The best place to catch a game is huge Río Plate stadium in Buenos Aires where Argentina plays internationals against arch rivals like Brazil and Uruguay. But you can also catch games in any large city. The regular season runs from early September through July.

Argentines also gravitate to a couple of other sports introduced by the British: rugby and polo. **Rugby** is popular at many school and private clubs around the country and Argentine teams often play in top international tournaments. While rugby hasn't quite reached the mass popularity of soccer, it's played with just as much passion and fervor.

Given the tremendous cost of raising, training and housing horses, **polo** remains an extremely elite game watched by well-healed spectators. Argentina continues to produce some of the world's best players, youngsters who literally grew up in the saddle on wealthy *estancias*. The best place to catch polo is the vaunted **Canchas Nacionales** (National Fields) in the upper crust Palermo district of Buenos Aires, in many respects the Wembley or Yankee Stadium of the game. There are two seasons: a low handicap season in the fall (March–May) during which many of the promising newcomers earn their spurs, and a high handicap season in the spring (September to December) when the stars strut their stuff. The season finale is the Argentine Open at Palermo in late November.

seals, southern sea lions and Magellanic penguins. Offshore is the domain of orcas, dolphins and right whales, while the peninsula's inland plains provide fodder for guanaco, rhea and other steppe species.

Other important local reserves include **Parque Provincial Aconcagua** near Mendoza, which surrounds South America's highest mountain; **Reserva Provincial Punta Tombo** and **Cabo Virgenes**, which harbor two of the country's largest penguin colonies; and **Parque Provincial Ischigualasto** in San Juan Province — about 170 km (106 miles) southwest of La Rioja via routes 38 and 150 — which embraces a stark desert landscape called the Valle de la Luna (Valley of the Moon).

Some of Argentina's most pristine areas are outside the park systems, like the fabulous **Quebrada de Cafayate** south of Salta. This 60-km (37-mile) long canyon contains scenery reminiscent of Arizona's Oak Creek/Sedona region — a vast red-rock wilderness rising above a lush wooden creek, *cardón* cactus set against weird rock formations. Most of the impenetrable **Esteros del Iberá** in northeast Argentina also lacks official protection. This enormous marshland — similar to Brazil's Pantanal — shelters myriad plant and animal species.

The popular parks — Iguazú, Nahuel Huapi, Los Glaciares and Península Valdés — are well endowed with tourist facilities, from luxury lodges to expansive campsites. The others boast facilities that are primitive at best. Unless you sign on with an adventure travel outfit, visiting the more remote parks for more than a couple of hours entails packing everything yourself — food, water, tent, medical supplies, etc. And don't expect a helicopter to pluck you off a mountaintop or out of the jungle if you get into trouble. This is wilderness in the true sense of the term.

Anybody who hankers to go **horseback riding** can find *cabalgatas* (stables) on the outskirts of just about any Argentine town. One of the best places is the gaucho town of San Antonio de Areco about two hours west of Buenos Aires where half a dozen *estancias* offer overnight stays or day visits with horseback riding. You can also ride through the jungle near Iguazú Falls, across the red-rock desert near Salta or into the foothills of the Patagonian Andes in Parque Nacional Los Glaciares and the Lake District.

With so many wide-open spaces, Argentina is ready made for **golf**. The country's most beautiful course is the 18-hole Llao Llao Country Club ((2944) 448525 or 448544 near Bariloche, surrounded by thick forest and overlooking an alpine lake with the Andes as a backdrop. The federal capital boasts more than a dozen links including the exclusive Miraflores Country Club ((3327) 454800 in suburban Garín and the low-cost municipal Cancha Golf Course ((11) 4772-7261 in Palermo.

Adventure sports are increasingly popular throughout the country. Flanked by several thousand miles of Andean peaks, Argentine is a paradise for **trekking** and **mountain climbing**. Top areas include Cerro Aconcagua (South America's highest mountain) near Mendoza, the Lake District near Bariloche, and the spectacular granite spires of the Fitzroy Range in southern Patagonia's Parque Nacional Los Glaciares. For more information on routes, conditions and guides contact the following organizations: Club Andinista Mendoza ((261) 431-9870; Club Andino Bariloche ((2944) 422266 FAX (2944) 424579; Fitzroy Expeditions ((2962) 493017 in Parque Nacional Los Glaciares.

Whitewater rafting is offered at many Argentine rivers including the Río Mendoza in the Central Andes, the Río Iguazú and Río Paraná in the northeast, and the Río Santa Cruz near El Calafate in Patagonia. But truth be told, these are little more than float trips. For real whitewater thrills run the Río Manso on the Argentine–Chilean border in the Lake District. A couple of Bariloche-based outfitters offer single or multiple day trips on this Class III–IV river, including Extremo Sur ((2944) 427301.

Argentina's premier winter recreation area and probably the best **ski resort** on the entire continent is Las Leñas ((2627) 471100 near Mendoza. Set in a charming Andean valley, the resort boasts 11 lifts and 41 downhill runs (with a maximum plunge of 1,230 meters) as well as ski school, equipment rental facilities and ski patrol for emergencies. Bariloche offers two snow sport areas: Piedras Blancas Ski Area ((2944) 441035 or (2944) 425720 on the side of Cerro Otto and the much more

challenging Gran Catedral ((2944) 460051 or (2944) 460062 with 67 km (41 miles) of sky trails spread across the eastern slopes of the Andes. At all of these resorts, the winter high season runs the last two weeks of July (during Argentina's winter school vacation). The low season spans late June to early July, and mid-September to mid-October.

The transition zone between the High Andes and the Pampas is also ideal for **mountain biking**. You can rent bikes in Mendoza, Bariloche or El Calafate and simply take off on your own across the rolling plains or the wooded foothills. If going solo isn't your cup of tea, join a guided mountain bike tour offered by adventure sports outfitters like Aymara Turismo y Aventura ((261) 420-0607 or (261) 420-5304 E-MAIL aymara@satlink.com, Calle 9 de Julio 983 in Mendoza; or La Bolsa del Deporte ((2944) 423529, Calle Elflein 385 in Bariloche.

Visitors also flock to Argentina for **sport fishing**. There are two popular area: the Lake District around Bariloche where trout, salmon and perch are the species of choice, and the muddy brown waters of the Río Paraná between Corrientes and Puerto Iguazú where huge fish like *dorado* and *surubi* are the top prizes. Outfitters in Bariloche and Corrientes offer equipment, bait, guides and boats.

OPPOSITE: The sands of Playa Bristol prove perfect for a game of bowls. ABOVE: Hikers make their way across the top of Patagonia's Perito Moreno Glacier.

The Open Road

Argentina has the best roads in South America, a comprehensive national and provincial highway network that stretches into just about every nook and cranny in the entire country. In fact, the automobile is a good way to explore Argentina's vast hinterland — assuming that you can tolerate hour upon hour of arrow-straight roads and monotonous scenery between major sights.

Other than ring roads around major cities like Buenos Aires and Córdoba, there is only one long-distance expressway — the wonderfully quick and easy toll road (Ruta 9) that links the federal capital with Rosario and Santa Fe. All other major roads are a single lane in each direction. However, this doesn't seem to hinder traffic flow, as passing is relatively easy.

Most of the national highways are in very good condition, with few of the potholes, rockslides or toppled trees that plague highways elsewhere in the continent. Many provincial roads (especially in Patagonia and the northwest) are all-weather gravel, which can be like driving on ice — vehicles tend to fishtail if you drive too fast. Four-wheel drive is recommended if you venture off-road into the Andes, the northwest desert or the jungle near Iguazú.

ABOVE: Fly-fishing the Río de los Conchas through the Quebrada de Cafayate. RIGHT: The Pan-American Highway winds into the Andes west of Uspallata.

Argentina offers a number of interesting road circuits. One of the easiest is a drive up the **Paraná Valley** from Buenos Aires, a route that runs past historic cities like San Antonio de Areco, Rosario and Santa Fe before culminating at Corrientes near the confluence of the Paraná and Paraguay rivers. Along the way you can explore the vast wetlands of the Paraná Delta, duck into Spanish mission churches or ride the range with real gauchos.

A far more intriguing route, and a much tougher motoring challenge, is the highway that runs across **northern Argentina** from Iguazú Falls on the Brazilian frontier to Salta, in the lee of the Andes. The roadside scenery takes in just about everything for which South America is famous — the pristine rainforest of Iguazú National Park, the impenetrable swamps of the Esteros del Iberá, a vast savannah wilderness called the Gran Chaco and finally the Andes rising along the Argentina–Chile frontier.

Most *porteños*, as the residents of Buenos Aires are called, shoot straight down Ruta 2 to the beaches at Mar del Plata. But you can take a much more leisurely path — **Ruta 11** as it meanders along the coast through La Plata and San Clemente del Tuyú. Another scenic coast road runs west from Mar del Plata, through Necochea and Tres Arroyos before terminating at Bahía Blanca.

With its vast distances, **Patagonia** is a real challenge for motorists, but nonetheless popular with overseas visitors who want to get a true feel for the region's wide open spaces. Picking up a rental car in Puerto Madryn, you can drive a huge circle route around northern Patagonia that takes you from the Atlantic seaboard across the Pampas to the Lake District and the Andes. You can start this same circle from Bariloche. Anyone on the outlook for real adventure drive Ruta 40 the entire length of the Patagonian Andes from Río Gallegos or El Calafate to Bariloche. But make sure you've got four-wheel drive to negotiate the mostly gravel roads.

There are many **shorter circuits** that can be accomplished in a single day. Heading north from Jujuy, Ruta 9 traverses the northwest desert via a deep canyon called the Quebrada de Humahuaca with its Andean Indian villages and quaint Spanish colonial churches. Heading south from Salta, Ruta 68 penetrates a red-rock wilderness called the Quebrada de Cafayate with scenery reminiscent of Arizona's Oak Creek Canyon. Heading west from Mendoza you can drive all the way up to the High Andes along Ruta 7 (the Pan-American Highway) with stunning views of Cerro Aconcagua and Cristo Redentor (Christ the Redeemer) along the way.

Backpacking

Argentina presents some stiff challenges when it comes to backpack travel. The biggest challenge is expense — the extravagant amounts demanded by so many hotels and restaurants. You could easily blow a week's budget in a single day if you're not careful. The second challenge is space — the fact that so many of Argentina's travel highlights are scattered so far apart.

But there are ways to tackle both problems. The best advice on saving money is to spend as little time as possible in Buenos Aires. Prices for accommodation and food drop appreciably outside the federal capital, to levels that make it possible for just about anyone to travel in Argentina for several weeks or months.

Most of the larger Argentine cities and all of the major tourist destinations — including

Iguazú Falls, Bariloche, Puerto Madryn and El Calafate — have youth hostels (*albergues*) that charge US$15 or less per night for simple bed and breakfast. These are among the cleanest, safest, most efficient hostels in all of South America. There are also loads of cheap hotels called *hospedajes* or *residenciales*. The quality of these establishments can vary greatly from one to another, and prices tend to be higher than youth hostels. Like hostels and cheap hotels the world over, expect to share your sleeping quarters and bathroom with total strangers. But that's the trade off for rock-bottom prices.

To many working-class Argentines, summer vacation means packing sleeping bags and tent into the back of the car and driving to some far-flung corner of the country. All of the popular national parks and nearly every provincial town offer excellent campgrounds where you can pitch your tent for next to nothing. The better campsites, most of them privately owned, offer shower blocks with hot water, picnic tables and barbecue areas, swimming pools and other recreation facilities, as well as snack shops and general stores.

Buenos Aires has wonderful restaurants, but unfortunately most of them are beyond the budget of most backpacking travelers. Fast-food restaurants proliferate in the central city, especially along pedestrian streets like Calle Florida and Calle Lavalle. Although there seems to be another McDonald's around every corner, Argentine fast-food embraces much more than burgers and fries. Other inexpensive delights include *empanadas, humitas, panchos,* and a hundred different types of pizza. Another low-cost alternative is *tenedor libre* or all-you-can-eat buffet, most common in Chinese restaurants. If you really crave a steak but the cost seems extravagant, remember that most *parrillas* give you a lot of bang for your buck — enough food to last several days if you pack the leftovers into a doggy bag.

Outside of Buenos Aires, food prices plunge to more moderate levels and budget travelers can actually afford to eat in proper restaurants every so often. *Confiterías* (snack bars) are ubiquitous in cities and towns throughout the provinces, with low-cost meals that can range from sandwiches to soup and salad to juicy steaks. Roadside diners are another good bet.

Unless you're going to pack six people into a single vehicle, renting a car is not a shoestring option. But that doesn't mean you can't see the sights. Like most Latin American countries, Argentina offers a

Living It Up

Although Argentina certainly has its fair share of wealthy citizens and visitors, it suffers from a distinct shortage of lavish hotels and restaurants. Many a traveler has uttered a gasp of dismay when entering a hotel that purportedly achieves five-star standards. Do not let the country's bizarre star system govern your choice of accommodations.

There are precious few truly modern hotels in the country, even in Buenos Aires. Instead, travelers find a few exceptional properties in nineteenth-century mansions and modern mountain lodges.

EXCEPTIONAL HOTELS

Buenos Aires claims the country's finest hotels, some rivaling their European peers. Many *porteños* say the best hotel in the country is the **Alvear Palace Hotel** in chic La Recoleta. Dignified doormen, butlers, and concierges set a formal tone, while French antique furnishings, glimmering chandeliers, and a lush abundance of velvet and silk speak of opulent comfort. Guests sleep between Egyptian cotton sheets, bathe with Hermes toiletries, and sip martinis beside a grand piano. It's easy to pretend you're a wealthy *porteño* at the height of the belle époque.

Nearly as sumptuous, the **Park Hyatt Buenos Aires** in La Recoleta combines Old World graciousness with modern amenities and spectacular views from its 13-story tower. Madonna chose to stay here while filming *Evita*. If it's good enough for this prima donna, who set the city on edge as she paraded about in grand costumes from the 1940s, it's definitely good enough for the average discerning traveler. Located near all the historical sights in downtown Buenos Aires, the **Claridge Hotel** is another grande dame with luxurious rooms, courtly service, and views over the city to the Río de la Plata. Though the hotels above are more prestigious, I enjoy the Claridge's somewhat quirky character and its proximity to the peaceful Plaza San Martín. Facing this same plaza, the **Marriott Plaza Hotel** retains some of the grandeur of the past. The 1909 German Baroque building has been remodeled several times, and the lobby and some rooms have lost their opulence. But the bar, restaurant, and ballrooms are still grand, and the service is impeccable.

comprehensive overland bus network with rates slanted toward students, families and working people. Most of the ultra-long-distance services are overnight, which save you the price of a hotel room. The better long-distance buses offer reclining airplane-type seats which make it easy to sleep, monitors that show old Hollywood films, and modest meals served by young attendants — all of this included in the basic price.

Argentina's domestic airfares are very expensive. The only routes you should fly are incredibly long distances like Buenos Aires–Ushuaia or Puerto Iguazú–Bariloche. Otherwise stick to ground transport. The "Visit Argentina" air pass offered by **Aerolíneas Argentinas/Austral (** (11) 4340-7777 or (11) 4340-7800 seems like a great deal at first glance. Available for purchase only outside of Argentina in conjunction with an Aerolíneas Argentinas international fare, the pass gives you four domestic sectors for as little as US$450. The coupons can be used over a one-month span and you can buy extra sectors for US$120 each. The problem is the "sectors." The only way to fly between most provincial capitals is doubling back through Buenos Aires. Which means that flying from Salta to Mendoza, for instance, would take two flight coupons rather than just one. At the end of the day, your air pass could get a lot more expansive than sticking to the ground.

OPPOSITE: Chaltén's modest hostels and cafés attract a steady stream of backpackers. LEFT: Biking around the edge of Bariloche's Lago Nahuel Huapi. ABOVE: San Telmo's cafés are rarely empty.

The hotels at Argentina's coastal resorts are geared more towards comfort than luxury. But Mar del Plata's **Costa Galana** succeeds on both fronts. Ocean-view suits have wraparound terraces with lounge chairs facing the blue horizon, and the top floor spa with hot tubs facing the view is outstanding.

You have to lower your standards a bit when traveling outside Buenos Aires. Even the finest hotels wouldn't stand out in Europe or the United States. But there are a few properties that certainly rise above the local competition. In Ushuaia, the **Las Hayas Resort Hotel** rises against a mountain backdrop on the road to the Martial Glacier. Fires blaze in stone fireplaces in the lounge areas; stream rises from the indoor lap pool. Guests feel like they're staying at a remote lodge, yet they're only a 10-minute drive from downtown. The **Llao Llao Hotel and Resort** in Bariloche benefits from an even more dramatic setting beside three lakes backed by soaring mountains. Architect Alejandro Bustillo created the mountain lodge with local woods, and designers filled it with local paintings and weavings. The hotel was renovated in 1993, and is now a national historic landmark. The possibilities for active play are seemingly endless — golf, tennis, boating, and even archery keep guests busy. The spa with sauna, steam rooms, indoor pool, massage, and beauty treatments takes care of the pampering.

If you've traveled all the way to Parque Nacional Los Glaciares you might as well stay at **Hostería Los Notros** in the park. The views of Moreno Glacier from most rooms and public spaces are mesmerizing, and the hotel's staff can arrange for you to get up close and personal on glacier hikes.

Sheraton is the only major international chain with several hotels in the country.

Its most outstanding property is the **Sheraton Internacional Iguazú**, where a third of the rooms face the spectacular Iguazú Falls. The same views captivate guests eating in the restaurants or swimming in the pool. The chain has hotels in Buenos Aires, Córdoba, and Mar del Plata. All have modern rooms and business centers.

You haven't really visited Argentina until you've spent a night at an *estancia*, preferably in the midst of gaucho land in San Antonio de Areco. The most lavish accommodations are at the nineteenth-century **Estancia La Porteña**, a classic ranch home with whitewashed walls draped with blazing pink bougainvillea. Take a dip in the swimming pool after a long horseback ride — real gauchos never had it this good. In Patagonia, the **Hostería Kau Yatun** outside El Calafate fulfills all expectations for an authentic gaucho experience.

EXCEPTIONAL RESTAURANTS

Beef reigns on all Argentine menus, and *parrilla*-style restaurants with open fire pits are by far the most popular choice for diners on all budgets.

Outstanding, melt-in-your mouth steaks are the specialty at **Cabaña Las Lilas** in Buenos Aires. The indoor restaurant with a patio overlooking the Río de la Plata at Puerto Madero is both elegant and extraordinarily busy. Suited waiters bustle about with sizzling platters of steaks, lamb chops, and beef ribs cooked to perfection. Salads are prepared tableside, and the wine list is outstanding. Also in Puerto Madero, **Katrine** offers a welcome change from the grilled meat theme. Chef Katrine Röed creates marvels with seafood and game, preparing light yet satisfying meals with a Mediterranean flair. The airy, minimalist decor is also a pleasant change from the wooden wagon wheel theme common in the beef restaurants.

The mainstream Crowne Plaza Panamericano Hotel is the unlikely home of one of the most exciting dining rooms in Buenos Aires. **Tomo I** attracts executives on expense accounts and theatergoers headed for the nearby Teatro Colón who want gourmet meals in sedate surroundings. Lobster, shrimp, duck, and quail are superbly prepared, and the vegetables and salads feature ingredients not usually found on local menus. Both travelers and locals enjoy a fine dinner combined with a professional tango show. The best choice for both is **El Viejo Almacén** in San Telmo. Precious few restaurants in Buenos Aires specialize in regional Argentine cuisine; tiny **La Querencia**

is the exception. It's neither fancy nor expensive, but the *empanadas*, *locro*, and *tamales* are as good (if not better) than in any countryside café.

Your choices for exciting dining diminish as you wander beyond the capital. If you're on the coast you must sample fresh fish and shellfish; I've yet to find an inland restaurant that excels in seafood. Mar del Plata has the widest array of seafood restaurants, from the all-you-can-eat buffets served in enormous dining halls at the port to intimate cafés. The chef at **Via Juancho** prepares exceptional salads and seafood cocktails featuring lobster and shrimp, and entrées with rich cream and cheese sauces. The desserts are superb as well. Mar del Plata's visitors delight in devouring fried squid rings and tentacles, steamed mussels, and *cazuela de mariscos* (seafood stew); perfect renditions of all three are served at **El Viejo Pop** at the port. Nearly everyone orders crab several times while visiting Ushuaia in Tierra del Fuego. At **Tía Elvira**, a small establishment with about a dozen tables packed close together, it seems every other diner opts for the chunks of cold crab served in the shell. The more refined **Kaupé** combines fine Argentine wines with crab and salmon entrées.

Puerto Madryn's restaurants also benefit from an abundance of local fish. At the waterfront **Placido**, the menu offers enough choices to keep you coming back again and again. Try the lobster omelet and *pulpo a la gallega* (octopus).

Italian canelone and *ñoquis* are among the highlights at **Circulo Italiano**, in the 90-year-old headquarters of the Italian Club in Santa Fe. The chef does a fine job with river fish as well — try the *surubi* or *lenguado*. River views enhance the romantic setting of the **Restaurant Turismo** in Corrientes. Choose an outdoor table on the stone terrace by the river, and sample the pasta chef's specialties or the *lomo Alaska*, smothered in a creamy mushroom sauce that's supposed to resemble a snow-covered mountain.

To the north, the indigenous character of Salta shines through at **El Solar del Convento**, where handwoven blankets and handmade masks add to the unusual decor. Beef is featured, though the preparations are so unusual they're actually daring. Patagonia's finest restaurant is **La Brida** at the Hostería Kau Yatun in El Calafate. The menu emphasizes Patagonian game, from venison to wild boar. The restaurant at **Los Notros** in Parque Nacional Los Glaciares benefits from stunning views of the glacier and regional cuisine featuring local lamb and trout. The chef at **La Cave** in Bariloche prepares some of the most innovative dishes available anywhere in the country. His sweet potato gnocchi with lamb *ragu* and chicken breast with prosciutto, sage and kidney bean salsa are far from ordinary.

OPPOSITE: Denizens of the Gran Café Tortoni linger over coffee and Cokes while visitors at the Bodegas Trapiche ABOVE in Maipú favor regional wines.

Family Fun

Argentina isn't an ideal place to travel with young children, especially those who don't adapt well to exotic food, extreme weather and long drives. But don't give up hope. The secret to success is creating an itinerary that includes activities and attractions that excite their interest.

Anything with animals is usually a big winner with children and Argentina has plenty of wildlife. The **Valdés Peninsula** of northern Patagonia is considered the "Serengeti Plains" of South America because of its numerous species and abundant numbers, from killer whales and giant elephant seals to guanacos and penguins. You can easily tour the major wildlife areas as a day trip out of Puerto Madryn, either in your own vehicle or part of a minibus safari.

Another great place to see indigenous wildlife is the **Complejo Ecológico Municipal** near Roque Sáenz Peña in the Gran Chaco region, a marvelous zoo and captive breeding center where animals from the Andes, Amazon and Pampas are studied and safeguarded. This is a wonderful opportunity to come face-to-face with all sorts of strange creatures including condors, jaguars, anteaters and boa constrictors.

Estancias are also ideal for a family visit. The huge ranches that cover so much of the Pampas and Patagonia offer kids a chance to ride horses, mingle with genuine gauchos, and maybe even brand a steer or two. Many of the

estancia houses feature swimming pools and other recreation facilities, and most of the meals are of the barbecue variety.

It's also hard to go wrong with dinosaurs. Patagonia has more fossil digs than just about any other place on the planet. The brand new **Museo Paleontológico Egidio Feruglio (MEF)** in Trelew offers one of the world's best bone collections: more than 5,000 in total from 30 different types of dinosaurs that once roamed Patagonia. The museum also has hands-on exhibits for kids, as well as film shows and educational courses. Nearby is a real-life dig, the **Parque Paleontológico Bryn Gwyn** near Gaimán, where you can delve 40 million years into the past.

Kids are also keen on boat trips. The wild ride that takes you right beneath **Iguazú Falls**, that gets you soaked to the bone, is cooler than any roller coaster. You can also try whale-watching boats that ply the deep-blue waters around the Valdés Peninsula, gentle float trips down the **Río Mendoza** and other Andes rivers, or the ferry ride across to **Isla Victoria** from Bariloche.

Cultural Kicks

Argentina's cultural attractions are diverse and far-flung, and differ greatly from those in other Latin American countries. There are precious few archeological sites, and no grand temples and fortresses like those built by the Inca in Peru. Evidence of **pre-Columbian**

civilizations exists in remote villages and canyons in the northern provinces, especially in Jujuy. A cluster of pre-Columbian ruins have been discovered, but barely excavated, in the northwestern town of Coctaca. A few small communities of Quechua Indians till the coarse earth in Humahuaca, growing their crops in terraced gardens similar to those in Peru's Sacred valley.

Other indigenous groups are honored in a cursory manner. Their names pop up in the landscape; Argentina's famed Pampas is named after the La Pampa Indians, and the Sierras de los Comechingones in Córdoba bear the name of the peoples who once lived in today's mountain resorts. Tierra del Fuego's **Museo del Fin del Mundo** has one of the country's best exhibits of pre-Columbian history in its detailed exhibits on the Yamana (also called Yahgan) tribes who settled on the inhabitable islands and along the waterfront. The museum also covers the history of Tierra del Fuego, including the tales of ships wrecked while sailing through the treacherous Beagle Channel.

Relics from Argentina's **colonial era** are more evident. Once again, the provinces north of Buenos Aires contain the bulk of the missions and fortresses built by the Spaniards during their march from Peru and Bolivia to Buenos Aires. Colonial churches, convents, and *cabildos* (city halls) have been preserved in Tucumán, Córdoba, Santa Fe, and Posadas. The seventeenth-century Convento de San Francisco in Santa Fe is one of the country's

most outstanding colonial structures, built by the Franciscans in 1680. La Iglesia de la Compañía de Jesús, built by the Jesuits in the mid-seventeenth century in Córdoba, is said to be the oldest church in the country. Both Córdoba and Buenos Aires were centers for Jesuit activity throughout South America, and both have preserved districts called the Manzana de las Luces. Intent on both conversion and education, the Jesuits built huge complexes including churches, cloisters, universities, and underground crypts.

Several **Jesuit missions** dot the countryside in the upper Paraná River basin outside Posadas. The most exceptional is San Ignacio Mini, one of the largest mission settlements in the country. Its central cathedral and cloisters were constructed in 1632; at its height the mission was home to some 4,000 Guaraní Indians. The settlement is one of Argentina's most important historical attractions, and includes a museum with life-sized replicas of the Jesuit *padres*.

Several **museums** around the country contain art and artifacts from the colonial period. One of the best is the Museo de Arte Española Enrique Larreta in the Belgrano neighborhood of Buenos Aires. Though the writer Lariat's home was built in 1916, it is styled after a colonial hacienda and contains a

LEFT: Face to face with a water buffalo in the Buenos Aires Jardín Zoológico. ABOVE: The strains of soulful tango tunes fill the streets of San Telmo.

valuable collection of religious art. The finest colonial-era home in Córdoba houses the Museo Histórico Provincial Casa del Virrey Marqués de Sobremonte and a collection of costumes and furnishings from the colonial period, along with Indian artifacts.

The most important icon in Argentine history is the **gaucho**, a romanticized, revered cowboy. The town of San Antonio de Areco outside Buenos Aires is a veritable living gaucho museum. The town's Museo Gauchesco Ricardo Güiraldes, named for the author of the gaucho novel *Don Segundo Sombra*, contains every imaginable gaucho implement and accoutrement.

Argentines are particularly enamored with the **early twentieth century**, when the country was at its economic peak and high society flourished. Nearly every museum in Buenos Aires is housed in a French palace or mansion,

and European furnishings are *de rigueur* in many a modern home. The whole era is lavishly displayed at the fascinating Museo Nacional de Arte Decorativo, housed in an over-the-top mansion designed by French architect René Sergent. The building alone boggles the mind with its excessively opulent decor, and the displays of fine crystal and china, fragile Louis XV tables and chairs, and European paintings and sculptures are overwhelming. I find it best to move on from here to the more subtle Museo de Arte Hispanoamericano Isaac Fernandez Blanco with its fine collection of **Latin American art** housed in and understated neocolonial building with flower-filled courtyards. Argentina's **premier art collection** is housed in the Museo Nacional de Bellas Artes, and includes works by Degas, Gauguin, and Manet. Contemporary painters, sculptors, and performance artists find a generous haven in the Centro Cultural Recoleta, a restored colonial Franciscan cloister.

Mausoleums at the Recoleta Cemetery — **Cementerio de la Recoleta** — are lavishly decorated with statues of the heroes buried within.

Shop till You Drop

Unlike nearby Bolivia and Peru, Argentina is not known for exceptional folk art. **Weavings** similar to those found in Brazil are available in the northern Andean provinces, where Quechua Indians live in Argentina's most authentic indigenous communities. Handwoven **ponchos** are the trademark souvenirs from Salta, and various small communities are known for their local **pottery**. The indigenous peoples of Patagonia also make distinctive weavings and pottery available in shops in Bariloche and San Martín de los Andes. A few shops in Buenos Aires carry handicrafts from throughout the country. Those truly devoted to folk art should schedule their travels to coincide with the folklore festival in Cosquín in January for the best overview of the country's crafts.

Argentina is known for its fine **leather** and its prices on leather goods. Several shops in Buenos Aires feature handmade shoes, jackets, briefcases, and purses; others specialize in saddles and equestrian gear. Some of the finest leather shops are located in La Recoleta and around the Plaza San Martín. San Antonio de Areco is the center for all things gaucho, including lassos and braided leather ornaments for saddles.

Silver and **alpaca** (a mix of silver and nickel) are also integral in the gaucho's accoutrements, and are used to make *facones* (long-bladed knives) with leather sheaths, silver belt buckles, and *rastas* (silver-studded leather belts). San Antonio's silversmiths also create lovely jewelry, often with equestrian themes. Silver is also used to decorate *matés*, the leather or gourd vessels used to drink the tea of the same name. Some *matés* are true works of art, especially when combined with delicate silver *bombillas* (straws). They can be found in almost any town, as they are essential items in many Argentine households.

Thanks to all the sheep, llama, and alpaca grazing in Patagonia and the Andes, Argentina is also known for its fine **wool sweaters**. Some are heavy, bulky items useful in mountain climes; others are more delicate and stylish. Bariloche and Mar del Plata are both known for their fine sweaters.

Short Breaks

Buenos Aires is a perfect base for long weekends or short vacations at many of Argentina's leading attractions. Other than Tierra del Fuego and Patagonia's deep south, most destinations are less than two hours flying time from the federal capital. Aerolíneas Argentinas and its domestic wing (Austral), plus smaller domestic carriers like LAPA and LADA, offer frequent service to outlying areas.

The most obvious choices for short breaks are the country's incredible natural wonders — Iguazú Falls, the high desert near Salta, the wine country around Mendoza, the Lake District beyond Bariloche, the Chubut Valley with its Welsh heritage and the inimitable wildlife of Puerto Madryn.

Three days in **Iguazú** gives you enough time to walk both the upper and lower circuits, take an adventure cruise to the base of the falls and pop over to Brazil for a little samba and shopping. A long weekend in **Puerto Madryn** is perfect for a drive around

OPPOSITE: "Energy stones" for sale at Puente del Inca in the High Andes near Mendoza. ABOVE: Jewelers display their wares at the Recoleta Sunday Market in Buenos Aires.

Festive Flings

Festivals in Argentina lack the frenzy and fervor of those of other Latin and South American countries, with a more sedate, European flavor. National holidays are celebrated more as a day away from work than cause for parades and parties. But every city and town has some sort of provincial celebration honoring a patron saint or significant historical event. Regional festivals offer more potential for getting a feel for the people and their customs. Since 1961, the city of Cosquín has held the **Festival Nacional de Folklore** (National Festival of Folklore) during the third week in January. For nine nights, invited musicians and dancers put on shows that blend Argentine and Latin American traditions. Concurrent with these events, the **Festival Provincial de las Artesanías** features works by Cosquín artists and those of nearby regions. A similar festival called **La Fiesta del Poncho** attracts artisans and musicians to Catamarca in July.

Carnival, celebrated in Brazil with wild exuberance, is a more modest affair in Buenos Aires, taking place only on the weekends, unlike other venues where the party continues for days on end. If you do happen to find yourself in Buenos Aires during late January and early February when Carnival is celebrated, take a drive up the Gualeguaychú, 220 km (132 miles) north of the capital, long considered to have one of the best Carnival festival in Argentina. Jubilant festivities with local floats, music and outrageous costumes take place during the weekends. Celebrations are also held in Salta, Corrientes, Mar del Plata, and Junín.

The **Fiesta Nacional de la Vendimia** (Festival of the Grape Harvest) in Mendoza, held annually for six decades, celebrates the ripening and harvest of the wine grapes. Argentina is a major international producer of wines, and Argentines take this holiday to heart, with parades, local bands, floats from each town in Mendoza Province, and the ultimate crowning of a local girl as Wine Harvest Queen. There is plenty of local wine available to liven up the party. The celebration takes place the last week in February and first week in March.

the Península Valdés and a whale-watching cruise on the South Atlantic. Three days is an ideal amount of time to explore **Mendoza** and environs; five days gives you enough time to include the **High Andes**. Three days is also a good duration for **Bariloche**, with time to explore the southern shore of Lago Nahuel Huapi and take a cruise over to Isla Victoria.

Flying isn't the only option. One of the most popular weekend trips is catching a **ferry to Montevideo**, the slightly rundown but always romantic capital of Uruguay. Anyone with a vehicle can choose from half a dozen destinations within a short drive from Buenos Aires including beach resorts, historic Pampas towns and fascinating cities along the Paraná River.

Four hours drive south of Buenos Aires is the sprawling Atlantic coast outpost of **Mar del Plata**, the country's most popular beach resort. Two hours west of the capital are the pilgrimage town of **Luján** with its huge neo-Gothic cathedral and the cowboy town of **San Antonio de Areco**, one of last bastions of true gaucho culture.

Another alternative is structuring a short break around a specific activity. For instance, you could fly into Puerto Iguazú for two or three days fishing for dorado and other game fish in the **Río Paraná**. Or devote an entire weekend to the annual and Salta **Carnival** celebrations in Corrientes and Salta. Or hop over to Mendoza or Bariloche for a few days of **skiing** and other winter sports.

ABOVE: Gauchos display their pride with silver coins and knives. RIGHT: Flamboyant costumes are *de rigueur* during Salta's boisterous Carnival.

Religious processions and a Passion Play are held in General Juan Madariaga during **Semana Santa** (Easter week). Thousands of pilgrims travel to the **Basílica Nuestra Señora de Luján** on May 8, the Virgin's feast day. In the northern provinces close to Peru, locals celebrate the Inca holiday of **Inti Raymi** in honor of the winter solstice at the end of June. August sees a month-long celebration of winter with the **Fiesta Nacional de la Nieve** (National Snow Festival) held in Bariloche and the Catedral ski area.

Gauchos are celebrated throughout the country with festivals and parades. In the Northwest, folkloric musicians and dancers, artists and artisans, and gauchos in full regalia turn out for the **Salta Gaucho Parade** held in mid-June. In San Antonio de Areco, the town's biggest bash is the annual **Día de la Tradición** in early November, a festival that draws genuine cowpokes and gaucho aficionados from around the world. More than 10,000 visitors pour into the tiny town to watch equestrian events like polo and cattle roping, as well as concerts, dances and parades. General Juan Madariaga holds a large **Fiesta Nacional del Gaucho** at the beginning of December, with parades, demonstrations of gaucho horseback riding skills, folkloric dancing, and plenty of *parrilla*-style meals.

Galloping Gourmet

Vegetarians beware! Argentina is the land of the carnivore, and it's not unusual to eat beef every day of the week. At first glance the country's cuisine seems fairly interesting, as long as you're a fan of steaks and organ meats. But a steady diet of steak, salad, and french fries (the single most popular meal in the country) soon wears thin — or fat in the case of those watching their weight. Fortunately, the country's enormous Italian population has heavily influenced the national diet, and pastas are prevalent everywhere. Pizza parlors are nearly as common as the ubiquitous cafés where Argentines avidly consume their two favorite treats — gossip and coffee.

Regional cuisine is largely ignored in the capital city, where restaurants follow the latest European trends. In the poorer, more indigenous provinces to the north, cooks stretch meager portions of meat and fish in savory soups and stews. Seafood rules along the coast. Lamb is a dietary staple in Patagonia, where Welsh immigrants are famous for their afternoon teas and pastries, and the Swiss and German settlers for their homemade chocolates and tortes.

BREADS
The best bread I've ever had in Argentina came from a roadside stand in Córdoba. Called *pan casero*, the bread was cooked in a wood-burning oven and had a smoky flavor and dense texture. Sandwiches are typically made with plain white bread, though you can ask for whole wheat (*pan integral*).

SNACKS
The best quick meal or snack is the *empanada*, a turnover stuffed with meat, cheese, and/or vegetables. *Empanadas* are sold in markets and restaurants; the ingredients vary with the region and the cook. Pizza parlors are even more prevalent than McDonald's. Many places sell pizza by the slice, and it's not unusual to see people walking down the street with a slice or two in hand. The pizza is usually excellent, and a great boon for those tired of sandwiches and burgers. Hotdogs, called *panchos* are also popular, and are sold at street stands and markets.

MEAT AND POULTRY
Beef may well be Argentina's national dish. It's certainly the most popular. Nearly every part of the cow appears on menus, much to the consternation of those confused by the

terminology. Some menus even offer pictures of the various breeds of cattle raised throughout the country so you can become better acquainted with your food. In its most familiar form, beef appears as steaks, called *bife*. *Bife de chorizo* is the thickest cut; *bife de costilla* is a T-bone steak; *bife de lomo* is sirloin; *churrasquito de entraña* is flank steak; *churrasco de cuadril* is a rump steak; and *asado de tira* is a short rib roast. As a rule, the portions are enormous — it's not unusual to order a steak weighing 550 grams (1.2 pounds). The steaks stand alone; side dishes cost extra. You can order your steak well done (*cocido*), rare (*jugoso* or *rojo*) or medium (*a punto*). Argentine *bife* has a mild flavor and less fat than that sold in the United States. It's often served with *chimichurri*, a savory and sometimes fiery hot marinade of oil, herbs, peppers, and garlic.

The most popular meat presentation is the *parrillada*, a mixed grill of *bife* and other meats best cooked over a wood fire. Meat cooked *a la parrilla* is grilled over hot coals; *al asador* means the meat is cooked on a spit. Restaurants specializing in these meat platters often display their fire pits and grills through street-front windows, allowing potential diners to view *chivitos* (young goats) and *lechónes* (suckling pigs) stretched on racks around the fire. Those with weak stomachs are well advised to ask for descriptions of the various meats before digging in (though you may be best off not knowing exactly what you're eating). I once shared a *parrillada* with a group of friends, and bravely sampled *chinchulin de ternera* (veal tripe or intestines), *riñones* (kidneys), *ubre* (udder), *mollejas* (sweetbreads or, if you must know, the thymus gland of a young cow), and *morcilla* (blood sausage). Fortunately, I managed to avoid the *criadillas* (testicles). Once was quite enough, thank you.

On the other hand, I've grown fond of *matambre*, a pounded flank steak rolled around hard-boiled eggs, spinach, and pieces of ham and usually served cold. *Milanesa de lomo*, a thin strip of flank steak breaded and fried, is usually the least expensive beef dish on the menu.

Chicken, called *pollo*, is also served *milanesa* style or *a la parrilla* (char-grilled). *Pollo deshuesado* is boneless chicken; a chicken breast is *suprema*. Lamb, called *cordero*, and is more commonly served in Patagonia than in the north. Pork usually appears as sausage (*chorizo* or *salchicha*).

Ham (*jamón*) is extraordinarily popular as an ingredient in meat dishes, sandwiches, pasta sauces, and egg dishes. Imported cured hams (*jamón crudo*) are served as appetizers (*tapas*).

FISH AND SHELLFISH

Fish is listed on menus as an afterthought in most of Argentina, and usually consists of a sole offering of grilled salmon. Ushuaia's king crab (*centolla*) may well be Argentina's finest seafood dish; it's certainly the most popular item on menus in Tierra del Fuego. Mar del Plata's commercial port has more seafood restaurants than any other one spot in the country. Specialties include *cazuela de mariscos* (seafood stew), fried squid, grilled *lenguado* (a mild white fish) or *merluza* (similar to cod), *pulpo* (octopus), and *langostinos* (crayfish). The Río Paraná in Corrientes is home to *surubí*, a type of catfish that grows up to 48 kg (100 lbs). The inland rivers also provide *pejerrey* (a white fish), *dorado*, and *sábalo* (shad).

REGIONAL DISHES

Regional cooking featuring traditional recipes is most common in Northwestern Argentina. Here you'll find excellent *tamales* (corn dough shaped around meet or fruit fillings) and spicy homemade *empanadas*. Stews are an integral part of the daily diet. The most famous is *carbonada*, a beef stew with vegetables and fruit, especially peaches. *Puchero*, another stew, typically includes beef, corn, and chickpeas along with whatever vegetables are available, while *locro* combine corn or wheat with meat.

OPPOSITE: An Indian woman sells garlic in Salta's Mercado Central. ABOVE: German immigrants have transformed Bariloche into a chocoholic's paradise.

VEGETABLES

At first glance the Argentine diet appears to lack *legumbres* (vegetables), which are usually hidden as side dishes on menus. Fortunately, salads are quite common, as are salad bars. Most menus offer *ensaladas comunes*, or simple salads, which are usually served in a large bowl and are shared by the table. The *ensalada mixta* typically includes tomato, lettuce, and onion, and may also contain hard-boiled egg and carrots. Most people dress their salads with a liberal dash of olive oil and salt; mixed salad dressings are a rarity. Endive (*endibia*), arugula (*rúcula*), spinach (*espinaca*), and hearts of palm (*palmitos*) often appear as salads as well. Many restaurants now have serve-yourself salad bars, though in some places you point to the ingredients you want and a server prepares your salad.

Steamed vegetables (*panaché de legumbres*) typically rely heavily on cauliflower (*coliflor*) and broccoli (*brócoli*). Some of the better restaurants also serve sautéed spinach, string beans (*chauchas*), and mushrooms (*champignones*). French fries (*papas fritas*) are extremely popular, as are fried potato slices (*papas a la española*). Baked potatoes are hard to come by, but mashed potatoes (*puré de papas*) are common. Most major cities have a few vegetarian restaurants, though you're hard put to find them in rural regions. Most menus include a few meatless pasta dishes.

BEVERAGES

Traditional Argentines are nearly addicted to *maté*, a tea made with *yerba maté* leaves. The tradition dates back to the Guaraní Indians. The preparation involves more than simply throwing a few tea leaves in boiling water, and the act of drinking *maté* is rife with symbolism. If someone offers you *maté* you can assume you've been accepted as a true friend.

The vessel for containing the tea is also called a *maté*, typically a gourd decorated with silver or leather. The tea is sipped through a *bombilla*, a metal straw with holes in the bottom to filter out the tea leaves. Argentines devoted to the drink carry their *matés* everywhere, along with thermoses containing the brewed tea.

Coffee is an essential part of the Argentine diet and lifestyle. It is served espresso style, in tiny cups. Coffee with milk is called *café con leche*. Another warm drink worth trying is the *submarino*, a glass of warm milk with a melting chocolate bar at the bottom. Sodas are called *gaseosas*; bottled water is *agua mineral*. *Licuados* are made with fresh fruit and water or milk.

Thanks in part to the large German population, Argentina has several good beers. Quilmes may well be the most popular, but you should also try Brahma and Bieckert. Draft beer is called *chopp*. A bottle is *porron*; can is *lata*.

Argentina's wines are gaining international attention, though they're still overshadowed by those from Chile. Most of the wine produced in Argentina comes from Mendoza, where vineyards thrive in a climate similar to that in the grape growing regions of California and France. Some say local wine hasn't received much outside attention because most of it is consumed right at home.

Hearty red wines are understandably popular in the land of beef; one variety stands out as an exceptional national product. The climate is particularly kind to the Malbec grape, and Argentina's Malbec wines are

among its top exports. A white grape, called Torrontés, also thrives in local vineyards, and produces and slightly sweet, light, fruity white wine. Chandon and San Telmo are the most popular labels. Etchart produces a fine Torrontés wine; Humberto Canale makes a tasty Malbec. Both red and white wines are used to make *clericot*, a fruit filled sangria.

SWEETS AND DESSERTS

Anyone with a sweet tooth will be delighted with the Argentine passion for sugar. Just one taste of *dulce de leche* (sweet, caramelized milk) is enough to send your blood sugar soaring. The thick caramel made of equal parts of sugar and milk is used in cookies, cakes, crepes, and ice cream; addicts order a side dish of *dulce de leche* with all sorts of desserts. Also popular is *dulce de batata* (sweet potato jam). *Dulce de leche* is used to fill maize-flour cookies called

alfajores, a local specialty in Mar del Plata and Córdoba. Homemade chocolates from Bariloche are excellent.

The sugar craving kicks in strongest in late afternoon, when Argentines settle over small cups of coffee and large slices of *torta* (cake) or pie. Tea houses serving lavish selections of sweets are popular in mountain resorts from Córdoba to Bariloche.

Argentine ice cream (*helado*) is wonderful, and ice cream is featured in all sorts of elaborate desserts. *Bombas*, scoops of ice cream coated with chocolate, are especially popular. You can find Freddo's ice-cream parlors nearly everywhere, but keep your eye out for smaller shops advertising *helado artesanal*, homemade ice cream.

Rosario's fruit stands are packed with seasonal fruits.

Special Interests

BIRD WATCHING

Antarctica's penguins and sea birds may well be the greatest draw for birdwatchers, but several other species are worth spotting.

Field Guides ((512) 263-7295 TOLL-FREE (800) 728-4953 FAX (512) 263-0117 E-MAIL fgileader @aol.com WEB SITE www.fieldguides.com 9433, Bee Cave Road, Austin, Texas 78733, are one of the leading tour companies in the world for birdwatchers, who consider the company's circumnavigation of the South Georgia Island and the Falklands to be a once in a lifetime adventure. Field Guides use Abercrombie & Kent's *Explorer* for the 18-day trip; scientists and naturalists assist passengers in spotting wandering albatrosses, snow petrels, and king penguins. The company also offers trips in the spring to the northern Andes, the pampas, and Patagonia.

HIKING AND BIKING

Backroads ((510) 527-1555 TOLL-FREE (800) 462-2848 FAX (510) 527-1444 WEB SITE www .backroads.com, 801 Cedar Street, Berkeley, California 94710, offers hiking and mountain biking trips that combine Chile's Lake District and Argentina's Patagonia.

FALKLAND ISLANDS (ISLAS MALVINAS)

Overnight stays on the Falklands are available through **Ladatco Tours** ((305) 854-8422 TOLL-FREE (800) 327-6162 FAX (305) 285-0504 E-MAIL tailor@ladatco.com WEB SITE www.ladatco.com, the best company I've found for information on these remote islands.

TANGO

To perfect their steps, tango aficionados head straight to Buenos Aires, where they'll see tango in the streets and can haunt *milongas* (dance halls) every night of the week. If you're lucky, you'll dance with old-timers. And if you're observant, you'll learn the intricacies of *la mirada*, those looks between woman and man that invite and accept dances.

It's easy in Buenos Aires to organize a whole trip dedicated to learning and dancing the tango. In addition to the places mentioned under TACKLE THE TANGO, page 17 in TOP SPOTS, and under NIGHTLIFE, page 96 in BUENOS AIRES, there are several other venues to see the real thing, or dance it, or learn it. **Club Almagro** ((11) 4774-7454, Madrano 522, has tango Tuesday and Friday, from 10 PM to 4 AM, with excellent music and good dancers of all generations, all dancing the close-embrace style. At Armenia 1366, you find both **La Estrella** ((11) 4307-5357 on Friday, and **La Viruta** ((11) 4832-4105 on Wednesday and Saturday. This is *the* hot spot for the young *porteño* tango crowd, and classes are often held before the dancing, which lasts until breakfast.

The popular, dimly lit **El Torquato Tasso** ((11) 4307-6506, Defensa 1575, in the San Telmo area, is one of the few places that frequently invites musicians. Check it out on Friday night or ask about classes held there. On Thursday and Saturday after 11 PM, **Niño Bien** ((11) 4496-3053 offers a more elegant atmosphere, where professionals can be seen dancing. Call to reserve a table near the dance floor.

For something truly authentic, try **Salon Canning** ((11) 4826-8351, Avenida R. Scalabrini Ortiz 1331, Sunday from 4 PM. The crowd is older, as it is at the somewhat kitsch **Viejo Correo** ((11) 4862-0520, Avenida Díaz Vélez 4820, on Tuesday and Friday. As can be expected, "in" places tend to change. Ask around.

Old ways still hold here and women who want to dance with regulars never sit with an accompanying man and they wait to be asked. Although it's hardly a demure wait, as it involves staring down a targeted man until he nods his *cabeseo* and comes to get his partner. It's recommended to sit near the entrance and/or not far from the bar. Every three dances is followed by *la cortina*, a musical interlude during which everyone sits down, meant for a change of partners.

Tango schools such as **La Escuela del Tango** ((11) 4383-0466, San José 364 Piso 3, offer classes for all levels. Lists of other classes and practice sessions can be found in the monthly *Tangauta*, which occasionally has an

English language section and is available in most tango venues. It lists all major tango activities as well as nightly dancing venues. The bimonthly *B.A. Tango* overviews tango happenings and can be found in many hotels.

Web sites for tango aficionados seeking information on tango happenings around the world include **www.abctango.com.ar**, which has articles on tango and listings of upcoming events in Buenos Aires, and **www.tangol.com**, the site for *Buenos Aires Day & Night*, a free publication listing arts events. In Spanish, **www.cybertango.com** lists classes and upcoming events along with worldwide tango links, and **www.tangoshow.com** highlights shows and venues with history and articles.

ANTARCTICA

Anyone with a bit of Gypsy in his or her blood is tempted to visit Antarctica. Explorers

have attempted to describe the beauty and isolation of the Great White Continent since 1775, when Captain James Cook called Antarctica "Lands doomed by nature to everlasting frigidness and never once to feel the warmth of the sun's rays, whose horrible and savage aspect I have no words to describe." Despite such dire observations, the continent continues to attract scientists and hardy adventurers, though most visitors now arrive via posh cruise ships. At least a dozen companies offer Antarctic cruises during the short summer season, which lasts from November to March. The best trips are lengthy affairs of two weeks or more.

OPPOSITE: Llamas graze the ruins of Quilmes in Tucumán Province. ABOVE: The Fitzroy Range looms above the shore of Lago Viedma.

Penguins may well be the continent's most popular inhabitants and biggest attraction. Most visitors grow almost addicted to penguin sightings and lament lost opportunities during days at sea. The 17 known species of penguins are all found in the Southern Hemisphere; most travelers spot at least a half-dozen breeds — chinstrap, gentoo, macaroni, king, rockhopper, and Adélies — during shore excursions. Humpback whales, Weddell's seals, giant albatrosses, and other mammals and birds keep binocular-bearing passengers on the ship's decks. Wildlife sightings are frequently broadcast over the ships' loudspeakers.

Antarctica's landscape is equally entrancing. Ice cliffs, pack-ice floes, glacier-lined fjords, and snow-covered mountains provide a scenic backdrop that changes both subtly and dramatically as the ship approaches islands and deep passages. There's even an underwater volcanic crater at Deception Island, where travelers swim in hot thermal springs.

Antarctica is extremely popular these days. Well-known cruises are sold out six months to a year before sailing. Make your reservations as far in advance as possible. Most cruises begin in Ushuaia; passengers typically spend a few days in Buenos Aires or Santiago before boarding. Several itineraries include stops at South Atlantic islands, including the Falklands and South Georgia.

Consider timing when planning your trip. Though the travel season is short, wildlife sightings vary considerably from beginning to end. During late spring and early summer (November), many species are engaged in serious courtship — birders are particularly entranced by the courting rites of wandering albatrosses, called "gamming." There are still a few hours of darkness each day, with ever-shorter nights between sunset and sunrise.

Daylight lasts 24 hours in the height of summer (December and January), when penguin chicks begin hatching from their eggs and toddling about their nests. By February, the chicks have shed their down and learned to leap (albeit awkwardly) into the sea. This is usually the best time for spotting whales.

Temperatures rarely climb higher than 4.4°C (40°F) degrees during the austral summer, and passengers often need parkas and rubber boots for shore excursions. Some ships provide cold-weather gear for passengers; others provide daunting packing lists. Read this information carefully. Boots are sometimes required, especially for wet landings in frigid water.

Lars-Eric Lindblad first chartered an Argentine naval vessel for an expedition to Antarctica in 1966. **Lindblad Special Expeditions** ((212) 765-7740 TOLL-FREE (800) 397-3348 FAX (212) 265-3770 E-MAIL travel@expeditions.com WEB SITE www.expeditions.com, 720 Fifth Avenue, New York, New York 10019, has been a leader in expedition travel in the region ever since. The company's *Caledonia Star* carries 110 passengers on two- and three-week voyages; some sailings include stops at South Georgia Island and the Falklands. Naturalists lead day hikes at landing sites and Zodiac boat trips around icebergs, and impart considerable knowledge about the region during frequent lectures. Another plus — all 62 cabins face outside.

Many passengers are devoted to **Clipper Cruise Line** ((314) 727-2929 TOLL-FREE (800) 325-0010 FAX (314) 727-6576 E-MAIL SmallShip@aol.com WEB SITE www.clippercruise.com, 7711 Bonhomme Avenue, St. Louis, Missouri 63105, and wouldn't consider traveling to Antarctica with any other company. This loyalty is largely the result of the company's policy of providing high-quality service, food, and accommodations without glamour or glitz. Well-heeled passengers shun fancy jewelry and ties and dress casually even in the dining room, though a few do don jackets and dresses for the captain's dinner. The passengers also tend to be highly educated; thus, the lecturers and guides are among the best in their areas of expertise. Clipper offers 15- to 23-day Antarctica cruises with frequent Zodiac landings and hikes among penguins. **Marine Expeditions** ((416) 964-5751 TOLL-FREE (800) 263-9147 FAX (416) 964-5751 WEB SITE www.marineex.com, 890 Yonge Street, Ontario, Canada M4W 3PN, offers a wide range of Antarctic expeditions and has a devoted following among international budget travelers. The *Marine Discovery* holds 128 passengers; all cabins have windows or portholes. One journey traces Sir Ernest Shackleton's expedition to South Georgia Island. Another includes four days at the Falklands (a longer stay than most cruises). Some passengers opt to board the ship in Ushuaia after traveling about the country on their own. The cruise rates are considerably lower in these cases, since airfare is not included.

South Georgia and Falkland Island cruises are also available with **Natural Habitat Adventures** ((303) 449-3711 TOLL-FREE (800) 543-8917 FAX (303) 449-3712 WEB SITE www.nathab.com, 2945 Center Green Court, Boulder, Colorado 80301.

Taking a Tour

Independent travel is more common than group travel in Argentina. Few companies offer organized, guided tours, and those that do typically combine Argentina with Chile. Some companies will set up an itinerary for you, booking all hotels and transportation in advance, and putting you in touch with local operators at each destination.

Tour operators in Buenos Aires prefer to work with travelers before they arrive in Argentina. Few have storefront offices. Instead, they work in secured buildings and do not accept drop-in visits. It's best to contact them by e-mail or fax before you travel to the country.

The best source for tour information in country is the local or provincial tourist information office. These offices usually have lists of companies offering general overview tours and special interest trips.

GENERAL INTEREST

Ladatco Tours ((305) 854-8422 TOLL-FREE (800) 327-6162 FAX (305) 285-0504 E-MAIL tailor@ladatco.com WEB SITE www.ladatco.com, 2220 Coral Way, Miami, Florida 33145, offers several itineraries covering all of Argentina's highlights including Iguazú Falls, Buenos Aires, and Bariloche. Itineraries can be tailored to individual interests. **Abercrombie & Kent** TOLL-FREE IN THE UNITED STATES (800) 323-7308 E-MAIL info@abercrombiekent.com WEB SITE www.abercrombiekent.com, 1520 Kensington Road, Oak Brook, Illinois 60523, offers individual and group itineraries emphasizing Patagonia. They can be reached in the United Kingdom at ((020) 7976-6176, 22 Chapter Street, London SWIP 4MP.

Republic Travel has offices in the United States ((310) 289-9944 FAX (310) 289-9948, 292 South La Cienega Boulevard, Suite 211, Beverly Hills, California 90211, and in Argentina ((11) 4322-9689 FAX (11) 4327-1774 WEB SITE www.republictravel.com, Avenida Córdoba 966, 1054 Buenos Aires, and can book airline tickets, hotel rooms, and tours.

Tour companies in Argentina that can organize your trip include **Argentina Guía** ((11) 4313-8448 FAX (11) 4312-3789 WEB SITE www.argentina-guia.com.ar, a well-organized company with extensive contacts throughout the country.

Hiking the ice fields of Parque Nacional Los Glaciares is serious business.

Bariloche. Passengers rave about the luxurious treatment they receive while on the plane and at the variety of destinations, which also include Machu Picchu and Easter Island.

SOUTH ATLANTIC CRUISES

Several companies offer cruises down Argentina's Atlantic coast, often when ships are in transition to and from Antarctica. Weather on the South Atlantic can wreak havoc with itineraries, closing ports all along the coast. Passengers should be prepared for a bit of seasickness; most ships provide medication. On the plus side, these cruises offer excellent wildlife experiences. Killer whales and southern right whales are easily spotted during the spring months off the coast of the Península Valdés; thousands of Magellanic and gentoo penguins nest in the Falkland Islands.

Clipper Cruise Line ((314) 727-2929 TOLL-FREE (800) 325-0010 FAX (314) 727-6576 E-MAIL SmallShip@aol.com WEB SITE www .clippercruise.com, also at 7711 Bonhomme Avenue, St. Louis, Missouri 63105, begins its Argentina cruise in Brazil's Amazon Basin, then continues on to Montevideo, Uruguay, before stopping in Buenos Aires. After tours of the city and *estancias*, the cruise continues on to the Valdés Peninsula and the Falklands, where naturalists lead excursions on several islands. The company's Clipper *Adventurer* handles South Atlantic storms with ease, and the cabins, library, and lounge are all comfortable and well stocked with all necessary amenities. Clipper's chefs manage to provide excellent and interesting meals that keep passengers satisfied even on the longest journeys.

Argentina itineraries are combined with stops in Uruguay and Chile on **Lindblad Special Expeditions** ((212) 765-7740 TOLL-FREE (800) 397-3348 FAX (212) 265-3770 E-MAIL travel@expeditions.com WEB SITE www.expeditions.com, 720 Fifth Avenue, New York, New York 10019. Lindblad's *New Caledonia* stops at Mar del Plata, Puerto Madryn and the Península Valdés en route to the Falklands, then sails through the Beagle Channel to Ushuaia and on to the Chilean Fjords. The trip lasts a little more than two weeks, and satisfies most sightseeing urges, though you may well be tempted to stay on board and continue on to Antarctica. **Marine Expeditions** ((416) 964-5751 TOLL-FREE (800) 263-9147 FAX (416) 964-5751 WEB SITE www.marineex.com, 890 Yonge Street, Ontario, Canada M4W 3PN, offers a land and sea tour around Patagonia, including the Moreno Glacier and Tierra del Fuego.

Fox Tours ((11) 4312-1001 FAX (11) 4315-6183, San Martín 910, Buenos Aires, tailors individual trips according your preference. Trekking or mountaineering, rafting or kayaking trips can be arranged to most parts of the country. English-speaking guides are available.

Pathfinder Tour Operator ((11) 4394-7982 or (11) 4327-3295 FAX (11) 4325-6826 E-MAIL mail@pathfinder-travel.com Avenida Paroissien 3715, Buenos Aires, is a multipurpose agency that specializes in group tours.

LUXURY TOURS

INTRAV ((314) 727-0500 TOLL-FREE (800) 456-8100 FAX (314) 727-0908 E-MAIL info@intrav.com WEB SITE www.INTRAV.com, 7711 Bonhomme Avenue, St. Louis, Missouri 63105, offers the ultimate South American odyssey for those with plenty of discretionary cash. The company uses a private jet to carry 88 guests all in first-class seating to South America's highlights. The Argentina portion of the trip includes a stay in La Recoleta (the loveliest part of Buenos Aires) and in San Carlos de

ABOVE: Cristo Redentor in the High Andes marks the boundary between Argentina and Chile. RIGHT: Mountains, valleys and glaciers all lure hikers into the Patagonia wilderness.

Welcome
to
Argentina

DESPITE ITS WELL-HONED IDENTITY, ARGENTINA IS REALLY A DOZEN COUNTRIES ROLLED INTO ONE, a rich concoction of Latin American culture, European civilization and primordial wilderness.

The subtropical northeast seems to take its cue from Brazil, languid towns that bask on the banks of muddy jungle rivers, waterfalls that plunge through basalt gorges and even a Carnival that mimics the annual hijinx in Rio. The arid northwest could not be more different: a land of adobe villages, *cardón* cactus and ruddy faced Indians that have more in common with their indigenous brethren in Bolivia and Peru than with anyone else in Argentina. Between these two extremes lies a largely uninhabited region called the Gran Chaco, thorn forest sprinkled with savanna that continues to resist human settlement.

Mendoza and the Cuyo region bear a striking resemblance to nearby Chile — lush vineyards set against snowcapped peaks — attributed not just to geography but also the fact that Cuyo was settled from Santiago rather than Buenos Aires. The picturesque Lake District around Bariloche is like a chunk of Switzerland that's been sliced off and somehow floated to the South Atlantic, a place of ski slopes, chocolate shops and Saint Bernards.

Patagonia is a different animal altogether, a rough and rugged land where earth forces continue to hold sway over human endeavors. The windswept landscapes of Tierra del Fuego, the Malvinas and the southern Andes draw their inspiration from the polar regions. Glaciers tumble down through mountain passes, melting into deep-blue lakes that feed into mighty rivers that churn their way down to the great bays and gulfs of the Patagonian coast. Wildlife abounds, a greater bounty of large animals than

anywhere else in South America — millions of penguins and seals, thousands of whales, and wandering herds of guanaco and rhea. If cities like Ushuaia and Río Gallegos have that end-of-the-earth feeling, perhaps it's because they really are, lying closer to the Antarctic than to Buenos Aires.

The heart and soul of Argentina is the Pampas, an incredibly flat grassland that spreads across the country's middle from Córdoba and Buenos Aires to the Atlantic coast and all the way down to the northern parts of Patagonia. Natural pampa with its lush endemic grasses has gradually given way to huge *estancias* — cattle and sheep ranches that dominated the Argentine economy until well into the twentieth century. Although cowboy culture has largely faded away, a victim of agro-business and motorized transport, the residents of the Pampas remain gauchos at heart, proud of their equestrian skills and their ability to eat copious amounts of beef.

Despite the existence of large provincial cities like Córdoba (1.3 million) and Rosario (1.1 million), nearly a third of Argentina's people live in Buenos Aires and environs. The federal capital dominates every aspect of modern Argentine life — politics, economics, sports, education and culture — a dynamic, bustling metropolis that ranks as one of the world's great cities. There is something unmistakably European about its broad boulevards, smartly dressed women and sidewalk cafés, as well as the flourish that *porteños* bring to nearly everything they do.

Quilmes was constructed by Argentina's most advanced pre-Columbian civilization.

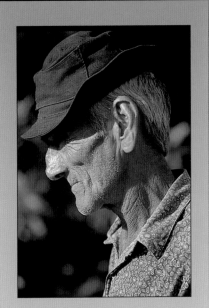

The Country and Its People

SPREAD ACROSS MORE THAN 2.8 MILLION SQ KM (1.08 million sq miles) at the bottom end of South America, Argentina ranks as the continent's second largest country (after Brazil) and the world's eighth biggest. If superimposed over a map of Europe it would stretch from Lisbon to Moscow, a distance of more than 3,500 km (2,200 miles).

But unlike Europe, Argentina is virtually empty. With a population of only 37 million (more than 88% living in cities) and a density of just 34 people per square mile, it also ranks as one of the planet's least crowded countries, vast tracts of land that harbor nothing more than sheep, cattle and isolated farmhouses.

largest glacier, a remnant of the time when most of Argentina was covered by ice.

DINOSAUR PARADISE AND GRAVEYARD

One hundred million years ago, the bottom end of South America was a rich breeding ground for dinosaurs and other ancient life forms. Much of the land was covered in jungle and swamp; volcanoes spewed out great lava flows and the Andes were just starting to push up from the seabed. During the Pleistocene period, four successive glaciations spurred by dramatic planetary climatic change transformed the landscape into the

The majority of Argentines trace their origins to Spanish settlers who came before independence and Italian immigrants who arrived in the late nineteenth and early twentieth centuries. Yet Argentina is a true melting pot that also includes ethnic Germans, Swiss, Welsh, Poles, Yugoslavians, Greeks, Lebanese and Syrians.

Argentina's geographical superlatives are also impressive. Cerro Aconcagua in the Central Andes is the highest peak in the western hemisphere (6,959 m/22,834 ft). Ushuaia in Tierra del Fuego is the world's southernmost city. Iguazú is the world's fourth largest waterfall in terms of mean annual water flow. Salina Grande in Patagonia is the lowest point in South America (42 m/137 ft below sea level). Tierra del Fuego is the continent's largest island. The Río Paraná (4,000 km/2,485 miles) is South America's second longest river, after the Amazon. Upsala is the continent's

high mountains and vast plains that characterize Argentina today.

Man didn't appear in Argentina until the end of the Ice Age, around 10,000 years ago, when primitive nomads came from farther north, attracted by the abundant game that grazed the Pampas. These early arrivals gradually evolved into distinct Indian groups like the Guaraní in the northeast, the Tehuelche on the Patagonian plains, the Ona in Tierra del Fuego and the Mapuche in the Lake District. By 500 BC, a few of the Andes tribes like the Diaguita had developed a sedentary civilization based on primitive pottery, metalwork and maize cultivation.

It was inevitable that the Argentine tribes would be influenced by more advanced peoples from the Central Andes, starting with the Bolivian-based Tiahuanaco civilization around AD 650. Trade flourished up and down the Andes, bringing all sorts of new products and innovations to the Argentine frontier. Hubs of culture began to appear in the northwest: the Humahuaca Valley of modern-day Jujuy Province, the Tafí Valley near Tucumán and the Jáchal Valley of San Juan.

The apex of the region's cultural development was the city of Quilmes, which flourished from around 1000 to 1667, supporting a population of 5,000 people in solid stone houses. By the end of the fifteenth century, Quilmes and other desert outposts had become nominal allies and trading partners of the giant Inca Empire, which probably would have swallowed up all of northwest Argentina were it not for an unexpected intervention from overseas.

Subsequent expeditions brought back stories of great civilizations and fantastic wealth beyond Argentina's relatively dismal shores. Although largely unfounded, the rumors set off a frenzied rush between Spain and Portugal to discover these "cities of gold" and claim the rich lands for their respective crowns. The Spanish got the jump on their rivals, founding a fortified settlement at Buenos Aires in 1536. After repeated Indian attacks, the nascent colony was abandoned. Most of the inhabitants sailed back to Iberia, but a small band of intrepid soldiers and pioneers under Juan de Ayolas made their way up the Río Paraná to present-day Paraguay, where they founded Asunción among friendly Indians.

THE EUROPEANS ARRIVE

Twenty-four years after Christopher Columbus "discovered" the New World, explorer Juan de Solís made the first European landfall in Argentina, in 1516. A Portuguese navigator working for the Spanish crown, De Solís set foot on the shores of the Río de la Plata long enough to claim this strange new land for Spain. Local Indians quickly rebuffed his men, and De Solís sailed off into historical obscurity. Ferdinand Magellan came along four years later, in 1520, on the initial leg of his landmark first circumnavigation of the globe. Magellan's ships probed the Plata estuary and sailed south, making one of their few landfalls near present-day Puerto San Julián where he executed a couple of mutineers and skirmished with the local nomads.

Over the next hundred years, Spanish civilization took route in northern Argentina. But very little of it derived from the Atlantic coast. Spaniards from Peru and Bolivia ventured across the *altiplano* to establish cities like Salta and Tucumán in the northwest. Other Spaniards crossing the High Andes from Chile founded Mendoza. Settlers coming down river from Asunción started Santa Fe and other outposts along the Paraná Basin. Not until 1580 did the Spanish make another attempt to establish a permanent presence in Buenos Aires, and this time they succeeded.

After so much effort, Spain then went about ignoring Argentina for several hundred years. As the capital of Spanish South America, Lima dominated politics, culture and trade to the detriment

OPPOSITE: A policeman catches up on current events at a Buenos Aires newsstand. ABOVE: Melon farmer Pedro Rubcich keeps the faith in Gran Chaco.

The Country and Its People

of provincial cities like Buenos Aires. Another major drawback to colonial development was the fact that Argentina couldn't boast any "get rich quick" schemes — very few gold or silver mines and nothing approaching a fabulous indigenous civilization like the Incas or Aztecs. All it seemed to have in abundance was grass, which the Spaniards divided into huge haciendas where the gaucho culture took root.

Argentina languished as a colonial backwater until the end of the eighteenth century. Just as the *norte americanos* were casting off the shackles of British colonial repression (1776), the good citizens of Buenos Aires were celebrating the fact that the Spanish crown had decided to create a new colonial entity with their hometown as the capital. But once again Argentine history was a little behind the curve: the Viceroyalty of the Río de la Plata and Buenos Aires's status as a colonial capital would both be short-lived.

NATIONAL LIBERTY OR DEATH

Following examples set during the American War of Independence and the French Revolution, South America's colonial elite was clambering for freedom by the early nineteenth century. Napoleon Bonaparte inadvertently kindled the fires of revolution in 1808 when he invaded Spain and deposed the king. With the head severed from the body of the Spanish Empire, the colonies were thrown into political and patriotic turmoil. Some of the more ambitious leaders saw Napoleon's intervention as an ideal chance to go their own way.

Throwing caution to the wind, the municipal government of Buenos Aires staged the continent's first coup d'état on May 25, 1810, overthrowing the Spanish viceroy and installing its own junta. Outlying provinces initially resisted the move, but a united Argentina finally declared independence in 1816.

Spain quickly rattled its sabers, threatened the newborn country with naval blockades and the possibility of invasion from Peru. The entire liberation movement might have quickly collapsed if not for the genius and daring of General José de San Martín, a native Argentine and Spanish military veteran.

Organizing a ragtag group of militia and volunteers into an efficient fighting machine, San Martín marched his Army of the Andes across the mountains in 1817. The move caught the Spanish completely off guard and Chile soon fell to San Martín. Next he turned his attention to Peru, where he combined forces with Simón Bolívar's army to vanquish the most important Spanish stronghold in the Americas.

THE REPUBLICAN PERIOD

The United Provinces of the Río de la Plata (as autonomous Argentina was initially called) were anything but united after independence. Constant bickering between the new country's strongest political groups marked the 1820s. The Unitarists, based in Buenos Aires, advocated a nation based on European models of free trade and strong central government. The Federalists, under the leadership of the wealthy landowners, championed an American-type system with strong provincial rights and agrarian economics.

Federalist leader Juan Manuel de Rosas took control of the government in 1829, parlaying his victory into a ruthless dictatorship that lasted until 1852. Even though his initial mandate was diluting the central government and securing power for the rural elite, Rosas actually accomplished the opposite in a brutal bid to strengthen his own power base. Rosas is also credited with establishing two government institutions that would flourish in Argentina until the end of the twentieth century — political torture and the secret police.

Rosas was so sadistic that many of his Federalist allies eventually turned on him. It took a bizarre alliance of rural landowners, urban intellectuals, European funding and military support from both Brazil and Uruguay, but Rosas was finally defeated at the Battle of Caseros outside Buenos Aires in 1852. A year later, a new federal constitution was inked in Santa Fe and the country officially became the Argentine Confederation. Bartolomé Mitre became the nation's first president and Buenos Aires its federal capital, setting the pace for rapid economic development and cultural progress over the latter half of the nineteenth century.

Much like the United States, Canada and Australia, the Argentine boom was fueled by massive immigration from Europe and the presence of a vast empty hinterland that furnished raw materials like wool, leather and wheat to the new urban factories. Buenos Aires began to transform itself into a world-class port. Steamboats plied the Río Paraná and railroads were built across the Pampas, connecting distant cities like Rosario, Córdoba and Mendoza with the federal capital.

Around this same time, Argentina also began to assert confidence beyond its traditional boundaries. The new federal army turned back a Paraguayan invasion of northern Argentina during the War of the Triple Alliance (1865–1870) and secured its claim to Patagonia during the controversial Conquest of the Desert (1879–1880), which doubled the size of Argentina.

By the turn of the twentieth century the population had reached four million and the economy was thriving, as one of the world's largest producers and exporters of beef, mutton, leather, wool and wheat. Buenos Aires had evolved in less than 100 years from a colonial backwater into a gleaming European-style city. And Argentina was ready to take its place among the great nations of the world. But once again, politics intervened.

TWENTIETH CENTURY ARGENTINA

Deep rifts in Argentine society boiled to the surface during the first decades of the twentieth century. The conservative rural elite, as arrogant as ever, resented the growing influence of the urban-based trade unions, comprised mostly of recent immigrants. The labor-supported Radicals came to power in 1916, shifting the national power base away from the provinces. But it wasn't long before the Conservatives reacted.

The military, in league with wealthy landowners, ousted Radical president Hipólito Yrigoyen in 1930, ending a half century of civilian rule. The new military junta banned opposition parties, rigged subsequent elections and drove their democratic rivals into exile via torture and intimidation — a pattern that would endure for another 50 years. The rise of Fascism in Europe bolstered the Argentine autocrats and led to the rise of Colonel Juan Domingo Perón, who engineered the military coup of 1943. Craving an official mandate from the people, Perón returned the government to civilian rule and was elected president in 1946 — with the aid of his wife Evita, who was treated almost like a saint by the working class.

Plagued by mismanagement and government intervention, the economy went into a nosedive in the 1950s. Almost overnight, Argentina went from being one of the world's richest countries to being an international basket-case. Perón's power base was severely undermined by the economic depression and his downfall almost ordained by

Getting up close and personal with a boa constrictor at the Complejo Ecológico captive breeding center in Roque Sáenz Peña.

the premature death of Evita in 1952. Three years later, Perón himself was ousted in a military coup and fled into exile.

After a rapid series of military juntas and military backed civilian governments, Perón returned from exile in 1972 and was promptly re-elected to the presidency in 1973. For one brief shining year, all of the various factions that grappled for control of Argentina seemed to come together, in peace, under Perón's guidance. But when he passed away in 1974, the country was plunged into political crisis again.

Into the vacuum stepped three competing groups: a militant, left-wing Peronist group called the Montoneros; a Trotskyist guerrilla outfit known

as the People's Revolutionary Army (ERP), and the United States-based Argentine Anti-Communist Alliance (AAA). Each group vied for power with similar tactics: intimidation and assassination. The country in chaos, the military assumed control again in 1976 and immediately started to eradicate any opposition, a notorious period of Argentine history called La Guerra Sucia (The Dirty War).

THE DIRTY WAR

Under the auspices of wiping out communism, the generals rounded up thousands of ordinary people—journalists, teachers, artists, trade union-ists, students and anyone else deemed a threat to their strong-arm rule. They were often kidnapped in the middle of the night by the secret police and paramilitary death squads, taken to detention centers where they were tortured and never heard from again.

Collectively they became known as the *desaparecidos* ("Disappeared"). Some were force to jump out of air force planes over the South Atlantic; most were simply shot and dumped in unmarked graves. The babies of women who gave birth during imprisonment were kidnapped by the state and secretly given out for adoption to military families and wealthy supporters. Although no official count has ever been released, it is estimated that somewhere between 9,000 and 30,000 perished.

Buoyed by the success in the Dirty War — and to diffuse growing global criticism of their domestic bloodbath — the generals decided to launch a genuine war in 1982. Attacking by land, sea and air, the Argentine armed forces invaded the British-held Falkland (Malvinas) Islands. The conflict lasted all of 74 days. British troops, much better trained and with superior equipment, quickly counterattacked and retook the islands. The Argentine generals were humiliated and subsequently resigned their political posts. Democracy was restored in 1983 with the election of Raúl Alfonsín.

Some of the ghosts of the Dirty War were exorcised in 1985, when several top generals were convicted of crimes against humanity and sentenced to prison terms. Trials related to the abductions and murders continue into the early twenty-first century, with the relatives of the Disappeared still demanding a full accounting of the atrocities.

ARGENTINA TODAY

Meanwhile, Argentina made a successful transition back to civilian rule. Alfonsín was replaced by Peronist leader Carlos Menem in free and fair elections in 1989. Menem's administration quickly moved to stem hyperinflation and other financial woes by introducing economic austerity programs, restructuring the country's massive foreign debt, curbing government spending, and pegging the Argentine peso to the United States dollar.

By the end of the 1990s, inflation was back to acceptable levels, foreign investment was flowing in again, and the economy was more buoyant than at anytime since the early 1950s. After two highly successful terms, Fernando de la Rúa succeeded Menem as president in the federal elections of December 1999.

ABOVE: The fine art of house painting in the waterfront La Boca district of Buenos Aires. RIGHT: El Cerro del los Siete Colores (Hill of Seven Colors) looms above Purmamarca.

The Country and Its People

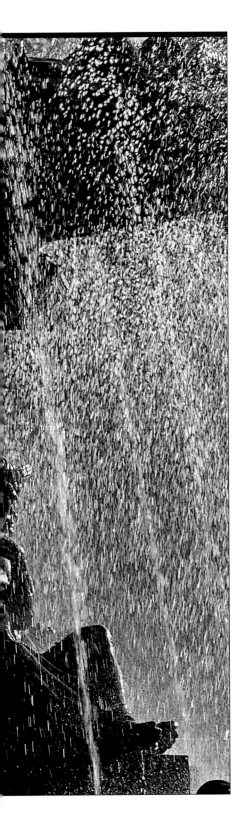

Buenos
Aires

THERE'S AN OLD SAYING THAT WELL DESCRIBES THE CHARACTER OF BUENOS AIRES: "An Argentine is an Italian who speaks Spanish, dresses like a Frenchman, and thinks like an Englishman." The same can be said for the city. Long called "the Paris of South America," Buenos Aires is far more European than Latin American. Its most important buildings are modeled after palaces in France; its major parks and plazas were designed by French landscape architect Charles Thays; and its café society resembles something along the Seine River.

Well-dressed women and men gossip over tiny cups of espresso at sidewalk cafés along broad avenues lined with jacaranda and rubber trees. Women wear stiletto heels and impossibly short

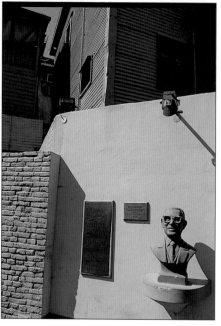

skirts even to work, and take great pride in remaining amazingly thin and beautiful. Men are equally vain in their custom-tailored suits and hand-stitched shoes. Cell phones are ubiquitous. On the surface, it appears that everyone in Buenos Aires is wealthy, young and attractive.

The city's architecture is similarly stylish, based for the most part on European designs. During Argentina's belle époque at the beginning of the twentieth century, Argentina's elite commissioned foreign architects, artists, engineers, and designers to create a modern city atop colonial ruins. In a few decades they transformed an eighteenth-century Latin American port city into a living museum of European architecture. French neoclassical mansions were all the rage; the more pillars, mansard roofs, caryatids, and chandeliers the better. Few colonial-era buildings were left intact, except for significant churches. The Buenos

Aires of today is barely a century old, its monuments largely the product of the early 1900s.

"A city like Buenos Aires seems to change more dramatically than other settled, historical cities like London or Paris because it demolishes its past in the rush to modernize," writes Jason Wilson in *Buenos Aires: A Cultural and Literary Companion.* Along the river in Puerto Madero, old warehouses now house chic restaurants. Gleaming skyscrapers represent a new wave of prosperity in the financial district.

The greater Buenos Aires region is home to over one-third of the country's population, many of whom are immigrants from the poorer provinces and nearby countries. Over three million people live within the city; 13 million reside in the sprawl extending into the nearby pampas. On the one hand, Buenos Aires is a microcosm of all things Argentine; on the other, it is a society unto itself. Its residents call themselves *porteños,* and claim a closer affinity to Europe than to Patagonia. "I feel more *porteño* than Argentine," writes Jorge Luis Borges, Argentina's most famous scribe.

Residents of the city have been called *porteños* for centuries; Buenos Aires began as a port city. *Porteños* are busy, fashionable, intelligent characters who speak an Italian-inflected Castillan Spanish that befuddles those from other Latin countries. Their vocabulary is liberally laced with French and German expressions, with a sprinkling of clever slang. ¡*Bárbaro!* describes all things fabulous; ¡*Qué Kafka!* eloquently characterizes the bureaucratic hell of city life. *Porteños* are philosophical, poetic, thoughtful, and self-involved. It's long been said that Buenos Aires has more psychoanalysts per capita than any other city in the world.

Certainly, there is much cause for concern. The past 50 years have been rough on residents. First came Eva and Juan Perón, whose government brought the disparities between rich and poor to an explosive peak. Then the *porteños* endured the ugliest period in Argentine history, during the Dirty War. Extraordinary inflation further demoralized the city's residents, challenging their survival.

But *porteños* are proud to live in one of the great cities of the world. El Capital, as they call their city, has no single famous monument and no world-class museums. Instead, it has a singular character, a flair and passion that spices daily life. It's a city for walking and watching drama unfold in the small acts of the street scene — the tango dancers performing in the parks, the uniformed waiters bearing trays of *café con leche* to offices, the men whispering *piropos* (compliments) to beautiful women slinking along the streets. It's a city celebrating life and the promise of the future.

ABOVE: Vivid colors brighten humble dwellings in La Boca. RIGHT: An ornate copper dome tops the Palacio del Congreso.

BACKGROUND

It took two tries to establish Buenos Aires as a viable city. Spanish explorer Pedro de Mendoza built a garrison on the hills above the Río de la Plata in the area now known as Parque Lezama in 1536. He called the settlement Buenos Aires in honor of the Virgen de la Buen Ayre, the Virgin of Good Wind, patron saint of sailors. The indigenous Querandí Indians were not pleased with the Spanish troops, and drove them away within five years. Basque explorer Juan de Garay established a presence by the river in 1580, near the present-day Casa Rosada. Both explorers chose this area for its location by the river and determined it would make a fine port city.

Garay laid out his new city in a grid pattern that prevails today, and placed the main plaza above the river. At that time, the Río de la Plata flowed through areas now covered with high-rises and warehouses; the Plaza de Mayo, Plaza San Martín, and Parque Lezama all overlooked the river from atop its *barrancas*, or banks. There are no traces of the early adobe houses used by Garay's soldiers; the oldest buildings in the city date to the mid-1700s.

Buenos Aires grew slowly. Its location and port made it a valuable settlement for silver miners in Peru and Bolivia, who found it easier to ship their wares on the river rather than cart them over the Andes. The Spanish settlers were a motley lot who had no-one to conquer (the Indians had moved on to more peaceful lands) and nothing of value to mine. Argentina's wealth lay in its fertile pampas, where enormous ranches, called *estancias*, were eventually established. The families who gradually gained riches and power were those who profited from cattle and agriculture. Within the city, life was bleak and smugglers gained the most profits. The residents, who numbered about 7,000 by 1700, had little loyalty to Spain, and were already forming a *porteño* identity.

Thanks to its port, Buenos Aires was named the capital of the Viceroyalty of the Río de la Plata in 1776. The British inadvertently strengthened *porteño* solidarity and identity in 1806, when General Beresford and his troops, who had overtaken the Dutch at the Cape of Good Hope, marched into Buenos Aires. The Spanish Viceroy quickly surrendered to Beresford and fled to Córdoba. Within days, Juan Martín de Pueyrredón and Santiago de Liniers led a resistance force into the city; Beresford was out in less than two months. The British returned in 1807 under the lead of General Whitlocke, who crossed the river after conquering Montevideo. *Porteños* assembled on the rooftops of houses along what's now called Calle Defensa and attached the soldiers with boiling water and stones. Whitlocke's troops took

refuge in the Convento de Santo Domingo, where their flag of surrender still hangs.

Emboldened by these two victories, the Argentines declared their independence from Spain. At that time, Spain was undergoing immense problems at home with a French invasion. The Argentines took advantage of Spain's distraction and appointed a *junta* with Cornelio Saavedra as its head. When Spanish monarch Ferdinand VII regained his throne, the Argentines refused to submit to his rule. In 1810, small group of less than 500 men gathered at the Cabildo (one of the oldest structures in present-day Buenos Aires) and voted for independence, appointing Carlos Alvear as independent Argentina's first President.

But the people of the provinces did not necessarily agree with decrees from the *porteños*, and battles ensued between those still loyal to Spain and those seeking independence. Britain and France made ongoing attempts to conquer the new government through river blockades and invasions. In July, 1816, Argentina's leaders met in the city of Tucumán in the north and hammered out a declaration of independence, which was presented to the country on July 9, 1816. July 9 remains a national holiday.

Disputes between the *porteños* and *provincianos* (residents of the provinces) continued, however, and there was little peace for independent Argentina's first presidents. The country's first dictator, Juan Manuel de Rosas, muscled his way into power in 1829. Representing wealthy ranchers and farmers, Rosas established a strong military and secret police, and embarked on a system of torture and political persecution that has been repeated far too often in Argentine history. Rosas set himself up in a large estate in the center of Buenos Aires on land that now makes up the city's largest greenbelt, Palermo Park. Rosas was deposed by General Justo José de Urquiza in 1852.

Subsequent presidents continued to concentrate their power in Buenos Aires, opening railways from the city to the provinces, establishing public schools, and encouraging foreign investment. But it wasn't until 1880 that Buenos Aires became the official capital of Argentina. By 1885 the city had over 600,000 residents and a weak infrastructure. Sewage ran down the streets, garbage was piled up everywhere, clean water was nearly nonexistent. Nearly 20,000 people died of yellow fever and cholera between 1867 and 1871, serving as a wake-up call to the government, which began an intense building campaign. The epidemic also changed the demographics of the city. Wealthy residents had built their mansions in the city's southern neighborhoods around San Telmo and the port, the epicenter of the plague. They fled to the northern suburbs of Recoleta and Retiro, leaving the south to the poor and to the city's ever-growing immigrant populace.

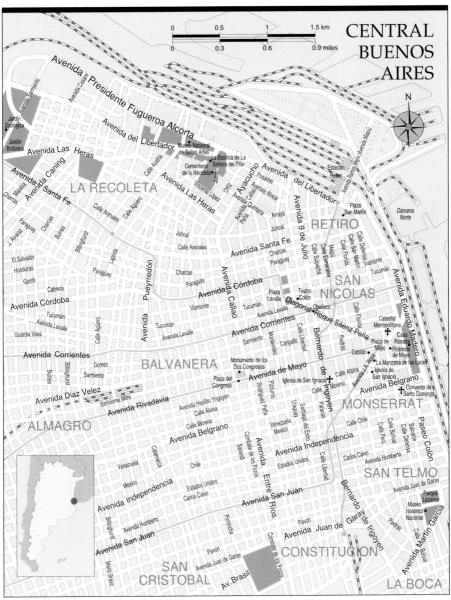

CENTRAL BUENOS AIRES

European immigration at the turn of the century caused enormous population growth throughout the country. Argentina received over six million immigrants between 1895 and 1912; Buenos Aires was their point of entry into the country. Immigrant neighborhoods took root in this period; some, like La Boca, have retained their Old World customs and traditions. San Telmo's mansions became flophouses and cheap hotels. With this ever-expanding labor force the city became the wealthiest, most populous metropolis in South America and its boundaries swelled far beyond the river and main plaza.

A few families attained great wealth during this era; much of their new money went into the creation of many of the finest buildings in Buenos Aires. European fabrics, furnishings, crystal, and art were imported for these grand mansions; visitors today get a sense of that gilded era when they tour the Museo Nacional de Arte Decorativo, designed as a private home by French architect René Sergent.

As the rich celebrated their importance by supporting the completion of the Teatro Colón and other landmarks of high society, the working class and poor immigrants began fomenting rebellion.

Labor unions were formed; socialists, communists, and anarchists championed workers' rights. The celebration of 100 years of Argentine independence in 1910 was accompanied by protest marches and demonstrations. Dissent grew until it exploded in 1919 during the *semana trágica*, when over 1,000 protestors were killed in the streets of Buenos Aires in just one week. The government made a few concessions during the presidency of Hipólito Yrigoyen, who established universal suffrage for men. Yrigoyen was overthrown in a military coup in 1930, and a series of conservative, isolationist, nationalistic leaders, some pro-Nazi, led the country with alternating aid and opposition from the military. The wealthy continued their pilgrimages

the vote in 1947. Unions gained strength, pensions were established; workers were given paid holidays and other benefits. Perón nationalized the railways, utility, and telephone companies. The Casa Rosada and Plaza de Mayo became focal points for enormous demonstrations supporting the Perón government.

The forces against Perón were equally vociferous. Business owners, writers, religious leaders, and the upper classes railed against what they called the Perón dictatorship. Evita's early death from cancer in 1952 was a harbinger of bad times. Argentina's economy was sliding into decline, thanks to decreasing grain prices on the international market and an increasing foreign debt. In

to Paris, London, and Rome, entrusting their interests at home to an unstable government. Then came Colonel Juan Domingo Perón and his wife, María Eva Duarte.

Perón was voted into power by the disenfranchised in 1946, beginning the lengthy rule by the Peronist party. His wife Evita became the saint of the masses, the savior of the *descamisados* (shirtless ones), and the most memorable character in Argentine history. Tourists today follow circuits tracing the Peróns' courtship, marriage, and government (see FOLLOW IN EVITA'S FOOTSTEPS, page 16, in TOP SPOTS). Evita's mausoleum has made the Recoleta Cemetery one of the most popular attractions in Buenos Aires.

The Perón presidency (he was reelected in 1952) forever changed the landscape of politics in Argentina. The working classes gained enormous attention and political benefits. Women were given

1955, the military bombed the Casa Rosada, and Perón was forced into exile. The country fell into decades of disastrous military rule. Buenos Aires seethed with discontent, as Peronists and revolutionaries fought a guerilla war with the military. Perón returned to power briefly in 1973; his return to Buenos Aires at the Ezeiza airport resulted in violence as supporters battled the opposition. The two sides engaged in gunfight. Without Evita by his side, a weak and sick Juan Perón proved an ineffectual president. When he died in 1974, his third wife, Isabel, became president of a radically divided country. Bombings, kidnappings, gun fights, and demonstrations became a part of daily life in the capital city; in 1976, Isabel Perón's presidency ended in yet another military coup.

The darkest period in Argentina's history was from 1976 to 1983 — La Guerra Sucia (The Dirty War). Military leaders declared a Proceso de

Reorginización Nacional (National Reorganization Process) that resulted in a reign of terror. The reorganization was declared in order to stabilize the economy and eliminate corruption. Instead, it became a means for the government to wage war against the citizenry. Revolutionary guerrilla groups were quickly defeated; anyone protesting the military's actions was subject to kidnapping, torture, and death. Just residing in Buenos Aires proved dangerous for anyone who looked like they might not agree with the government. University students, artists, and writers were targeted and lived in terror. Unmarked dark sedans sat on neighborhood streets from Recoleta to La Boca, reminding residents that the government was always watching. The term *desaparecidos* became part of everyday vocabulary as more and more people "disappeared," never to return. Some estimates put the number of persons who disappeared during the Dirty War at 9,000; others say as many as 30,000 people lost their lives. The courageous *Madres de la Plaza de Mayo* (Mothers of the Plaza de Mayo) began their marches in the plaza, silently bearing witness to their disappeared children.

Two events unified Argentines during this period — Argentina's 1978 victory in the World Cup, and the 1982 invasions of the Islas Malvinas (Falkland Islands). On both occasions *porteños* demonstrated solidarity and pride on the streets of Buenos Aires, and new monuments rose in the parks. A wall bearing the names of Argentines killed in the ill-fated war sits at the base of Plaza San Martín. Finally, in 1983, Argentina returned to civilian rule under Raúl Alfonsín, who commissioned a report on the Dirty War called *Nunca Más*. A few high-ranking military officers were jailed, and the plight of the *desaparecidos* gained international attention. Students returned to the universities and cafés of Buenos Aires, and city life took on a patina of normalcy. Severe inflation colored any sense of stability, however, and Argentines found themselves literally struggling for financial survival.

As we enter the twenty-first century, Buenos Aires is once again a vital cosmopolitan city veering toward prosperity. The Casa Rosada has a new pink façade, the Plaza de Mayo hosts concerts as well as protests, and *porteños* are once again the fashionable trendsetters of South America. The economy appears to be stabilizing, and an ever-larger segment of the city's populace can now afford to dine in the new restaurants in Puerto Madero and shop in the fancy boutiques in Recoleta and Palermo. Overpopulation continues to challenge the city's infrastructure; greater Buenos Aires, with 13 million residents, is home to one-third of the country's population. Though democracy and freedom are the catchwords of the day, some Argentines, especially journalists, writers, and political activists, retain a realistic fear of

the military and the government. But a spirit of hope and happiness seems to be gaining strength as *porteños* adjust to peace.

GENERAL INFORMATION

The best place to obtain information and maps on Buenos Aires is at the **Secretaría de Turismo de la Gobierno de la Ciudad de Buenos Aires** ((11) 4372-3612 FAX (11) 4374-7533, Avenida Sarmiento 1551. In addition to *The Golden Map*, a large street map with tourist sights marked, the office also distributes the *Quick Guide*. The best up-to-date source for museum hours and special events is the brochure *Disfrutando Buenos Aires*.

Another excellent street map is available at most *subte* (subway) stations. The city tourism department has kiosks at the airports, the bus station, on the top floor of the Galerías Pacífico shopping center, and at the Café Tortoni.

The daily *Buenos Aires Herald* is Argentina's oldest English-language newspaper. Its Friday edition has a special events section; restaurant reviews are published on Sundays. The newspaper also has a web site at www.buenosairesherald.com. A few newsstands on Calle Florida carry the *International Herald Tribune*. Many also sell good city and country maps.

The telephone area code for Buenos Aires is 11; local numbers have eight digits, which always

OPPOSITE: Eva Perón's followers decorate her tomb in Recoleta with flowers and memorial plaques. ABOVE: The Casa Rosada has maintained a rosy hue since 1873.

start with 4. Not all brochures and tourist information booklets have incorporated these new phone numbers. Make sure the number you're dialing has eight digits. Many *porteños* use portable phones; you must dial 15 before a portable number.

Locutorio and *Telecentro* telephone offices are scattered all over the city; many have Internet access. There are several Internet cafés on the pedestrians-only blocks of Calle Florida and Avenida Lavalle. Rates are especially low at **Internet Café Galería Paseo Lavalle** ((11) 4322-5660, Avenida Lavalle 835, located on the first floor (the floor above street level). At **Café Pernambuco** ((11) 4383-4666, Avenida Corrientes 1686, drinks are served at the computers.

Dollars are nearly as common as pesos in Buenos Aires. Cab drivers and cashiers tend to examine bills closely, as forgeries are common. Travelers' checks are only accepted at expensive hotels and restaurants, and few hotels will convert travelers' checks to pesos. **American Express** ((11) 4312-1661, Calle Arenales 707, will exchange their travelers' checks. Several banks along Calle Florida offer currency exchange; banks open 10 AM to 3 PM, Monday through Friday. There are ATMs all over the city.

Nearly every province in Argentina has a tourist information office located in Buenos Aires where you can get maps and brochures. Some also display and sell regional crafts; others will book hotel rooms for you. For a full listing, see TOURIST INFORMATION, page 272 in TRAVELERS' TIPS.

GETTING AROUND

Buenos Aires is a walker's paradise — and you can always buy a fashionable new pair of shoes if yours wear out. Since the city is divided into *barrios*, or neighborhoods, you can easily concentrate your exploring in one area, then move on to the next. Pedestrians pay little heed to traffic lights when crossing streets, and dodge through any tiny space between vehicles.

The *subte* (subway) is easy to negotiate and an efficient means of transportation. The first line opened in 1913; called Line A it begins at the Plaza de Mayo and still uses old wooden cars. There are five lines covering the central areas of the city, and other lines are under construction. Tokens cost less than US$1; you need only one token to transfer between lines. The *subte* runs Monday through Saturday, 5 AM to 10 PM, Sundays and holidays 8 AM to 10 PM.

Buses are easy to use as well, though their routes are confusing at first. Signs at the bus stops list the areas each line covers; if you don't see your

The Teatro Colón adds a touch of class to the frenzied evening traffic on Avenida 9 de Julio.

destination on the sign, ask those in line for assistance. *Porteños* are orderly bus passengers, and form long queues at bus stops. Passengers pay their fare at an electronic machine behind the driver's seat and receive a ticket. The buses run 24 hours daily, though appear infrequently on weekends.

Cars are a hindrance rather than a help in the city. Taxis are fairly inexpensive and are metered. Private taxis, called *remises*, are more comfortable and the drivers offer safe, personalized service. *Remise* companies usually have a few drivers who speak English, French, Italian, or German; they often act as unofficial guides adding commentary along the way. I sometimes hire a driver if I'm racing about the city in various directions. The hourly fee can be less than numerous cab rides. The hotels will assist you in finding a driver or you can contact **Manuel Tienda León** ((11) 4314-3636.

TOURS

Several tour operators offer city tours worth taking for an initial orientation, along with a wide range of special interest tours and trips to the countryside. Most companies prefer that you call for reservations rather than visiting their offices. As a rule, business offices are in locked, guarded buildings, and visitors are required to have appointments. Most do not accept credit cards, and expect payment in cash during the tour. Guides and drivers welcome tips.

Most companies offer bus tours of the city; night time walking tours around Recoleta and Puerto Madero; group visits to tango shows including admission and drinks; and day-long trips on the Tren de la Costa to San Isidro and Tigre. It's not unusual to run across groups from competing tour companies doing the exact same thing at the same place. The prices are all similar as well, and most companies use bilingual guides. The biggest difference is the quality of the guides and the mode of transportation.

I've had good experiences with **Travel Line** ((11) 4393-9000, a company that advertises heavily in the hotels. They prefer clients make reservations through the hotel desk. The guides know their stuff, and willingly answer questions. Their Evita tour combines a history of Buenos Aires with details of the Perón presidency; it's extremely worthwhile. Travel Line also offers a tour to La Plata, the capital of Buenos Aires Province, 58 km (36 miles) outside the city.

It's a good idea for first-timers to sign up for an inexpensive bus tour of the city just to nail down the layout and neighborhoods. **Buenos Aires Turs** ((11) 4371-2304 or (11) 4371-2390 WEB SITE www .sectur.gov.ar/trans/bat/index_g.htm, Calle Lavalle 1444, is one of the larger companies offering a variety of bus tours of the city and surrounding areas. The San Telmo tour on Sundays takes in the antiques market, followed by lunch and a tango show.

Buenos Aires Vision ((11) 4394-2986/4682, Calle Esmeralda 356, also has a wide array of tours, including their City Tour, highlighting the parks of Palermo, May Square, the Teatro Colón and the neighborhood of La Boca.

For those with an interest in architecture, **Espacio Verde** ((11) 4374-2222, Calle Viamonte 1454, presents tours of the city's structures, focusing on edifices with a foreign influence. With an architect as your guide, you will visit buildings of French-, English-, or Italian-style architecture and learn about their history.

Historical Tours ((11) 4311-1099, Calle Paraguay 647, is another company which offers a variety of excursions throughout the city, focusing on the history of Buenos Aires and its neighborhoods. They also offer several tours highlighting art museums and the Teatro Colón.

Most agencies offer day tours to *estancias* (ranches) in Buenos Aires Province, about an hour or two outside the city. You can arrange these tours yourself if you have transportation, but they're most enjoyable when a large group is attending. The visit typically includes a demonstration of horse-riding and roping skills by gauchos who work the ranches when not attending to tourists, along with a traditional *asado criollo* barbecue lunch and folkloric and tango dancing. You can arrange a visit on your own by contacting **Estancia La Margarita** in General Rodriguez ((11) 4322-1406. Always ask for detailed instructions, as the *estancias* are usually located in rural areas without street addresses.

The **Secretaría de Turismo de la Gobierno de la Ciudad de Buenos Aires** ((11) 4372-3612 FAX (11) 4374-7533, Avenida Sarmiento 1551, offers an excellent array of weekend walking tours at various spots of interest around the city. The tours are held in Spanish, though guides typically speak some English. Even if you don't understand everything, the tours are a great way to mingle with locals and see areas you wouldn't usually explore. Call ((11) 4374-7651 for information on upcoming tours, and ask for the brochure listing tours in the tourist office.

WHAT TO SEE AND DO

Buenos Aires is an enormous city, yet relatively easy to explore. Most sites of interest are clustered in specific areas, many within walking distance of each other. Tourists must deal with one significant complication as they plan their days: Argentina's museums keep some odd hours. Many in Buenos Aires don't open until 10 AM or 11 AM; some are only open from 3 PM to 7 PM; many are closed on Mondays. It's not unusual to go out

of your way to visit a museum, only to find it closed for no apparent reason. The monthly edition of the tourist brochure *Disfrutando Buenos Aires* is the most valuable resource museum lovers can find, as it lists current hours and tells if a museum is closed for renovations. Unfortunately, this brochure isn't as readily available as the seasonal city guides. Check with the city's tourist offices and kiosks for a copy.

PLAZA DE MAYO

The historic and political heart of the nation, the Plaza de Mayo extends for two blocks. Unlike the city's other plazas, this imposing concrete square is somewhat austere, with a few clusters of trees, lawns, flower gardens, and benches breaking up the expanses of cement. A few vendors display small flags of Argentina, postcards, and photos of Che Guevara and Evita Perón on their carts, but

there's a distinct absence of frivolous balloon sellers or hot-dog carts.

The plaza is the forum for the *Madres de la Plaza de Mayo* (Mothers of the Plaza de Mayo), who march here on Thursday afternoons at 3 PM. The mothers wear white scarves embroidered with the names of their missing loved ones, and pay witness to one of the country's most disgraceful periods, the Dirty War, which lasted from 1976 to 1983. Argentines and visitors gather to observe and march with the mothers, who mourn the *desaparecidos*. Today, the mothers also mourn the loss of their grandchildren. Many of the babies born to mothers in captivity were placed with military or wealthy families; some of the grandchildren of the *Madres de la Plaza* may well be growing up with their parents' torturers.

The *Madres de la Plaza de Mayo* circle the plaza's fountain on Thursday afternoons.

The **Pirámide de Mayo**, a simple obelisk, rises above the center of the plaza, which is named for Argentina's May 1810 uprising against Spain. A severe bronze statue of **General Manuel Belgrano** astride a charging horse, created by French artist Albert in 1873, rises at the east end of the plaza. Belgrano's statue faces the **Casa Rosada** ((11) 4344-3051, Calle Hipólito Yrigoyen 219. Spanish Conquistador Juan de Garay chose this position atop a slight hill overlooking the Plate River for his original fort, and the government has ruled the country from here ever since. Similar to Washington DC's White House, the Casa Rosada (Pink House) is the presidential headquarters; the president, however, lives in a far grander mansion on the northern outskirts of the city. The façade facing the plaza was painted a vivid pink just before the 1999 inauguration of President Fernando de la Rúa; the other three walls of the structure were left a faded rosy beige, as if the paint ran out. In 1873, President Sarmiento chose the color pink for the building to represent the union of the two political factions of the day, the Federals (presented by the color red) and the Unitarians (white).

The current structure is actually made up of two buildings—the Secretaría de Comunicaciones (Communications Secretariat and post office) and the Casa de Gobierno (Government House), which were connected via a series of arches and upper level offices in the late 1800s by architect Francisco Tamburini. Two elaborately dressed guards of the Grenadiers regiment are posted on each side of the main arch used as the building's street-side entrance. A barrier prevents pedestrians from strolling right up to the Casa Rosada; police are posted here during functions taking place in the Plaza de Mayo. The **Museo de la Casa Rosada** ((11) 4344-3051, Calle Hipólito Yrigoyen 219 within the building, is open to visitors for free; there is a charge for guided tours. The exhibits focus on a history of Argentina's presidents and the ruins of the colonial-era fort. Hours are erratic, and the museum is closed during official events. When the president is present, a small flag is raised just below the large flag atop the building.

The president addresses the public from a second-story balcony in the original Casa de Gobierno at the north side of the entrance; Madonna belted out "Don't Cry for Me Argentina" from this balcony for the film *Evita*, but only after intense negotiations with the government.

A short detour across Avenida Rivadavia to the corner of Avenida de Mayo takes you to an office building that once housed the Hotel Argentino, where José Hernández finished his epic poem *Martín Fierro*. The building is closed to the public, but a small plaque outside commemorates the event.

North of the Casa Rosada is the **Banco de la Nación Argentina**, taking up an entire block on Avenida Rivadavia. The formal neoclassical mansion was designed by architect Alejandro Bustillo in 1940. The next block is consumed by the **Catedral Metropolitana** ((11) 4331-2845, Avenida Rivadavia and Calle San Martín. The rather dull façade topped with an elaborate frieze depicting biblical scenes was designed in the 1830s by French sculptor Joseph Dubourdieu as an addition to the original building, constructed in 1745. The façade dwarfs the original building, whose tiled dome rises almost like an afterthought at the very back. An eternal flame burns at the south side of the entrance to honor General José de San Martín, whose mausoleum inside the cathedral is the building's main attraction.

Soldiers from the Grenadiers Regiment, established by the general in 1811, guard Martín's mausoleum, which sits in a circular domed room beside the main altar. The marble tomb was designed by French sculptor Carrière Belleuse, and depictions of the battle for independence are painted around the bronze dome. Guided tours (usually in Spanish) are available on weekday afternoons.

The city government operates from the **Legislatura de la Ciudad de Buenos Aires** at the intersection of Calle Perú and Diagonal Julio A. Roca. White pillars front the neoclassical building, which appears wedged into the V-shaped intersection. The public is allowed to enter the building during weekday office hours.

One of the city's few remaining colonial buildings sits at the west end of the plaza. The simple white **Cabildo** (Town Council) ((11) 4334-1782, Calle Bolívar 65, was constructed between 1748 and 1764. The building (and the fact that it has remained long after most of the city's other colonial structures were destroyed) is a revered symbol of Argentina's independence. In May 1810, Argentines gathered at the Cabildo to protest Spanish rule; the subsequent revolution is detailed in exhibits inside the building. Pieces of the original structure were demolished as the city grew, but the remains were restored in 1939 and the Cabildo is now a designated historic monument. A crafts fair is held most days in the patio behind the building, where a walkway connects Avenida Hipólito Yrigoyen and Avenida de Mayo.

The **Palacio Gobierno de la Ciudad de Buenos Aires** ((11) 4224-8323 WEB SITE www.buenosaires .gov.ar, Avenida de Mayo 575, is located in the original offices of La Prensa. The city operates a cultural center in the building and offers tango lessons, art exhibits, band concerts, and guided tours of one of the most ornate buildings by the plaza. Three blocks down Avenida de Mayo is the most important café in Buenos Aires, **Gran Café Tortoni** ((11) 4342-4328, Avenida de Mayo 829 (see WHERE TO EAT, page 96). As much a cultural center as it is a café, Tortoni is well worth several visits.

A door next to the café leads to an underground space called **La Bodega**, where tango shows are held. Behind the café on Avenida Rivadavia, enormous *palo borracho* trees shade Plaza Roberto Artl.

The area surrounding the Plaza de Mayo is the epicenter of historical Buenos Aires; the neighborhood is sometimes called El Centro (the center) but is officially called Monserrat. It also contains one of the city's most confusing intersections, as the main streets change names at the plaza. Two diagonal streets — Diagonal Roque Sáenz Peña and Diagonal Julio A. Roca (which ends at an equestrian statue of General Roca, who led the conquest of Patagonia) also end at this point, as do several subway lines. Calle Florida, the pedes-

oldest church in the city. Behind it are a few remaining cloisters from the **Procuradía de las Misiones** that housed the Jesuit headquarters for the society's South American missions. Other early buildings were destroyed as a series of schools were constructed. The block gained its name in 1821 to denote its significance as the intellectual center of Buenos Aires; many of the leaders of the fight for independence were educated here. In 1911, the **Colegio Nacional** was built as the centerpiece of the Manzana de las Luces; it remains one of Argentina's leading public high schools. A series of tunnels was constructed by the Jesuits to link churches and cloisters; guided tours of the tunnels and the block's buildings are sometimes

trian thoroughfare that connects Plaza de Mayo with Plaza San Martín, ends at Diagonal Roque Sáenz Peña (also called Diagonal Norte) beside the ornate neocolonial Bank of Boston. It is a good idea to walk the perimeter and become familiar with street names when you begin touring the area, as you'll probably return here several times to visit museums.

La Manzana de las Luces (The Block of Bright Lights) ℂ (11) 4342-6973 covers an entire block between Perú, Alsina, Bolívar and Moreno streets southwest of the plaza. Jesuit missions congregated here in 1630, but most of the remaining important buildings were constructed after the Jesuits were expelled in 1767. The **Iglesia de San Ignacio** ℂ (11) 4331-2458, at the corner of Bolívar and Alsina, is the only intact Jesuit-era structure remaining. The Baroque-styled church was constructed in 1713 and is said to be the

offered by the city. The tours are usually held in Spanish and begin at the corner of Perú and Alsina streets. Call ℂ (11) 4331-9534 or (11) 4342-9930 for the current schedule.

Calle Defensa runs south from the Plaza de Mayo to San Telmo (see below) and is one of the more fascinating streets in the city. At the corner of Defensa and Alsina, the **Museo de la Ciudad** (Municipal Museum) ℂ (11) 4331-2123, Calle Alsina 412, is housed in a typical late nineteenth century residence. Temporary and permanent exhibits portray life in the city in past centuries; the museum's collection includes household furnishings and appliances, bits of pieces of destroyed historic buildings, and a reproduction of a nineteenth century pharmacy. Museum staff are also responsible for the reconstruction of the **Calle Perú**

La Boca's many artists find inspiration in their colorful surroundings.

Subte subway station at the corner of Calle Perú and Avenida de Mayo. This replica of the original 1910 underground station includes some of the original wooden subway cars.

Also on Defensa, the **Basílica y Convento de San Francisco** ((11) 4331-0625, Calle Defensa at Calle Alsina, is one of the city's oldest and loveliest churches. It was originally designed by Jesuit architect Bianchi in 1730, and completed in a German Baroque style in 1911. The exterior is decorated with relief statues of San Francisco de Asís and Cristóbal Colón, and the interior was refurbished in 1955. **Capilla San Roque** (San Roque Chapel), beside the main entrance, was built in 1775. The small square in front of the church is a

SAN TELMO AND LA BOCA

One of the most delightful ways to spend a Sunday in Buenos Aires is to stroll down Calle Defensa to the south-side *barrio* of San Telmo and its riotous Sunday market. Until the 1870s, San Telmo was one of the most desirable neighborhoods in the city, filled with the colonial homes of aristocratic families. When yellow fever broke out in the area in 1871, the wealthier families quickly fled for the northern neighborhoods, leaving San Telmo to poor immigrants. The fine houses became tenements, and the neighborhood classed one of the most dangerous areas in the city. It wasn't until

pleasant place to rest your feet for a few minutes. The **Convento de Santa Domingo** ((11) 4331-1668, Calle Defensa 422, was built in the 1750s. In front of the convent the **Basílica Nuestra Señora del Rosario** is home to flags taken from British troops who invaded the city in 1806, and others taken from Spanish troops during the War of Independence. The basilica was fired upon during the English invasion, as evidenced by bullet holes in the tower (deliberately copied when the tower was remodeled).

A marble mausoleum designed by Italian sculptor Ettore Ximenes holding the remains of General Manuel Belgrano is located at the atrium entrance to the church. Belgrano designed the flag of Argentina. Inside the church, one wall is devoted to San Martín de Porres (patron saint of the city); it is covered with plaques and handwritten notes thanking the saint for his help.

the 1970s that artists and writers began moving into the quarter, refurbishing the old homes for studios, shops and apartments. Today, the neighborhood is one of Buenos Aires's cultural hubs, filled with fascinating shops, tango halls, and historic sites. It still has a reputation as a magnet for pickpockets and petty thieves, however; keep a close hold on your belongings, especially as you reach the market area.

Several of the homes along Calle Defensa bear plaques telling the stories of their famous former residents. Bernardino Rivadavia, the first president of Argentina, lived at Calle Defensa 350. The **Museo Nacional del Grabado** ((11) 4345-5300, Calle Defensa 372, is devoted to engravings. The exhibits include works by Picasso, Miro, and Argentine artist Alfredo Benavídez Bedoya. The museum was founded by Professor Oscar Pécora in 1960.

The preponderance of antique shops after you cross Calle Chile is a sign that you're entering the market district. San Telmo's famed Sunday market is centered at **Plaza Dorrego** at the intersection of calles Defensa and Carlos Calvo, though vendors spread their wares on sidewalks all around the area. The sellers' stands display a seemingly endless array of antiques and collectibles, some of questionable authenticity. Browsers are discouraged from touching the merchandise unless they're serious about purchasing something. The regular customers and dealers are well acquainted; if you understand Spanish you'll be entertained by their banter. Though it's hard to see on Sundays, the plaza is

tango hall in an eighteenth-century colonial building that once housed a general store. **Casa Blanca** ((11) 4331-4621, Calle Balcarce 668, is also colonial in style, while **Michelangelo** ((11) 4328-2646, Balcarce 433, is housed in a converted warehouse. If you plan on a late night round of the tango clubs it's a good idea to check out the neighborhood in daylight; this isn't the safest place to wander around lost at night.

Calle Defensa continues past Plaza Dorrego to **Parque Lezama** at the intersection with Avenida Brasil. Site of a more crafts-oriented Sunday fair, the park was once the highest point on the Plate River's shores and is said to have been the place where explorer Pedro de Mendoza landed

usually a peaceful spot where old men play chess under rubber trees. The buildings surrounding the square are a hodgepodge of architectural styles; some house outdoor cafés offering shady umbrellas and cool drinks to the weekend crowds, while others contain souvenir shops. The best place to quench your thirst and take a much-needed break from the cacophony is the **Bar Dorrego** ((11) 4361-0141 at Calle Defensa and Avenida Humberto. The dark bar with wooden walls interspersed with mirrors has been a neighborhood hangout since the 1920s. Patrons settle in over mugs of *chopp* (draft beer) and bowls of peanuts, whose shells cover the floors.

Calle Balcarce, one block east of Calle Defensa, is the heart of today's tango scene and home to many tango clubs. **El Viejo Almacén** ((11) 4307-7388, on Balcarce at Avenida Independencia, is a

in 1536. It held the estate of Enrique Lezama in the 1880s; his collection of life-sized sculptures still stands atop the park's steep slopes. The ochre-colored Lezama home now houses the **Museo Histórico Nacional** ((11) 4307-1182, Calle Defensa 1600. Built like an Italian palazzo with a square tower, the house had 32 rooms; many are filled with exhibits detailing Argentina's history. Among the most striking exhibits are the enormous, violently realistic oil paintings by Cándido López depicting Argentina's war with Paraguay, and the room devoted to General José de San Martín. Covered with a mosaic of blue-and-white tiles, the five egg-shaped domes of the **Iglesia Ortodoxa Rusa**, Avenida Brasil 315,

OPPOSITE: *Porteños* enamored with the past search for bargains at San Telmo's weekend antique market. ABOVE: One San Telmo shop features musical memorabilia.

tower over the park. The church was built in 1901 and is filled with icons and works of art donated by Czar Nicolas II.

Two blocks northeast of Plaza Dorrego is the intimidating **Facultad de Ingeniería** at Paseo Colón and Avenida Independencia. Built by the military government of the 1930s and 1940s, the German neoclassical building with a series of severe columns at the entrance was used by Eva Perón for her foundation to serve the poor and is now the College of Engineering. In front of the building, on an island in the middle of Paseo Colón, is a sculpture by Argentine artist Rogelio Yrurtia called *Canto al Trabajo* (Song to Work). It is said Juan Perón planned to build a large mau-

Despite the dangers, La Boca is still fascinating and fun. Tourists gravitate to **Calle Museo Caminito** at Avenida Pedro de Mendoza across from Buenos Aires's first port. Created in 1959 at the urging of artist Benito Quinquela Martín, the Caminito is an open-air museum and art gallery. It also serves as a living tribute to the Italian immigrants who have made this area the Little Italy of Buenos Aires. These immigrants, including a majority from Genoa, imported a Mediterranean flair to their neighborhood that endures today. Tango dancers perform at the entrance to the Caminito, offering impromptu lessons to passersby. Painters set up their easels under an array of ramshackle houses painted vivid shades of red, yellow, blue,

soleum for Evita on this spot; instead, the park-like traffic island is called the Plaza Eva Perón and the monument represents her dedication to the workers of Argentina. Behind the Engineering College on Avenida Azopardo is the **CGT** (Confederation of Workers) building, where Evita's body was held for two years while being embalmed by Dr. Pedro Ara. A tiled portrait of Evita is inlaid on one wall, near a torch with an eternal flame.

South of San Telmo on the edges of the river is **La Boca**, the starting point for all immigrants who entered the city by ship in the 1800s. A working-class, port-oriented *barrio*, La Boca is both intriguing and dangerous. Visitors are warned not to wander from the tourism areas heavily patrolled by police; poverty is rife here, and outsiders bearing thick wallets and expensive cameras are easy prey.

and green. The structures, which look like they could collapse at any moment, are typical immigrant houses made of wood and corrugated sheet metal with rooms added on as an afterthought and stairways leading to small porches and clotheslines. **Vuelta de Rocha** across Mendoza from the Caminito has some cafés and souvenir shops.

The **Museo de Bellas Artes de la Boca de Artistas Argentinos** ((11) 4301-1080, Avenida Pedro de Mendoza 1835, is located in the upper floors of the Quinquela Martín elementary school. The painter's studio remains intact in the third-floor watchtower, while other rooms are devoted to the paintings of several Argentine artists from the early twentieth century. The museum's hours are unpredictable, so it's best to call ahead. The most important edifice in the neighborhood for locals is the **Estadio del Club Boca Juniors** ((11) 4362-2050, Calle Brandsen 805. Home to the wildly popular Boca Juniors *fútbol*, or soccer, team, the stadium holds 50,000 wild fans and is practically a cathedral in their minds. A team museum is in the planning stages.

In years past tourists and *porteños* took great pleasure in visiting La Boca's restaurants and cantinas long into the night, partaking in informal tango shows and general revelry. Unfortunately, most locals say the neighborhood is just too dangerous for such frivolity these days, and taxi drivers are reluctant to cruise the streets after midnight. If you're determined to check out the scene, carry the number of a cab or private car company with you and call for transportation rather than loitering in the street.

architect Levacher modeled the building after Milan's Galleria Vittorio Emanuele. The massive building served as part of the National Museum of Fine Arts and the headquarters of the Buenos Aires–Pacific Railway before falling into disrepair in the 1960s. Renovations began in earnest in 1989, and today the Galerías is surely one of the fanciest shopping malls in the world. A glass dome covers much of the building; murals by famed Argentine artists enhance five of the walls. A tea shop and bar on the third floor provide a pleasant respite from the bustle within the plaza, and the lower level food court is one of the best spots in the area for inexpensive dining. In addition to dozens of shops, the plaza contains a large movie

PLAZA SAN MARTÍN AND RETIRO

The most important pedestrian street in the city is **Calle Florida**, which runs north from the Plaza de Mayo neighborhood to Plaza Libertador General San Martín. Lined with banks, shopping arcades, restaurants, cafés, and at least four McDonald's franchises, Florida was the first paved street in Buenos Aires and the first to have electric lights. *Porteños* have gathered here since the mid-1800s, strolling past fashionable shops and gossiping over coffee in club-like cafés.

All street signs on Calle Florida point the way to **Galerías Pacífico** ((11) 4319-5118, Calle Florida 753. Bordered by Córdoba, Florida, San Martín and Viamonte streets, Galerías Pacífico is a giant shopping center in a historic building. The structure was originally designed in the late 1800s to house a French-themed market; designing

theater complex and the **Centro Cultural Borges** ((11) 4319-5359, Viamonte and San Martín. The center, named for Argentina's most famous writer, houses temporary art exhibits and holds art and culture lectures in its large auditorium.

At the intersection of Calle Florida and Avenida Alvear, liveried doormen greet guests under the portico at the **Marriott Plaza Hotel** ((11) 4318-3000. Ernesto Tornquist, one of Argentina's leading bankers and the head of one of the country's most powerful families, hired German architect Alfred Zucker to design the hotel, which opened in 1909. The German Baroque façade retains the original design, though the hotel's public spaces and rooms have been remodeled several times.

OPPOSITE: Tango clubs line San Telmo's most famous streets. ABOVE: Bright neon lights and loud music entertain crowds of pedestrians on Calle Florida.

The best rooms in the hotel face the **Plaza Libertador General San Martín**, the loveliest park in Buenos Aires. Once a muddy field where bullfights were held on Sunday afternoons in the early 1800s, the plaza was transformed into a verdant oasis by French landscape architect Charles Thays in 1883. In spring, a border of jacaranda trees provides a lacy screen of lavender blossoms; in summer, thorny *palo borracho* trees burst forth with thousands of orchid-like pink flowers. Clusters of pine, magnolia, and palm trees serve as miniature forests providing lovers a sense of privacy as they flirt on the benches. Naturally, an enormous monument to General San Martín dominates one end of the plaza. Created in 1862 by French sculptor

politics. Across the broad avenue, vendors and crowds mingle in front of the massive **Estación Retiro** train station ((11) 4311-8704, Avenida Ramos Mejía. Built upon the riverbed in 1915 (after the original train depot burned to the ground), the Retiro was designed by British architect Ambrose Pointer. Iron girders forged in Liverpool support a high vaulted ceiling above the tracks, giving the building the appearance of an open-air cathedral. Commuter trains to the northern suburbs depart from this station and run past the shantytowns where immigrants from Bolivia and Paraguay live in makeshift hovels.

The Plaza San Martín is the focal point for the inner city's most prestigious neighborhood, Retiro.

Luis José Daumas, the sculpture depicts the victorious general atop his horse; the base of the statue is a popular impromptu café for office workers picnicking in the sun.

A railing of ornate concrete posts edges the east side of the plaza, which sits atop a steep hillside leading down to the Plate River. Stairways lead down the hill to **El Cenotafio a los Caídos en la Guerra del Atlántico Sur**, the War Memorial to the Fallen in the South Atlantic War (better known as the Malvinas War between Great Britain and Argentina in 1982). An honor guard is posted beside a curving marble wall listing the names of 649 Argentines killed in the war. Ironically enough, the memorial faces the **La Torre de los Ingleses**, a replica of Big Ben donated to the city by the British in 1916. The tower was renamed La Torre Monumental after the Malvinas War; plans to open its lookout tower appear to have become mired in

In the early 1900s, several families constructed French-style mansions facing the plaza; several now house government agencies. The **Circulo Militar** (Officers' Club) ((11) 4311-1071, Santa Fe 750, was originally called the Palacio Paz, and was designed by Louis Sortais in 1902 for José C. Paz, founder of the newspaper *La Prensa*. An ornate bronze and wrought-iron gate guards the entry to the palace, which now houses a military club and the **Museo Nacional de Armas** ((11) 4311-1071, Avenida Alvear 745, open to the public from March through December. The stately French neoclassical **Palacio San Martín** ((11) 4819-8092, Calle Arenales 800, was designed in 1909 by Alejandro Cristophersen for the powerful Anchorena family. The complex was composed of three residences, each with a subtly different style. As a result, the building combines belle époque, Baroque, art nouveau, and neoclassical elements, and is the architect's masterpiece. The Argentine Ministry of Foreign Affairs took over the building after a public auction in 1936. After many years of restoration, the palace was opened to the public on a limited basis in late 1999. The interior alone is staggering with its gilded dome ceilings, glistening chandeliers, and original French furnishings. In addition, the ministry's extensive art and archeology collections are on display. The hours are erratic; call ahead or check with the tourist office.

Argentina's first skyscraper also faces the plaza. The 120-m-high (394-ft) **Edificio Kavanagh** (Kavanagh Building), Avenida San Martín, was built in the 1930s. The highly stylized building

sides of downtown and the *barrios* of Monserrat, San Nicolas, and Balvanera. Avenida de Mayo is one of the main routes linking this area with the Plaza de Mayo in a diagonal line from the Casa Rosada to Congress. Avenida de Mayo becomes Avenida Rivadavia at the grand **Palacio del Congreso**, Avenida Callao, its architecture strikingly similar to that of the Capitol Building in Washington DC. Architect Victor Meano chose a classic Greek-Roman theme for the palatial building which houses the nation's legislature. A green copper dome dominates the elaborate white marble and granite façade topped with trumpeting angels. Classic caryatids frame the side doors; Doric pillars with elaborate capitals

narrows to a star shape in a series of terraces; it's one of the most prestigious apartment buildings in the city. Down towards the river is one of the city's small treasures. The **Museo de Arte Hispanoamericano Isaac Fernandez Blanco(** (11) 4327-0228, Calle Suipacha 1422, is dedicated to Latin American art. Architect Martín Noel designed the neo-Colonial building as his home in the 1920s, and filled it with religious art, sculpture, and Peruvian silver. Evening concerts are sometimes held in the courtyard garden. A small admission fee is charged.

THE CITY CENTER

Several of the most important neighborhoods in Buenos Aires are clustered on both sides of Avenida 9 de Julio, said to be the broadest avenue in the world. The avenue divides the east and west

abound. Visitors are usually not allowed to tour the congress building.

The congress building faces the Plaza Congreso and **Monumento de los Dos Congresos**, an enormous frothy confection of sculpted horses straining to mount granite steps said to represent the Andes. The monument honors the two congresses in 1813 and 1816 that led to Argentina's independence. It looms over the long plaza with precious few benches and small gated lawns (the gates do not keep kids from running about on the grass). Several ornate early twentieth-century buildings with domes, balustrades, towers, and gargoyles face the plaza. Most of the buildings house government agencies or private residences; some have

OPPOSITE: Small neighborhood shops stock cigarettes, beer, lotto tickets, and postal stamps. ABOVE: A soaring obelisk towers over the widest avenue in the world.

fallen into disrepair. Check out the stained-glass minaret and metal windmill atop the defunct Confitería de Molino at the corner of avenidas Callao and Rivadavia, and the building without a name topped by two full-grown stone men striking a bell. There are several upscale apartment complexes along the park; on Sunday afternoons, women in fur coats and high heels walk arm in arm about the neighborhood.

Avenida Callao runs north from the Congress building to Avenida Córdoba and the most outrageous building in all Buenos Aires. The **Palacio de Aguas Argentinas** (originally called Palacio de Aguas Corrientes) ((11) 4379-0105, Avenida Córdoba 1950, is a massive confection designed by Swedish engineer Carlos. A.B. Nystromer, Norwegian architect Olaf Boye, and the British design firm of Bateman, Parsons and Bateman. Though it looks as if it should house several royal families, the palace is actually home to an intricate series of pipes and 12 metal tanks containing 72,000 tons of drinking water. Work began on the building in 1887 and finished in 1894 with a façade of over 170,000 ceramic pieces and 130,000 enameled bricks provided by London's Royal Doulton & Company. The terracotta glazed bricks cover the first floor of the building; other sections have various shades of ochre, green, and blue. An overabundance of cornices, pilasters caryatids, and the shields of Argentina's first 14 provinces contribute to the building's ornate opulence; black mansard roofs with towers rise high above the palm trees planted in narrow, gated gardens.

If the building captures your fancy, visit **El Museo del Patrimonio Histórico** hidden down an upstairs corridor (a guide will lead the way). Copies of the original building plans cover the walls, and a few pieces of the Royal Doulton ceramic decorations are on display. The museum also contains a curious array of old toilets, bidets, sinks, and faucets.

Walk east on Calle Viamonte from the Aguas Argentinas building to Avenida 9 de Julio to reach the **Plaza Lavalle**. The plaza's gardens were planted in the mid-1800s, and several century-old ficus trees shade its benches. Palaces in the Greek, art nouveau, and French neoclassical styles frame the park. Until streets and traffic were rerouted, the plaza served as the entryway to the **Teatro Colón** ((11) 4382-6632, Calle Libertad 600. Italian architect Francisco Tamburini began drawing his plans for the theater in 1829, but the entire project was not completed until 1908. The main theater seats 2,500 in a horseshoe-shaped arrangement with boxes and balconies rising in several levels under the central dome. The Golden Hall upstairs is modeled after Versailles and is replete with chandeliers and tapestries. Until recently, the theater was one of the main tourist attractions in Buenos Aires, and visitors could tour the under-

ground workshops where all costumes and props are created. But in early 2000, officials decided the building was unsafe, and workmen began reinforcing critical areas. The theater was closed to tourists (though open for a limited season of concerts and plays). The building's future is insecure, and theater staff are concentrating on obtaining funding for major renovations.

The theater district along Avenida Corrientes has long been the hangout for the intelligencia and artsy set. This long, crowded stretch is a mix of Manhattan's Times Square, Broadway and Forty-second Street, filled with theaters, bookstores, cinemas, and porn palaces. On weekend evenings the street is filled with art-loving *porteños* headed out for a night on the town. Lines form in front of theaters where the latest plays are. Impromptu bookstores fill warehouse spaces, while more formal shops showcase the latest novels in elaborate window displays attracting crowds. Its seems there's a café on very corner, including some of the most famous gathering spots for the literati. The **Teatro San Martín** ((11) 4371-0111, Avenida Corrientes 1530, is a large complex with a live theater stage, film halls, and art and photo galleries. The rather plain building was designed by Mario Roberto Alvarez in 1960. Most of the attention went to the theaters and galleries, which host international artists year round. Upcoming events are posted on the front doors and in a pamphlet available at the theater and in some tourist offices. **La Plaza** at Avenida Corrientes 1660 offers a pleasant respite from the street action. Small coffee shops, galleries, theaters, and boutiques fill the landscaped passageway.

At the heart of Avenida 9 de Julio is the soaring white **Obelisco** (Obelisk), a peaked 67-m-tall (221.5-ft) tower that is one of the city's most prominent landmarks. Built in 1936 as part of a major public works program, the obelisk marks the place where the flag of Argentina first hung.

LA RECOLETA

Firmly established as the most cultured neighborhood in Buenos Aires, La Recoleta is worth exploring again and again. Most of the city's finest hotels are located on its broad avenues, near fashionable boutiques and restaurants. The name comes from the Franciscan monks, who called their outlying churches *recoletas*, or retreats. Though La Recoleta is no longer a country parish, it retains a sense of separateness from the larger city.

The most popular tourist attraction is the brick-walled **Cementerio de la Recoleta** on Avenida Mariscal López, where magnificent mausoleums sit atop the most expensive land in the city. Once the garden for the adjacent eighteenth-century

The Teatro Colón's Golden Hall is modeled after Versailles.

convent, this city of the dead was laid out along a pattern of streets by engineer Felipe Bertres in 1822. Several generations of Argentina's wealthiest families are buried in elaborate miniature marble castles replete with flying angels and life-sized statues of favorite saints. The small narrow structures usually have several lower levels where coffins and urns are stashed; the main rooms typically have elaborate altars.

Tombs bear the names of several past presidents, generals, and literary figures. But the most famous mausoleum in Recoleta is hardly the fanciest. The family Duarte commissioned a plain black building fronted by a brass gate for their remains, not knowing Argentina's most famous celebrity would one day be interred here. Hundreds stop by daily to visit the final resting place of Evita Perón, whose death served to enhance her mystique (see FOLLOW IN EVITA'S footsteps, page 16 in TOP SPOTS). Other significant personages entombed in Recoleta include President Sarmiento (who lies beneath a bronze condor), President Mitre, and José Hernández, author of the gaucho poem *Martín Fierro*.

Visitors wander the cemetery to visit their loved ones or explore this open-air art and architecture gallery, where famed sculptors display their more elaborate works. Some of the guests have the future in mind as they shop around with newspaper clippings listing mausoleums for sale. *Porteños* find nothing unusual about the practice of selling off the family vault to the nouveau riche seeking permanent prestige. After all, a square meter of land alone in Recoleta cemetery is worth about US$20,000 before you add on the cost of a scaled-down Greek temple.

The cemetery grounds were once part of **La Basílica de La Señora del Pilar** ((11) 4803-6793, Calle Junín 1898, one of the most beloved churches in Buenos Aires. Built in 1732 for the Franciscan friars, the Baroque colonial church and cloister complex is painted a soft white, which flatters the many brides who pose at its portals. The wrought silver altarpiece was created in Peru, and appears more regal and refined than the gold ones found in most important churches. Guided tours of the cloisters are available.

The adjacent **Centro Cultural Recoleta** ((11) 4803-9744 or (11) 4803-1041, Calle Junín 1930, was also a creation of the colonial Franciscans. Designed as a convent in the mid-1700s, the center has a series of long hallways with vaulted ceilings connecting a maze of rooms; several small gardens and a main courtyard divide stable buildings. After serving as a home for the elderly, the center was renovated in 1978 by architect Jacques Bedel and painter-architects Luis Benedit and Clorinda Testa to serve as a cultural center for the entire city. Art exhibits, lectures, performances, and concerts attract crowds on weekends

and a steady stream of visitors throughout the week. The small shop has an excellent selection of books on Buenos Aires, Argentina, and the arts. Admission is charged. The city occasionally offers free walking tours of various neighborhoods, which begin in front of the center on Sunday mornings.

The lower level arched passageway of the cloisters faces a row of outdoor cafés atop the **Buenos Aires Design Center** ((11) 4806-1111, Avenida Pueyrredón 2501. Anchored by a Hard Rock Café, the restaurant row incorporates everything from traditional *parrillas* to an outdoor Wendy's burger franchise and is one of the most popular places in the city for leisurely see-and-be-seen weekend lunches. The Design Center descends down as steep slope and houses dozens of furniture, carpeting, fabric, and house-wares shops. Just try to combat your envy as you window-shop; at least you'll get a sense of how wealthy *porteños* furnish their homes.

Avenida Alvear, facing the cemetery, basilica and cultural center across the **Plaza Intendente Alvear**, is the social center of Recoleta. Its anchor is the **Alvear Palace Hotel** ((11) 4808-2100, Avenida Alvear 1891, which has remained the city's most glamorous hotel since its opening in 1932. Stop in the Lobby Bar for tea or a cocktail, if you are properly dressed. Even guests must wear "smart casual" clothing when in the lobby. Avenida Alvear and the surrounding streets are lined with designer boutiques and old mansions, some of which now house embassies. La Biela ((11) 4804-0449, Avenida Quintana 596, is the most important see-and-be-seen café, with plastic tables scattered about under a huge *gomero*, or rubber tree. This section of Junín and the adjacent pedestrian walkway on Calle Ortíz are lined with classy restaurants and bars popular as late-night gathering spots. Calle Posadas, one block north of Alvear, is another good street for a stroll. Juan and Eva Perón either lived together or shared adjacent flats in an unmarked apartment building at Calle Posadas 1500. Madonna set up house during filming of *Evita* at the luxurious Park Hyatt at Calle Posadas 1086, attracting hordes of protestors and celebrity watchers. **Patio Bullrich** ((11) 4815-3501, Avenida Libertador 750, is one of the most exclusive shopping centers in town.

A series of parks cover the sloping hillsides from the center of La Recoleta to Avenida del Libertador. Artists and artisans display their works in the parks on weekends, attracting crowds. Several fine museums line the avenue, which runs northwest from the Plaza San Martín through La Recoleta and on to the northern suburbs. The **Palais de Glace Salas Nacionales de Cultura** ((11) 4804-1163 or (11) 4805-4354, Calle Posadas 1725, holds temporary arts and crafts exhibits; a banner hanging from the building tells what's happening.

The city's main art museum is the red **Museo Nacional de Bellas Artes** ((11) 4803-3390, Avenida del Libertador 1403, which housed water pumps before being redesigned by architect Alejandro Bustillo in 1930. Along with a comprehensive collection of Argentine painting and sculpture, the museum displays several pieces by European masters including Rodin, Degas, Manet, and Gauguin. Rotating exhibits by contemporary artists are displayed near the entrance.

A far more impressive building houses the eclectic collection of the **Museo Nacional de Arte Decorativo** ((11) 4806-8306, Avenida del Libertador 1902. French architect René Sergent designed several important mansions in Buenos Aires; this

— Francisco Bullrich, Clorinda Testa, and Alicia Cazzaniga — worked on the design; the result is an angular slab of concrete and glass perched atop pillars overlooking Avenida del Libertador. It took over 30 years for the library to be completed. The architects won the commission in 1962; Jorge Luis Borges laid the foundation stone in 1971 and the doors finally opened in 1992. Visitors are allowed to use the library and its adjacent room filled with computers; Internet access is free, but there's usually a long line. The Internet room is part of the Plaza del Lector, a large expanse of grass and reading benches behind the building; there's also a café here selling inexpensive sandwiches and snacks.

one, built for the Errázuriz family, is the most outstanding. Designed much like late eighteenth-century mansions in Paris, the Palacio Errázuriz is a study in excess financed by the family's success in cattle raising and agriculture. A wrought iron and bronze gate opens to a driveway framed by pillars; a stairway leads to the foyer and an enormous Renaissance-style reception hall. Each splendid room contains a wealth of *objets d'art*, from Lalique vases to Rodin sculptures to Louis XV chairs. Exhibits for the small **Museo de Arte Oriental** ((11) 4801-5988 in the bedrooms and hallways of the upper floor include swords, pottery, and lacquered furnishings from the Far East. Admission is charged for both museums.

In startling juxtaposition to the avenue's opulent architecture, the **Biblioteca Nacional Mariano Moreno** ((11) 4807-0090, Calle Agüero 2510, is modern and austere. Three Argentine architects

The grounds on which the library stands were once part of the Casa Unzué, where Juan and Eva Perón lived and where Evita died. In late 1999, at the very end of his administration, President Carlos Menem dedicated the city's only monument to Evita in front of the library on Avenida del Libertador. Most of the Unzué estate was destroyed during the military regime's purge of all things Peronist, but a small part remains and houses the **Instituto Nacional Juan D. Perón** ((11) 4802-8010 WEB SITE www.jdperon.gov.ar, Calle Austria 2593. Call in advance for a tour of the building and a viewing of a film made up of news clips from the Perón administration.

Argentine folk art is featured at the small **Museo de Motivos Argentinos José Hernández** ((11) 4802-9967. Though the museum is named

Chic *porteños* gather under the umbrellas at La Recoleta's sidewalk cafés.

for the author of *Martín Fierro*, Hernández had nothing to do with the collection. Instead, the displays of arts and crafts from pre-colonial days to the present was collected and donated by a expatriate American, Carlos Daws.

PALERMO AND BELGRANO

Another north-side neighborhood filled with turn-of-the-century mansions, Palermo is home to the city's largest parks, collectively called **Palermo Park**. Much of the land was part of the estate of President/Dictator Juan Manuel de Rosas, who built an extensive *estancia* with a colonial-style mansion here in 1838. After his downfall, Rosas

kindly, the exhibits are old fashioned, with an Indian-style palace for the elephant exhibit and dusty enclosures for monkeys, tigers, and bears. Admission is charged.

The frothy white marble **Monumento a los Españoles** (Monument to the Spaniards) rises above the intersection of Avenida Sarmiento and Avenida del Libertador. Nearby is the main entrance to the largest section of the park complex, **Parque Tres Febrero** (Third of February Park) on Avenida Sarmiento between Avenida del Libertador and Avenida Presidente Figueroa Alcorta. The name commemorates the Battle of Monte Caseros in 1852, in which Rosas led the victors. The park includes mini forests, lakes, lawns, and

was banished to England and his estate destroyed in 1899. President Domingo Sarmiento took over the estate for the country and had the land cleared and landscaped.

The greenbelt begins at the **Plaza Italia**, at the intersection of Avenida Santa Fe and Avenida Sarmiento. *Porteños* eager to escape the city's pandemonium head for the shady **Jardín Botánica** ((11) 4832-1601, Avenida Santa Fe and Avenida Las Heras, laid out in 1897 by landscape architect Charles Thays. A maze of trees and pathways leads to a small brick castle and a long greenhouse sheltering tropical plants; lily ponds, statues, and private benches are scattered about. Admission is free. Nearby, the **Jardín Zoológica** ((11) 4804-7412, at Avenida las Heras and Avenida Sarmiento, was another Sarmiento project from 1888. Enormously popular with school groups and families, the zoo is packed on spring weekends. To put it

plenty of winding trails for joggers, cyclists, and in-line skaters. Paddleboats are available for rent at the park, and horse-drawn carriages provide transport from one end to the other (though they charge upwards of US$20 an hour for a ride). If you visit in spring, don't miss the **Paseo del Rosedal** on Avenida de la Infanta Isabel. A white bridge leads over the lake to a wonderland of more than 400 perfect rose bushes blooming with pink, lavender, scarlet, and peach flowers. A white pergola serves as the prettiest wedding chapel in the city, and sculptures and benches are scattered about lawns facing the rose beds. The **Jardín Japonés** ((11) 4804-4922, at Casares and Adolfo Berro, is a peaceful oasis of streams, fishponds, and whispering bamboo fronds that encourages silent meditation. Designed by civil engineer Isakari and landscape architect Yatsuo Inomata, the park incorporates graceful bridges and Japanese sculptures. Admission is US$2. A moon rock presented to the Argentines by United States ex-president Richard Nixon and a meteorite that fell in the province of Chaco in 1965 are prominently displayed at the **Planetario Galileo Galilei** ((11) 4771-6629, Sarmiento and Roldán. Designed by architect Enrique Jan in 1962, the domed planetarium presents space films on weekend afternoons. Admission is charged.

A version of a county fair called the **Exposición Rural** is held every August in the **Sociedad Rural Argentina** ((11) 4777-5501, Avenida Santa Fe and Avenida Sarmiento, a fairgrounds for agricultural exhibits. Horses rule at the **Hipódromo Argentino** ((11) 4777-9001, Avenida del Libertador 4205, which sprawls along the northern edge of the park. The racetrack is the epicenter of Buenos Aires's equestrian set, and dates from 1882 when President Carlos Pellegrini founded the Jockey Club.

The park dominates Palermo, but the neighborhood's residential and commercial streets are worth exploring as well. The neighborhood of Palermo Chico, east of the park along Avenida Presidente Figueroa Alcorta, is lined with French neoclassical mansions dating from the early 1900s, many now used as embassies and diplomats' residences; Argentine architect Alejandro Bustillo created several of the masterpieces in this upscale neighborhood.

The northeastern edge of Palermo gives way to the **Costanera Norte**, where a wide sidewalk runs along the shores of the Plate River. Once a fashionable area where wealthy *porteños* strolled on weekend afternoons, the Costanera is now a haven for the city's less fortunate residents. Families gather along the walkway to fish, picnic and play as private yachts and sailboats glide by on the river. The peak-roofed building at the end of a long pier at the north end is the private **Club de Pescadores**, a prestigious fishing club.

A classy, private neighborhood northwest of Palermo, **Belgrano** isn't on the standard tourist itinerary. But it is well worth a visit. The suburb became a desirable enclave for artists, writers, and diplomats after the yellow fever epidemic of 1871 drove thousands from the center city. Limestone cliffs called **Las Barrancas de Belgrano** at La Pampa and Avenida Virrey Vertiz were transformed into a park by Charles Thays in 1892; the residential streets between here and Avenida Cabildo are filled with an eclectic array of homes built in the early 1900s.

Belgrano is named for Manuel Belgrano, who designed the pale blue and white flag of Argentina, and is home to one of the prettiest plazas in Buenos Aires. **Plaza General Belgrano**, bordered by Juramento, Echeverría, Cuba and Vuelta de Obligado streets, is a modest square with eucalyptus and jacaranda trees sheltering benches and sculptures; a crafts fair is held here on weekends.

Facing the square is the **Parroquia de Nuestra Señora de las Inmaculada Concepción** ((11) 4300-5547, Avenida Independencia 910, a circular church topped with a dome. The gray exterior gives way to a more colorful interior, with paintings covering the interior of the dome.

More interesting is the **Museo de Arte Española Enrique Larreta** ((11) 4783-2640 or (11) 4748-4040, Juramento 2291, former home of novelist Enrique Larreta. Author of *The Glory of Don Ramiro*, Larreta served as Argentina's ambassador to France in the early 1900s, but refrained from joining his fellow *porteños* in their passion for French architecture. Instead, his home was designed in 1916 by Martín Noel in a colonial style as an addition to a house designed by Ernesto Bunge in 1882. The museum contains the original illustrations for Larreta's novels, copies of the books' many translations, family portraits hanging on silk-covered walls, and a sixteenth-century altar and *retablos* sectioned into religious scenes with nearly life-sized statues imported from Spain. The formal garden is a delight with its boxwood and lavender hedges, Moorish fountains, magnolia, citrus, and palm trees, and small stage where concerts are occasionally held. Admission is charged. Also facing the plaza, the **Museo Histórico Sarmiento** ((11) 4783-7555, Juramento 2180, honoring one of Argentina's most beloved presidents. The colonial-style building is filled with memorabilia from Sarmiento's life, including furnishings, portraits, and uniforms. Some rooms are used for cultural workshops and lectures. Admission is charged.

Belgrano's old-fashioned ambience is evident in its **Mercado** at Juramento and Ciudad de la Paz streets. Vendors bring produce, fish, flowers, and meat to one of the few open-air markets in the city daily; on weekends their displays attract shoppers from throughout Buenos Aires. There are several excellent delicatessens in the market displaying imported cheeses, salami, ham, olives, and salads, all perfect for a picnic lunch. The market is open daily from 8 AM to 1 PM and 5 PM to 8:30 PM. **Las Cañitas**, a small neighborhood between Palermo and Belgrano, has become one of the city's hottest nightspots, with over 30 restaurants within a few blocks of each other.

PUERTO MADERO

Engineer Luis A. Hüergo designed the city's original port on the Río de la Plata in 1897; the street along the waterfront bears his name. Eduardo Madero was granted the concession to build the port—little did he know his name would eventually reign over one of the city's most fashionable dining districts. By 1910, Puerto Madero's four

Belgrano's ethnic restaurants and trendy clubs are packed long past midnight.

docks were unable to handle the port's commerce, and a new, more functional port area, called *Puerto Nuevo* was constructed to the north. In 1990, the city's leaders decided to transform Puerto Madero's red brick warehouses into livable spaces. The buildings now house residential apartments, offices, over two dozen restaurants and a university campus. Future plans include expensive office and condominium towers, and a shopping center. Puerto Madero became the forty-seventh *barrio* in Buenos Aires in 1999; developers and city officials are hoping it will bring new life to the riverfront.

Porteños spend weekend afternoons strolling along the riverfront, riding bikes on the wide pathways, and lingering over coffee and pastries at riverfront cafés. Children are particularly entranced with the **Buque Museo Fragata A.R.A. Presidente Sarmiento** ((11) 4334-9386. The tall-sail battleship was constructed in 1898 and serves as a floating museum. Private yachts fill the marina in front of the yacht club, and this section of the river is filled with boaters on weekends.

As Puerto Madero was remodeled, much of the debris was discarded in the river. It gradually was covered with dirt and indigenous plants and trees. Now the junk heap is called **Costanera Sur**, Avenida Costanera and Avenida Macacha Güemes, and is informally termed a biological reserve. Birds, ducks, and fish have begun to return to the city to inhabit the reserve, and *porteños* find it a pleasant natural escape. Unfortunately, fires are common here. Some say the land is too valuable to be used as a wildlife refuge; according to the gossip grapevine (a vital force in *porteño* life), the frequent wildfires may have a devious purpose.

SPORTS

A recent newspaper poll asked Argentines what brings the most pleasure in their lives. Family and money got decent ranking, but the number-one joy for all was *fútbol* (aka soccer). *Fútbol* star Diego Armando Maradona is nearly as sacred a personage as tango singer Carlos Gardel or Evita, and the soccer stadiums of Buenos Aires are somewhat akin to cathedrals. The whole country celebrated when Argentina won the World Cup in 1978; the parties and parades in Buenos Aires were particularly poignant as they provided a brief glimmer of joy during the Dirty War. Argentina won again in 1986. Soccer is played year round. The two most popular teams are the Boca Juniors (Maradona's club) and the River Plate; the city comes to a halt when these two teams oppose each other. Attending a game is to see *porteños* in their most passionate state. Fans, called *"hinchas,"* cram both the cheap and expensive seats (tickets cost US$20 to US$100), and televisions all over the city are tuned to the game.

Given the historic importance of horses and horsemanship in Argentina, it's natural that the elite would turn to **polo** as a form of recreation and skill. English ranch owner David Shennan introduced polo to Argentina in 1875, and the sport quickly caught on in the *estancias* of the pampas. Several polo clubs started in late 1800s. Polo games are held at the Canchas Nacionales in Palermo; games are held from March to May and September to December. Contact the Asociación Argentina de Polo ((11) 4331-4646, 4342-8321 for schedules and tickets. If you're a polo fanatic consider visiting La Martina Polo Ranch ((11) 4576-7997, near Vicente Casares, 60 km (37 miles) from Buenos Aires. The ranch has over 80 polo horses and is a training center for horses and players. **Horse racing** is also understandably popular. Races are held at Hipódromo Argentino ((11) 4777-9001, Avenida del Libertador 4205.

Visitors interested in **golf** can arrange transportation and tee times through their hotels or by contacting the Asociación Argentina de Golf ((11) 4394-2743. TGG — The Golden Golf ((11) 4322-0352 or (11) 4322-8547 specializes in golf for tourists. They can arranges tee times and transfers to course and club rentals. The most popular courses are Cancha Municipal de Golf ((11) 4772-7261, Tornquist and Olleros in Palermo, and Jockey Club Argentino ((11) 4743-1001, Marquéz 1700 in Olivos.

SHOPPING

Porteños love to shop and have plenty of places dedicated to this passion. Shopping centers abound, from the fashionable Galerías Pacífico (see WHAT TO SEE AND DO, page 77) to cramped arcades on busy streets. Shops are clustered on Calle Florida, Avenida Santa Fe by Plaza San Martín, Avenida Alvear, and Avenida Quintana in Recoleta. Stores are generally open 9 AM to 8 PM on weekdays, 9 AM to 1 PM on Saturday, with many closed on Sunday except in shopping centers. The 21% tax on goods is refundable if you spend more than 200 pesos. There are Global Refund Offices at the international airport where you can show your receipts and obtain your refund. Just be sure to show up at the airport well in advance of your flight, as the system is a tad complicated and slow.

Buenos Aires isn't a big folk-art center, though there are a few shops selling crafts from the northern provinces and Tierra del Fuego. **Chamote** ((11) 4300-0352, Calle Defense 845 in San Telmo, is one of the nicest. They display a large selection of wooden animals carved by the Guaraní Indians from the north, and fine silver and gourd *matés* (used for making tea) with delicate silver straws, called *bombillas* (see GALLOPING GOURMET, page 40 in YOUR CHOICE, for information on *maté*). The displays are equally enticing at **La Buena Tierra** ((11) 4823-1712, Calle Agüero 1608, where Peruvian handicrafts are mixed in with those from northern Argentina. Wool shawls and weavings are on display at **Raíces Artesanías Argentinas** ((11) 4803-2588, Calle Vicente Lopez 1929 in La Recoleta. Tango posters, CDs, and videos are sold at **Almacén de Tango Generales** ((11) 4362-7190, Don Anselmo Aieta 1067. The shop is in the first story of one of the old mansions overlooking San Telmo's Plaza Dorrego. **Artesanías Salta** ((11) 4815-7841, Avenida Peña 1771, carries alpaca (nickel and silver) objects and jewelry from Salta. Wood carvings, gourd *matés*, and handcrafted jewelry are displayed at **Wayra** ((11) 4319-5343, Calle Viamonte 555, the best souvenir shop in Galerías Pacífico. **Rincón Gaucho** ((11) 4325-7341, Calle Suipacha 985, sells gaucho crafts, ponchos, silverware, and *matés*, at reasonable prices.

Bookstores are an integral part of *porteño* life; everyone reads everywhere. Books are expensive (especially those not in Spanish), and the second-hand bookshops and stalls along Calle Corrientes are immensely popular, as are the vendors selling used books most days at Plaza Lavalle. **El Ateneo** ((11) 4325-6801, Calle Florida 340, is an enormous shop with a good selection of books on Argentina and English-language novels.

Young *porteños* are entranced with furnishings, jewelry, and clothing from the Golden Age of Buenos Aires, circa 1900 to 1920. Dozens of shops in San Telmo cater to their tastes. **El Buen Orden** (4307-8608, Calle Defensa 894, is an enchanting shop stocked with dresses, shoes, buttons, lace, hats, evening bags, and medals; as the owner says, it is "el único en el mundo" (the only such place in the world). **Paseo del Anticuarios**, Calle Defensa 900, is filled with independent vendors displaying everything from old newspapers to chandeliers. Even if you're not interested in buying antiques, take a look at the fabulous displays at **GIL Antigüedades** ((11) 4361-5019, Calle Humberto 412; you'll wish you'd been around in the 1920s.

Argentina's wines are gaining international attention, and a few fine shops specialize in teaching locals and visitors how to find the best vintages. Most also stock a wide range of imported wines and gourmet foods. **La Maison du Vin** ((11) 4361-2907, Calle Defensa 891 in San Telmo, holds wine-tasting classes; its wine cellars are used by several fine restaurants for storage. Looking for a gift for a friend? Check out the imported and regional liquors, wines, champagnes, and chocolates at **Savoy** ((11) 4371-1995 at Avenida Callao 35. A back room is filled with pricey gift baskets, while tins of caviar, pâté, and sardines line the shelves beside imported Italian cakes.

Polo aficionados know the best boots and saddles are displayed at **La Martina** ((11) 4576-7997, Calle Paraguay 661, and **Arandú** ((11) 4816-6191, Calle Paraguay 1259. **Fortín** ((11) 4812-2731, Avenida Santa Fe 1245, specializes in handmade leather shoes and boots. High quality leather goods, saddles, and elaborately handcrafted silver *matés* are on display at **La Querencia Talabartería** ((11) 4312-1879, Calle Esmeralda 1018. Fine leather jackets, shoes, and purses are also available at **Rossi & Caruso** ((11) 4811-1965, Avenida Santa Fe 1601, **Beretta** ((11) 4813-9258, Calle Arenales 1654, and **Welcome** ((11) 4312-8911, Avenida Alvear 500.

Fine jewelry shops are clustered around Plaza San Martín and in Recoleta; the gold district

is located around Calle Libertad at Avenida Corrientes. There are bargains to be found in 18-caret gold, Brazilian emeralds, and semiprecious stones; bargaining is expected. Respected jewelers include **Santarelli** ((11) 4322-4170, Calle Florida 688, **Jean-Pierre** ((11) 4804-6668, Avenida Alvear 1892, **H. Stern** ((11) 4312-4595 in the Marriott Plaza Hotel and the Alvear Palace Hotel, and **Antonio Belgiorno** ((11) 4811-1117, Avenida Santa Fe 1347, known for their silver pieces.

Browse through the **Buenos Aires Design Center** ((11) 4806-1111, Pueyrredón 2501, for an overview of some of the latest imported and domestic household items. **Morph** ((11) 4806-3226 has a great selection of china and glassware; some of their smaller pieces make wonderful, usable souvenirs.

Shoppers stroll through the opulent Galerías Pacífico mall.

WHERE TO STAY

The hotel selection in Buenos Aires is a bit odd, especially for travelers accustomed to modern accommodations. Nearly all the hotels in all price ranges are housed in older buildings, some barely renovated. The finest have been modernized without losing their Old World charm; most, however, are simply refurbished every so often in a haphazard manner. Don't be fooled by grand lobbies with sparkling chandeliers and gleaming wood counters. The grandeur often ends at the creaky elevator. Many rooms are small and dark, though most have air-conditioning or fans (essential in the stifling summer heat and humidity). Televisions don't always have cable channels or satellite service; if you're hooked on CNN ask if it's available before booking your room. Direct-dial, long-distance telephone service is only available in the more expensive hotels, and the charge for calls (even those made with a calling card) is usually quite high. Nearly all bathrooms have a bidet, and many now have hairdryers. Most hotels, even those without restaurants, offer some kind Continental breakfast included in the room rate.

VERY EXPENSIVE

New in the summer of 2000, the **Buenos Aires Hilton** ((11) 4891-0000 FAX (11) 4891-0145 WEB SITE www.hilton.com, Avenida Macacha Güemes 351, sets a whole new standard for style and luxury in Buenos Aires. The soaring glass and steel building rises above the river across the water from Puerto Madero in the city's newest district. In fact, the area is so new the hotel has its own street — which greatly confuses the average cab driver. Nothing else in the city compares with the hotel's dazzling atrium lobby, glass elevators, and chic restaurant. The 413 rooms and suites all have walk-in closets, large desks, two phone lines with direct-dial service, mini bars, safe-deposit boxes, and separate shower and tub areas in the large bathrooms. The gray and beige color scheme enhances the modern style — you won't find antiques and floral linens here. A separate building houses Hilton Residences, which are similar to apartments and fulfill the needs of business travelers on extended stays in the city.

Naturally, chic La Recoleta claims the city's most elegant belle époque hotel, the lavish **Alvear Palace Hotel** ((11) 4808-2100 TOLL-FREE IN THE UNITED STATES (800) 448-8355 FAX (11) 4804-9246 WEB SITE www.alvearpalace.com, Avenue Alvear 1891. Opulent and sedate, the Palace is guarded by doormen in high hats who frown upon slovenly tourists — the dress code requires "smart casual" clothing in the public spaces. Guests luxuriate in soft beds with light down comforters, and bathe

with Hermes toiletries. The decor is high French with loads of velvet and silk. Amenities include a health club and pool, gourmet restaurant, afternoon tea in the atrium, and attentive concierges and butlers. If you're not staying here, stop by (properly attired, of course) for a drink in the formal lobby bar.

Also in Recoleta, the **Park Hyatt Buenos Aires** ((11) 326-3736 TOLL-FREE IN THE UNITED STATES (800) 233-1234 FAX (11) 326-3736, Calle Posadas 1086, combines a nineteenth-century mansion with a 13-story tower. After scouting the city for appropriate digs, Madonna chose the Hyatt as her home base while filming *Evita*, much to the neighbors' dismay. Crowds clogged the streets after her arrival, either to protest the film and her role in it or to do a bit of stargazing. The hotel's enormous suites and personalized butler service make all guests feel special, and its huge pool and health club are added perks. Though not quite as elegant, the **Caesar Park** ((11) 819-1100 TOLL-FREE IN THE UNITED STATES (800) 228-3000 FAX (11) 819-1165, Calle Posadas 1232, is well located near La Recoleta's fanciest shopping center, Patio Bullrich. The rooms are large and decorated with period antiques.

EXPENSIVE

Despite several renovations, the **Marriott Plaza Hotel** ((11) 4318-3000 TOLL-FREE IN THE UNITED STATES (800) 228-9290 FAX (11) 4318-3008 WEB SITE marriotthotels.com/buear, Calle Florida 1005, is still the grandest hotel in downtown Buenos Aires. Built in 1909 by Ernesto Tornquist, the building was designed by German architect Alfredo Zucker as the city's first luxury hotel. Some rooms can be splendid, with glorious views of Plaza San Martín. Others are cramped and dark, and face walls or alleyways. The service is top-notch, and the concierges are extremely helpful in guiding confused tourists. The Plaza Hotel Grill is a fine gourmet restaurant popular with elite business travelers.

With only 75 rooms, the **Aspen Suites** ((11) 4313-9011 FAX (11) 4313-8059 E-MAIL info@aspen suites.com.ar WEB SITE www.aspensuites.com.ar, Calle Esmeralda 933, has a friendly, intimate feeling and a great location, just two blocks from the Plaza San Martín. All rooms have huge whirlpool tubs, carpeting, antique furnishings and plenty of closet space. Breakfast, which is included in the rate, is substantial, and the rooftop pool is a delight after hours of walking about the city.

Though the competition is stiff in this category, the **Claridge Hotel** ((11) 4314-7700 TOLL-FREE IN THE UNITED STATES (800) 223-5652 FAX (11) 4314-8022 E-MAIL reservations@claridge-hotel.com WEB SITE www.claridge.com.ar, Tucumán 535, stands out for its tasteful renovations and devotion to style. A bright white entryway replete with columns and brass fronts the tall brick building. Inside it's all glowing burnished wood and cushy carpets and the rooms are elegant yet comfortable. The health club and pool are major pluses. Aim for a room at the top for views over the city to the river.

The **Sheraton Buenos Aires Hotel & Convention Center** ((11) 4318-9000 TOLL-FREE IN THE UNITED STATES (800) 325-3535 FAX (11) 4318-9353, Calle San Martín 1225, is the largest hotel in the city, with over 600 rooms. Popular with conventioneers and tour groups, the hotel has several restaurants catering to travelers' tastes and dining schedules (you won't feel completely out of place dining before 9 PM). The adjacent Park Tower is more luxurious, with spacious suites and butler service. Another familiar chain hotel with predictable rooms and

.com.ar, Calle Esmeralda 542. The restaurant and lobby give the impression of a modern hotel, though the rooms are renovated versions of an older property.

MODERATE

Many of the city's best hotels in this price range are located around Avenida 9 de Julio near the Congress building and the Teatro Colón. Fancier than most hotels in this category, the **Gran Hotel de la Paix** ((11) 4381-8061 E-MAIL hotel-delpaix @sinectis.com.ar, Avenida Rivadavia 1155, is a pleasant choice. The older building with stained glass ceiling panels and a burnished wood front

service is the **Crowne Plaza Panamericano** ((11) 4348-5000 FAX (11) 4348-5250 WEB SITE www.pan americano-bue.com.ar or www.crowneplaza .com.ar, Calle Carlos Pellegrini 525. Its two towers rise above Avenida 9 de Julio across from the Obelisco; a room high up at the front offers the best city views you can get from any hotel in the city. All the state-of-the-art comforts are available, from direct-dial phones and voice mail to cable television and whirlpool baths. The decor sticks with the traditional Buenos Aires style, with antique reproductions and heavy drapes. The restaurants are all good; the best is Tomo I (see WHERE TO EAT, below). The best views of all keep exercisers entranced as they work out in the fitness center on the top floor of one of the towers.

Argentina business travelers outnumber tourists at the pleasantly efficient **Rochester Hotel** ((11) 4326-6076 E-MAIL info@rochester-hotel

desk has been updated and the 70 rooms and suites have in-room safes and cable television. The simplest rooms are in the budget range, though it's possible the rates will rise as word gets out about the comfort and the hotel's grand breakfast buffet eggs, cheeses, and pastries included in the room rate.

Another reasonable choice is the **Hotel de los Dos Congresos** ((11) 4372-0466 FAX (11) 4372-0317 E-MAIL hdoscong@hotelnet.com.ar, at Avenida Rivadavia 1777 directly across from the monument of the same name. Formerly called the Mar del Plata, the hotel has a colonial façade and totally modern interior. The rooms have a refreshing, clean simplicity. Ceiling fans are a welcome change from air-conditioning (which is available), and lamps over the beds are perfect for reading.

The city's grand hotels display its finest architecture.

The location is ideal. Family heirlooms fill the lobby and rooms at the **Lancaster Hotel** ((11) 4312-4061 FAX (11) 4311-3021, Avenue Córdoba 405. The guests are treated as family as well; this is one of the most pleasant older hotels in this category.

Exuding faded elegance, the **Hotel Castelar** ((11) 437-5000 FAX (11) 325-6964, Avenida de Mayo 1152, seems quite grand upon first glance. But the 200 rooms are rather ordinary, though they do have cable television and direct-dial phones. The gym with Turkish baths is an unusual feature that pleases guests in need of some pampering. A grand exterior also greets guests at the **Hotel Crillon** ((11) 4310-2000 FAX (11) 4310-2020, Avenue Santa Fe 796. The location across the street

hotels. Wagon wheels and wood paneling prevail, though the 40 rooms are bright and cheery. Some rooms have hot tubs, and the hotel has a pool and a sauna.

INEXPENSIVE

My vote for the best budget rooms in the country goes to the **Phoenix Hotel** ((11) 4312-4845 FAX (11) 431-2846 E-MAIL info@hotelphoenix.com.ar WEB SITE www.hotelphoenix.com.ar, Calle San Martín 780. The grand old building holds rooms with high ceilings, antique armoires, and French windows opening to tiny balconies, some with views of the river. A former ballroom has been

from the Plaza San Martín is ideal, and the public spaces carry out the classic French theme of the building's architecture. The rooms are less elegant; try for one on an upper floor facing the plaza. Location is the main reason for choosing the **Bristol Hotel** ((11) 4382-5400 FAX 4382-0061, Calle Cerrito 286. The Obelisk, Teatro Colón, and Avenida Corrientes theater district are all nearby; thus, the hotel is popular with tour groups. The old-fashioned rooms are adequate, though it's best to see a few before settling in. I once checked in late at night only to find the next morning that the drapes actually covered a boarded-up window blocking out all daylight. The complimentary breakfast is more filling than most, thanks to the addition of egg dishes.

The country-inn theme at **Posta Carretas** ((11) 4322-8534 FAX (11) 4326-2277, Calle Esmeralda 726, is a pleasant change from the city's European-style

converted into a dining room where a Continental breakfast is served (included in room rate). Tango lessons are offered on several evenings. The rooms have ceiling fans and televisions; the air-conditioning is operated from the front desk. The staff members are all helpful; those working at the front desk speak English. Taxi drivers are often confused by foreign pronunciations of the hotel's name; ask for the intersection of San Martín and Córdoba if the driver doesn't understand what you want.

When guests standing at the front desk chime in praising their rooms and the friendly staff, you can tell you've found a great budget hotel. Such is the case at the **Nuevo Hotel Callao** (/FAX (11) 4374-3861 E-MAIL hotelcallao@infovia.com.ar, Avenida Callao 292. The 40 impeccably clean rooms with private bath are often booked solid. Japanese managers oversee the **Suipacha Inn** (/FAX (11) 4322-0099 E-MAIL suipachainn@ciudad.com.ar,

Calle Suipacha 515. The rooms are tiny, but clean, and have small closets, air-conditioning, and ceiling fans and mini refrigerators; some bathrooms have tubs as well as showers. Four rooms have kitchenettes. Those seeking lodgings in a quiet neighborhood will appreciate the **Guido Palace Hotel** ((11) 4812-0341 or (11) 4312-3789, Calle Guido 1780 in La Recoleta. The 46 simple, clean rooms have air-conditioning and cable television, and there's a small restaurant by the entrance. If you're not interested in staying in the downtown historic district, this hotel is a great find.

Rock-bottom rates attract backpackers to the **Buenos Aires International Hostel** ((11) 4300-9321 E-MAIL info@aaj.org.ar WEB SITE www.aaj

.org.ar, Avenida Brasil 675, in San Telmo. A member of Hostelling International, the converted house has 90 beds in dorm rooms, pay phones, laundry facilities, and a central lounge. The neighborhood is somewhat dangerous, so take advantage of the free security box for your passport and valuables.

WHERE TO EAT

There's no shortage of restaurants in Buenos Aires, though most serve the same thing — grilled meats and/or Italian pastas and pizzas. Restaurants specializing in platters of meat (*parrilladas*) abound in every price range; most serve salads and a few fish dishes as well. Japanese restaurants are becoming popular, though sushi is outrageously expensive. Given the Argentine passion for beef, vegetarian restaurants are hard to find.

As a rule, *porteños* don't eat large breakfasts, usually getting by with coffee and *medias lunas*, small pastries similar to croissants. A few tourist restaurants serve American-style breakfasts with bacon and eggs, but most hotels offer free Continental breakfasts that keep guests satisfied. Lunch is served from noon until 3 PM, and is usually a large meal. The cafés fill up around 4 PM, when it seems everyone in the city stops for coffee and a few small sweets or a cocktail and plate of chips, nuts, and cheese. Ice cream is an especially popular mid-afternoon snack. Be sure to stop by one of the ubiquitous Freddo's ice-cream stands and try *helado dulce de leche* — made with the Argentines' most popular sweet of equal parts of milk and sugar boiled together. Dinner doesn't begin until after 9 PM; woe to the traveler who prefers dining far earlier, American style. Restaurants are open and empty until the clock chimes nine; gradually, clients arrive until seats at the most popular spots are all taken by 11 PM. Expensive and moderate restaurants usually accept credit cards. Some of the more expensive restaurants include a cover charge (*cubierto*) in your bill, which is not meant to replace the tip.

The city's best restaurants are clustered in several popular nightspot areas. La Recoleta has long been a dining haven, with eateries lining the walkway by the Buenos Aires Design Center and across from the cemetery and parks on Junín and Ortíz. Puerto Madero has become one long restaurant row, with over 30 eateries, most in the expensive category. Las Cañitas on the border between Belgrano and Palermo is the newest hot spot, with ethnic restaurants lining a few residential streets.

VERY EXPENSIVE

Ada and Ebe Cóncaro preside over one of the city's most prestigious restaurants: **Tomo I** ((11) 4326-6698, Calle Carlos Pellegrini 525 in the Crowne Plaza Panamericano hotel. Long recognized as an outstanding gourmet restaurant, Tomo I is the place for a splurge. Start with the *ensalada langostinos*, a mix of arugula, raddichio, and other greens topped with Parma ham, mushrooms, and fresh shrimp. Move on to the duck, lamb, or quail entrées with the vegetable timbale on the side, and finish with the marinated peaches topped with meringue. Executive menus combining several courses are usually less expensive than ordering à la carte. Some say **Cabaña Las Lilas** ((11) 4313-1336, Avenida Alicia Moreau de Justo 516 in Puerto Madero, has the best beef in town. It's certainly among the most expensive restaurants around, with steaks priced over US$15 sans side dishes. The beef is flavorful and perfectly prepared to

The Museo Nacional de Bellas Artes contains a fine selection of paintings and sculptures by European masters.

order, and among all the usual cuts are T-bone and rib-eye steaks and lamb chops familiar to American travelers. The desserts are excellent — try the homemade almond ice cream over a crisp chocolate cookie.

Chic in design, **Katrine** ((11) 4315-6222, Avenida Alicia Moreau de Justo 138, also in Puerto Madero, is a welcome change for diners weary of standard Argentine fare. Chef Katrine Röed specializes in light Mediterranean cooking. Great dishes include octopus salad with gazpacho sauce; grilled salmon with wasabi, duck *confit* with peach chutney, and king crab ravioli. The minimalist black and white decor and refreshingly light cooking are a pleasure worth revisiting.

EXPENSIVE

Those unaccustomed to Argentine dining are thrilled to read the English/Spanish menu at **Las Nazarenas** ((11) 4312-5599, Calle Reconquista 1132. The colonial-style building is dwarfed by office towers in the business district close to Plaza San Martín, and the dining room is packed with bankers and professionals at lunch. At night it's a bit more sedate. Dinners begin with a tasty *empanada* and end with a small glass of Mariposa, a honey-flavored liqueur. Though the menu offers several fish dishes, most diners prefer the *parrilla* platters heaped with beef, veal, sausages, and sweetbreads or the spit-roasted *chivito* (goat).

A life-sized fake cow guards the front door at **Los Troncos** ((11) 4325-0156, Calle Suipacha 732, where cooks tend wood-burning grills by the front window. Heavy wooden chairs and tables, metal chandeliers, and uniformed waiters all represent the most traditional Argentina dining experience; the menu is completely focused on grilled meats.

Harper's Recoleta ((11) 4801-7155, Calle Junín 1763, has a long-standing reputation for fine dining. The intimate dining room has exposed brick walls, and the outdoor café is separated from its neighbors by a bougainvillea-covered arbor. King crab au gratin with caviar, chateaubriand, and sole with cabernet sauce are all standout dishes; the profiteroles and chocolate chip mousse are well worth the calories.

Restaurante Munich Recoleta ((11) 4804-4469, Calle Ortíz 1871, is another standout. Despite the German name, the cuisine is traditional Argentine, with an emphasis on meats. The steak is unusually tender and tasty, and the creamed spinach is deservedly famous. Some diners rave about the *sesos en salsa verde* (brains in green sauce) and the chicken Kiev. Deer and boar heads are mounted on the walls, and the leather and wood decor gives the place a hunting lodge ambience. One drawback — credit cards are not accepted.

While other Puerto Madero restaurants cater to a wealthy clientele, **La Caballeriza** ((11) 4514-4444, Avenida Alicia Moreau de Justo 580, is boldly geared toward the masses. The enormous dining room is often packed with families, tourists, and couples out for a reasonably priced feast. This is a good place to dine with a group, as the menu offers several dishes worth tasting. For a starter try the *tablita de achuras* (assorted entrails), and share a selection of entrées including *pamplona de pollo* (a thin chicken breast rolled around a stuffing of olives, bacon, peppers, and cheese), *matambrito de cerdo* (pork brisket), and juicy *asado de costilla* (beef ribs grilled on a spit). This is one of few steak houses serving baked potatoes with sour cream; they also have baked sweet potatoes. The menu has English translations. A service charge is included in the check.

In San Telmo, **La Casa de Esteban de Luca** ((11) 4361-4338, Calle Defensa 1000, is both a historic site and a restaurant. The building was the home of Estaban de Luca, composer of Argentina's national anthem. The peaceful restaurant that now occupies several rooms serves Argentine and Italian dishes, including *lomo* (steak) in red wine sauce and spinach-stuffed ravioli. Another historic home has been transformed into the **Restaurant Antigua Tasca** ((11) 4832-1155, Avenida Carlos Calvo 319. A plaque at the front of the eighteenth-century home tells the story of a sad romance that ended with a father killing his own daughter. Fortunately, the mood of the gracious restaurant is more upbeat. An outdoor patio and several small rooms are pleasant on Sunday afternoons; the menu features steaks and seafood.

MODERATE

Restaurants around the Plaza de Mayo and the Plaza San Martín are packed during the weekday lunch period, when office workers devour enormous meals and bottles of wine before returning to work. Some are more popular at night, as is the case with **Filo** ((11) 4311-0312, Calle San Martín 975. The wild decor and blaring rock music attract a young, hip crowd who devour gourmet pizzas baked in a red and green striped wood-burning oven. The salads are huge and fresh. The unusual linguini with sweetbreads and clams sounds odd but actually tastes good. Pizza lovers take note — the pepperoni pizza is loaded with roasted peppers, not the meat Americans expect. Similar in attitude and cuisine, **Memorabilia** ((11) 4322-7630, Calle Maipú 761, emphasizes its Italian theme with green and white checked tablecloths and photos of Sophia Loren. The menu features pizzas, pastas, and salads. **Broccolino** ((11) 4322-7652, Calle Esmeralda 776, is more refined, sedate, and traditional and serves satisfying pastas.

Gran Victoria Café and Restaurant ((11) 4342-3725, Hipólito Yrigoyen 500, is conveniently located across the street from the Plaza de Mayo. The busy, trendy restaurant is a popular lunch spot and serves reasonably priced executive menus (three-course meals with beverage) along with salads, sandwiches, pastas, and steaks. It's a popular after-work spot as well, and a good place to grab a window-side table and watch the busy street scene. The same can be said for **Scuzi** ((11) 4322-9543, Avenida Córdoba 800. The enormous bright and cheery restaurant is packed at midday, thanks to the all-inclusive menu featuring something for every taste. There are several great salads, a good Thai chicken curry, steaks, thick sandwiches, and several vegetarian dishes including vegetable lasagna and a soy-based imitation of *pollo milanesa*

work crowd sipping imported wines and beers and sampling tapas. You can order half portions of the oily octopus salads, olives, mushrooms, and red peppers or, if you're with a group, get the Great Plank of the Tasca — an array of tapas to satisfy four people. Entrées include grilled albacore tuna, pink salmon, tortilla, and several inexpensive rice dishes filled with vegetables and shellfish. Travelers dining alone needn't feel lonely if they sit at the bar; the bartenders and customers are quite chatty. Another plus — you don't have to wait until the magic dining hour to have a satisfying meal.

One doesn't expect to find an imaginative menu in an Argentine Irish pub. As a result, **John John** ((11) 4313-1428, Calle Reconquista 924, is a

with a soy patty breaded and fried. The menu is translated into French and English, but tourists are a small part of the clientele. Instead, this is a see-and-be-seen hangout for trendy *porteños*, who also pack the place for late afternoon coffee and excellent desserts.

Sushi is all the rage these days, but it's often prohibitively expensive. The prices are fairly reasonable at **Sensu** ((11) 4393-9595, Calle Florida 528. In addition to California rolls, niguiri sushi, and sashimi, the chefs whip up salmon, beef, shrimp, and chicken combos with fresh vegetables and white rice. There's a branch of Sensu in the food court at the Galerías Pacífico shopping center.

Dark red walls and balsa wood lamps cast a sleek air over **Tancat Tasca** ((11) 4312-6106, Calle Paraguay 645, a tiny tapas bar with a grand menu. A curving bar runs the length of the narrow restaurant; by mid-evening it's filled with the after-

pleasant surprise. The bar menu includes a great grilled chicken and guacamole sandwich, toast with smoked salmon, warm brie and capers, and fried squid. Full dinners are served in a small upstairs dining room or in the comfortable bar and include pork chops marinated in Guinness, crab cakes, salmon tartare, and a Bailey's Irish ice cream parfait. The menu is so delightfully unique you'll be tempted to dine here frequently. Those wishing to sample a typical *parrilla* without spending a fortune should check out **La Estancia** ((11) 4326-0330, Avenida Lavalle 941.

The newest hot nightspot is Cañitas, a Belgrano neighborhood. The area is beyond trendy, and businesses compete with wildly eclectic decor emphasizing bright colors and a modernistic industrial style. Unfortunately, the menus are less

Argentina's most famous writers haunt the Gran Café Tortoni.

adventurous, and the *parrilla* restaurants are the consistent favorites. Restaurants come and go here, but you're sure to find unusual German, French, and even Irish eateries.

La Fonda del Polo ((11) 4772-8946, Calle Báez 301, stands out among the beef houses, and families fill the outdoor tables before the trendy young crowd arrives. The platters of sweetbreads, steaks, and sausages are reasonably priced. At **Club Zen Wok and Roll** ((11) 4772-8866, Calle Hüergo 366, the "Asian Fusion" menu offers surprisingly successful dishes. The spring rolls stuffed with beef, gazpacho with oysters, and salmon with sautéed vegetables are all quite pleasing — the sushi and sashimi, however, don't live up to their extraordinary prices. **Indochine** ((11) 4772-4159, Calle Báez 165, is equally exciting — try the sweet potato won tons and prawn curry. **Santino** ((11) 4779-9060, Calle Báez 194, is the best Italian trattoria with a great list of imported wines and a peaceful back patio.

The hip set also congregates in Palermo, where fans of Mexican food find perfect margaritas and *carne asada* (marinated beef) at **Cielito Lindo** ((11) 4832-8054, Calle El Salvador 4999.

One of Buenos Aires's most popular dining areas sits between the Recoleta Cultural Center and the Buenos Aires Design Center. The **Café Rix** ((11) 4806-1111, Avenida Pueyrredón 2501, stands out for its enthusiastic wait staff and outstanding chefs. The outdoor café is packed for Sunday lunch, with families and couples feasting on enormous salads, sandwiches and omelets. The spinach and ricotta crepes are superb, as is the huge fruit salad topped with ice cream.

The aptly named **Museo del Jamón Restaurant** ((11) 4382-4144, Avenida Cerrito 8, has a different take on the all-pervasive meat theme. Hunks of ham hang incongruously in the decorous dining room, and the appetizer list is filled with selections of imported hams. The menu features tapas and traditional Argentine dishes, including the substantial *gran bife del museo* with steak, peas, string beans, asparagus, and stuffed potatoes.

A few shaded outdoor tables allow diners to watch the action in the Plaza de Congreso from the **Plaza del Carmen** ((11) 4573-2733 at Avenida Rivadavia 1795 on the corner of Callao. The interior dining room is just a bit less noisy than the sidewalk café, so one might as well sample everything from beef brochettes to cheese crepes while watching pedestrians pass by. The restaurant offers an unusual and refreshing twist on the endless list of sweets, the *espuma de limón*, a sort of ice cream soda made with lime sorbet and champagne. The waiters are especially accommodating here, and the newsstand next door carries the *Buenos Aires Herald*. Thick slices of pizzas and fat *empanadas* are available for takeout or are served in the noisy, bright restaurant at **La Americana** ((11) 4371-0202

at Avenida Callao 83. Those unfamiliar with local menus will be delighted by the window display, where pastries such as the mysterious *sopa inglesa* (actually a moist cake rather than a soup) are labeled and temptingly displayed.

INEXPENSIVE

It takes some creativity to dine inexpensively in Buenos Aires. Fortunately, most hotels include Continental breakfast in the room rate — don't miss it. You can pick up a quick lunch of *empanadas*, pizzas, or *panchos* (hotdogs) all over the city. Many markets post signs advertising *empanadas* and one *lata* (can of soda) for US$2 or so. The food court in the basement level of the Galerías Pacífico Shopping Center is packed with takeout stands offering everything from chow mien to tabbouleh — most have lunch specials.

A wooden awning shades the sidewalk tables at **Puerto del Carmen** ((11) 4322-1054, Avenue Córdoba 628 near Calle Florida. Ficus trees block the view of the traffic, making this one of the most pleasant outdoor cafés in the city. Waiters present a tray of cheese and ham cubes and a platter of nuts and chips as you order your meal; with those filling starters you can have a satisfying dinner of pizza or any of the large salads. The complete *milanesa ternera* (breaded pork) dinner for two includes french fries and vegetables and costs what most restaurants charge for one serving. The waiters are kind, and most speak some English.

You can dine fairly inexpensively at **El Palacio de la Papa Frita** ((11) 4393-5849, Calle Lavalle 735, if you stick with the daily specials. A full meal of *pollo milanesa* (breaded and fried chicken) with puffy fried potato slices and a fried egg costs less than US$6, as does rice sautéed with squid and mushrooms. As the name suggests, potatoes are featured in many guises, mashed, baked, soufléd, and fried.

Everywhere you go in Buenos Aires you see people eating pizza, often while walking down the street. One of the oldest pizza parlors in the city is **Pizzeria Güerrin** ((11) 4371-8141, Avenida Corrientes 1368. Customers line up at the counter for a slice of pizza with a variety of toppings, then straddle a stool at the counter or head back out the door, lunch in hand. There are tables in back as well. The pizza is great, with a thick crust and plenty of melted cheese. **Pizzeria Mi Tío** ((11) 4362-1244, Calle Estado Unidos 900 in San Telmo, is another traditional pizza parlor with a few tables by an open window overlooking the street. Most Italian restaurants serve inexpensive plates of gnocchi, which are so popular with *porteños* that some families traditionally eat these potato dumplings on the last Thursday of the month, when money is tight. Also in San Telmo, **Mitos** ((11) 4362-7810, Calle Humberto 1, offer special lunch tango shows on weekends, with the dancing accompanied by inexpensive *parrillas*.

Budget travelers should be on the lookout for signs offering *Tenedor Libre*, which translates into free fork and means the restaurant serves a low-cost buffet. **Nuevo Restaurante Dragon del Cielo** ℂ (11) 4053-3526, Calle Defensa 1156, is a good example, with a seemingly endless lineup of salads, pizza, pastas, chop suey, chow mein, fried rice, chicken and beef dishes, and desserts. They also have inexpensive set menus, including drinks.

Shun the ubiquitous McDonald's on Calle Florida in favor of **Bonpler** ℂ (11) 4325-9900, Calle Florida 481. The fast food has a French flair — croissant sandwiches, chilled soups — and the

are hard to come by in this fancy neighborhood. There's only a counter here, but you can take your *empanadas* and have a picnic at the park.

A *parrilla* for four at **La Vieja Rotisería** ℂ (11) 4832-9835, in San Telmo, costs less than steak for one at Puerto Madero's restaurants. On weekend afternoons the restaurant is packed to the rafters with families feasting on platters of grilled meats and heaping bowls of salad and french fries. You may have to wait for a table, but be patient. The meal, especially when combined with a bottle of San Telmo Merlot and the genial chatter of the crowd, may well be a highlight of your trip. Neighbors and artists stop by for a beer and burger at **Hipopótamus** ℂ (11) 4300-8450, Calle Defensa 1493,

dining area is cool and quiet. **Yin-Yang** ℂ (11) 4311-7798, Calle Paraguay 858, delights vegetarians with platters of steamed rice and veggies and tofu-based entrées. A natural food store fronts **La Esquina de las Flores** ℂ (11) 4813-3630, Avenida Córdoba 1587. Stairs at the back of the bright yellow shop lead up to one of the city's best natural foods restaurants. Along with a wide variety of soups, salads, and pastas, the cooks prepare tall *tartas* (quiche-like cakes) filled with cheese and veggies, baked eggplant, soy burgers, and regional stews including *locro* and *guiso*. The setting is simple — a counter with a few stools — but the food is quite tasty at **La Querencia** ℂ (11) 4393-3205, Calle Esmeralda 1392. *Tamales*, *empanadas*, stews and simple beef and chicken plates taste like those you find in the countryside.

The fare is similar at **El Sanjuanino** ℂ (11) 4804-2909, Calle Posadas 1515 in Recoleta. Cheap meals

across the street from Parque Lezama. The cool, dark is a great place to escape the Sunday afternoon market crowds. Liverwurst and sardine sandwiches are available along with the decent burger, and the bar stocks several imported beers. Food and drink prices rise after 8 PM.

CAFÉS AND *CONFITERÍAS*

Porteños love their coffee and sweets, and have turned the coffee break into an art form. The city is loaded with famous cafés where stylish women and men in business suits pass many hours chatting over tiny cups of espresso-strength coffee, with or without hot milk. The coffee is usually accompanied by a small glass of water, a glass of orange drink, and a few small cookies or candies.

Large cafés provide private billiard rooms for the after-work crowd.

The practiced *porteño* can linger over this diminutive snack for hours, perhaps ordering a glass of champagne or a pastry along the way. Cafés and *confiterías* play an important part in the workday. Their waiters can be seen bearing trays of coffee cups down the sidewalk at all hours, delivering a jolt of caffeine to weary office workers.

Confiterías fill up from 4 PM to 6 PM. Tourists who despair of waiting until 9 PM for dinner can safely order small sandwiches or plates of cheeses and cold meats to tide them over.

The most famous such hangout in Buenos Aires in **Gran Café Tortoni** ((11) 4342-4328, Avenida de Mayo 829. The café opened in 1858 and remains quite grand, with gilded mirrors, polished wood bars, marble tables, stained glass ceiling and black suited waiters, some of whom seem to have been among the original staff. Pictures of nearly every famous Argentine artist, musician or writer adorn the walls — Jorge Luis Borges and Carlos Gardel are both said to have been regulars. Wander about the many rooms, including the handsome pool hall and grand salons, where tango performances and concerts are held on weekends. The food is surprisingly inexpensive, but the service is agonizingly slow.

Confitería Ideal ((11) 4326-0521, Calle Suipacha 384, is a faded rendition of Tortoni. The decor is equally grandiose but almost ghostly in its state of disrepair. But there's a whole other world in the upstairs ballroom, where tango lessons are held on weekday afternoons. Argentine, European, American, and Japanese locals and tourists practice their steps under the watchful guidance of professional dancers and a sprinkling of elderly *porteño* men eager to guide young women through the seductive dance. Ceiling fans whir madly as music blares over the speakers and dancers dip under the crystal ball — a surreal scene in all. The pros show up late on weekend nights.

More sedate and genteel, the **Café Richmond** ((11) 4322-1341, Calle Florida 468, is a study in wood and brass. Chess players linger over their boards on the lower level, while society matrons stack their purchases on several chairs by their tables. Save this one for a time when your sweet tooth is at its most demanding, then order a slice of the *torta Richmond*, an outrageous chocolate cake layered with cherries and chantilly cream. Neighborhood cafés are good refuges for those staying in hotels with expensive or nonexistent restaurants; if you just want a quick snack without all the restaurant fuss, find a café you like and get to know the waiters. I've grown fond of the patient *mosos* (waiters) at **Confitería St. Moritz** ((11) 4311-7311, Calle Paraguay 802, who seem amused by tourists' odd appetites. Sandwiches, pastries, and fruit salads are all inexpensive and can be ordered anytime of day. A young crowd frequents **Café Pernambuco** ((11) 4383-4666, Avenida

Corrientes 1686. Cocktails, wine, and beer are more popular than coffee, though those seeking nonalcoholic drinks are happy with the *licuados* made with fresh fruit and water or milk. Best of all, you can have your beer and surf the net simultaneously at the computers in the back of the room.

Reading is an important part of café life. At **Clásica y Moderna** ((11) 4812-8707, Avenida Callao 892, the two are combined in a bookstore and café long known as one of the leading gathering points for the literati.

La Recoleta's idle rich while away the hours in green plastic chairs at **La Biela** ((11) 4804-0449, Calle Quintana 596, under the shade of an enormous rubber tree. The cemetery is right across the street, and the finest boutiques nearby. Everything on the menu costs more if you sit outside, and the prices are outrageous. Order an agua mineral or a soda and take your time watching the crowd.

NIGHTLIFE

Tango shows are at the heart of Buenos Aires's nightlife; tourists and locals alike fill dance halls on weekend nights. The cover charge for the most popular shows runs between US$30 and US$60 and sometimes includes a drink or two. Many of the tango halls are located in San Telmo, said to be the birthplace of the dance. **Casa Blanca** ((11) 4331-4621, Calle Balcarce 668, holds several highly professional shows nightly; its program has photos of important politicians and celebrities who have attend shows here. The performances include folk dances from the northern provinces. **El Viejo Almacén** ((11) 4307-6689, Calle Balcarce at Avenida Independencia, puts on a very traditional tango show for typically upscale audiences; dinner is served in the restaurant next to the theater.

Tango is just part of the show at **Michelangelo** ((11) 4328-2646, Calle Balcarce 433, a trendy nightspot in a converted warehouse. Modern dance, folkloric dance, singing and magic are all part of the act; some say it has a Las Vegas flair. Puerto Madero also has a tango hall at **Tangoteca** ((11) 4311-1988, Calle Alicia Moreau de Justo 1728. Some of these clubs have special shows for tour groups at 9 PM or 10 PM, then open to the public for late-night performances.

Thanks to tango's ever-increasing popularity, you needn't spend a fortune at a formal club in order to watch the dance. **Café Tortoni** (see CAFÉS AND *CONFITERÍAS*, above) holds tango shows most nights in La Bodega, its main dance hall. The café also hosts jazz and classical music performances, and publishes a monthly pamphlet called *Buenos Aires Cultural* listing upcoming events. You can stop by here any night of the week and find something exciting on stage. Some of the professional dancers end their nights at **Confitería Ideal** (see CAFÉS AND *CONFITERÍAS*, above) dancing with the amateurs in the upstairs ballroom. **El Chino** ((11) 4807-7624, Calle Beazley 3565, is located in a converted warehouse and offers tango performances and open dancing on Friday and Saturday nights.

Tango isn't the only popular dance in Buenos Aires. Fancy discos are also part of the frenetic nightlife scene. Most places don't open until 10:30 PM or 11 PM and close around 5 AM; customers are expected to dress stylishly — no jeans or T-shirts. **Sodoma** ((11) 4807-7622, Calle Vicente López 2233 in Recoleta, is one of the more elegant dance clubs, as is **Buenos Aires News** ((11) 4778-1500, Avenida Infanta Isabel in Palermo. **El Living** ((11) 4811-4730, Avenida Marcelo T. Alvear, is also in Palermo, home to an ever-changing array

HOW TO GET THERE

Ezeiza International Airport ((11) 4480-6111 is located about 34 km (21 miles) south of downtown Buenos Aires. More than two dozen international carriers serve the airport with daily flights from Europe and North America as well as large South American cities including Lima, Bogota, São Paulo, La Paz, and Santiago. Regional flights from other parts of the country arrive at the **Aeroparque Jorge Newberry** ((11) 4514-1515 in the Costanera Norte, just 10 minutes from downtown. Both airports are served by **Manuel Tienda León** ((11) 4314-3636 TOLL-FREE (800) 777-0078, Avenida Santa Fe 790, a

of clubs and bars. Purple and blue lights illuminate the sail-like roof (a miniature replica of the Sydney Opera House) at **El Divino** ((11) 4315-2791, Calle Cecilia Grierson 225 at Puerto Madero. **La Morocha** ((11) 4778-0050, Avenida Dorrego 3307, is extremely popular. Act like a tourist and arrive early; otherwise you might never get in.

A half-dozen pubs attract shoulder-to-shoulder crowds hoisting pints of Guinness and Harp. The **Kilkenny** ((11) 4312-7291, Avenida Alvear 399, is possibly the most popular. An Englishman rules over **Sedón** ((11) 4361-0141, Avenida de Mayo and Avenida Córdoba, where you can often partake in a tango lesson with your beer. **La Cigale** ((11) 4813-8275, Avenida de Mayo 722, hosts a wide range of musical groups on weekend nights. **The Spot** ((11) 4811-8955, Calle Ayacucho 1261, has live jazz and special drink nights — martinis are the latest rage.

transfer service that provides bus and private car transportation to and from downtown. Transport from Ezeiza costs US$14 one way; from Aeroparque it's US$5. Taxis are also available, though the ride from Ezeiza costs about US$40. From the Aeroparque a taxi ride to most hotels should cost less than US$10.

International and regional buses arrive at the **Estación Terminal de Ómnibus** ((11) 4310-0700, Avenida Ramos Mejía 1680. Hydrofoils and ferry boats travel across the Río de la Plata between Buenos Aires and Uruguay several times daily. **Buquebus** ((11) 4317-1001 is a popular carrier with daily trips to Montevideo and Colonia. Ferries depart from Dársena Norte (the North Dock) at Avenida Moreau de Justo and Avenida Tres Argentinos.

Calle Lavalle is the Buenos Aires version of Piccadilly or Times Square.

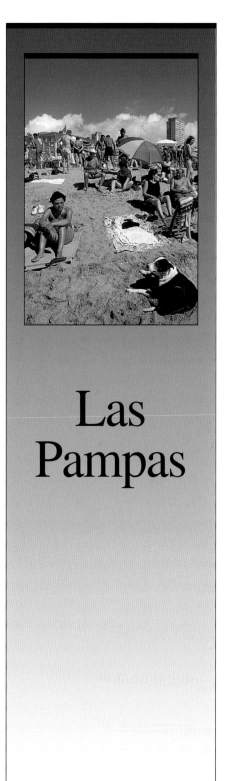

Las Pampas

GRASSY FLATLANDS BLEND INTO WAVES OF HEAT AND LIGHT UNDER THE BLUE HORIZON in the seemingly endless region of Las Pampas. Named for the Pampas Indians who once roamed this vast land, the Pampas extends from the Andes to the Atlantic Ocean between the Highlands and Patagonia. Its boundaries are as hazy as its landscape, as the grasslands range through the provinces of Buenos Aires, La Pampa, San Luis, Córdoba, and Entre Ríos. The eastern sector is the most heavily populated, with major settlements around the cities of Buenos Aires, San Luis, and Córdoba.

The Pampas flows eastward to the coastal cities, railroads, and ports of Mar del Plata and Bahía Blanca. It is Argentina's breadbasket and one of

its most valuable natural resources. Its fertile fields produce soybeans (Argentina is one of the world's largest soybean and soy oil exporters), corn, wheat, and miles of sunflowers, valued for their beauty and their oil. Cattle, an integral part of the country's history and economy, range over enormous *estancias* (ranches) established in the nineteenth century. Though many of the largest *estancias* have been divided and subdivided over the years and towns and cities have grown up along rail lines and highways, the western part of the region still feels wild, open and free.

Some visitors find the pampas disappointing at first glance. Visions of endless fields of golden pampas grass (*cortadera*) waving in the breeze are rarely a reality, except in swamp areas along the rivers and coast. I have seen gauchos galloping atop *caballos* on the range; I've also seen them cantering along paved highways.

In reality, the Pampas is somewhat like a never-ending Kansas. No one city can claim dominance over the region, though a few are essential to the Pampas experience. San Antonio de Areco is Argentina's most important gaucho center, home to several fine *estancias* and a gaucho museum. Luján is home to the nation's most important church, La Basílica Nuestra Señora de Luján. Coastal Pampas is one enormous playground for Argentines and their guests.

Between these cultural and natural hubs lies the soul of the Pampas, visible from highways and country roads. The monotonous terrain is broken by vivid surprises and scenes. Clusters of cattle grazing under a canopy of *sombra de toro* trees. Women and children selling homemade cheese at rustic roadside stands. Horses racing in whirls of dust; gauchos whipping their bolas in the wind. Narrow pine forests beside sand dunes. It takes time, money, and a tolerance for boredom to explore the Pampas, but the experience *vale la pena* (is worth the effort).

SAN ANTONIO DE ARECO

Nearly everyone who ventures to Argentina for the first time expects to find gauchos riding across the open plains, roping cattle and wielding bolas as if the nineteenth century had never ended. And naturally they're disappointed. Cattle ranching is still big business, but these days the "dogies" are rounded up by helicopters and herded to market in the back of 16-wheeler trucks.

One place where the bygone gaucho culture persists is a small Pampas town called San Antonio de Areco, about two hours west of Buenos Aires. This is largely due to the fact that Ricardo Güiraldes — the beloved bard of gaucho culture — lived and wrote at Estancia La Porteña, on the outskirts of San Antonio. Born in Buenos Aires in 1886 the son of a wealthy land owner, the dashingly handsome Güiraldes lived life in a grand manner. Despite his wealth, he bore an amazing affinity for common working folk like gauchos and fishermen. His bestselling *Don Segundo Sombra*, published a year before his death in 1926, enshrined gaucho society in the same manner that novels by American scribes Zane Grey and Louis L'Amour romanticized life in the Wild West. Güiraldes was only 42 when he died in Paris in 1927 under somewhat mysterious circumstances — nobody is sure of the exact cause of death, a fact that no doubt adds to his enduring popularity. But his ghost seems to haunt much of San Antonio and the local citizens go to great lengths to keep his memory — and the cowboy customs he wrote about — alive through museum displays, historic buildings and special events.

The town's biggest bash is the annual **Día de la Tradición** in early November, a festival that draws genuine cowpokes and gaucho aficionados from around the world. More than 10,000 visitors pour into the tiny town to watch equestrian events such as polo and cattle roping, as well as concerts, dances and parades.

The area was wilderness until the seventeenth century, when Roman Catholic missionaries built a chapel dedicated to Saint Anthony near the banks of the Río Areco. The church was later destroyed by Indians and the area abandoned by Europeans until 1730, when rancher José Ruiz de Arellano established an *estancia* on the site. He picked the spot largely at the behest of his wife — a devotee of Saint Anthony — who promised to build a new chapel if their ranch was spared the fate of the old mission. The ranch survived, the *señora* built her chapel and the *estancia* evolved into the gaucho town of San Antonio de Areco.

GENERAL INFORMATION

San Antonio's **Dirección Municipal de Turismo** ((2326) 53165 or (2326) 53105 WEB SITE www.arecoturismo.com.ar is situated in the riverside park near the junction of Zerboni and Arellano. They are extremely helpful and can arrange walking tours of the city. Open weekdays 7 AM to 2 PM and weekends 10 AM to 5 PM.

If you need to change money, there are several **banks** along Calle Alsina south of the main plaza. Correo Argentino is at the corner of Alvear and Del Valle near Plaza Belgrano.

For medical emergencies try **Hospital Emilio Zerboni** ((2326) 52391 or (2326) 52345 at the corner of Lavalle and Moreno. The town's only pharmacy is **Kiosco** ((2326) 54276, Arellano 185.

OPPOSITE: The gaucho culture survives in parts of the Pampas. ABOVE: Sunflower oil is one of Argentina's main exports.

WHAT TO SEE AND DO

San Antonio's downtown area is compact and easy to explore on foot with a map from the tourist office. A good place to start is the **Plaza Ruiz de Arellano** (also called the Plaza Mayor) with its various historic buildings. The two-story **Casa de los Martínez** occupies the site of the original *estancia* homestead while the nearby **Iglesia San Antonio** is the progeny of Señora Arellano's chapel. The church is staffed by amiable Irish priests who tend a flock that includes immigrant Irish, Slavic and Italian Catholics as well as old-time Spanish families. Like many Argentine churches, San Antonio is rather plain except for the hundreds of light bulbs that illuminate the main altar.

Dominating the plaza's opposite side is the Intendencia (town hall). A block farther north is the **Museo Usina Vieja** (Old Power Plant Museum) at Calle Alsina 66, a permanent exhibit of local art and handicrafts including exquisite silver, leather and wood work. Open weekdays 8 AM to 1 PM and weekends 10 AM to 5 PM.

For a slice of authentic gaucho culture duck into the **Despensa Bar Bessonart** at Calle Segundo Sombra 151. Divided in half by a long wooden bar, the establishment doubles as a saloon and general store that sells fresh fruit, homemade bread and canned goods. The real-life Don Segundo Ramirez, the hero of Güiraldes' novel, used to come here once a week to have a drink and buy his provisions. Gauchos, most of them way beyond retirement age, gather at Bessonart each evening to down shots and chat about the good old days. Many of them don traditional Argentine cowboy wear including berets, big silver belt buckles, leather boots and silver-handled daggers. One regular patron is Juan Güiraldes, the author's grand nephew and the current owner of Estancia La Porteña.

You can cross the Río Areco on the new **Puente Tapia** or the historic **Puente Viejo** (Old Bridge) built in 1857. The bridge empties onto a dirt road called Calle Ricardo Güiraldes, which was part of the original ox cart road from Buenos Aires. Pleasant parks with shade trees and picnic areas line both sides of the river.

Dead ahead after crossing the old bridge is the San Antonio's top attraction, the **Museo Gauchesco Ricardo Güiraldes** ((2326) 52583 in Parque Criollo. This shrine to gaucho culture features numerous galleries in a reproduction *estancia* house called the Casa del Museo, plus historic buildings moved from elsewhere in Argentina. The museum entrance hall is decorated with iron cattle brands including the famous "La Guardana" — the first brand registered in Argentina (1822). Another gallery is dedicated to gaucho silverwork including daggers, belt buckles, whip handles

and *maté* mugs. Two rooms are filled with Güiraldes mementos including his favorite guitar and a plaster cast of the author's hand made in Paris after his death. Paintings of rural life by early twentieth-century Argentine artist Pedro Figari decorate many of the walls. Next door to the museum is the **Pulpería la Blanqueada**, an original nineteenth-century tavern filled with typical furniture and decorations from the early gaucho days. Scattered around the **Parque Criollo** are other historic buildings including a small chapel, an old flour mill and a carriage barn. The museum is open daily (except Tuesday) 11 AM to 5 PM.

For those who want to delve into local history even farther, the **Municipal Cemetery** near the southern edge of San Antonio contains the grave of both Ricardo Güiraldes and Don Segundo Ramirez.

On the western edge of town is **Estancia La Cinacina** ((2326) 52773, Bartolomé Mitre 9, which caters to day visitors more than other ranches in the area with horseback riding, folklore performances and barbecues. It can seem artificial at times, but for most folks this is the easiest way to get a quick introduction to gaucho culture. Anyone who wants a short horseback ride in the countryside around San Antonio can contact local stables like **La Aurora** ((2326) 55147, Alvear 345, and **El Fortín** ((2326) 55963 in the Costanera Norte park.

SHOPPING

No other Argentine city can eclipse the traditional silver and leather handicrafts produced by the skilled artisans of San Antonio. Their workshops and showrooms cluster along the narrow streets on all sides of the main plaza. Among the items made locally are silver belt buckles, traditional gaucho daggers, *maté* mugs and spoons, and equestrian gear.

One of the country's most renowned silversmiths is **Raul Horacio Draghi** ((2326) 55499 or (2326) 54207, Calle Guido 391. Other amazing artists include **Raul Marchi** ((2326) 54345 at Calle San Martín 83, and the **Rigacci Brothers** ((2326) 54016 at Calle Quetgles 333. All of these men will create custom-made jewelry and other silver pieces to your specifications. Near the Parque Criollo on the other side of the river is **Fabiana Devereux Plateros** ((2326) 55395 on Calle de los Horneros.

A great place for gaucho gear is **Casa Dimattia** at Calle Alsina 252, which sells a wide range of ponchos, hats, boots and equestrian accoutrements. Also consider the leatherwork at nearby **El Moro** at Calle Alsina 322, which also sells silverwork.

Pampas weavings and tapestries are the specialty at **Christina Giordano de Bincaz** ((2326) 52829, Calle Sarmiento 112. For antiques try **Cosas de Ayer** at Calle Zapiola 143. **Toque Sutil** at Calle

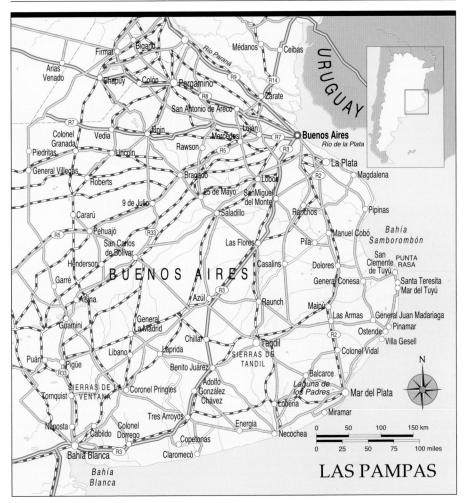

LAS PAMPAS

Arellano 230 is an art gallery devoted to modern Argentine paintings.

Anyone with a sweet tooth should pop into **La Olla de Cobre** ((2326) 53105, Calle Speroni 433, a combination chocolate factory and chocoholic boutique.

WHERE TO STAY

San Antonio has a rather limited supply of accommodation, with half a dozen places in the same general prize range (low moderate to high inexpensive). My personal pick in San Antonio is **Hotel Los Abuelos** ((2326) 68-758367, which occupies a strategic position at the corner of Zapiola and Zerboni. Rooms feature private baths, cable television and telephone, as well as parking right outside. The staff is friendly and there's a pleasant riverside park right across the street. Directly across Calle Zapiola is another good bet, **Hotel San Carlos** ((2326) 53106, which offers modest rooms and a small tea salon. Up the road is the popular and often fully booked **Hostal de Areco** ((2326) 54063, Zapiola 25. Despite its reputation as a favorite with foreign visitors, I find the staff rather snooty and withdrawn.

Almacén de Ramos Generales ((2326) 56376, Bolívar 66, is rightly famous for its restaurant, but the rooms are nothing to sneeze at although this is one of the few places in urban San Antonio that offers something akin to a "gaucho" atmosphere. One of the few places to stay in the heart of town is **Residencial El Hornero** ((2326) 52733, at the corner of Moreno and San Martín.

Prices are a bit lower than other local abodes, but you still get private baths with hot water and parking for your car. **La Posada de Ceibo** ((2326) 54614, on Calle Irigoyen between Ruta 8 and Avenida Smith, has rooms with private baths, hot water and cable television, as well as a garden with barbecues, bicycles and playground equipment. Anyone who craves peace and quiet should check out **Posada Los Paraisos** (2326) 53541 FAX (2326) 55995 on Camino del Quinton, about 10 km (six miles) north of town in the countryside near Estancia El Encuentro. Rooms are equipped with double beds, private bathrooms and kitchen area.

Places where you can pitch a tent in San Antonio include a **municipal campground** at the intersection of Zerboni and Bolívar (near the river) and **Auto Camping La Porteña** (2326) 53402, eight kilometers (five miles) from town on the Güiraldes *estancia*. The latter is situated in a thick grove of trees on the banks of the Río Areco. Facilities include shower blocks with around-the-clock hot water, soccer and volleyball, fishing, barbecues and picnic tables, as well as a small store.

Estancias

A number of cattle ranches in the San Antonio region welcome visitors for overnight stays. But expect to pay top dollar: an average of US$150 to US$200 per night per person. The most extravagant is **Estancia La Porteña** (2326) 52583 FAX (2326) 52101 about 20 minutes by car or taxi from the main plaza. Built in the middle of the nineteenth century, this gorgeous property features whitewashed walls and red tile roofs draped in purple and pink bougainvillea, wrought-iron furniture beneath the cool verandas and big shade trees all around. It's often so quiet all you can hear are birds chirping. There's a swimming pool, a trophy room full of polo memorabilia, and stables where you can mount a horse for a tour of the sprawling *estancia* and a ride along the banks of the Río Areco. Upstairs in the main building is the Writer's Corner where Ricardo Güiraldes penned *Don Segundo* and other works. Another room dedicated to General Rosas, a very controversial figure in Argentine history because of his brutal conquest of the Patagonian Indians.

Another authentic property is **Estancia El Rosario de Areco** (2326) 56239, originally built in 1892 and still a working ranch where cattle and polo ponies are bred. Activities include horse-

back riding, sulky trips, tennis, cycling; there is a swimming pool and a polo school. Other ranches in the San Antonio area include **Estancia El Ombu** (2326) 92080 and **Estancia La Julia** (2326) 53401.

Reservations are required for overnight stays at all of the above *estancias*. Two of them — La Porteña and El Rosario — use a central booking office in Buenos Aires: Patricia Acuña (11) 4312-7104 FAX (11) 4312-3789 E-MAIL pacuna@ipsa.com.ar.

WHERE TO EAT

San Antonio's best restaurant is the charming **Almacén de Ramos Generales** (2326) 56376, Calle Bolívar 66. The decor is an updated version of a nineteenth-century Argentine general store and if the weather's nice you can also sit outside on the veranda. The menu is dominated by tasty homemade pasta, but there are also *parrilla* meat dishes and superb desserts. Reservations are highly recommended, even on weekday nights. Another good bet is **La Vieja Tortuga** (2326) 56080, Calle Alsina 60, which offers a wide variety of pizzas (35 different kinds) as well as traditional Argentine dishes like *empanadas* and *pollo al horno*. *Parrillada* is offered on Saturday and Sunday and there is live folk music on Friday and Saturday nights.

Diehard meat eaters should check out **Parrilla La Costa** (2326) 52481, at the corner of Belgrano and Zerboni, which also offers pasta dishes. **Dell'Olmo** (2326) 52506, Calle Alsina 365 is another local favorite both for its pizza and Italian-style ice cream. On the other side of the river is another tasty little place called **El Nueva Rosada** (2326) 68-758643, opposite the Parque Criollo. The heavily Argentine menu includes beef, pork and chicken specialties as well as salads and local desserts.

If you wake up in the middle of the night with a raging hunger or want to pick up a quick bite before you drive back to Buenos Aires, **Don Pancho** (2326) 56220 on Ruta 8 at the edge of town is open around the clock.

HOW TO GET THERE

San Antonio de Areco lies on the Pampas 113 km (70 miles) northwest of Buenos Aires via Ruta 8. There is almost hourly bus service from the huge Retiro terminal in Buenos Aires. San Antonio's funky little **Terminal de Ómnibus** (2326) 56387 or (2326) 55010 is located on Ruta 8 near the intersection of Calle General Paz. Another option is daily train service from Lacroze station in Buenos Aires. San Antonio's **Estación Ferrocarril Mitre** is on the western side of town, at the intersection of Güiraldes and Quetgles.

LUJÁN

Gauchos played a major role in creating Argentina's most important cathedral in the small town of Luján, 65 km (40 miles) from Buenos Aires. According to local lore, in 1630 an ox-drawn cart destined for a ranch in Sumampa in Santiago del Estero came to a halt beside the Río Luján. Despite all efforts by the gauchos accompanying the cargo, the cart would not budge. Even after all the cargo was emptied, nothing happened. Then someone suggested unloading just one box and leaving the rest on the cart. Suddenly, the oxen were able to pull the cart. The passengers opened the single box and found a statue of the Virgin Mary. The gauchos decided the Virgin wished to remain exactly at that spot, and the cargo's owner proceeded to clear the land and build a church.

The miracle of Luján has become Argentina's most treasured religious legend, and the town its most important religious center. Every Catholic in the country feels the need to visit Luján, and thousands of pilgrims make the journey each year. Pilgrimages were particularly important during the years of the Dirty War, when thousands of *porteños* frequently paraded from Buenos Aires to Luján's basilica to draw attention to the plight of the disappeared. These mass processions no longer occur, but Luján remains one of the most popular destination in the country.

GENERAL INFORMATION

Luján's **Tourist Information Office (** (2323) 434666 or (2323) 420453 WEB SITE www.lujanbsas.com.ar, Avenida 9 de Julio 938, operates an excellent information booth with maps and information on the basilica's history.

WHAT TO SEE AND DO

Two small churches occupied the sacred land until 1887, when the first cornerstone was laid for the **Basílica Nuestra Señora de Luján (** (2323) 435101, Avenida San Martín 1. Padre George M. Salvaire, the parish priest, was instrumental in the design, choosing an eighteenth-century French Gothic style with two bell towers rising 106 m (348 ft) into the sky. In 1930, 300 years after the statue arrived in Luján, the Virgin was named the patron saint of Argentina, Uruguay, and Paraguay and the church was declared a basilica. Construction was completed in 1930, and 15 bronze bells made in Milan rang in the towers. Today, the towers are visible from the highway into town, and the church looms over a block-long cement plaza lined with trees and vendors' carts. A carnival atmosphere prevails, as self-

appointed traffic cops wave cars into parking spots (they charge a fee for the spot) and photographers beckon families to pose in front of their church for instant Polaroid portraits. Music blares from loudspeakers. Hotdogs, sodas, *empanadas*, and bottled water are sold at stands around the plaza, as are balloons, dolls, and ice cream. Those selling religious medals, statues, and candles have the prime spots in front of the church. It's the only place in Argentina I've seen children begging for money, and they're not timid in their efforts.

The basilica itself is impressive, both for its architecture and for the intense devotion of those who believe in the Virgin's miraculous powers.

Life-sized statues of the 12 apostles are mounted above the three bronze doors at the front of the church, along with gargoyles representing the Devil running from God. Inside, plaques bearing the names and prayers and devotees are mounted all over the walls, demonstrating the gratitude of a legion of worshippers from all over South America. Other plaques bear the names of families who donated thousands and millions of pesos for the church's construction and maintenance. Several side chapels honor various saints; one of the largest is devoted to St. Patrick.

The statue of the Virgin found by the gauchos in 1630 sits in a chapel up a stairway behind the main altar. Made of clay in Brazil, the diminutive

OPPOSITE: Grilled sausages are part of a typical *asado*. ABOVE: Gauchos are among the country's most beloved characters.

figure stands just 43 cm (17 in) tall, and is painted blue and white, backed with gold rays like sunlight. Flags from all over the world hang around the chapel, and pilgrims pack the small area, leaving flowers and gifts. Thousands of pilgrims travel to Luján on May 8, the Virgin's feast day. Guided tours of the basilica are available, and mass is held seven times a day.

Beside the church, the eighteenth-century *cabildo* (city hall) and *casa del virey* (viceroy's house) have been combined for the **Complejo Museográfico Enrique Udaondo (** (2323) 42-0245, Avenida Lezica at Avenida Torrezuri. The complex includes a **Museo Histórico Colonial** with exhibits from colonial times to the twentieth century.

The adjacent **Museo del Transporte** contains antique wagons, carts, and stagecoaches and a plane that is said to have been the first to travel from Europe to South America. Two stuffed horses, Gato and Mancha, add a bit of comedy to the displays. The horses were part of an expedition from Argentina to Washington DC that took place in the 1920s. A **Museo Devocional de la Virgen** contains a collection of offerings brought by pilgrims. The museums are closed on Monday and Tuesday.

WHERE TO STAY AND EAT

Most visitors reach Luján on day trips from Buenos Aires, or stay at the *estancias* and hotels in San Antonio de Areco. There are several small, inexpensive hotels near the basilica if you wish to spend the night. Snacks and full meals are available at restaurants on the streets facing the plaza.

HOW TO GET THERE

The **Terminal de Ómnibus (** (2323) 420044, Avenida Nuestra Señora de Luján 600, receives buses from Buenos Aires hourly. Some tour companies in Buenos Aires offer day tours to Luján. Drivers can reach Luján via Ruta 7 from Buenos Aires.

LA PLATA

Capital of the province of Buenos Aires, La Plata is a political and industrial town with few tourist attractions. Most travelers visit the city on day trips from Buenos Aires, taking in the major attractions in a few hours.

GENERAL INFORMATION

The **Tourist Information Office (** (221) 482-9656, Calle 6 at Calle 50, has a few brochures and maps. The staff seems a bit befuddled by foreign tourists, however, and information is sketchy at best.

WHAT TO SEE AND DO

Plaza Moreno, bordered by calles 14 and 12 and avenidas 50 and 54, is the main plaza. In the park, the **Piedra Fundacional** (Foundation Stone) marks the geographical center of the city. It was laid in 1882 under the direction of Governor Dardo Rocha, when politicians in Buenos Aires decided to create a new capital for the province rather than having Buenos Aires be both the national and provincial capital. As was common in burgeoning cities, construction began almost immediately on the **Catedral**, Calle 14 at Avenida 51. The first stone for the neo-Gothic cathedral was laid in 1885, but it wasn't until 1999 that the towers were completed. The church is one of the country's most impressive, and was modeled after cathedrals in France.

The **Museo de La Plata (** (221) 483-9125, Paseo del Bosque 1900, also called **Museo de Ciencias Naturales** (Natural Science Museum), is one of the most important museums in the country. It houses archeological and anthropological collections covering the history of South America. The exhibits could be more imaginatively displayed and are labeled only in Spanish.

Eva Perón left her mark on La Plata by supervising the design and construction of **La República de los Niños (** (221) 484-0194, Camino General Belgrano Km. 7 north of downtown. This odd miniature city contains replicas of Argentina's most important historical buildings, along with scenes from fairy tales. A miniature train carries children past the buildings. Kids accustomed to more sophisticated theme parks might find this one boring.

HOW TO GET THERE

Several tour companies offer day trips from Buenos Aires to La Plata (see TOURS, page 70 under BUENOS AIRES). Several buses travel between Buenos Aires and La Plata daily. The **La Plata Terminal de Autobus (** (221) 421-0992 is on Calle 4 at Calle 42. If you're driving, La Plata is 58 km (36 miles) south of Buenos Aires off the Autovía 2.

MAGDALENA

The Río de la Plata empties into the Atlantic Ocean at the Bahía Samborombón south of La Plata. The region at the north of the bay is an excellent bird-watching area and is dotted with tiny towns and large *estancias*. Magdalena is the closest town to two *estancias* that incorporate private nature reserves and accept overnight guests.

El Destino ((11) 4806-3051 FAX (11) 4804-6997 E-MAIL pacuna@ipsa.com.ar WEB SITE WWW .argentina-ranches.com.ar MAILING ADDRESS Marcelo T. de Alvear 590, 1058 Capital Federal, Buenos Aires, is home to the Fundación Elsa Shaw de Pearson. The foundation supports a 4,500-hectare (11,100-acre) nature reserve used by biologists and naturalists to study the region's flora and fauna. Guests at the *estancia* can roam through the reserve on foot, horseback, or horse-drawn carriage, following trails to the riverbanks where egrets and herons fish alongside human anglers. The main ranch house is unlike any other I've seen, designed in an austere Bauhaus style with little ornamentation. Several guest rooms, some with private bath, are lovingly decorated with family antiques, photographs, and linens. Meals are served in the main dining room, and guests have use of a book-lined living room with comfortable couches and a fireplace. The grounds are a botanist's delight. Reservations are essential, as are detailed directions to the ranch.

Also in the area **Estancia Juan Gerónimo** ((11) 4937-4326 FAX (11) 4327-0105 is a 162-hectare (400-acre) nature reserve with a Tudor-style ranch house. Hiking, bird watching, and horse riding are available to day-trippers and overnight guests alike. Reservations are essential. A map to the property is provided when reservations are confirmed.

THE NORTH COAST

Nearly a dozen small towns line the coast south of Bahía Samborombón between La Plata and Mar del Plata. Several are included in an area called the **Municipalidad de la Costa**, and share a joint **Tourist Information Office** ((2246) 434474 FAX (2246) 434387 WEB SITE www.costa.mun .gba.gov.ar, Avenida Costanera 8001, Mar del Tuyú. All are located on Ruta 11, which winds and curves along the coastline south from La Plata to Mar del Plata. The drive along this rural highway is sometimes scenic, sometimes perilous, and often boring. It takes about six hours to cover the distance of about 350 km (217 miles) between the two cities, as opposed to 3.5 hours on the inland Autovía 2, a high-speed toll road. There are many places to stop and spend the night along the way, and the trip gives travelers a better sense of coastal life than they get from a quick visit to Mar del Plata.

The first beach town in the chain is **San Clemente del Tuyú**, located at the south end of the bay below Punta Rasa. Migratory birds flock to this area, and can be spotted from the hiking trails in the **Reserva de Vida Silvestre**, a 1,214-hectare (3,000-acre) reserve at Punta Rasa. Far more popular, thanks to constant advertising, is **Mundo Marino** (Marine World) ((2252) 430300, Avenida Décima 157. Marine World is part amusement park, part nature park, with rides, carnival games, dolphin and whale shows, and aquariums. It's immensely popular with families and is packed in the summer months. Admission is charged; hours vary with the season. Another theme park, **Bahía Aventura** ((2252) 423000,

Centro Comercial Faro San Antonio 9, is beside the lighthouse Faro San Antonio. Built in 1892, the lighthouse is said to have been the first on the coast, and is still operational. The park's *elevador panorámico* sky tower carries visitors in a glass elevator to a lookout 60 m (197 ft) above the ground. The area is especially interesting for naturalists, since it marks the point where the Río de la Plata enters the Atlantic Ocean. An audiovisual display provides information on the many species of birds that migrate to the area; hiking trails along the bay give birdwatchers the opportunity to spot rosy spoonbills, eagles, and flamingos. Admission is charged; hours vary with the season.

OPPOSITE: Gauchos herd cattle in the vast Pampas. ABOVE: An Argentine beauty on the beach.

PINAMAR

While San Clemente and the nearby towns of Santa Teresita and Mar del Tuyú attract *porteños* vacationing on limited budgets, chic Pinamar is the purview of the elite. Pine forests edge the sand on the outskirts of town, which resembles a mountain village nestled beside the sea. The area was developed as a resort in 1944 by architect Jorge Bunge; the main street through town bears his name. Stylish boutiques and cafés line the broad Avenida Bunge leading to the beach. The **Tourist Information Office** ((2254) 491680, Avenida Bunge 654, distributes an excellent tourist guide booklet listing hotels, restaurants, and facilities.

Pinamar has one of the loveliest beaches along the coast, with carefully raked sand backed by pine trees. The shore, especially north of Avenida Bunge, is lined with *balnearios*, beach clubs with a variety of facilities. Some have restaurants, bars, and beach gear rental. Others have all the above plus pools, gyms, and volleyball courts. The town lacks the intense party scene of Mar del Plata, which makes it an attractive choice for those who prefer a peaceful setting.

Just south of Pinamar, the small community of **Cariló** is even more exclusive and scenic. Visitors must pass through a security gate and drive down a long dirt road to reach the beach, which is rarely crowded. Vacation homes are tucked in groves of pines and palms down side roads, most unmarked. A commercial center provides all the necessities, including a small market and several restaurants and sportswear boutiques. **Ostende**, a bit farther south, is a small town with several buildings dating back to the early 1900s. A brochure available at the Pinamar tourist office describes some of the historic buildings, and includes a map of their locations.

General Juan Madariaga, 14 km (nine miles) northwest of Pinamar on Ruta 74, was once the railroad hub for southern Buenos Aires Province and the coast. Today it's a popular day-trip destination from the coastal resorts. Boating and fishing are available on two lakes — Laguna Salada Grande and Laguna Los Horcones. Both have boat and fishing gear rentals. Los Horcones is also popular for windsurfing and kayaking; rentals are available at the lake. Locals have dubbed their town "La Ciudad Guacha" (The Gaucho City) in honor of the many old *estancias* in the area. More than half a dozen are open to visitors with reservations. For information contact the **Tourist Information Office** ((2267) 42-1058 FAX (2267) 42-0057 E-MAIL culturamadariaga @telpin.com.ar WEB SITE www.madariaga .mun.gba.gov.ar, Calle General Martínez Guerrero 2039.

General Juan Madariaga holds a large Fiesta Nacional del Gaucho at the beginning of December, with parades, demonstrations of gaucho horseback riding skills, folkloric dancing, and plenty of *parrilla*-style meals. During Semana Santa (Easter week) nearly 300 locals participate in a musical passion play called "Pasión Según San Juan," recreating the death and resurrection of Jesus. Both festivals attract enormous crowds; if you plan to attend, book a room in Pinamar well ahead of your stay.

Where to Stay

Pinamar's hotels are smaller than those in Mar del Plata and reservations are absolutely essential in summer.

Set in a small forest of eucalyptus trees, the moderately priced **Hotel del Bosque** ((2254) 482480, Avenida Bunge at Calle Júpiter, is a peaceful spot with only 47 rooms. Facilities include a pool, tennis courts, sauna, and full restaurant. Though it's a few blocks from the beach, the setting and service make this a good choice for those seeking peaceful relaxation. **Hotel Arenas** ((2254) 482621 E-MAIL arenas@telpin.com.ar, Avenida Bunge 700, is closer to the beach, in the commercial area of the town. The bright yellow building includes both hotel rooms and apartments with full kitchens, and has a gym, sauna, hot tub and restaurant. Rates are moderate.

The beach is just a few steps away from the inexpensive **Taorima Hotel** ((2254) 481171, Calle San Martín at Calle Sarmiento. The hotel resembles a modern brick Tudor-style motel, and the rooms have brick walls and private baths. In the same price category, the **Soleado Hotel** ((2254) 490340 E-MAIL soleado@telpin.com.ar, Calle Sarmiento at Calle Nuestras Malvinas, is also close to the beach. Some rooms in the two-story building have ocean views, and the hotel has a full restaurant.

Where to Eat

Avenida Bunge is lined with cafés, restaurants, and ice-cream parlors, and the beach with casual open-air cafés. Prices are a bit steep during tourist season, and many places close down in winter. For a moderately priced meal, **Parrilla Parada Uno** ((2254) 481386, Avenida Bunge at Avenida Shaw, is one of the most popular beef houses in town. The large A-frame wood restaurant is packed for weekend lunch, when families devour huge platters of grilled meats. **Abuela María** ((2254) 493922, Avenida Bunge 999, specializes in homemade pastas, and offers set menus for a reasonable price.

Inexpensive dining can be found at **Cocodrilo** ((2254) 489885, Avenida del Mar at Fragata 25 de Mayo, a fun spot at the beach serving good breakfasts, sandwiches, and burgers. One of the more popular pizza spots, **Pizzería San Carlos** ((2254) 484380, Avenida Shaw 672, is open year-round.

How to Get There

There are flights from Buenos Aires to Villa Gesell (25 km or about 15 miles south of Pinamar) in the summer; taxis are available for transport from the airport to Pinamar. Frequent buses from Buenos Aires and Mar del Plata arrive at the Terminal de Ómnibus ((2254) 482247 at Avenida Shaw at Calle del Pejerrey. Drivers can reach Pinamar via Ruta 11 from La Plata and the north coastal towns or by taking the Dolores exit from Autovía 2.

VILLA GESELL

The most scenic stretch of the drive along the coast is around Pinamar and the next significant town, Villa Gesell. On the west side of the road, fields of wheat, corn, alfalfa, and sunflowers stretch as far as the eye can see. On the east, stands of pines and eucalyptus edge golden sand dunes topped with tufts of green grass. An occasional gaucho appears in the distance, riding amid the fields. The pampas are at their best here.

Don Carlos Idaho Gesell chose wisely when he picked this area for a nature reserve and vacation resort in 1931. He purchased 1,648 hectares (4,072 acres) of coastal land, planted more trees along a maze of streets, and left the dunes protected by the trees and undisturbed by development. It wasn't until 1959, when a road was constructed to link Villa Gesell with Buenos Aires, that tourists began to arrive. Today, the town has a population nearing 20,000 and a loyal following of visitors who treasure its natural beauty and abundant tourist services. Like Pinamar, Villa Gesell resembles an alpine village with A-frames and chalets housing hotels and shops. Unfortunately, success has left its unsightly mark, and the jumble of businesses close to the waterfront is appallingly unattractive.

General Information

The **Tourist Information Office** ((2255) 456859 WEB SITE www.gesell.com.ar, Boulevard Silvio Gesell at Avenida Buenos Aires, is located in a chalet-style building at the first traffic circle as you enter town. The staff is extremely helpful.

What to See and Do

Many of the town's attractions are clustered around the **Reserva Forestal Pinar del Norte** at Avenida Buenos Aires and Alameda 202, a central park that resembles a small forest growing atop a sand dune. Over 100 species of plants are protected in the park, along with several types of trees introduced by Gesell to guard the dunes from erosion. Acacias, cypress, pines, eucalyptus, and fruit trees shade the trails through the reserve and offer a haven to dozens of species of birds. The **Museo y Archivo Histórico Municipal** ((2255) 468624, Alameda 202 at Calle 301, is located within

the park. Displays on the city's development fill the first house Gesell built at his resort. The house is also called La Casa de las Cuatro Puertas for the doors Gesell built facing the four cardinal points. Gesell built a second home, a chalet by the sea, in 1952. It was turned over to the city after he died in 1979 and is now used as the **Centro Cultural Chalet de Don Carlos** ((2255) 450530, Alameda 202 at Calle 301.

The forest experience has been commercialized at **Aventura en el Bosque** ((2255) 454881, Boulevard Silvio Gesell at Paseo 101. Six hectares (15 acres) of forest have been transformed into a theme park with a miniature train ride through the trees, a small zoo and aviary, artisans' work-

shops, and song and dance shows. Hours vary with the season; admission is charged.

Villa Gesell's greatest attraction is its beach, a long stretch of sand dotted with towering dunes. A long pier popular with fishermen stretches 15 m (49 ft) over the water at the south end of the beach. The **Faro Querandí**, 15 km (nine miles) south of town, rises above the forest and dunes on an isolated stretch of beach accessible only by four-wheel-drive vehicles. Built in 1922 with material carted in by horses, the lighthouse is one of the highest in the country; visitors are welcome to climb the 276 stairs to the top. The views (and wind gusts) are extraordinary.

You can drive to the lighthouse on your own; jeep rentals are available at **Pedro Cuevas Villa Gesell 4X4 Rent** ((2255) 458604. Guided tours to the lighthouse are available through **El Costero** ((2255) 468989, Paseo 110 between avenidas 3 and 4. **Moto X Fox** ((2255) 454646, Avenida Buenos Aires at Alameda 212, offers trips to the lighthouse from Villa Gesell and Cariló. Horseback riding on the beach and to the lighthouse is available with **Escuelas de Equitación San Jorge** ((2255) 454464, Avenida Circunvalación and Paseo 102.

Wide parasols called *sombrillas* shade vacationers on Playa Bristol.

There is another attraction well worth visiting south of Villa Gesell in the town of Balcarce. The **Museo del Automóvil Juan Manuel Fangio** ((2266) 43-0758, Calle Rocha at Calle Mitre, Balcarce, is named for Argentina's most famous race car driver. The excellent automotive museum contains a collection of antique cars and racing cars, and traces the history of the automobile through well-designed exhibits.

Where to Stay

It seems like every other building in Villa Gesell is a hotel or vacation apartment complex, and you should be able to find a room even without reservations. Many places are closed from May to October.

MODERATE

Located just 50 m (just under 55 yards) from the sea, **Tequendama Spa & Resort** ((2255) 462829 E-MAIL tequendama@gesell.com.ar, Paseo 109 at Avenida 1, is a full-service resort with large air-conditioned rooms. Many have balconies looking out over the ocean, and all have safe-deposit boxes and small refrigerators. Within the spa are a gym, sauna, steam room and hot tubs. There is a full restaurant with 24-hour room service. The hotel is the headquarters for the tour company America 4X4, which offers lighthouse trips. Tequendama is open year round. **Terrazas Club Hotel** (/FAX (2255) 462181, Avenida 2 at Paseo 104, is similar in price and services. Its spa, located at the beach five minutes from the hotel, has a pool as well as the facilities listed above. The hotel is open from October through April.

INEXPENSIVE

The **Hotel Atlántico** ((2255) 462253, Avenida Costanera at Paseo 105, has several ocean view rooms, which are higher in price than those at the back of the hotel. Suites and apartments have kitchen facilities. The hotel is open from October through Easter week. The **Merimar** ((2255) 46-2243 FAX (2255) 46-2539 E-MAIL merimar@hotmail .com, Avenida Costanera at Paseo 107, has ocean-view rooms, apartments, and very inexpensive rooms without a view. It's open year round.

Where to Eat

Restaurants abound in town and along the beach; many are closed in winter. The following moderately priced restaurants are open year round. A country theme prevails at **La Casa de Antonia** ((2255) 458666, Calle 303 and Boulevard Gesell. The stone cottage restaurant is best known for its fondues (try the seafood fondue) and afternoon teas. **Ariturito** ((2255) 463037, Avenida 3 at Paseo 126, serves traditional grilled meats and pastas. **Dogos Café** ((2255) 468780, Avenida 2 at Paseo 104, is a cheery, casual café serving full

breakfasts, sandwiches and burgers at lunch, and grilled meats or pasta at dinner.

How to Get There

Villa Gesell's small airport is served by Aerolíneas Argentinas during the summer months. Frequent buses from Buenos Aires and Mar del Plata arrive at the **Terminal de Ómnibus** ((2255) 476058 at Avenida 3 and Paseo 104. Drivers can reach Villa Gesell via Ruta 11 from La Plata and the north coastal towns or by taking the Dolores exit from Autovía 2.

MAR DEL PLATA

In the winter, Mar del Plata is a peaceful seaside city with a population of about 600,000 full-time residents. Come summer, it's a madhouse. The population triples as *porteños* escape the city's heat and humidity and head for the beach. Traffic

comes to a halt, pedestrians take over the streets, and the sand is barely visible beneath a mass of nearly bare bodies. Prices in restaurants and hotels rise as the season peaks in December and January, then gradually decline in February and March. By April, the vacationers have returned to work and Mardel (the city's nickname) becomes habitable once again.

Newcomers have a hard time discovering Mardel's charms; at first it just looks like a big, crowded city that happens to sit beside the sea. Part of the fault lies with city planners, who looked the other way as developers littered the waterfront with unsightly highrise hotels and condo complexes. The clutter detracts from the coast's natural beauty and clashes with Mardel's traditional architecture. The wealthy *porteños* who built their summer homes on Mardel's hills in the early twentieth century favored European-style chalets and mini palaces, many built with the stones

unearthed when the port was dredged. Today's buildings resemble 1970s concrete slabs blocking sea views and breezes. Many wealthy *porteños* have abandoned Mar del Plata for the more scenic shores of Punta del Este in Uruguay, and several of the loveliest private homes have been turned into museums.

Still, thousands of Argentines thrive on the crowds and excesses that are the hallmarks of a Mardel vacation. But travelers seeking the roar of the surf and long walks on the beach are best off visiting in the off season. Winter has its drawbacks, since the area is subject to fierce coastal winds — hence the metal and wood shutters on most buildings. But in the spring and autumn, when the water is warm and hotel rates fall, Mar del Plata offers a pleasant respite from the bustle of Buenos Aires.

Mar del Plata's fishing fleet shares the port with hundreds of sea lions.

BACKGROUND

Juan de Garay, who founded Buenos Aires in 1580, is believed to have traveled along the coast of Mar del Plata, but Europeans found little reason to settle here. The Jesuits arrived in 1851 and founded the mission of Nuestra Señora del Pilar at Laguna de los Padres, but had limited success converting the Indians of the Pampas. In the mid-1800s a few settlers from Spain and Portugal began developing the area; in 1860 they sold their land holdings to Don Patricio Peralta Ramos, who is credited with establishing the city.

national economy faltered in the 1940s and 1950s, Mar del Plata reached the end of its belle époque. Families found it difficult to maintain their lavish vacation homes; several were donated to the city. By the 1960s, Mardel had lost its exclusive luster and become a working-class resort. Some wealthy families have retained their vacation compounds and memberships in the city's exclusive clubs, and Mardel remains Argentina's largest and most popular seaside resort.

GENERAL INFORMATION

The headquarters for Emtur, the **Mar del Plata Tourism Office** ((223) 495-1777 WEB SITE WWW

At that time, Mar del Plata's main enterprise was a large slaughterhouse serving the nearby *estancias*. Ramos and other settlers gradually developed agricultural plots, built residential neighborhoods and a school, and received permission from the regional governor to establish the city of Mar del Plata. A rail line connecting the city with Buenos Aires was completed in 1886, and *porteños* began visiting the coast on holidays. Mardel's cathedral, one of the most impressive in the country, was completed in 1905, and in 1907 the settlement was officially designated a city. Wealthy *porteños* commissioned European architects to design vacation homes on the hills above the best beaches, and Mar del Plata became a fashionable resort. The port, now the largest on Argentina's Atlantic coast, was dredged in 1923.

Like the rest of the country, Mar del Plata thrived in the 1920s and 1930s. Then, when the

.argenet.com.ar/emtur, Avenida Belgrano 740, is geared more toward national tourists than foreigners, and there may not be English-speaking clerks on duty. The most useful **Puesto de Información Turística** (Information Booth) is located in the Hotel Provincial at Boulevard Marítimo 2400. The airport desk is staffed only when flights arrive.

GETTING AROUND

You can walk to most attractions if you stay in downtown, and public buses run along the waterfront past all the beaches.

One factor above all causes the most confusion for first-time drivers. The main street running along the waterfront is labeled one thing and called another. In all its grandeur, the street is called Boulevard Marítimo P. Peralta Ramos, shortened to Boulevard Marítimo by most businesses. Yet the street signs read Boulevard Peralto Ramos, leaving the uninitiated to drive about in frustration until they catch on. Just to drive you a little more insane, the street changes names to Avenida Martínez de Hoz when it reaches the Navy base south of town.

If you're entering town by car from the airport or highway, you reach the beach at the north end of the boulevard, which suddenly becomes a one-way street in the direction opposite that which you're driving. Southbound traffic is routed to Avenida Colón, which runs inland along the edge of Plaza Colón into the hills above the waterfront. But don't despair. Colón eventually leads back to Boulevard Marítimo and the beach.

WHAT TO SEE AND DO

Naturally, one must first go to the beach. In high season the sand is packed with brightly colored umbrellas, awnings, and tents and the water is overcrowded with hundreds of bobbing bodies. In the center of the action is the **Muelle Club de Pesca** (Fishing Club Pier) at the foot of Avenida Luro, with a famous restaurant and café (see WHERE TO EAT, below). **Playa Popular** (just north of the pier) and **Playa Bristol** (just south) are the most popular stretches of sand. Vendors hawk rental umbrellas and tents all along the sand; others vie for the right to braid young girls' hair with ribbons and beads in the Jamaican style. It's an absolute mob scene that everyone loves. Families on budgets book apartments for weeks on end all around downtown and walk back and forth between their air-conditioned rooms and the sand from dawn until long past sunset.

The beach lies just off the main streets in downtown. As you travel south, the coast becomes hilly and rocky, and sandy beaches are interspersed with small jetties and stretches of rock-strewn beaches. Small streets called *paseos* dip down from Boulevard Marítimo to the shoreline. A few blocks south of the main beaches on Boulevard Marítimo is the **Torreón Del Monte** (also spelled Monje) ((223) 451-5575, Paseo Jesús de Galíndez and Viamonte. An incongruous miniature castle with towers and turrets, the Torreón was constructed in 1904 as a landmark along the coast. It's still an impressive building, now divided into bar areas and dining rooms where fashionable types impress their friends over leisurely (but not particularly outstanding) lunches. The beach here, called **Playa de los Pescadores**, is popular with surfers.

Farther south the hotel prices rise and the beaches are a bit less crowded, until you reach **Playa Grande**, between calles Garay and Formosa. Above the beach is **Parque San Martín**, where kids love to roll down a grassy hill. The sand below is lined with rows of semipermanent tents like little canvas rooms sitting side by side all the way to the

water. Some of the areas are open to the public (the umbrella and tent rentals are more expensive than at the other beaches), but many are the purview of Mardel's wealthy inhabitants, members of exclusive private beach clubs. Families have belonged to these clubs for generations and gather every summer, with grandparents regaling grandkids with tales of the good old days. This area is one of the best for serious swimmers (you needn't belong to a club to walk one of the pathways to the water's edge and lay your towel on the sand).

Lifeguard towers are scattered along the beaches and a colored flag system warns bathers of rough currents. Stay out of the water if a red flag is posted nearby.

A manmade jetty separates the swimming beaches from the Navy base; another separates the base from the port, one of Mardel's biggest attractions. As one of the country's main fishing ports, Mardel is home to a huge community of fishermen and their bright orange skiffs, which float and bob in a colorful panorama at the **Dársena de Pescadores**. Seafood restaurants and souvenir shops fill the **Centro Comercial del Puerto** at the entrance to the port at Avenida Martínez de Hoz and Calle Vertiz. Be sure to stop by **Pescadería Mellino** ((223) 480-0806, Centro Comercial del Puerto 12, a fascinating fish market stocked with the catch of the day displayed on piles of ice. The market also sells seafood cocktails and shells. Tickets for boat cruises are sold at various stands in the center. **Anamora Yate Fiesta** ((223) 484-2744, offers daytime, sunset, and night boat tours, as does **Turimar Paseos Marítimos** ((223) 489-7775.

A maze of potholed streets at the port leads to the fishing docks and the **Reserva de Lobos Marinas**, a cluster of rocks that are home to a large colony of sea lions. Knowing a good thing when they see it, the sea lions live among the fishing boats, feeding upon what they can steal from the catch. The stench is horrendous, but the sight worth the discomfort. The sea lions, who growl and lumber about as if posing for photographers, are separated from onlookers by a wire fence.

There's far more to Mar del Plata than the beach. A *rambla* (seaside sidewalk) runs along the waterfront in downtown between two large brick buildings designed by architect Alejandro Bustillo in 1938. One of the red hulks houses the **Casino Central** ((223) 495-7011, Avenida Marítimo, one of Mardel's biggest draws. Slot machines create a constant clang in the lower floor gaming room, while the more restrained concentration on poker, blackjack, and roulette rules over the upper floor. The adjacent building once housed the **Hotel Provincial**, and now is used for offices. Tango dancers, magicians, and reggae bands perform on the *rambla* between the two buildings.

The catch of the day on display at the fish market.

Plaza Colón, which faces the casino between Boulevard Marítimo and Avenida Colón, separates the waterfront from the busy streets of downtown. Calle Rivadavia and Calle San Martín are both pedestrian-only streets leading to the impressive neo-Gothic **Catedral**, also called Iglesia San Pedro, at the intersection of Calle San Martín and Avenida San Luis. Somewhat modeled on Paris's Notre Dame with flying buttresses and an abundance of stained glass, the cathedral is one of the most impressive churches in the country. It faces **Plaza San Martín**, the city's main plaza, where a statue of General José de San Martín, sculpted in bronze by Luis Perlotti, looms over roses, flowerbeds, and lawns.

Just a few blocks inland are some of the finest chalets and villas in the country. Mar del Plata's original families were entranced with the country homes in Normandy, and copied the architecture in their seaside city. Wander through the neighborhood of Los Troncos, especially the streets around the intersections of Avenida Güemes and Calle Quintana for a glimpse of grandeur. A few homes are now used as museums. The **Villa Mitre** ((223) 495-1200, Calle La Madrid 3870, was built to resemble a Spanish hacienda in 1931 for the Mitre family. In 1979, the home was donated to the city and became the **Archivo Museo Histórico Municipal Don Roberto Barili**. Several rooms contain historic photographs, city plans, antique furnishings and art; the library has bound volumes of local and national newspapers.

The nearby **Villa Victoria** ((223) 492-0569, Calle Matheu 1851, was constructed in 1912 and designed by a British architect. Unlike most of the city's fine homes (which were constructed of stone and stucco) this yellow wood bungalow is awash with gables, balconies and porches. It sits amid rose and herb gardens, and houses the **Centro Cultural Victoria Ocampo**, dedicated to Argentina's most famous female author. Exhibits include some of her original manuscripts, photographs

of the country's literary elite, and sculptures and paintings by modern-day women artists.

Constructed in 1909, the extraordinarily ornate Normandy-style **Museo Municipal de Arte Juan Carlos Castagnino** ((223) 486-1636, Avenida Colón 1189, was originally the home of the Ortíz Basualdo family. The museum is named for the Mar del Plata-born artist whose paintings illustrated *Martín Fierro*, the famous gaucho poem by José Hernández. Over 100 of the painter's works are included in the museum's collection; some are exhibited in the villa's many rooms. Admission is charged; closed on Wednesday.

On a far different level, the **Museo Guillermo Vilas** ((223) 451-1903, Calle Olavarria 2134, is devoted to Argentina's most famous tennis player and Mardel's favorite son. A modern glass-enclosed restaurant fronts the original villa, which resembles a Tudor castle. Several of the original rooms contain Vilas' tennis trophies and other memorabilia, including his Harley Davidson motorcycle. There's even a Vilas boutique, with logo hats, shirts, and racquet bags.

The **Museo Municipal de Ciencias** (Science Museum) ((223) 478-8791, Plaza España at Avenida Libertad and Catamarca, attempts to woo Mardel's returning visitors with temporary exhibits aimed at children. Admission is charged.

The beach is secondary to some visitors, who travel to Mar del Plata on pilgrimages to the **Gruta de Nuestra Señora de Lourdes** ((223) 480-3072, Calle Magellanes 4000. Modeled after the shrine in France, the site includes a statue of the Virgin set above a cave dripping water. Devotees gather the water in jars, plastic bags, and plastic bottles in the shape of the Virgin, and splash the water onto their bodies wherever illness or injury is present. Thanks to the Virgin are displayed on hundreds of tin and tile plaques mounted on rocks along a walkway leading past tiled stations of the cross. The shrine also includes models of the cities of Bethlehem and Jerusalem; drop a coin in a machine beside the dioramas and the figures of humans and donkeys move along tracks up streets and hillsides. The tacky displays hold the attention of school kids parading through on field trips. Several large shops display statues, prayer cards, and other religious mementos.

The biggest attraction for kids is the **Mar del Plata Aquarium** ((223) 467-0700, Avenida Martínez de Hoz 5600, south of the city. Dolphins, whales and water skiers perform in hourly shows, and mussels, clams and starfish endure constant prodding in the hands-on tide pool. The park has a beach and several sea-life exhibits, including sea lions, penguins, and crocodiles. You can swim with dolphins for an extra fee; call ahead for reservations. Admission is charged. Trolleys offering transport to the aquarium line up along the Plaza Colón. You can't miss them — just look for the

waving cartoon characters beside garishly painted buses blaring loud music. Nearby, the **Parque del Faro** ((223) 467-4400, Paseo Costanera Sur Presidente Arturo Illia 5600, is billed as a "fantasyland" and includes interactive exhibits focusing on the sea. Admission is charged.

SPORTS

Sport-fishing boats depart from the Club Náutico on the Espigón Comercial Puerto (Port Jetty) off Avenida Martínez de Hoz. Turimar ((223) 480-9372 at the jetty offers half-day fishing trips including gear; the catch can include small sharks, corvina, grouper, and sea bass.

Mar del Plata's waves are far from extreme, but they're good enough for diehard **surfers** and **body boarders**. Tournaments are held at Playa Grande in March. **Windsurfing** is best at Playas del Balcón on Paseo Costanera Sur. **Scuba diving**

trips are offered by Oceanica Expediciónes ((223) 4484-0325, Club Náutico on the Espigón Comercial Puerto (Port Jetty) off Avenida Martínez de Hoz. **Horse races** are held at the Hipódromo de Mar del Plata ((223) 487-4001, Ruta 226 Km. 5.

SHOPPING

Beach gear is sold at stands and in shops along the waterfront. The largest shopping center, **Los Gallegos** ((223) 499-6900, Calle Rivadavia 3050, is just a few blocks inland. Arts and crafts are displayed daily in front of the cathedral. Mar del Plata is known for its handmade sweaters, which fill the front windows at boutiques along Calle Martín. And it seems everyone visiting Mardel must purchase at least one box of *alfajores* (wafer cookies

OPPOSITE: Families play in the Plaza Colón when the sun sets. ABOVE: High-rise condos and hotels line the urban stretch of Playa Bristol.

filled with *dulce de leche*) made by the Havana company. There are shops boasting the Havana sign all over town.

Cabrales, Alberti 1343, looks like it's just a fancy wine shop until you walk through the doors. Then you realize there is far more to this store. Cabrales specializes in imported coffees, pastas, cheeses, caviar, liquors and other gourmet products; it's also an art gallery and concert space. Jazz groups play in a second-story room lined with crates of wine. Artists display their works in a second Tudor-style building behind the store. The building itself is worth checking out and it's a lovely place to sip a fine cup of coffee.

WHERE TO STAY

Hotel rates vary drastically with the season, rising to their peak in January. You may get a better deal if tourism is low, especially for midweek stays. Most hotels offer complimentary Continental breakfast. Many have a few rooms with kitchenettes, which are popular with vacationing families.

Expensive

The best rooms in town are the oceanfront suites at **Costa Galana** ((223) 486-0000 FAX 486-2020 E-MAIL reservas@costagalana.com.ar. The sleek tower above Playa Grande is a popular setting for weddings and business meetings, thanks to its stylish marble and brass decor and its professional service. The large rooms have all the amenities one could desire, from large bathtubs to mini bars, cable television, and safe-deposit boxes. The hotel's best feature is its top-floor spa, including a lounge area with two large hot tubs and cushioned chairs facing the ocean view. The rooftop pool is heated, and the spa includes an exercise room and beauty salon.

The location is far from ideal, but the **Sheraton Mar del Plata Hotel** ((223) 499-6000 TOLL-FREE (800) 325-3535 FAX (223) 499-9009 WEB SITE WWW .sheraton.com, Avenida Alem 4221, is so popular, reservations are essential in summer. The hotel sits beside the golf course way above the ocean, but its large pool area, fitness center, good restaurants, and comfortable rooms make it a desirable headquarters for business travelers and tour groups. **Torres de Manantiales** ((223) 486-1999 FAX (223) 486-2222, Calle Alberti 445, is extremely popular with families, thanks to its full apartments with kitchens and several bedrooms. The building is the highest along the waterfront; many rooms have great views of the sea. Facilities include an outdoor pool. One of the biggest draws is the hotel's full-service spa offering massage, body wraps, facials, and hydrotherapy treatments. The spa is on the south coast about a half-hour drive from the hotel; transportation is provided.

Moderate

The best reasonably priced rooms in town are at the **Hotel las Rocas** ((223) 451-5362 E-MAIL lasrocas @satlink.com, Calle Alberto 9. The blue and white building is on a hillside overlooking the ocean, and the pounding surf provides constant background music for guests in the 50 rooms. Most rooms have small balconies facing the sea; the beach is across the street and down a slight hill.

A portrait of Don Quixote greets guests at the **Hotel Dos Reyes** ((223) 491-2714 FAX (223) 491-2916, Avenida Colón 2129. The lobby and lounge areas gleam with marble and polished wood. Rooms and suites have mini-bars and room service, and the furnishings are modern. The service and accommodations are better than at most hotels in this category. Rates at the **Hotel Argentino** (/FAX (223) 493-0091, Belgrano 2225, fall to the inexpensive category in low season, but the hotel is very popular in midsummer and rates rise

accordingly. The highrise building is just two blocks from the casino and beach, and right across the street from a laundromat. Rooms are larger than most, and have television and safe-deposit boxes. The decor is rather dark and the staff a bit imperious. A sense of faded grandeur prevails at the **Hotel Astor** ((223) 492-1616, Calle Entre Ríos 1649. You may need to check a few rooms before unpacking—some are cleaner than others. Music is piped into all rooms, but you can switch it off.

Inexpensive

Guests rave about the complimentary breakfast at **Benedetti Hotel** ((223) 493-0031 FAX (223) 492-0523, Avenida Colón 2198. The buffet spread surpasses most by offering egg dishes, cheeses and meats, fresh fruit, and yogurt, and the tables look out on to the street. The hotel's decor is an eclectic blend of floral fabrics, pillars covered with abstract

tiled murals, dark wood walls, and modernistic chandeliers. The rooms are simpler and have safe-deposit boxes, phones, and televisions. The staff is friendly and helpful. Low rates are the biggest attraction at the **Gran Hotel Continental** ((223) 492-1300, Avenida Córdoba 1929. A closet-sized elevator transports guests to surprisingly large rooms with televisions mounted on the walls, thin mattresses on the beds, and bright blue and white tiled bathrooms.

WHERE TO EAT

Expensive

Casually elegant and intimate, **Via Juancho** ((223) 496-1513, Calle Santiago del Estero 1330, is the best place for a romantic splurge. Begin your dinner with the shrimp, avocado, and palm

The entire country seems to migrate to Mar del Plata in summer.

hearts cocktail, followed by *langostinos a la Jarry*, a piping hot dish of shrimp in an egg, cream, and cheese sauce, or the *caya Chilena pero Argentina*, a rice, chicken, and mushroom dish popular in Chile. Save room for the *bombas a la Mostiero*, scoops of vanilla ice cream with a chocolate mint sauce, or the outrageously sweet *Juanita López* combining ice cream, *dulce de leche*, mousse, and meringue. The proprietor tends to name dishes after friends and famous personalities, which makes the menu a tad confusing. End your meal with a small glass of *limoncello*, a lemon liqueur made in Mar del Plata. A sedate setting in a Tudor house on a slight hill above the sea makes **Trenque Lauquen de la Costa** ((223) 451-4269,

Boulevard Marítimo at Calle Bernardo de Irigoyen, a favorite with upscale locals. Seafood dominates the menu.

There's a certain charm to **Espigón Pescadores Restaurant** ((223) 493-1713, Boulevard Marítimo and Avenida Luro, at the edge of the fishing pier. The restaurant is housed in a replica of the 1927 Fishermen's Club; the current two-story structure looms over the end of the pier like a white wooden hulk topped with billboards. The scene is more pleasant indoors, where tables covered with green and white cloths sit against large windows overlooking the sea. The menu is much like Mardel's other seafood eateries — one dines here for the scenery more than the cuisine.

Moderate

Hip restaurants and bars line the back streets above Playa Grande. One of the best is **El Anticuario** ((223) 451-6309, Calle Bernardo de Irigoyen 3819. The decor combines aspects of an Irish pub, German beer hall, and American brew pub with surprising success. Tables and booths are set far enough apart for privacy; those seeking companionship gather at the long bar. The *tabla de picadas Mediterráneo* is a platter of cheese, ham, mussels, olives, anchovies, sardines, and squid that easily satisfies a party of four. The large garlic-laced

spinach salad and a couple of *empanadas* stuffed with cheese and tomatoes make a fine meal for one. Other standouts include chicken marinated in honey and beer and *cazuela de mariscos* (seafood stew similar to cioppino).

Set menus are the best choice for those dining on a budget at **Restaurant Miglierina** ((223) 495-7024, Calle Belgrano 2361. Like most restaurants in downtown, Miglierina is a noisy, busy affair with something for everything on the menu. The shrimp crêpes and grilled salmon are good choices. Couples crowd **La Tranquera** ((223) 479-3098, Avenida Constitution 6576, late at night before visiting neighborhood discos. A classic *parrilla*, La Tranquera specializes in huge platters of barbecued meats served with national wines and the requisite mixed salads and french fries. **El Viejo Pop** ((223) 480-0147, Centro Comercial del Puerto 7, is the nicest restaurant amid the hodgepodge at the port. Designed to resemble the interior of a handsome yacht, the restaurant has dark wood paneled walls, red velvet curtains, a collection of brass ship's lamps and an overabundance of nautical props. Lunch is a formal affair featuring salmon pâté, smoked trout, fried squid, and steamed mussels for starters. Splurge on the sole with prawn and clam sauce or the Marseillaise bouillabaisse for an entrée, followed by lemon sorbet with champagne.

Inexpensive

Located in the middle of the action, **La Casona** ((223) 493-8943, Calle Rivadavia at Avenida Córdoba, dominates one corner of the pedestrian walkway. Frantically busy most times of day, the bright, clamorous restaurant serves a bit of everything — sandwiches, pizza, salads, calzones, pastas, and grilled meats. A plate of fried chicken, french fries, and salad costs just US$5; strangely enough, the pizzas and calzones are the most expensive items on the menu. You may end up returning here often for a quick burger or a bowl of vegetarian ravioli. Arrive early in the evening and claim one of the tables on the second-story balcony overlooking the sidewalk — a great spot for people-watching. Most items are available for takeout.

Surfers hang out at **La Princesa** ((223) 451-9845, Calle Bernardo de Irigoyen 3816. This open-air café is filled with surf photos. Sandwiches and burgers are the main fare, and waves the focus of conversation.

The Centro Comercial at the port is lined with restaurants, many offering all-you-can-eat seafood and beef buffets. Customers pile their plates high with grilled fish and shrimp and share long wooden tables with strangers all intent on the feeding frenzy. **La Nona Rosa** ((223) 480-0806, Centro Comercial del Puerto 13, is among the most popular and inexpensive.

NIGHTLIFE

Once the sun goes down, vacationing Argentines take a short rest in preparation for long nights of vigorous partying. Most of the city's main clubs are located away from the beach on Avenida Constitución. **Sobremonte** ((223) 479-2600, Avenida Constitución 6698, is an enormous complex with several dance clubs featuring techno-rock, Latin, and romantic music. **Azúcar Salsoteca** ((223) 495-7938, Avenida Constitución 4478, is the best spot for salsa and other Latin music. The best tango shows are at **Malena Club de Tango** ((223) 495-8533, Calle Rivadavia 2312. Live Latin music is played at **Mirador Waikiki** ((223) 484-0966, Avenida Martínez de Hoz 4320. Concerts and tango shows are held at the **Teatro Municipal Colón** ((223) 494-8571, Hipólito Yrigoyen 1665.

HOW TO GET THERE

There are several daily flights between Buenos Aires and Mar del Plata during the summer. Planes arrive at the **Aeropuerto Internacional Brigadier B. de Colina** on Ruta 2 north of town. There is daily service from Buenos Aires and Córdoba, and weekly service from Bariloche, Salta, Mendoza, and Tucumán. Several bus companies travel the route between the main terminal in Buenos Aires and Mar del Plata. Nonstop deluxe service is offered by **Plusmar** ((223) 451-4367, Calle Bolivia 18. The **Estación de Ómnibus** ((223) 451-5406, Calle Alberti 1602, is served by dozens of lines reaching all parts of the country. Trains run between Buenos Aires and Mar del Plata during the summer high season, and seats should be reserved in advance. The **Estación Terminal de Ferrocarril** ((223) 475-6076 is at Avenida Luro and Calle Italia.

It takes about four hours to drive from Buenos Aires to Mar del Plata on Autovía 2, a multi-lane toll road where most drivers far exceed the speed limit. It takes about six hours to reach Mar del Plata from La Plata on Ruta 11, a narrow curving back highway along the coast.

LAGUNA Y SIERRA DE LOS PADRES

The Laguna de los Padres, 10 km (six miles) east of Mar del Plata on Ruta 226, is a nature reserve and popular day trip for visitors to Mar del Plata. The lake is a particular favorite with birdwatchers; at least 90 species of birds inhabit the area. Fishermen, boaters and kayakers stick to the water, while hikers head into the Sierra de los Padres, a nearby forest reserve. Facilities in the area include picnic grounds, a small zoo, and several *parrilla* restaurants. Those interested in gaucho culture should visit the **Museo Municipal José Hernández** ((223) 463-1394, Ruta 226 Km 14.5, located in a colonial style ranch house near the Laguna de Los Padres. Permanent exhibits of rural life include antiques and costumes from *estancias* in the 1920s. Author of the epic poem *Martín Fierro*, José Hernández, lived in the ranch house turned museum for several years; locals claim it was here that he learned the gaucho lifestyle and accumulated the knowledge of ranch life incorporated in his writing. Hernández fans gather here on November 10 to celebrate the author's birthday with displays of gaucho horsemanship and a traditional *parrilla* feast.

A small map of the area is available at the tourist office in Mar del Plata. Camping is available at **La Serranita** ((223) 463-0003, Ruta 226 Km. 24.5.

TANDIL

The **Sierras de Tandil**, a low mountain range northwest of Mar del Plata, may well be the most scenic area in the boring pampas landscape. Rounded hills rise like humps of rock 800 m (2,624 ft) above groves of trees and fields of corn and wheat outside the city of Tandil, an important agricultural hub. One of the oldest geological formations in South America, the Sierras de Tandil were once the province of guanaco, fox, eagles, hares and ostrich, and are believed to have been one of the first inhabited areas in Argentina. Today, they are extremely popular with hikers, rock climbers, mountain bikers, and spelunkers, who visit on weekend excursions from Buenos Aires and the coast.

Tandil is home to about 100,000 residents, and is a modern, orderly city with few historical attractions. Locals have long had an interest in the curative powers of herbs and native plants and all forms of natural healing; Tandil was home to a legendary healer named Gerónimo de Solané, fondly called Tata Dios, in the late 1800s. It's also an important religious center. The city is packed with visitors during Semana Santa (Easter week), because many believe **Monte Calvario**, just a few blocks from the central plaza, resembles Golgatha, where Christ was crucified. A tall cross stands atop the hill, along with the **Gruta de Lourdes**, a shrine to the Virgin of Lourdes.

The area is also known for its homemade cheese and chocolates. Regional cheeses and candies are sold at **Época de Quesos** ((2293) 448750, Calle 14 de Julio at Calle San Martín, a restored ranch house. The most important sight in town is the **Cerro La Movediza**, a large rock formation northwest of downtown where Tata Dios lectured his followers. For many years an enormous triangular-shaped boulder sat precariously atop the small hill; though the boulder has fallen, it remains a popular attraction. **Dique y Lago del Fuerte**, a

Fishermen cast their lines in the surf at Playa de los Pescadores.

large lake and water reservoir with public swimming pools on the south side of town, also draws crowds, especially on weekends. But the majority of visitors head for the hills.

Tandil's **Tourist Information Office** ((2293) 432073, Calle 9 de Julio 555, distributes a good map and some brochures. The staff is very helpful with setting up excursions to the mountains. Tours of the city and mountain areas are offered by **Barbini Tourism** ((2293) 428612, Calle Maipú 1375; they can also arrange overnight stays at mountain cabins and ranches. Similar services are available from **Organización Turismo Serrano** ((2293) 431894, Calle San Martín 186. **Cabalgatas Gabriel Barletta** ((2293) 427725, Calle Avellaneda 673, offers horseback riding trips into the mountains.

Most visitors prefer to stay at *cabañas* outside the city. The tourist office has information on the best places and can help make reservations. You can also check with the Buenos Aires Province Tourist Office in Buenos Aires. The **Posada de los Pájaros Spa Hotel** ((2293) 431108, Avenida Don Bosco at Calle Namuncurá, is a full service resort with offices in Buenos Aires ((11) 4812-2777, Calle Uruguay 1064.

THE SOUTH COAST

Ruta 11 runs south along the coast from Mar del Plata, past a series of unremarkable beaches, the aquarium, and the red-and-white striped *faro* (lighthouse). Once away from the city, the landscape changes dramatically, with clusters of trees bent by the wind sheltering a few *balnearios* (beach clubs) and campgrounds. Rural restaurants beckon drivers with enormous signs; on weekends tourists congregate at the picnic tables near the fire pits where the aroma of roasting beef and goat stimulates appetites. A series of barrack-like red brick buildings appear suddenly at the side of the road, one of the results of Peronism's devotion to workers. These incongruous buildings are actually seaside hotels for members of labor unions.

Watch out for the treacherous *lomadas* (speed bumps) outside **Miramar**, about 45 km (28 miles) south of Mar del Plata. The city is called "The City of Children" and endless road signs and *lomadas* encourage drivers to proceed cautiously. The antithesis of Mar del Plata, Miramar has just 20,000 full-time residents and a completely relaxed attitude. Bicyclists ride in the middle of the street, often linking arms with friends riding motor scooters. The biggest thrill here is surfing — Miramar consistently has the highest, strongest waves along the coast. A few unsightly 1970s-style highrise apartment and condo buildings line the street across from the waterfront. The **Parque los Patricios** is a pleasant, grassy park with a small lake. Restaurants and shops line Calle 9 de Julio,

a pedestrian-only street running perpendicular to the sea. For a good, small hotel, try **Hotel Marina** ((2291) 420462, Avenida 9 No. 744.

The coastal road ends at Miramar, and Ruta 88 heads a bit inland as it runs south to **Necochea**, 130 km (80 miles) south of Mar del Plata. In summer, vast fields of sunflowers line the road like a scene from a Van Gogh canvas; Argentina is one of the world's main producers of sunflower oil.

Tiny Necochea has little interest for tourists seeking excitement. Its main attractions are the grass-covered sand dunes by the sea (popular with dune buggy enthusiasts) and the small waterfalls of the Río Quequén. The river is a favorite spot for boaters and for anglers seeking trout and mack-

erel. A cluster of shipwrecks litters the sand where the river meets the sea, and a colony of sea lions live nearby. Those wishing to spend a night in these calm surroundings have a few inexpensive hotels to choose from. The best are the **Hotel León** ((2262) 424800, Avenida 79 No. 229, and **Hotel Necochea** ((2262) 433255, Avenida 79 No. 217. The city has a WEB SITE www.necocheanet.com.ar.

BAHÍA BLANCA

Bahía Blanca is the largest city in the southern part of Buenos Aires Province, and marks the beginning of coastal Patagonia. It is home to an important Navy base and a large port and has about 300,000 residents. Few tourists visit this area, since the beaches are less attractive than those farther north and the nearby mountains less impressive than the Andes.

The most interesting attraction is the **Museo del Puerto** ((291) 457-3006, Calle Cárrega at Calle Torres. Devoted to detailing the history of immigration, the museum's exhibits focus on the history of the port, the railroad, and the beginnings of communities in the pampas. It's open on Saturday and Sundays only. The **Museo de Bellas Artes** ((291) 456-4157, Calle Alsina 65, displays works by Argentine artists, many focusing on gaucho themes. Several historical buildings are clustered around the **Plaza Rivadavia** at the center of downtown at Calle San Martín and Calle Alsina. Many copy the style of the belle époque palaces in Buenos Aires.

Bahía Blanca's **Tourist Information Office** ((291) 456-4234, Calle Alsina 45, is located close

Adventure travelers are drawn to **Sierra de la Ventana**, a small mountain village northwest of Bahía Blanca in the Sierras de la Ventana mountain range. The mountains peak is at 1,300 m (4,265 ft), though most of the range is far lower. The town is 124 km (77 miles) northwest of Bahía Blanca on Ruta 33. There are several hotels and restaurants in the town, and tour operators offer guided hikes in the mountains. There is public bus service from Bahía Blanca.

WHERE TO STAY AND EAT

Bahía Blanca's hotels are mainly geared toward business travelers. **Hotel Belgrano** ((291) 456-4404,

to the plaza. The information booth at the airport is open when flights arrive.

The Sierras de la Ventana mountain range breaks up the monotonous pampas terrain and provides worthwhile diversions for both locals and travelers. Just outside the small town of Tornquist, 76 km (47 miles) northwest of Bahía Blanca, the **Parque Provincial Ernesto Tornquist** is a 6,700-hectare (16,556-acre) natural park donated to the country by the wealthy Tornquist family. It is one of the most popular hiking areas in the region. A well-marked trail leads over 914 m (3,000 ft) up to **Cerro de la Ventana**, a 1,134-m-high (3,720-ft) peak that is a national historic monument. It takes about two hours to reach the top; rangers sometimes collect an entry fee. There is a campground at the entrance to the park. Tornquist is located on Ruta 33 and is accessible by public bus.

Calle Belgrano 44, is an inexpensive option just one block from the main plaza. Its 100 rooms are well maintained and have air-conditioning and private baths. There are several pizzerias and *parrilla* restaurants around the main plaza.

HOW TO GET THERE

Aerolíneas Argentina, Austral, and LAPA all serve the **Bahía Blanca Aerostación Civil Airport** ((291) 486-0319, located on the Navy base north of town. Buses from throughout the country arrive at the **Terminal de Ómnibus** ((291) 486-0319, Calle Brown 1700.

A traditional lifestyle prevails at *estancias* in the Pampas.

Meso-
potamia
(The
Northeast)

LIKE THE ORIGINAL FERTILE CRESCENT in the Middle East, Argentina's Mesopotamia is bounded by two great rivers, the Río Paraná and the Río Uruguay, which come together about 30 km (20 miles) north of Buenos Aires to form the Río de la Plata. Despite an abundance of big cites and sprawling farms, the region is still dominated by wetlands — marshes and swamps, lagoons and lakes, and thundering cascades like the incomparable Iguazú Falls. Two immense areas remain largely wild and untamed: the myriad islands and tributaries that comprise the Paraná Delta and the Esteros del Iberá marshes.

More than any other great river in South America, the Paraná was an avenue of conquest for the early Spanish, who established a string of forts and missions along her shores at places like Rosario, Santa Fe and Corrientes. Years later, the river provided convenient passage for the waves of European immigrants who arrived after independence, ambitious settlers who helped nurture these steamy subtropical outposts into the large modern cities they are today.

Three large provinces — Entre Ríos, Corrientes and Misiones — nestle along the Paraná's eastern bank while along its western edge sprawls another immense province called Santa Fe. Despite their geographic proximity, each flaunts a distinct personality. Much like neighboring Uruguay and the Pampas on the other side of the Río Paraná, Entre Ríos is dominated by large cattle *estancias*, a place where the gaucho culture endures — in spirit if not in fact. With its famous Carnival and laissez-faire attitudes, Corrientes likes to fancy itself as the country's "Little Brazil." Swathed in subtropical jungle and populated by a strange mix of Guaraní Indians and Germanic settlers, Misiones feels more like the Amazon than anything you would expect of Argentina. Santa Fe is a different animal altogether, an agricultural and industrial powerhouse with Mediterranean panache.

ROSARIO

Perched along the slow-flowing Río Paraná, Rosario is revered by Argentines as the "cradle of the flag" — the city where General Manuel Belgrano conceived the blue-and-white national banner in 1812. The city's most prominent feature is the Monumento Nacional de la Bandera, a waterfront landmark on the spot where the flag first fluttered.

But Rosario is more than just a historical footnote. With more than a million residents, it's Argentina's third largest city (after Buenos Aires and Córdoba) and in many respects the country's industrial hub.

Spaniards built a fort here in 1689 to protect navigation along the Paraná. Over the next century, a modest civilian settlement grew up outside the walls, a market town for the nearby haciendas and a thriving port for agricultural goods bound for Buenos Aires and beyond. Rosario didn't blossom into a full-blown city until after independence when it began to attract a steady flow of European immigrants. In 1870, the Central Argentine Land Company decided the best way to tansport the agricultural bounty of the Pampas — and stimulate even more settlement on its vast land tracts — was to build a railroad between Rosario and Córdoba.

The iron horse had the desired effect: hundreds of thousands of immigrants poured into the northern plains via Rosario and the city quickly burgeoned into a powerhouse of transport and industry. By the early twentieth century the population had breached 200,000 and Rosario had been dubbed the "Chicago of Argentina" because of its grain and beef exports and myriad factories that churned out steel, textiles, chemicals and leather goods.

The boom transformed Rosario from a rough-and-ready frontier town into a graceful European-style city with broad avenues and elegant architecture, inspired by French and Italian themes. Although many of the old buildings have given way to modern highrise structures over the last 30 years, much of the past remains intact, an enduring monument to Rosario's golden age. The city also has the distinction of being the birthplace of Communist revolutionary (and cultural icon) Ernesto "Che" Guevara, born in 1928 in an upper middle class townhouse at the corner of Entre Ríos and Urquiza in downtown Rosario.

Rosario hosts several annual festivals including **La Semana de la Bandera** (Flag Week) the third week in June which features patriotic speeches, parades and solemn ceremonies. The **Fiesta Nacional de las Colectividades** in November pays tribute to the nation's immigrants with two weeks of cultural events including traditional dance, music and art.

GENERAL INFORMATION

Ente Turistico Rosario (the tourist information center) ((341) 480-2230 FAX (341) 480-2237 E-MAIL etur@rosario.gov.ar is in the riverside park near the intersection of Belgrano and Buenos Aires. The staff is extremely helpful with hints on how to enjoy both the city and the Upper Paraná Delta. Be sure to pick up a free map with information on local beaches and islands. Open daily 9 AM to 7 PM.

Correo Argentina is on the south side of Plaza 25 de Mayo at Calle Córdoba 721. **Telefónica** on Calle Córdoba between San Martín and Maipú offers overseas and domestic calls as well as fax, Internet and stamps. **R.S. Computadoras** at Calle Roca 743 offers Internet access at US$2 per hour.

There are a number of places to change money along both pedestrian streets in downtown Rosario. If you need to top up your medical kit pop into the 24-hour **Farmacia Rosario** ((341) 426-1110, Calle San Lorenzo 1315.

WHAT TO SEE AND DO

Guide books tend to ridicule the huge **Monumento Nacional de la Bandera** (National Monument of the Flag) along Rosario's waterfront, but I've always found it rather striking, especially the robust murals and sculptures around the base. Erected between 1943 and 1957, the boat-shaped structure centers around a 70-m (230-ft) concrete "mast" on the spot where General Manuel Belgrano first raised the Argentine flag in 1812. An elevator zips visitors to the summit for panoramic views of the city and the broad Río Paraná. Other features include the **Cripta Belgrano** (where

the beloved general is buried) and the **Sala Banderas** where flags from various nations are on display. The monument is open Tuesday to Sunday 9 AM to 6 PM and Monday 2 PM to 6 PM.

Directly behind the monument is the **Pasaje Juramento**, a bridge that takes pedestrians across a large fountain garnished with imposing statues by Argentine sculptor Lola Mora. The passage empties onto the leafy **Plaza 25 de Mayo**, the heart of old Rosario and still surrounded by stout colonial and republican buildings. Dominating the square's eastern flank is the French-style **Cathedral of Our Lady of Rosario**, a late eighteenth-century basilica with an alter hewn from Carrera marble and a statue of the Virgin Mary brought from Spain in 1773. Next door is the attractive neo-renaissance **Palacio de los Leones** (Lions Palace), built in 1898 and now the Rosario city hall. The

A retired artillery piece proves a cool playground at the Monumento Nacional de la Bandera in Rosario.

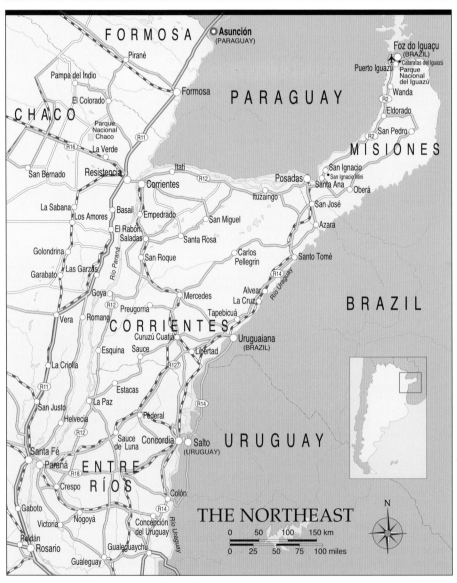

THE NORTHEAST

0   50   100   150 km
0   25   50   75   100 miles

N

Museo de Arte Decorativo Firma y Odilio Estevez
((341) 448-2544 on the plaza's north side contains
an eclectic collection that includes colonial paintings, Flemish tapestries, Bolivian silverwork and
Peruvian ceramics.

Downtown Rosario is dominated by two lively
pedestrian malls: **Calle Córdoba**, which runs from
Plaza 25 de Mayo to Calle Paraguay, and shorter
Calle San Martín. The streets are flush with restaurants, boutiques and department stores and are
especially busy in the late afternoon and early
evening when local university students crowd the
sidewalk cafés. A 15-block stretch of Córdoba
between Plaza 25 de Mayo and Boulevard Oroño
has been designated the **Paseo del Siglo** (Passage

of the Century) because it boasts so much of the
city's bygone architecture including the majestic
Bolsa de Comercio (stock exchange) which blends
art deco and neoclassical elements, the lovely
Victoria shopping arcade (even the McDonald's
fast-food outlet on the ground floor can't diminish its belle époque beauty), and a wonderfully
restored **Edificio Falibella** (1889) with its mock
Paris train station façade.

Rosario offers a number of other museums,
but only a few are really worth a look. The **Museo
Municipal de Bellas Artes Juan B. Castagnino**
((341) 480-2542, at the corner of Pellegrini and
Oroño close to the Parque de la Independencia,
boasts a small but impressive collection of Latin

American and European paintings and sculpture. El Greco and Goya are among the Old Masters represented here, but many of Argentina's best-known artists are also featured. Close by is the **Museo Histórico Provincial Doctor Julio Marc** ((341) 421-9678 in the Parque de la Independencia which details the history of Santa Fe Province from the pre-Colombian era through colonial times and the heady post-independence period.

Once dominated by warehouses and other port facilities, Rosario's waterfront has undergone major urban renewal in recent years. Pleasant riverside parks now stretch north and south from the Monumento Nacional de la Bandera. In the Parque de la Bandera is one of the best natural science collections on northern Argentina, the **Museo del Paraná y Sus Islas** ((341) 448-2136, which highlights the flora and fauna of the Paraná River and its myriad islands. Farther south is the sprawling Parque Urquiza, which has a small planetarium and various athletic facilities called the **Complejo Municipal Astronómico Educativo Rosario** ((341) 448-3084.

Farther upstream is a popular riverside beaches like **Rambla Catalunya** and **Balneario la Florida**, the latter at the foot of a red-rock ravine carved by a branch of the Río Paraná. The strands are crowded with sun-seekers on summer weekends and during school vacations, but virtually empty the rest of the year. **Paseo del Caminante**, a brand new riverside promenade, takes walkers and joggers along the ravine.

Daily in summer (weekends only the rest of the year) ferries run between Balneario la Florida and several islands in the Paraná Delta including **Isla Verde** (swimming, camping, restaurant) and **Isla Buenaventura** (swimming, fishing, walking trails, horseback riding). **Hayra S.R.L.** ((341) 449-8688 or (341) 425-1530 offers two-hour **river cruises** through the Paraná Delta on the modern *Ciudad de Rosario* from a wharf near the flag monument. Departures on Saturday at 5:30 PM; Sunday and holidays at 3 PM and 5:30 PM. The price is a steal: just US$5 per person.

SHOPPING

With very little in the way of local arts and crafts, Rosario isn't the best place in Argentina for a shopping spree. But the prices sure beat the pants off just about anything in Buenos Aires.

A broad range of regional handicrafts can be found at **Quebracho Artesanías** ((341) 449-5700 in the Galería del Paseo at San Martín 861. The selection includes ponchos, daggers, ceramics, *maté* paraphernalia, leatherwork and tapestries. There's even more gaucho gear at **Talabartería La Posta** ((341) 430-6359, Calle San Juan 3493.

Las Trancas ((341) 426-1658, in the Galería La Favorita at Calle Sarmiento 846, is one of the few shops that offers typical Argentine leather items including shoes, sandals, travel bags, breeches and vests, as well as traditional *criollo* silver items. Modern leather fashion including jackets, skirts and trousers is the forte at **Fabbro Factory** ((341) 482-2990, Calle Necochea 1760.

One of the city's most intriguing shops is **El Coleccionista** ((341) 449-2028, Calle Córdoba 884, which sells antique stamps, postcards, coins and paper money.

WHERE TO STAY

For a place of its size and stature, Rosario offers rather meager accommodation in every category. The best choices are the lodgings that keep you near the action of the thriving pedestrian malls. But none are very upscale.

Expensive

With hordes of visiting businessmen, Rosario boasts a number of good apartment hotels with facilities and prices that often surpass the local four-stars. For instance, the spiffy **Pringles Apart Hotel** ((341) 447-4050 E-MAIL pringles@lidernet .com.ar, Calle Santa Fe 1470 in downtown Rosario, offers rooms with air-conditioning, kitchenettes, and cable television and Internet connection with common facilities such as a solarium, swimming pool, laundry service and 24-hour room service.

Similar amenities and prices are found at the **Urquiza Apart Hotel** ((341) 449-4900 FAX (341) 449-1677 E-MAIL uah@apart-urquiza.co.ar, Calle Urquiza 1491. Both hotels slash their rates 40% to 60% on weekends for anyone who books ahead and stays at least two nights.

The **Hotel Presidente** ((341) 424-2545 FAX (341) 424-2789 E-MAIL solans@impsat1.com.ar, Avenida Corrientes 919, features both executive and regular suites. The marble-pillared lobby is rather cramped with the bar and dining area just a few meters apart. However, the secluded rooftop swimming pool seems much further away from the madding crowd.

Moderate

The city's best value for money is probably the **Hotel Plaza Del Sol** ((341) 421-9899 FAX (341) 426-4432 E-MAIL plaza@satlink.com.ar, in a red-brick tower at Calle San Juan 1055. Although they lack anything resembling a Latin American character, the rooms are certainly up to global standards of comfort and cleanliness. A gym and pool on the eleventh floor allow you a bird's-eye view of the city — you can ride a stationary bike while you people-watch along the pedestrian mall.

Once the pride of downtown Rosario, the **Hotel Libertador** ((341) 424-1158 TOLL-FREE (800) 5554-6835 E-MAIL solans@interactive.com.ar, at Avenida Corrientes 752, threw open its doors again in

February 2000 after a major renovation. Now part of the flashy Solans Empresa hotel chain, the modern makeover should put the Libertador back among the city's elite choices.

The **Nuevo Hotel Europeo** ((341) 424-0382 FAX (341) 424-0432 E-MAIL nuevonet@hotelnet .com.ar, Calle San Luis 1364, offers adequate rooms at moderate prices, although the lobby's musty aroma takes a bit of getting used to. There's a gym on the property.

If you don't mind screaming red decor, the **Benidorm Hotel** ((341) 421-9368 FAX (341) 426-5584, Calle San Juan 1049, is a very convenient place to stay in the heart of Rosario. Rooms here feature air conditioning and there is a cafeteria on

they're all clean and large enough to keep you from feeling claustrophobic like so many budget hotels. Some rooms don't have private baths.

Inexpensive bungalows are offered on several islands in the nearby Paraná Delta including **Isla Buenaventura** ((341) 156-425607 and **Isla del Frances** ((341) 453-1324 or (341) 155-473045. Camping is available on **Isla El Coyote** ((341) 481-4923 and **Isla Verde** ((341) 454-4684.

WHERE TO EAT

Expensive

In terms of both ambience and edibles, my choice for Rosario's best restaurant is **Amarra 702** ((341)

the ground floor. **Savoy Hotel** ((341) 448-0071 FAX (341) 480-0075, Calle San Lorenzo 1022, is located away from the pedestrian malls, but still within walking distance of all the important places in town. The lobby's threadbare carpet makes the place seem less inviting, but the belle époque façade is most pleasing to the eye. Rooms have air-conditioning, but no television.

Inexpensive

If a simple environment will suffice, try the **Hotel Bahía** ((341) 217271 FAX (341) 491290, Calle Maipú 1262. It's located across the street from one of the pedestrian malls and offers 24-hour room service and bar.

Hotel Normandie ((341) 421-2694 FAX (341) 440-0385, Calle Mitre 1030, is popular with young backpackers from all over the world. Some rooms don't have television or air-conditioning, but

421-0082, down along the riverfront at Avenida Belgrano 702. Like many Argentine restaurants, the menu runs a broad gamut from pasta and salad to humongous steaks and river fish. My favorite dishes include boneless chicken cooked in champagne, skewers of pork soaked in cognac and roast pork stuffed with a sweet fruit sauce. The location is equally enticing: a whitewashed colonial mansion cloaked in terracotta tiles.

The simple wooden tables and bright red table clothes conceal the fact that **Valentino** ((341) 482-6955, at the corner of Corrientes and Cochabamba, serves up the city's best Italian cuisine. Many of the pasta dishes are divine, and there's a fine selection of Argentine and Italian wines to wash everything down.

Rosario offers dozens of *parrilla* restaurants but the most elegant is **Nueva America** ((341) 426-9679, Calle Córdoba 2302. Don't let the name fool you: this is an Old World dining experience that includes great service and fine cuisine. The menu includes wonderful steak, river fish, seafood and pasta dishes.

Moderate

Rosario has a wealth of good mid-range restaurants, but the place I keep going back to again and again is **Puebla ¢** (341) 426-4988, Calle Mitre 715. The Franco-Iberian peasant decor — a melange of pottery, baskets and Toulouse-Lautrec prints — is what first caught my eye. But the food is equally appealing, hearty country dishes such as chicken with broccoli and potatoes, vegetable ravioli, and steak with stuffed tomato, bacon and spinach.

As the name suggests, **Puerto Picasso ¢** (341) 447-1037, Calle 3 de Febrero 2417, also draws its inspiration from the Mediterranean. The menu includes some of the city's most imaginative fare: *spaghettis negros a la calamarettis* (black pasta in squid sauce), *carre de cerdo en mostaza, oporto y miel* (roast pork in mustard, port and honey), and *tournedo de lomo as las cuatro pimientas* (loin of beef cooked in four different types of peppers).

Fratelli Express ¢ (341) 430-9700, in the Patio de la Madera at Calle Cafferata 729, combines a fun atmosphere (wacky modern mobiles and sculptures) with a tasty menu. Owners Guillermo and Marcelo Megna suggest the Mediterranean seafood salad followed by Patagonian style lamb and finished off with their famous tiramisu.

There are a number of restaurants along the Río Paraná waterfront that offer both indoor and al fresco dining. **Hemingway ¢** (341) 449-4626, on Avenida Belgrano near the flag monument, offers the city's best aquatic fare including delicious river fish and seafood. **La Misión del Marinero ¢** (341) 447-2315, at Calle Sarmiento 209 across the street from the riverside Parque España, offers one of Rosario's most romantic outdoor settings, especially after dark. Farther upstream is **Señor Arenero ¢** (341) 454-2155 on Avenida Costanera near the Balneario La Florida.

Inexpensive

One of the few places in northern Argentina that doesn't obsess on beef is **Rincón Vegetariano ¢** (341) 425-9114, Calle Mitre 720. That is not to say they don't have meat on the menu — there are a few low-calorie chicken and beef dishes — but vegetables, fruits, nuts and beans take center stage. Among the delectables are *milanesa de berenjena* (breaded eggplant), *canelone verdura* in white or mixed sauce, and *ensalada de arroz* (rice salad) with lettuce, tomato, eggs, carrots, mushrooms and beets.

La Vendetta ¢ (341) 424-2124 at the corner of Jujuy and Oroño is a diehard Italian pizza parlor

with funky decor and 40 different types of pie. Everything is made "al mejor estilo argentino" (the best Argentine way) which means that all pizza meats are barbecued in traditional *parrilla* style.

My favorite sidewalk café along the downtown pedestrian streets is **Francisco** at Calle Córdoba 1470, a great place to pick up an inexpensive breakfast, a sandwich in the middle of the day, or a quick bite in the evening. Their menu includes burgers, pizzas and steak sandwiches, plus an extensive drinks list that ranges from cognac and Cinzano through delicious *licuados* (fruit smoothies).

If it's fresh hot java you crave, pop into **Coffee Break** at Calle Paraguay 829. This cozy café, tucked between brick walls with vaulted arches, resembles a ruined monastery filled with the aromas of freshly brewed coffees from around the world. Ice cream and other frozen delights are the specialty at **Freddo** on the corner of Juan Alvarez and Roca. Buy something cold and munch on it across the street in the plaza.

NIGHTLIFE

One of the city's most happening spots in the **Shark Bar** on Calle Santa Fe (between Paraguay and Roca) where you can down ice-cold beer to the sound of current Latin American and gringo hits.

Philippe Starck meets Wild Kingdom in a trendy downtown bar called **Miscelanea ¢** (341) 447-0014 at Calle Roca 755. The decor is outrageous: entire walls painted like zebra stripes and cheetah spots, plush red velvet seats around wrought-iron tables. An extensive snack menu features the likes of onion rings, pasta and steak. But the best thing about Miscelanea is the after-dark people watching.

HOW TO GET THERE

Rosario is 312 km (200 miles) northwest of Buenos Aires in the Upper Paraná Delta. The quickest way to get there from the federal capital is via Ruta 9, a four-lane *autopista* (toll road) similar to a United States interstate highway but with a posted speed limit of 110 kph (about 75 mph). The drive takes about three hours.

Rosario's wonderfully restored **bus terminal** (Estación Terminal de Ómnibus Mariano Moreno) ¢ (341) 437-2384 is about 20 blocks west of downtown at the intersection of Santa Fe and Cafferata. There is frequent service to other northern Argentine cities including Buenos Aires (four hours), Santa Fe (two hours), Córdoba (six hours), Mendoza (10 hours) and Salta (16 hours). Companies with offices in Rosario include

The bounty of Argentina's heartland is sold along the streets of central Rosario.

Chevallier((341) 438-6034, **ABLO**((341) 439-7186, **TATA** ((341) 439-8493 or (341) 439-0901, and **La Unión** ((341) 438-0038.

Civic authorities like to brag that **Aeropuerto Internacional Rosario** ((341) 451-2997 is second only to Buenos Aires in overseas business, but in reality there are very few international flights other than to Rio de Janeiro and São Paulo in Brazil. There are daily flights to and from Buenos Aires on **Aerolíneas Argentinas/Austral** ((341) 424-9332 or (341) 424-9461, Calle Santa Fe 1410, and daily commuter service on regional airlines to Córdoba, Salta, Tucumán, and Mendoza.

SANTA FE

Long overshadowed by Rosario in terms of economic power and cultural stamina, Santa Fe has retained its political power as the capital of sprawling Santa Fe Province. And while its arch-rival Rosario fancies itself as the birthplace of the Argentine flag, Santa Fe cherishes its role as the guardian of the country's constitution. The historic Constitutional Congress of 1852–1853 took place here and the city has played host to four other conventions to amend the document, including a landmark meeting in 1994 that restored basic human rights after the downfall of the generals.

Despite its modern sheen, Santa Fe de la Vera Cruz (its full name) is one of the region's oldest settlements, founded by Juan de Garay and a Spanish military expedition dispatched from Asunción in 1573. The original site was about 30 km (20 miles) north of the present city, but it was difficult to defend and prone to flooding. A century after its birth, Santa Fe was moved lock, stock and barrel to the confluence of the Salado and Paraná rivers where it soon prospered into a market town and transportation node.

Modern-day Santa Fe is home to more than 350,000 people. But it still shoulders a certain small-town flair, a street-level congeniality absent from so many Argentine cities.

GENERAL INFORMATION

The best place to pick up maps and brochures is the **Dirección de Turismo** ((342) 457-4123 or (342) 457-1881 in the Terminal de Ómnibus at Calle Belgrano 2910. Open daily 8 AM to noon and 3 PM to 6 PM.

Correo Argentina's main branch is at the corner of Mendoza and 27 de Febrero near Plaza Blandengues. The **Telefónica** office at the corner of San Martín and Irigoyen Freyre offers international telephone service plus fax, stamps and Internet access.

There are numerous places to change cash and travelers' checks along Avenida San Martín

including **Citibank** at the corner of La Rioja. Medical supplies and prescription drugs are available at **Farmacia Cerda**, Avenida San Martín 2472.

WHAT TO SEE AND DO

Santa Fe has only one outstanding landmark, but it's one of the best historic sights in northern Argentina — **Convento de San Francisco** ((342) 459-3303 at the corner of San Martín and Amenábar, one block south of Plaza 25 de Mayo. Finished in 1680 and built to last, the complex boasts thick, whitewashed adobe walls and heavy wooden ceilings — the spitting image of the Californian missions erected almost a century later by the same

Franciscan order. The chapel is one of the most beautiful churches in Argentina, filled with ornately carved altars and capped by an intricate cedar roof that fits together like a puzzle. The remarkable central dome is called the *"cupula media naranja"* because it resembles a half orange. And don't be surprised if you suddenly hear tango tunes wafting from the chapel loudspeakers — the resident priests are big music fans.

The central courtyard is flush with all sorts of plants cultivated by the padres — corn, bananas, grapevines and dozens of flowers. Part of the cloisters is still used by the Franciscans as living quarters and is off-limits to the public. The convent **museum** offers an eclectic collection of spiritual and secular memorabilia including musical instruments, vestments, silverware, historical books and documents, portraits of colonial-era bigwigs and a full-scale wax diorama of the Constitutional

Conference of 1852–1853, which took place in this very building. The church and museum are open daily from 10 AM to noon and 3:30 PM to 6:30 PM. Admission free.

Outside the convent is the **Paseo de los Dos Culturas**, a leafy historical park dedicated to the indigenous and colonial inhabitants. Taking pride of place in the center of the park is a statue of Juan de Garay, the city's founder. In the park's northeast corner is the **Museo Etnográfico y Colonial (** (342) 459-5857 with displays on local Indian culture and colonial life. In the northwest corner and housed in a mission-style structure erected in the same year as the convent is the **Museo Histórico Provincial (**(342) 459-3760, which highlights the history and lifestyle of nineteenth-century Santa Fe including period furnishings, clothing and decorative arts.

Adjacent to the historical park is the city's most important square, the **Plaza 25 de Mayo**, surrounded by many of Santa Fe's most important civic and religious structures. The **Casa de Gobierno** (1909), built in the neo-Renaissance style so reminiscent of late nineteenth-century Paris, houses offices of the provincial government. The **Catedral Metropolitana** (1751) with its sky blue cupolas dominates the plaza's northern flank but isn't nearly as interesting as the much smaller and older **Iglesia de Nuestra Señora de los Milagros**, a whitewashed Jesuit church with Moorish domes that dates from the 1690s. One block west of the plaza is another fine colonial church, the **Iglesia de Santo Domingo** at the corner of 9 de Julio and 3 de Febrero, part of a Dominican convent.

Avenida San Martín runs north from the plaza into Santa Fe's modern commercial and entertainment area. Most of the action centers along a seven-block pedestrian mall between Garay and Eva Perón along which many of the city's finer shops and restaurants are arrayed. Many of the structures along this stretch date from the late nineteenth and early twentieth centuries, such as the attractive **Teatro Municipal Primero de Mayo (** (342) 452-1653 or (342) 453-7777 at San Martín and Garay. Built in 1905, the French belle époque-style landmark was heavily restored in 2000 and puts on a regular slate of drama, music and dance (including tango).

WHERE TO STAY

Moderate

Warm earth tones and pre-Columbian decorations greet you in the lobby of the **Hostal Santa Fe de la Veracruz (** (342) 455-1740 FAX (342) 455-1742 E-MAIL hostal_santafe@ciudad.com.ar, Avenida San Martín 2954. Each of the seven floors has a lovely stained-glass window at the end of the hallway, while the rooms are all air-conditioned.

Other perks include late checkout until 6 PM and cable television.

Hotel Conquistador ((342) 455-1195 FAX (342) 455-1196, Calle 25 de Mayo 2678, takes itself a bit too seriously. It's located a block off the main street in downtown. **Hotel Río Grande (** (342) 500700, Calle San Gerónimo 2586, is the priciest place in town, but worth it for the comfort.

The atmosphere is pleasant both inside and outside the **Castelar Hotel (** (342) 456-0999 FAX (342) 456-0999 WEB SITE www.hotelnet.com.ar, at the corner of 25 de Mayo and Cortada Falucho. With convenient access to the pedestrian mall, the 50-year-old hotel offers a tranquil patio area right outside the front door. The lobby is decorated with

cherry wood accents and it has a restaurant on the ground floor. Rooms have a clean and cozy feel with a small bathroom; the larger rooms have bathtubs and hardwood floors. **Gran Hotel España (** (342) 455-2264 WEB SITE www.ssdfe.com .ar/linverde, Calle 25 de Mayo 2647, offers comfortable rooms with breakfast included. The hotel has a swimming pool and gym for those who want to work out or relax.

Inexpensive

The eccentric **Hotel Emperatriz (** (342) 453-0061, Calle Irigoyen Freyre 2440, is my favorite in Santa Fe. Many of the rooms are small and dark, and both the air-conditioning and the bathrooms could do with a bit of modernization. But the building is a treasure: a rambling republican mansion built by nineteenth-century Spanish immigrants and decorated with heavy wooden furniture, wrought-iron chandeliers and antique mirrors.

Another good choice in the budget category is the **Hotel Hernandarias (** (342) 452-9752 FAX (342) 453-8188, Avenida Rivadavia 2680, which has 37 rooms.

OPPOSITE: Santa Fe's Convento de San Francisco reflects the region's Spanish colonial heritage. ABOVE: Pioneer days come alive at Santa Fe's Museo Histórico Provincial.

WHERE TO EAT

For genuine Old World atmosphere and wonderfully rich Italian cuisine it's hard to beat **Restaurant Circulo Italiano (** (342) 456-3555, on the ground floor of the Santa Fe Italian Club at Calle Hipólito Yrigoyen 2451. Nearly everything I have tried is absolutely delicious: fresh pasta dishes such as *canelone* and *ñoquis,* broiled or baked river fish such as *surubi* and *lenguado*, the *brochette de pollo* (chicken kebab) and the amazing *ensalada circulo italiano* with carrots, asparagus, ham and pineapple. They also offer a three-course *parrillada completa* at a very reasonable price. After dinner take a stroll through the 90-year-old club building.

Another good bet, especially for traditional barbecued meats, is **Parrilla La Brigadier (** (342) 458-3367, situated in an old mansion at Avenida San Martín 1670. Dig into a juicy *colita de cuadril* (beef cutlet) or *pollo agridulce* (sweet and sour roast chicken) in an atmosphere redolent of the city's golden days.

One of the city's most eclectic eateries is **Mi Casa (** (342) 456-4712, tucked in an ancient building at 2777 Avenida San Martín. The menu ranges from pampas favorites like *pechito de cerdo* (roast pork breast) to salads, fish and Chinese dishes.

Opposite the municipal theater at the lower end of the San Martín pedestrian street is a trendy joint called the **Ole Coffee Bar (** (342) 459-2083 with floor-to-ceiling windows and bright yellow, purple and turquoise decor. It's open from dawn until dusk serving great coffee and breakfast in the morning, light snacks throughout the day and then quick meals to the theater-going audience.

On a hot summer day duck into **Via Verona** at San Martín 2563, where ice cream becomes an art form. There are 24 flavors available in cones, sundaes or one-kilo (2.2-lb) drums.

HOW TO GET THERE

Santa Fe is 476 km (295 miles) north of Buenos Aires and 164 km (100 miles) north of Rosario via Ruta 9.

The **Terminal de Ómnibus** is on Calle Belgrano one block east of Plaza España. There is frequent bus service to Buenos Aires (six hours), Rosario (two hours), Córdoba (five hours), Corrientes (10 hours) and other northern cities. There is hourly service to the city of Paraná on the river's eastern bank. **Tata Rapido (** (342) 452-9953 offers frequent service to Rosario and other nearby destinations.

Aerolíneas Argentinas offers daily flights between Santa Fe and Buenos Aires from tiny **Aeropuerto Sauce Viejo**, 17 km (11 miles) south of the city center.

CORRIENTES

Famed both for its rowdy annual Carnival and sweltering subtropical climate, the pleasant riverside city of Corrientes lies near the confluence of the Paraná and Paraguay rivers. Although the highrise apartment buildings give it a modern gleam, this is actually one of Argentina's oldest towns, founded in 1588 by a military expedition dispatched from Asunción with orders to establish a garrison near the confluence of the Paraná and Paraguay rivers. Over the last 400 years, Corrientes has grown into a city of more than a quarter million people with an economy based on serving a vast agricultural hinterland and transporting commodities like beef, timber and *yerba maté* down river to Buenos Aires.

Carnival takes place the two weekends prior to Ash Wednesday and the start of Lent, usually in February, and the Corrientes version is considered the most risqué in all of Argentina. Grandstands are erected along a seven-block stretch of Avenida Ferré for fabulous Corso parade that includes samba bands, wonderfully decorated floats and thousands of scantly clad male and female dancers. The parades take place on Friday, Saturday and Sunday nights, starting around 9 PM and running until two or three in the morning. Admission prices range from US$3 for the worst grandstand seats to US$200 for special VIP boxes that include all-you-can-down champagne and caviar.

Although few people you meet on the street could tell you anything about Graham Greene, Corrientes is the sleepy riverside setting of *The Honorary Consul*, his fictional account of a backwater British diplomat kidnapped by Paraguayan revolutionaries. Graham visited the city twice, in 1966 and 1971, and also mentions Corrientes in *Ways to Escape*, his 1981 autobiography.

GENERAL INFORMATION

The folks at the **municipal tourist office (** (3783) 464504 are friendly and helpful, although they really don't have much in the way of maps or brochures. You'll find them in the Casa de la Ecología overlooking the waterfront on Avenida Costanera, one block south of the casino.

Corrientes is one of the few Argentine cities where United States dollars are not readily accepted outside of major hotels, so it's advisable to buy some pesos before wandering around. **Citibank (** (3783) 479607 offers money exchange and a 24-hour ATM machine at Calle Hipólito Yrigoyen 1602 (on Plaza Cabral) but there are lots of *cambios* throughout the downtown area.

Correo Argentina's main branch is at the corner of San Martín and San Juan. **Telefónica** offers overseas calls, fax and Internet service from offices at Calle Junín 1543 on Plaza Cabral and Avenida 3 de Abril 903.

WHAT TO SEE AND DO

Despite its age, Corrientes retains few of its colonial buildings. Most of the important civic and religious structures date from the post-independence period and are not nearly as striking as those found in Rosario or Santa Fe.

The city's oldest structure is the **Convento de San Francisco** overlooking the intersection of Mendoza and Quintana, not far from the river. Originally constructed in 1608, the convent was largely rebuilt in the early nineteenth century and then heavily restored in the 1930s. The chapel and the small museum are worth a quick look. Adjacent to the complex is a strange little park called the **Monumento a la Gloria** that honors local Italian immigrants. Running the length of the park and covering one of the outer walls of the convent is a extraordinary mural that details local history from pre-Hispanic times through the Republican period.

Two blocks west is the **Plaza 25 de Mayo**, the heart of nineteenth-century Corrientes. Among the structures surrounding the square are the Italian Renaissance-style **Casa de Gobierno** (1886) and **Iglesia La Merced**.

There are several small museums in the central city. The **Museo Histórico de Corrientes** at Calle 9 de Julio 1044 details the city's colonial and republican era with maps, documents, weapons, uniforms, furniture and decorative arts. The **Museo de Bellas Artes** at Calle San Juan 634 features a limited collection of Argentine painting and sculpture.

Perhaps the best thing to do in Corrientes is just stroll along the **waterfront** between Parque Mitre and the bridge. Day or night there's always something happening: fishermen mending their nets or setting off into the muddy Río Paraná; young lovers smooching on park benches; weekend revelers cruising up and down the Avenida Costanera in pickup trucks.

WHERE TO STAY

Expensive

The city's best and brightest is the brand new **Corrientes Plaza Hotel (** (3783) 421346, Calle Junín 1549, overlooking Plaza Cabral, which opened just in time for Carnival 2000. It's thoroughly modern and very friendly with a spacious lobby (that includes a restaurant and bar) and rooms with panoramic views of the plaza and downtown. Breakfast and parking are included in the rates.

Moderate

It may not be the best hotel, but the venerable **Hotel Turismo (** (3783) 433174 or (3783) 433190, Calle Entre Ríos 650, is still the city's most distinctive property. Opened in 1948, this waterfront hotel looks like something out of 1930s Southern California — swimming pool surrounded by slender palms, whitewashed walls cloaked in red-tile roofs and a spacious patio that overlooks the river. The lobby and corridors bask in dark, polished wood. Unfortunately the guest rooms aren't nearly as spiffy: peeling paint, clamorous air-conditioners, battle-weary furniture and threadbare carpets might detract from the romantic allure. But the price is right.

Smarter — but not nearly as romantic — accommodation is offered at the 12-story **Hostal del Pinar (** (3783) 429726 or (3783) 436100, a bit further up the waterfront at Calle Placido Martínez 1098. Rooms are rather blandly decorated, but still modern and comfortable; many offer superb river views. There's a rooftop terrace with swimming pool and a popular *parrilla* restaurant on the ground floor.

Visiting businessmen flock to two efficient hotels in the downtown area. The 67-room **Hotel Orly (** (3783) 420280 or (3783) 427248, Calle San Juan 867 off Peatonal Junín, offers rooms with cable television, air-conditioning, mini bar and direct-dial phones. A block away, the **Gran Hotel Guaraní (** (3783) 433800 FAX (3783) 424620 E-MAIL hguarani@espacio.com.ar, Calle Mendoza 970,

The mighty Paraná and Paraguay rivers flow together near Corrientes.

offers 143 well-appointed rooms as well as swimming pool, solarium and café.

Hotel San Martín ((3783) 421061 or (3783) 421068, Calle Santa Fe 955, occupies a commanding position overlooking Plaza Cabral, but it's a shadow of its former self, now a dark and dreary place that is best avoided unless nothing else is available.

Inexpensive

One of the best budget inns is **Hospedaje Brasil** ((3783) 442199, Avenida Maipú 2400, near the bus station; rooms come with private baths and hot water.

Alternative backpacker hangouts include the nearby **Hotel Caribe** ((3783) 469065, Avenida Maipú 2590, and **Residencial Necochea** ((3783) 426506, Calle Heroes Civiles 1898.

WHERE TO EAT

Restaurant Turismo ((3783) 433174 or 433190, Calle Entre Ríos 650, in the hotel of the same name is the city's most romantic dining venue, with outdoor tables on a stone terrace overlooking the Costanera boulevard and the river. Fresh pasta including gnocchi, vermicelli, ravioli and cannelloni is made twice a week by the resident pasta chef, but there are also lots of delicious beef and chicken dishes. Another specialty is grilled *surubi*, a huge Paraná river catfish that grows up to 48 kg (100 lbs).

Corrientes sports a number of good *parrillas* including **Las Brasas** ((3783) 435106 overlooking the river at the junction of Avenida Costanera and San Martín, where the steaks are always juicy and beer always ice cold. Another good choice is **Estancia Dona Ana** ((3783) 432657, Avenida 3 de Abril 1052, a big place with huge portions of various *asado* dishes and homemade pasta.

Surubi and other local river fish are prepared to perfection at **La Cueva del Pescador** ((3783) 422511, Calle Hipólito Yrigoyen 1255.

If you want really cheap eats, try the **food trailers** permanently parked along the Costanera opposite the casino and the Hotel Turismo. *Empanadas*, super *panchos* (hotdogs), sandwiches and ice cream dominate the menus.

Casino del Litoral has an outdoor beer garden called **La Chopería** that overlooks the busy Costanera waterfront.

HOW TO GET THERE

Corrientes is 1,041 km (645 miles) north of Buenos Aires via Rosario, Santa Fe and its sister city Resistencia, which lies on the west bank of the Río Paraná across the hulking Puente Belgrano bridge.

There are frequent buses to and from the city's **Estación Transporte Gobernador Gonzalez** ((3783) 462243 including service to Resistencia (30 minutes), Buenos Aires (14 hours), Posadas (five hours), Puerto Iguazú (10 hours). The terminal is on Avenida Maipú in the southern suburbs, a good taxi ride from most hotels.

Aeropuerto Camba Punta is just off Ruta 12 about 10 km (six miles) east of Corrientes. Aerolíneas Argentinas/Astral ((3783) 427442 or (3783) 423918 offers daily service to Buenos Aires (90 minutes).

POSADAS

Nestled on the south bank of the Río Paraná about halfway between Corrientes and Puerto Iguazú, the sleepy riverside city of Posadas has known three reincarnations. It was originally founded in 1615 as a Jesuit mission for the local Guaraní Indians, but the padres later move their compound over to Encarnación on the opposite bank. The remains of Posadas were later occupied by Paraguayan troops during that country's ill-fated attempt to cede northeast Argentina. The interlopers were expelled during the War of the Triple Alliance (1865–70), after which the modern town of Posadas was founded as a means to secure Argentine sovereignty over the region.

Like so many Argentine cities, waves of European immigration have given Posadas a decidedly Continental ambience with pleasant sidewalk cafés and leafy tree-lined streets. The quarter million inhabitants are the descendants of Italian, Spanish, German, Swiss and Eastern European immigrants, and they are most welcoming to the handful of travelers who manage to get this far off the beaten path. No shortage of hospitality here.

Truth be told, there are not that many reasons for lingering in Posadas itself. The city is primarily a gateway into southern Paraguay, the nearby Jesuit missions and the vast Esteros del Iberá marshlands.

GENERAL INFORMATION

As the capital of Misiones Province, Posadas is home base for the extremely efficient provincial tourist office — the **Secretaría de Turismo** ((3752) 447539 which maintains an information desk at Calle Colón 1985. English language brochures and maps are available in abundance. Open daily 8 AM to noon and 2 PM to 8 PM. There's also a tourism hotline TOLL-FREE (800) 555-0297 with information daily from 8 AM to 8 PM.

Cambio Mazza ((3752) 440505, Calle Bolívar 1932, can take care of most of your money-changing needs. Proper banks cluster around the Plaza 9 de Julio; several offer ATM machines and credit card cash advances.

The main **post office** is two blocks west of Plaza 9 de Julio, at the corner of Bolívar and Ayacucho. **Telecom** maintains an outlet for long distance calls, fax and e-mail service at the corner of Colón and Santa Fe.

For medical emergencies try **Hospital Madariasa (** (3752) 447000 at the junction of Lopez Torres and Cabral.

WHAT TO SEE AND DO

Strolling along the river has become problematic since the Yacyretá Dam starting backing up water along the Río Paraná in the mid-1980s, but you can still catch a pretty good glimpse of the water-

You can hop a local bus from the Terminal de Ómnibus at the corner of Mitre and Uruguay (they run about every 15 minutes between sunrise and sundown) or catch a taxi across the lengthy Puente Beato Roque Gonzalez. The view from the bridge is superb. Taxi driver **Julio Cesar (** (3752) 443553 charges US$20 for a morning or afternoon in Encarnación; he will assist with border formalities but speaks minimal English.

In the tradition of so many Latin American border towns, much of **Encarnación** is thoroughly rundown and most of the historic buildings are either gone or should be demolished. The main attraction here is shopping at prices that are often a third or half of comparable items in Argentina.

front from the **Parque República del Paraguay** at the good of Calle Colón (which turns into Calle Alberdi).

The city's oldest buildings (from the Republican period) cluster on or around the **Plaza 9 de Julio** in the middle of town, including the French neo-Gothic **cathedral** and the nearby **Gobernación** (provincial capitol). Although opinions differ, the only one of the local museums that merits a visit is the **Museo Arqueológico (** (3752) 435845, Calle General Paz 1865, which boasts artifacts from areas flooded by the Yacyretá project as well as exhibits and objects from the Jesuit period.

Posadas is the best place to pop across into **Paraguay** for the day. The border crossing at Asunción is often backed up with local traffic and the crossing to Ciudad del Este requires a detour through Brazil. By comparison, the traverse from Posadas to Encarnación is quick and painless.

Don't expect antiques and high-quality crafts. Most of the merchandise is unequivocal junk — cheap electronics and clothes, counterfeit CDs and knock-off watches, Chinese-made toys and Mexican-style black velvet paintings of Inca warriors or naked maidens. Once in awhile you come across something truly strange: musical condoms or Amazonian aphrodisiacs. But for the most part it's all fairly tame. The main shopping area is the crowded **market** which sprawls for blocks along Avenida Estigarribia between the waterfront and the bluffs. The shops around **Plaza Artigas** in the middle of town are a bit more upmarket. And you can pick up some good deals on traditional orange-colored ceramics at stalls near the Paraguayan end of the international bridge.

Rent a bike in Posadas and cycle across the international bridge into Paraguay.

The huge **Represa de Yacyretá** hydroelectric project, 90 km (54 miles) west of Posadas, is a whole different ball game, the introduction of ultramodern technology into what had previously been pristine wilderness and secluded ranchland. Slated to supply 40% of Argentina's electricity, the dam is often cited at a paragon of Third World graft and corruption. When construction started on the 1.5-km (one-mile) dam in 1983, the cost estimated was US$1.5 billion. The final cost will be something in the neighborhood of eight times that amount. Another controversial aspect of the project is the fact that the 200-km-long (124-mile) reservoir has displaced more than 40,000 people and drowned millions of animals along the Upper Paraná.

(there is no small irony in the fact that they called themselves the *Company* of Jesus).

Much like cattle, the Indians were rounded up and herded to the mission compounds where they were "broken" by a nefarious system called *reducción*, which included the abolition of their pagan ways and nomad lifestyles in favor of Christianity and economic slavery. The Jesuits taught the Guaraní all sorts of European skills — cultivation, animal husbandry, forestry, boat building, ceramics, carpentry, stonework and weaving — and then made huge profits from the goods produced by Indian labor.

Almost from the start, the missions were plagued by raids from Brazilian slavers, epidemics

Anyone who gets off on incredible engineering can take a free guided tour of the dam and hydroelectric by taking a public bus or taxi from Posadas to the **Centro de Relaciónes Publicas de Yacyretá-Apipe** ((3786) 420050 in the town of Ituzaingó. After a 10-minute video, a hydro company minibus whisks you off for an hour-long excursion. There are four tours daily Monday to Saturday and two tours on Sunday.

Jesuit Missions

Starting in 1607, the Jesuits created a network of 30 missions in the Upper Paraná Basin over a massive area of what is now northeast Argentina, southern Paraguay and southwestern Brazil. Ostensibly their main objective was converting the Guaraní and other local tribes to Catholicism. But the Jesuits were also keen businessmen who knew a golden opportunity when they saw one

of various European diseases (like smallpox) and squabbles with Spanish settlers who coveted the Jesuit's vast labor pool and land holdings. The Spanish crown expelled the Jesuits in 1767, the missions soon fell into ruin and the Guaraní wandered back to the forest, where they had to learn to fend for themselves in the jungle again after 150 years of Jesuit protection. The Jesuit era is somewhat romanticized in *The Mission*, a Hollywood film starring Robert De Niro, but it gives a good idea of what life for the *padres* and *indios* must have been like.

The best preserved of the Jesuit missions — and perhaps the most outstanding historic sight in all of Argentina — is **San Ignacio Mini** ((3752) 470186 in the village of San Ignacio, 59 km (32 miles) east of Posadas via Ruta 12. Heavily restored in modern times, the mission was founded in 1632 and thrived for more than a hundred years on *yerba maté* and other cash crops. Its central focus is a huge red-stone cathedral, now largely in ruins, that overlooks a grassy central plaza. Flanking the church are cloisters where the Jesuits lived and workshops for Guaraní artisans, and spread around the plaza are the remains of barracks where as many as 4,000 Indians once lived.

Don't miss the **museum** and its many creative displays, including a "jungle room" that shows what the area must have been like in pre-Hispanic times, a full-scale replica of a Paraná River caravel, and a spooky diorama that features 18 life-sized Jesuits. English-speaking guides loiter near the front gate. Admission. Open daily 7 AM to 7 PM.

WHERE TO STAY

One of the few places that affords views of the Río Paraná is **La Aventura** ((3752) 465555 or (3752) 460951 E-MAIL aventuraclub@arnet.com.ar at the junction of Urquiza and Zapiola. The wood-paneled *cabañas* have a rustic feel but not without sacrificing modern conveniences like air-conditioning and cable television. Other features include a small beach, kidney-shaped pool, outdoor snack bar, tennis courts and a restaurant that doubles as an after-hours pub.

You can't get any more central than the **Posadas Hotel** ((3752) 440888 FAX (3752) 430294 E-MAIL

Mission Santa Ana is mostly unrestored, an Argentine version of Angkor Wat — stone walls cloaked in jungle or cleaved by massive roots, lizards sunning themselves on tombstones and snakes slithering through the undergrowth. It was founded in 1660 and grew into one of the largest missions in the Jesuit realm, with a reputation for fine metalwork including arms with which the padres fended off their many enemies. Archaeologists didn't start reclaiming Santa Ana from the jungle until 1993 and the task is far from complete. The small site museum offers metal and ceramic artifacts, photos and maps. There are no English-speaking guides, but the curator is happy to give a full-length account of the Jesuit era in Spanish. Santa Ana is 45 km (27 miles) east of Posadas; look for the dirt road beside the CBSe Yerba Maté factory on Ruta 12 just before the village of Santa Ana. Admission. Open daily 7 AM to 7 PM.

hotelposadas@arnet.com.ar, situated just half a block off the Plaza 9 de Julio at Calle Bolívar 1949. It's hard to find two rooms with matching decor, but don't let that bother you. The hotel is clean, comfortable and convenient. Rooms include cable televisions, air-conditioning and mini bars, and there's a small snack bar/pub on the ground floor.

Best of the budget places is the cheerful **City Hotel** ((3752) 439401 or (3752) 433901, Calle Colón 280 overlooking the Plaza 9 de Julio. Rooms feel a little cramped, but some have balconies with views over the square and downtown Posadas. And there's a pretty good restaurant downstairs.

One of the few decent abodes on the Paraguay shore is the **Hotel Paraná** ((595-71) 4440 at Avenida Estigarribia 1414, just off the Plaza Artigas in

OPPOSITE: Mission San Ignacio Mini was the jewel in the Jesuits' crown. ABOVE: Sunset colors the watery wilds of the Esteros del Iberá wetlands.

downtown Encarnación. The rooms seem a little cramped and are badly in need of refurbishing, but downstairs you can sink into huge brown leather sofas or rack 'em up on the single billiards table. There's a spiffy French-run **Novotel** ((595-71) 4131, along Ruta 1 on the outskirts of town, but it's far away from the market areas and geared more toward business people on the Asunción–Encarnación circuit.

There aren't a lot of good campgrounds in the Posadas area, but one exception is **Paraíso de Ester** ((3752) 491012, Ruta 12 km. 11.5, about 500 m (550 yards) from the Garita de Posadas. You can pitch your tent in four hectares (nearly 10 acres) of parkland with picnic tables, barbecues, swimming pool, and shower blocks.

WHERE TO EAT

Posadas has its fair share of *parrilla* restaurants. Two of the best are along Calle Bolívar near the Plaza 9 de Julio: the highly recommended **La Ventana** at Bolívar 1725 and **La Querencia** at Bolívar 322. Expect huge portions and moderate prices at either establishment.

The trick is finding someplace that isn't totally dominated by meat and pasta dishes. **Mikele Bistro** ((3752) 423110, Calle Córdoba 474, offers a wide range of Southern European specialties including local river fish prepared with Mediterranean sauces or garnish. **La Aventura Restaurant** ((3752) 465555 or (3752) 460951, in the hotel of the same name at the junction of Urquiza and Zapiola, offers tasty *surubi* and *dorado* with views of the Río Paraná.

For lunch or dinner in Encarnación, try the lively **Cuarajhy** at the northwest corner of the Plaza Artigas. There's al fresco dining on the front terrace (if you can stand the traffic noise) and much quieter eating inside. The menu doesn't differ all that much from a typical Argentine *parrillada* with barbecued meats as the central focus. But the prices are conspicuously lower than the on other side of the river.

HOW TO GET THERE

Posadas is 310 km (192 miles) east of Corrientes and about 300 km (185 miles) southwest of Iguazú Falls along Ruta 12.

Buses run frequently to both cities from the new **Terminal de Ómnibus** at the junction of Ruta 12 and Avenida Santa Catalina. Express buses take about five hours to either Corrientes or Iguazú. Many of the Iguazú services stop in Santa Ana and San Ignacio, where you can visit the missions and then hop the next bus that comes along. A number of companies offer long-distance service to Buenos Aires (15 hours) and other major Argentine cities including **Via Bariloche**

((3752) 455599 or (3752) 434737, **Río Uruguay** ((3752) 455833 and **Expreso Singer** ((3752) 424771.

Aeropuerto San Martín ((3752) 451903 on the outskirts of Posadas offers daily service to Buenos Aires (90 minutes) on Aerolíneas Argentinas/Austral ((3752) 433340 and LAPA ((3752) 440300. There is also weekly air service to Corrientes, Formosa and Iguazú.

PUERTO IGUAZÚ

This sleepy town at the confluence of the Iguazú and Paraná rivers anchors Argentina's northeast corner. Most people use Puerto Iguazú as a staging point for visits to the cataracts and nearby Brazil rather than as a destination in its own right. But that's not to say the place doesn't have its own special small-town charm. Local residents seem to be a lot more amiable to visitors than in Foz do Iguaçu across the border. Due to low-priced competition in Brazil, prices for accommodation, food and other expenses are incredibly reasonable in Puerto Iguazú compared to the rest of Argentina. Gas, for instance, is 50% less expensive than in other Argentine cities.

GENERAL INFORMATION

There's a very friendly and informative **Secretaría de Turismo** information office ((3757) 420800 in the heart of town at Avenida Aguirre 396. The English-speaking staff can give out maps and brochures as well as information on local hotels, travel agencies, adventure sports and formalities for crossing to the Brazilian side. Open weekdays 8 AM to noon and 3 PM to 8 PM and weekends 8 AM to noon and 4:30 PM to 8 PM. Misiones Province tourism authorities also offer a free tourist **information hotline** TOLL-FREE (800) 555-0297, which operates daily 8 AM to 8 PM.

The local branch of **Correo Argentina** is at Avenida San Martín 780. The **Telecom** office at the corner of Aguirre and Eppens offers long-distance calls as well as fax and Internet service.

There are a number of places to change money along Avenida Aguirre in the middle of town including **Cambio Dick** ((3757) 420778 at No. 471. There's another *cambio* next to the Aerolíneas Argentinas office on Avenida Aguirre and a local branch of **Banco Nación** at the corner of Aguirre and Schwart. Just down the block from the bank is the **Puerto Iguazú Hospital** for medical emergencies.

The **Brazilian Consulate** near the corner of Guaraní and Esquiu is where citizens of the United States, Australia, Canada, Mexico, Japan and Russia can pick up their Brazilian visas. The fee for United States passport holders is a whopping US$58, even if you're only going across the border for a couple of hours. The consulate staff is generally unfriendly, unhelpful and unsympathetic.

TOURS

Puerto Iguazú is chock full of travel agents who specialize in cataract tours and adventure trips into the wilds of Misiones Province. **Turismo Dick** ((3757) 420778 FAX (3757) 420152 E-MAIL turismo dick@interiguazu.com.ar, Avenida Aguirre 226, is one of the oldest and most reliable, with daily excursions to both the Argentine and Brazilian falls. They also offer trips to the Wanda mines, San Ignacio ruins, Ciudad del Este in Paraguay and jungle horseback riding.

Explorador Expediciónes ((3757) 421600 E-MAIL rainforest_exp@interiguazu.com.ar, Calle Perito Moreno 217, specializes in ecological tours and photo safaris into the national park and other jungle areas. They can also arrange bird watching, rafting, biking and kayaking trips.

One of the best for arranging visits to Guaraní Indian villages is **Pasto Verde** ((3743) 493178 E-MAIL pasto_verde@yahoo.com in Salto Capiovi. **Aguas Grandes** ((3757) 421140 FAX (3757) 423096 E-MAIL aguasgrandes@interiguazu.com.ar can also arrange Guaraní visits as well as excursions to the Saltos del Moconá waterfalls in eastern Misiones Province, the longest cascade in South America.

Iguatur ((3757) 420004 FAX (3757) 421116 offers one of the area's best all-inclusive tours: an 11-hour marathon journey to the Brazilian falls, the town of Foz do Iguaçu, the Itaipú hydroelectric project and Ciudad del Este, Paraguay all for only US$30.

Private car tours across the border into Brazil and Paraguay can be arranged through **Remises Ecología** ((3757) 421852. A full-day excursion to the Brazilian side costs US$75; for another US$15 you can tack on Ciudad del Este and Itaipú Dam in Paraguay. Remember that citizens of many countries (including the United States, Canada and Australia) require a visa to enter Brazil, even for a few hours (see GENERAL INFORMATION, above).

WHAT TO SEE AND DO

If you take away the falls, there really isn't much reason to visit Puerto Iguazú. Foremost among local attractions is **Guira-Oga**, a center for the study and captive breeding of raptors and other endangered birds located off Ruta 12 behind the Orquídeas Palace Hotel. Launched in 1997, the center sprawls across 22 hectares (54 acres) of jungle under the aegis of nonprofit Asociación Ornitológica del Plata (AOP) and includes special enclosures for birds confiscated from collectors or found injured. It offers an excellent chance to see species like the black-hawk eagle that are usually difficult to observe in the wild.

There are a couple of small, very specialized museums that could warrant a visit. **Museo Automotor** at Camping Viejo Americano on Ruta 12 displays the private vehicle collection of the campground owner including vintage race cars and motorcycles. **Museo Mbororé** at Avenida San Martín 231 showcases local Guaraní Indian culture with photos, artifacts and handicrafts. **Museo Imagenes de la Selva** at the corner of Los Cedros and Guatambú (one block up from Avenida Aguirre) sports a small but interesting collection of native woodcarvings.

For stunning views of the confluence of the Iguazú and Paraná — the place where Argentina, Brazil and Paraguay come together — take a stroll through the park along Avenida Río Iguazú. The Argentina side is marked by a small blue-and-white pyramid called the **Hito Tres Fronteras**. Adjacent to the monument is a small collection of souvenir stalls called the Corredor Artesanal.

The **Wanda Mines** (Minas de Wanda) make a great half-day trip from Iguazú. Semiprecious stones like agate, topaz, quartz and amethyst are extracted from massive geodes formed millions of years ago by gas or water bubbles trapped inside lava flows. The lode was accidentally discovered in the 1950s by a couple of brothers farming a small patch of land overlooking the Río Paraná.

The lighthouse-like observation tower in Parque Nacional del Iguazú.

They later had a falling out, hence the presence of two separate companies working a single mineral field — **Compañía Minera Wanda** and **Compañía Tierra Colorada**.

There is very little difference between the free tours or the overstocked gift shops at either location. Merchandise runs a gamut from elegant jewelry pieces and exquisite geodes to tacky paperweights and raw chunks of stone. Prices are lower than for comparable items in Buenos Aires, but not much. Wanda is 43 km (26 miles) from Iguazú along Ruta 12. The mines are about two and a half kilometer (one and a half miles) down a bumpy dirt road, but the turnoff is well-marked and there are always touts or children more than glad to show you the way for a small fee.

SHOPPING

With so many tourists, especially from neighboring Brazil, one would figure that Puerto Iguazú would overflow with tacky souvenir outlets. Such is not the case. The pickings, in fact, are a little slim.

The arcade at the **Hotel Esturión**, Avenida Tres Fronteras 650, offers half a dozen shops with good-quality Argentine arts and crafts. Just up the road at the Hito Tres Fronteras monument is the **Corredor Artesanal** with more than a dozen open-air stalls selling low-price souvenirs.

The stretch of **Avenida Aguirre** between the tourist office and Calle Alvar Núñez has several small artisan shops as well as street vendors selling inexpensive bangles, necklaces and earrings made with semiprecious stones from the nearby Wanda mines. A little, nameless, gift shop at No. 286 hawks a small but good variety of local souvenirs like T-shirts, baskets and *yerba maté* packets.

You may not be able to take them home, but the **Orquídiario del Indio Solitario** at Calle Jangadero 719 sells a wonderful selection of orchids and other regional plants. The nursery is located in the Villa Nueva neighborhood, three blocks from the Hito Tres Fronteras monument.

WHERE TO STAY

Expensive

When all factors are taken into consideration, the best place to stay in town is the **Hotel Esturión** ((3757) 420020 or (3757) 420232 FAX (3757) 420414 on a bluff overlooking the Iguazú River at Avenida Tres Fronteras 650. The Esturión has everything I demand of a large, modern hotel including expansive gardens, large pool, good-sized rooms (many with balconies overlooking the river), a pretty good restaurant,

good souvenir shops, and a friendly staff. The rooms are a little worn (they could do with new carpets and furniture) but they are clean and comfy. This is also a good place to stay if you're traveling with the kids: the Esturión has its own playground and small petting zoo with ponies, rabbits and monkeys.

On the highway down to the falls is the huge **Hotel Cataratas** ((3757) 421100 or 421090 E-MAIL hotel.cataratas@fnn.net, Ruta 15 km 5, which offers similar architecture but none of the Esturión's quirky charm. However, sports facilities are excellent, including swimming pool, tennis courts, health club, volleyball and sauna.

Anyone who can't leave their luxury behind during a trip to the wilderness can check into the five-star **Iguazú Grand Hotel & Casino** ((3757) 498000 or (3757) 498050 FAX (3757) 498060 on Ruta 12 near the Argentina–Brazil border station and bridge. There isn't much in the way of rainforest ambience, just plenty of ways to lose your money.

Moderate

With so much competition from Brazil, Puerto Iguazú offers loads of hotels in the moderate category. My personal favorite — maybe one of the best little hotels in Argentina — is the **Orquídeas Palace** ((3757) 420472 or (3757) 420195 E-MAIL orquideashotel@orquideashotel.com WEB SITE www.orquideashotel.com. Situated in lush gardens on the southern edge of town, this is actually the second closest hotel to the falls (after the Sheraton). But that's not the only reason to stay here. Run by a congenial Swiss-Italian woman named Andrea, the place is both immaculate and charming. Rooms are outfitted with lovely bedspreads and matching drapes, as well as mini bar, air-conditioning and cable television. *Cabañas* are also available. The hotel restaurant offers a good tourist menu at lunch and dinner. Even though she's largely confined to a wheelchair, Andrea still tends most of the orchids and other tropical plants in the garden and makes local treats like *dulce de mamón* and *guayaba*, sold at the front desk.

Another good bet is the **Hotel Saint George** ((3757) 420633 FAX (3757) 420651 E-MAIL hotel saintgeorge@interiguazu.com.ar WEB SITE www .hotelsaintgeorge.com, Avenida Córdoba 148 in the middle of town. The rooms are modern, comfortable and nicely decorated; the staff is helpful and the swimming pool is surrounded by verdant tropical gardens. If the Saint George is full, try the nearby **Alexander Hotel** ((3757) 420249 or (3757) 420566, Avenida Córdoba 222, which has similar amenities and prices.

Inexpensive

Best of the bargain abodes is the popular **Hostería Los Helechos** ((3757) 420338, which is surrounded by tropical trees at Calle Paulino Amarante 76. The architecture is sort of Spanish Mission meets 1950s Arizona, with a restaurant/bar off the lobby and a small pool out back. Rooms are simple but clean and have private baths. Rooms with cable television and air-conditioning are slightly more.

A couple of blocks away is another good budget bet called the **Hotel Tierra Colorada** ((3757) 420572 or (3757) 420649 at the corner of Avenida Córdoba and Calle El Uru. All of the 30 rooms have private baths; some have air-conditioning and others fans. Nearby is the highly recommended **Residencial Paquita** ((3757) 420434, Avenida Córdoba 158, which has rooms with private bath, air-conditioning and balconies.

There are lots of small hostels scattered around town where overnight prices barely breach double digits. One of the most central is **Hotel Bompland** ((3757) 420965, Avenida Bompland 33, near the tourist office. Nothing fancy, but the price includes private bath and breakfast.

Other choices include **Residencial El Trebol** ((3757) 420356, Calle Curupi 53 near the Anglo American College; and **Residencial Familiar Noelia** ((3757) 420729, Calle Fray Luis Beltran 119, a couple of blocks from the bus station. Both offer rooms with private bath. All offer simple rooms with private bath.

Puerto Iguazú offers a number of places where you can pitch a tent. **Camping Viejo Americano** ((3757) 420190, at the southern end of town at Ruta 12 km 5, primarily caters to auto campers, but also has space for backpackers and walk-up visitors. Facilities include showers with hot water,

a swimming pool, a playground and general store. Bungalows and *cabañas* are also available. Nearby is the smaller but similar **Camping El Pindo** ((3757) 421795, Ruta 12 km 3.5. Half an hour south of town, on the shores of Lake Uruguai, is **Camping Uruguai** ((3757) 420380 or 420778 which offers horseback riding, nature trails, swimming, fishing and other recreation. There's also a small *parrilla* restaurant and a general store.

WHERE TO EAT

Moderate
One of the most popular places in Puerto Iguazú (and my personal favorite) is **La Rueda** ((3757)

422531, Avenida Córdoba 28. The extensive menu includes freshwater fish dishes like *dorado a la rueda* with a pepper, onion, tomato and cheese sauce, and *surubi garganta del diablo* stuffed with palm hearts, prawns, mushrooms and beans. There's loads of homemade pasta dishes (try the scarparo or pesto sauces) as well as *parrilla* meats. For dessert try a local sweet called *dulce de mamón* (fresh papaya slices smothered in *dulce de leche*). Sit in the air-conditioned dining room or outside on the terrace.

Right up the road is another veteran eatery, **Gran Parrilla Charo** ((3757) 421529, Avenida Córdoba 106, with a full range of barbecued meats and pasta dishes like vegetarian cannelloni and chicken or meat gnocchi. They've also got *surubi* and other local river fish.

The Wanda mines are a treasure trove of semiprecious stones formed inside geodes.

Inexpensive

Another stalwart of Puerto Iguazú's "restaurant row" is **Parrilla Pizza Color** ((3757) 420206, Avenida Córdoba 135. Barbecued meat is the specialty here including *bife de chorizo, mollejas, chinchulin* and roast chicken.

El Quincho Tío Querido ((3757) 420027, on Avenida Bompland next to the hulking Hotel Libertador, is a pleasant little place with al fresco dining beneath papaya trees. It's a cool place to hang on a hot night, and there's often music wafting across the patio. The menu includes *lomitos, empanadas*, various *milanesas*, river fish, burgers, hotdogs and ice cream. The three-course "menu turistico" is very reasonably priced.

Municipal workers flock to a modest little restaurant called **El Criollito** ((3757) 421622, in the red-brick building at Avenida Tres Fronteras 106 next to the city hall, for inexpensive pasta, *milanesas*, sandwiches and burgers. If you like loud music and lively atmosphere with your food, try **Blanco Parais** ((3757) 422534, Avenida Aguirre 262, where you can munch pizza, steaks and burgers in the outdoor beer garden to the strains of live *cumbia* music in the evenings.

HOW TO GET THERE

Puerto Iguazú is 1,464 km (907 miles) north of Buenos Aires via Rosario and Corrientes. An alternative route is taking Ruta 14 up the Río Uruguay valley via Gualeguaychú, Concordia and Santo Tomé.

Puerto Iguazú's overland **bus station** is located on Avenida Córdoba in the heart of the city. Several companies make the long haul (22 hours) to Buenos Aires including **Expreso Singer** ((3757) 421581, **Via Bariloche** ((3757) 420916, and **Crucero del Norte**. More than a dozen companies make the short haul from Puerto Iguazú to Posadas (six hours). There is also daily service to other northern cities like Corrientes, Resistencia, Córdoba, Santa Fe and Salta. **Pluma** is the only bus line with direct service from Puerto Iguazú to Brazilian destinations including Rio de Janeiro, São Paulo, Curitiba and Florianápolis.

Most international visitors reach Puerto Iguazú by air from Buenos Aires and elsewhere. The **airport** is situated about 15 minutes outside town near the entrance to the national park. **Aerolíneas Argentinas/Austral** ((3757) 420036 or (3757) 420168 offers daily service to Buenos Aires and Córdoba. Their ticket office is at Avenida Aguirre 295 near the tourist office. There is an inexpensive shuttle bus from the airport to the bus terminal in the middle of town.

Long-distance bus service and flights to various Brazilian destinations are also offered from Foz do Iguaçu on the Brazilian side of the border.

IGUAZÚ FALLS

The name means "big water" in the language of the Guaraní Indians, but you don't realize just *how* big until you see Iguazú Falls for the first time. Angel Falls in Venezuela might be higher, but this is South America's most spectacular cascade, a raging wall of water that plunges 80 m (230 ft) off the edge of a basalt plateau. The average flow isn't nearly as great as Niagara Falls (5,663 m^3/200,000 ft^3 versus 1,727 m^3/61,000 ft^3 per second), but Iguazú is much more impressive at close range — a shimmering necklace of 275 separate falls divided by emerald-green jungle islands that stretches four kilometers (two and a half miles) between the northeast tip of Argentina and one of the southern extremes of Brazil.

The Guaraní believe the falls were formed by supernatural beings that once walked the earth. An evil forest god kidnapped an Indian maiden and took her deep into the jungle. Her boyfriend, a young Indian warrior, eventually rescued the maiden. They escaped in a canoe down the Río Iguazú, but the forest god used his magic powers to cleave the riverbed, creating a giant waterfall over which the Indian warrior and maiden plunged to their deaths.

Geologists spin a much different tale. About 100,000 years ago, during the Triassic Era, a massive lava flow covered much of southern Brazil, Paraguay and northern Argentina. Plate tectonics created a huge fault in the lava along the path of the present-day Río Paraná. Over thousands of years the Paraná gradually wore away the soft bedrock covering the basalt, creating precipitous cliffs on either side. The tributary called the Río Iguazú began to plunge over one of these cliffs, creating the great falls. Slowly but surely, erosion carved a deep gorge along the Río Iguazú, pushing the falls farther and farther east to their preset location, 29 km (20 miles) upstream from the confluence of the Paraná and Iguazú rivers.

The Guaraní and other local Indian groups have known about the falls for thousands of years. The first Europeans didn't arrive until 1541, when an expedition under the command of Alvar Núñez Cabeza de Vaca stumbled upon the cataracts during a journey from the Atlantic coast to Asunción in Paraguay. The Jesuit missionaries who dominated the upper reaches of the Paraná Basin during the seventeenth and eighteenth centuries knew about the falls. Their closest mission was at Santa María, only a few kilometers upstream from the cascade, and the falls featured prominently in a Robert De Niro movie called *The Mission* about the Jesuit epoch.

In 1882, Swiss Italian explorer Giaccomo Bove "rediscovered" the falls with help from local guide Carlos Bossetti. Twenty years later, the Argentine government dispatched an expedition to study and survey the falls. This was around the same time that John Muir and Teddy Roosevelt were advocating protection of natural wonders in the United States. Picking up on that rift, expedition leader Carlos Thays recommended that Iguazú Falls be turned into a national park for the enjoyment of future generations. The national park on the Argentine side was created in 1934 and now covers about 67,000 hectares (165,560 acres).

The banks of the Río Iguazú above and below the falls are cloaked in thick subtropical rainforest that harbors an incredible variety of plant and animal species, many of them endemic to the region. More than 2,000 plant species (including

deciduous trees. For an in-depth discussion of Iguazú's flora and fauna, get a copy of *Iguazú: The Laws of the Jungle*, by Argentine naturalist Santiago G. de la Vega (available in Spanish and English).

GENERAL INFORMATION

An entrance fee of US$5 per person is collected at the national park **entrance station** on the road from Puerto Iguazú. Payable in Argentine pesos or United States dollars.

The **Centro de Informes** visitor center ((3757) 420180 near the falls is a treasure chest of information on the falls and the surrounding forest. Multilingual rangers staff an information desk,

85 different orchids), 500 types of butterfly, 448 bird varieties and 80 kinds of mammals have been recorded in the national park.

Among the animals that call the Iguazú forest home are predators like jaguars and pumas, large terrestrial browsers like tapirs and peccaries, arboreal mammals like capuchin monkeys and tree anteaters, and a wide variety of spectacular birds including toucans, parakeets, falcons and vultures. Below the falls, the Río Iguazú teams with amazing fish like the piranha, *dorado* and *surubi*, as well as caiman and numerous aquatic bird species.

Iguazú's subtropical forest differs from tropical forest in several ways: there are no distinct dry and rainy seasons, which means that Iguazú's average annual rainfall of 2,000 mm (79 in) is spread evenly across the year; humidity and temperatures are lower than tropical rainforest; there is less biodiversity but a much greater number of

passing out free maps and brochures. Open daily 7 AM to 8 PM. The complex also houses a natural history museum, a small theater with slide shows on various aspects of the park, a snack bar and a scientific research station that specializes in subtropical rainforest studies. Souvenirs are available at a small craft shop and Guaraní Indians who spread their wares across blankets on the visitor center veranda. Nearby is a small food court with about half a dozen stalls. A **Telecom** kiosk in the parking lot offers long-distance and overseas telephone service.

A huge new visitor center is currently under construction south of the present site with scheduled opening sometime in 2001. It will include a natural history interpretation center and visitors services including craft shops and food outlets.

River trips are the best way to experience the power and glory of Iguazú.

Also in the works is a natural-gas powered tramline from the new visitor center to a future network of foot bridges above the falls, which will lead visitors to a point directly above the Garganta del Diablo.

Rangers occasionally lead **guided walks** along the edge of the falls and through the nearby forest. One of the most popular is a night walk along the Upper Circuit on full-moon evenings. Check the bulletin board at the visitor center for current schedules.

Private guides are also available. They usually lounge on the veranda right outside the visitor center's main entrance and are fully licensed by the Argentine national park service. Expect to pay about US$30 for a two to three hour stroll along both the Upper and Lower Circuits. If you need an English speaking guide try **Ingrid Zabala** ((3757) 423195, a naturalist (originally from Buenos Aires) who's been showing people around Iguazú for more than a dozen years.

WHAT TO SEE AND DO

Pick up a map at the visitor center and strike off on one of the trails leading to the falls. Plan your own route or take one of the well-worn circuits. No matter which way you walk, make a point of climbing to the top of the lighthouse-like **observation tower** near the visitor center for a panoramic view of the falls and the Brazilian shore.

Much of the 1.8-km (slightly over a mile) **Lower Circuit** (Circuito Inferior) has been replaced since 1992, when a flood wiped out most of the old trails and bridges. Brand-new metal stairs plunge down the jungle-shrouded hillside to a tourist service area with an air-conditioned snack bar, restrooms and outdoor tables. From there, the trail leads off to the left to an observation platform next to **Lanusse Fall**, which tumbles straight into the reddish-brown Río Iguazú. A metal bridge leads across the front of **Alvar Núñez Fall**, named after the Spanish explorer who "discovered" Iguazú in 1541. This is a great place to catch a glimpse of the swifts that nest behind the curtain of water.

Continuing along the same trail, you eventually round a bend onto a stunning view that takes in almost all of Iguazú in a single glimpse, from super-wide **San Martín Fall** on the right and straight up the gorge to the Garganta del Diablo (Devil's Throat). Farther along is a mist-drenched observation platform at the base of **Bossetti Fall**, a great place to cool off if you're already drenched with sweat. From here a secondary trail leads down to the river where you can catch a free shuttle boat over to Isla San Martín (see below). The main trail loops back through thick tropical forest — with glimpses of **Dos Hermanos Fall** — to the Lower Circuit snack bar where you can chill out with an ice-cold drink.

The 800-m (half-mile) **Upper Circuit** (Circuito Superior) follows wooden catwalks across the top of several major cascades including Bossetti and **Mbigua Fall** to an observation deck that poises precariously above **Adam and Eve Fall**. The catwalk once continued to a perch above San Martín Fall, but was washed away in the 1992 flood and is currently being reconstructed. Still, the views from the Upper Circuit bridges and platforms are incredible, a panorama of rainbows, rising mist and raging water that seems to stretch into infinity.

For an altogether different view, hop the free shuttle boat to **Isla San Martín**, not really an island so much as a basalt peninsula that protrudes from the middle of the falls. From the beach, a steep trail leads up and across the island to a point where you can view San Martín Falls at close range. Isla San Martín's little sandy beach provides the only safe swimming in the Río Iguazú. The boat service operates daily from 8 AM to 4:30 PM. The last return is at 5:30 PM.

Anyone craving an amazing bird's-eye view of **Garganta del Diablo**, the tallest and wettest of the 275 cataracts that comprise Iguazú, venture to **Puerto Canoas** on the Upper Iguazú River, where you can catch a motor boat across to a small island behind the savage falls. A catwalk leads to the very edge of the abyss, a vertigo-inducing glimpse right down through Satan's jaws. The boat trip costs US$4 per person and takes about five minutes. From the visitor center you can take a taxi (US$10 round trip) or the Transportes Cataratas shuttle bus (US$2) to Puerto Canoas.

Away from the cataracts, Iguazú National Park offers several hiking routes through virgin rainforest. The most accessible is the **Sendero Macuco**, a five-and-a-half-kilometer (three-mile) path that leads from the park's main access road to Arrechea Falls on the Lower Iguazú. The trailhead is adjacent to the Centro de Investigaciones Ecológicas Subtropicales (Center for the Investigation of Subtropical Ecology) between the park entrance station and the Sheraton hotel. Far from the madding crowds that frequent trails adjacent to the falls, the Macuco is an excellent means to explore the local flora and fauna. The birdlife and butterflies are especially rich along this trail, but you might even catch a glimpse of a coati or agouti darting across your path. Like most jungle trails, the Macuco is best at dusk and dawn, when it's cooler and there are more animals about. Bring plenty of water, binoculars and sunscreen. The complete round trip takes about three hours.

Don't leave Iguazú without venturing onto the **Río Iguazú**, a rare chance to get an up close and personal look at a giant waterfall. Zodiacs take you right into the spray zone below San Martín

RIGHT: Garganta del Diablo (Devil's Throat) plunges 80 m (230 ft) off the edge of a basalt plateau. OVERLEAF: Iguazú comprises 275 separate waterfalls.

and other cascades, a thundering crash of white water that almost literally takes your breath away.

A number of adventure tour operators on both sides of the border organize river trips of one sort or another. **Iguazú Jungle Explorer** ((3757) 421600 FAX (3757) 420311 offers several options from a 12-minute cruise that takes you right up beneath San Martín Falls and into the Garganta del Diablo canyon (US$15) to a one-hour "Gran Aventura" that includes a four-wheel-drive jungle run, a six-kilometer (four-mile) journey up the Lower Iguazú and a complete drenching at San Martín Falls (US$33). Iguazú Jungle Explorer has an office in the shopping arcade at the Sheraton hotel and an outdoor desk at the ferry landing to Isla San Martín.

Eleven kilometers (seven miles) into the park is the renowned **Hotel Tropical das Cataratas** ((45) 521-7000, which resembles a Mediterranean palace poised on a bluff above the Iguazú Gorge. Take a walk through the hotel's public areas and lavish gardens, and maybe even have lunch there before you take off on the series of catwalks and stone stairs that leads down to the Brazilian falls. The trail winds past Floriano and Santa María falls — with amazing views of the Argentine cascades — before coming almost face to face with **Garganta do Diabo** at the very end of the catwalk. You can walk the entire distance or avail yourself of the **glass-enclosed elevator** that shoots up the side of Floriano Falls.

Brazilian Side

Although only about a quarter of the falls lies within Brazilian territory, the north shore offers a whole different perspective on one of nature's greatest wonders, including much better views of Garganta do Diabo (the Portuguese version of Devil's Throat) and numerous other jungle trails.

The north shore is protected within the confines of **Parque Nacional do Iguaçu**, an expanse of subtropical rainforest more than twice the size of the Argentine park but with much of the same flora and fauna. The park entrance station is about 14 km (nine miles) from both Puerto Iguazú and Foz do Iguaçu, the main town on the Brazilian side. There is a US$6 per person entrance fee payable only in Brazilian currency. The entrance station has free maps and brochures and there's a small visitor center nearby called the **Centro de Visitantes** where more information is available.

Only tour operators on the Brazilian side offer "**Macuco Safari**" boat trips to the foot of Devil's Throat; national park authorities on the Argentine side prohibit these trips because they are considered too dangerous. **Ilha do Sol Turismo** ((45) 574-4244 offer this exhilarating one-hour river trip for US$32. Likewise, only the Brazilian side offers **helicopter flights** over the falls; Argentine park authorities think the noisy choppers are too disruptive to the wildlife. Arrange flights (US$50) through the tour desk at the Cataratas hotel.

You can reach the Brazilian side by taxi, bus or private car via Ruta 12 and the Ponte Internacional Tancredo Neves. If traveling by public bus from Puerto Iguazú, you have two options: venture all the way into Foz do Iguaçu town and transfer to another bus heading into the national park; or ask the bus driver to let you off at the roundabout beyond the Brazilian immigration station, from where you can catch another bus heading into the park.

Private cars with drivers to the Brazilian falls can be arranged through **Remises Ecología (** (3757) 421852 at the Sheraton hotel. A full-day excursion costs US$75.

Shopping

Guaraní Indians sell various arts and craft items on the veranda outside the **visitor center**, which also includes a small shop selling locally made souvenirs.

The **Sheraton shopping arcade** features several good souvenir, craft and clothing shops including Artesanías Nahu, El Indio and Vida Deportiva. Prices are higher than the visitor center or shops in Puerto Iguazú, but the quality is often higher.

Where to Stay

The **Sheraton Internacional Iguazú (** (3757) 421600 or (3757) 421602 FAX (3757) 491848 overlooking the falls is the only overnight accommodation inside the national park and probably the best place to stay in all of northeast Argentina. All guestrooms have balconies; those with cataract views are slightly more expensive than those with jungle views. But I think you really get bang for your bucks — sweeping vistas of the hotel gardens and the Iguazú Gorge with the mist-shrouded falls in the distance. The Sheraton has just about everything you expect from a posh resort hotel including a gourmet restaurant, swimming pool, tennis courts, health club with massage and sauna, putting green and a very good shopping arcade (see above). Major renovations were underway in early 2000.

On the opposite shore is the classy **Hotel Tropical das Cataratas (** (55-45) 521-7000 TOLL-FREE (800) 452266 FAX (55-45) 574-1688 WEB SITE www.tropical hotel.com.br, PO Box 34, Foz do Iguaçu, looking out over the falls in the Brazilian national park. The Mediterranean architecture — pink walls and red-tiled roofs — is a stark contrast to the Sheraton's stark white modern lines. The hotel's gourmet restaurant offers more ethnic diversity — spicy Brazilian fare rather than Argentine beef. The lush tropical gardens are punctuated by a wonderful swimming pool where you can bask for hours.

There's only one place to pitch a tent in the Argentine park, a primitive **campground** at El Nandú, 600 m (just over a third of a mile) upriver from Puerto Canoas on the Upper Iguazú. There's no running water or electricity. But you can't beat the price: it's free. Cooking fires are allowed. There's a snack bar at Puerto Canoas for anyone who forgot to bring their own grub.

Where to Eat

I'm one of those travelers who doesn't expect gourmet food in the wilderness. But if you can't live without, the Sheraton's **Garganta del Diablo Restaurant (** (3757) 420296 offers a full spread of delicious Argentine and international dishes. The steaks are especially good and there are a couple of very good choices on the one menu. My only complaint: they could tone down that bright overhead lighting. They are open for dinner only.

The nightly buffet at the Sheraton's **Oasis Restaurant** isn't nearly as good as it should be — "watered down" in an attempt to cater to a wide variety of tourist palates — and really not worth the US$25 per head. However, the buffet breakfast and lunch are much better in terms of both victuals and value. I also like the restaurant's afternoon tea with freshly squeezed fruit juices and delicious cakes. With its lofty ceiling and soothing air-conditioning, this is a good place to lounge after a trek along the Lower and Upper circuits.

Argentine and Brazilian tourists flock to **El Fortín** restaurant at the visitor center for *parrilla* dishes centered on steak, chicken and pork. Prices are moderate and the portions usually huge. Open for lunch only.

There are inexpensive **snack bars** with sandwiches, ice cream and cold drinks along the Lower Circuit and at Puerto Canoas on the Upper Iguazú River, plus a cluster of food stalls near the visitor center.

How to Get There

Iguazú Falls is 17 km (11 miles) east of Puerto Iguazú. Take Ruta 12 east from town as far as the turnoff to Posadas and then Ruta 101 into the park. The route is well sign posted.

Transportes Cataratas buses run about every half hour from 6:30 AM to 7:30 PM from the Terminal de Ómnibus in downtown Puerto Iguazú to the parking lot at the national park visitor center and on to Puerto Canoas on the Upper Iguazú River. The last return bus to the city is 8 PM from the visitor center.

Taxis between Puerto Iguazú and the park visitor center or Sheraton hotel run about US$30. The trip takes 20 minutes. The directions to Iguazú Falls from elsewhere in Argentina are essentially the same as for Puerto Iguazú (see page 142).

Semiprecious stones and jewelry from the Wanda mines are popular souvenir items at Iguazú.

The Northwest

WITH ITS STATELY *CARDÓN* CACTUS AND RED-ROCK CANYONS, northwest Argentina is a complete contrast to the rest of the country, a wonderfully winsome desert landscape of oasis towns with mountains as a backdrop. Farther east are small subtropical mountain ranges that harbor flora and fauna found nowhere else on the planet, and then a vast wilderness of thorn trees and high savanna grass called the Gran Chaco, which stretches all the way into Paraguay and Brazil. But the difference doesn't end with scenery.

Outside the provincial capitals, the culture is remarkably indigenous, a land of ruddy-faced Indians who seem to have much more in common with their brethren in neighboring Bolivia

than with the Euro-centric residents of Buenos Aires or Patagonia. Argentina's most advanced pre-Hispanic civilizations took root in the fertile valleys of the northwest, spurred by an exchange of goods and ideas with more advanced societies around Lake Titicaca farther north.

The region also came under the sway of the powerful Inca Empire and would probably have become an integral part of the Inca realm if not for the arrival of the Spanish Conquistadors. But even the colonial history of this region is different; pueblos and missions were settled from the Pacific Coast and supplied from Peru rather than via the Río de la Plata.

Today the region is split between seven different provinces: Salta, Jujuy, Tucumán, Catamarca,

ABOVE: Salta's Iglesia San Francisco is one of Argentina's more flamboyant churches. RIGHT: Baroque prevails inside Salta's huge cathedral.

Santiago del Estero, Chaco and Formosa. The city of Salta, with its grand colonial architecture and artisan shops, is the primary tourist destination. But the intrepid traveler will find plenty of interest in the other areas ranging from the desert villages and Jesuit churches of Jujuy to the ancient stone ruins of Catamarca to the bizarre wildlife that inhabits the Gran Chaco region.

With its stanch *indio* heritage, the northwest is endowed with all sorts of religious festivals that aren't celebrated anywhere else in Argentina, or at least without so much gusto. Among the highlights of the spiritual calendar are the **Virgen de Candelaria** procession in Humahuaca on February 2, the **Pachamama** (Mother Earth) festival in Purmamarca and Amaichá del Valle on February 6, the **Día de los Muertos** (Day of the Dead) in Humahuaca on October 31, as well as the Brazilian-style **Carnival** in Salta city on the two weekends preceding Lent.

SALTA

In the fertile Valle de Lerma, Salta was founded in 1582 by Conquistador Hernando de Lerma. It's regarded as Argentina's finest colonial city.

With cobblestone streets, leafy squares and a refreshing lack of highrise buildings, Salta feels much smaller than its 400,000-person population. The city is a fine base for exploring further afield in the northwest, with excellent highways that lead north to Jujuy and south to Tucumán and Catamarca, as well as the remarkable *Tren a los Nubes* (Train into the Clouds) that leads into the High Andes.

GENERAL INFORMATION

The place to head for maps, brochures and other resources is the provincial **Secretaría de Turismo** ℂ (387) 431-0950 FAX (387) 431-0716 WEB SITE WWW .turismosalta.com in the colonial-era building at Calle Buenos Aires 93, about a half a block south of the Plaza 9 de Julio. In addition, there's a small **municipal tourist office** two blocks away at the corner of Buenos Aires and San Martín.

The main branch of **Correo Argentino** has moved into a sparkling new post office building at Calle Dean Funes 140. Open Monday to Friday 8 AM to 8 PM, Saturday 8:30 AM to 12:30 PM. **Telefónica** has several locations in the downtown area for long-distance calls, Internet hookups and fax service including Calle Caseros 760, Calle Florida 17, Calle España 406 and Calle Alvarado 686. The outlets are open Monday to Saturday 7 AM to 2 AM and Sunday 8 AM to 1 PM. You can also get Internet service at a number of cybercafés around town including **Chat Café** at Calle Vicente Lopez 117 and **Artesanías Owet** at the corner of Caseros and Catamarca.

Numerous banks in the central city will change cash, travelers' checks and dispense ATM money including **Citibank** ((387) 431-4972 at the corner of España and Balcarce. Across the street are branches of **Banco de la Nación** and **Banco Galicia**.

Hospital San Bernardo ((387) 422-4255, Calle Tobis 69, is the place to head for emergency medical treatment.

A number of travel agents can assist with city tours, excursions to outlying areas and tickets to the *Tren a los Nubes* including **Altiplano Tur** ((387) 431-4677 or (156) 831787, Calle Buenos Aires 94, and **Tastil** ((387) 431-1103 FAX (387) 431-1223 E-MAIL tastil@ish.com.ar, Calle Zuviría 26. Outfitters specializing in adventure tours through desert and mountains regions include **MoviTrack Safaris** ((387) 431-6749 FAX (387) 431-5301 E-MAIL movitrack @arnet.com.ar, Calle Buenos Aires 68, and **Clark Expeditions** (/FAX (387) 421-5390 E-MAIL yuchan@ arnet.com.ar, Calle Caseros 121. **Panta Aventuras** ((387) 429-0554 or (156) 057084 organizes guided

trips to see Andean village Carnival celebrations and Holy Week festivities.

WHAT TO SEE AND DO

Everything in Salta radiates from the **Plaza 9 de Julio**, a leafy town square surrounded by hotels, sidewalk cafés and exquisite colonial buildings. The huge **Iglesia Catedral de Salta** dominates the plaza's northern flank but isn't nearly as ancient as it looks; finished in the 1870s, it's a fine example of late Baroque. Inside are the remains of liberation hero General Martín Miguel de Güemes, a native *Salteño* who turned back seven Spanish invasions from Bolivia with a ragtag army of gaucho horsemen. Open Monday to Friday from 6:30 AM to 4:30 PM, Saturday and Sunday from 7:30 AM to 5 PM.

On the plaza's southern side is the charming **Cabildo** with its thick whitewashed walls and heavy wooden beams. Originally constructed in

154

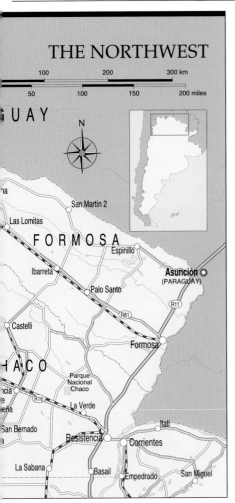

THE NORTHWEST

charged. Across the street is the beautifully restored milk-chocolate façade of the **Municipalidad** (City Hall). Duck inside for a quick look-see; it's free. Next door the **Casa de Arias Rengel**, a white-washed building that resembles a Foreign Legion fort in the Sahara Desert. It is now home to the **Museo Provincial de Bellas Artes (** (387) 421-2384, Calle Florida 20, with galleries on twentieth-century painting and sculpture. Open Monday to Saturday 9 AM to 1 PM and 5 PM to 9 PM, Sunday 9 AM to noon. Admission is charged. At the corner of Florida and España is a wonderful old red-washed building called the **Casa de Leguizamón** with an ice-cream shop on the bottom and an antique wooden balcony wrapped around the second floor.

Heading east from the plaza the first structure that really catches your eye is the **Casa de Uriburu (** (387) 421-5340, Calle Caseros 417, preserved much as it was when President José Evaristo Uriburu lived here in the nineteenth century. Open Tuesday to Saturday 9:30 AM to 1:30 PM and 3:30 PM to 8:30 PM. Admission is charged. Dominating the intersection of Caseros and Córdoba is Salta's most magnificent church, the ornate **Iglesia San Francisco** (1796) with a startling blood-red and ocher façade, lofty bell tower and statue of the pious Saint Francis in the square out front. Check out the unusual murals on the façade of the annex buildings to the right of the main church. Open daily 7 AM to noon and 5 PM to 9 PM.

Another couple of blocks east along Calle Caseros is the **Convento San Bernardo**. Established in the sixteenth century as a hermitage and hospital, it's still a beehive of Carmelite nuns and not open to the public. You'll have to appease yourself with a view of the magnificent gateway, carved from *algarrobo* wood by native craftsmen in 1762.

Looming above central Salta is a 1,400-m (4,590-ft) mountain called **Cerro San Bernardo**, which offers splendid views of the metropolis, and even the snowy Andes in the west if the weather's clear enough. There are three ways to reach the top: you can flag a taxi, huff and puff up 1,136 steps, or ride the **Teleférico (** (387) 431-0641 cable car, which rises from a terminal in Parque San Martín near the corner of Avenida San Martín and Avenida Yrigoyen; daily 10 AM to 7:45 PM (US$6 return). At the summit are a small snack bar, an old wooden cross and various viewpoints. Indian artisans often set up shop on weekends, their crafts spread across blankets and benches.

Tren a los Nubes

The famed *Tren a los Nubes* (Train into the Clouds) is one of region's foremost attractions, a day-long excursion into the rocky *quebradas* (canyons) west of Salta that culminates in a journey across the sky-high viaduct at **La Polvorilla** and a stop at

1582 as the seat of local political power, the current building dates from 1783 and now houses the **Museo Histórico del Norte (** (387) 421-5340 with exhibits on the heritage and lifestyles of the pre-Hispanic, colonial and republican periods, as well as local architecture. Open Tuesday to Friday 9:30 AM to 1:30 PM and 3:30 PM to 8:30 PM, Saturday 9:30 AM to 1:30 PM and 5 PM to 8 PM, Sunday 10 AM to 1 PM. Through the **Asociación Artística ARSIS (** (387) 431-8898, Avenida Santa Fe 90, the museum offers on ongoing schedule of classes in various disciplines including flamenco dancing, drama, cooking, music, science, pottery, wood-work, photography and children's art.

A block west of the plaza along the pedestrian part of Calle Florida are a number of other eighteenth-century colonial structures. **Casa de Hernández (** (387) 437-3352 or (387) 422-0317, Calle Florida 97, houses a small museum devoted to Salta's urban history. Open Tuesday to Saturday 9 AM to 12:30 PM and 4 PM to 8:30 PM. Admission is the old mining town of **San Antonio de los Cobres** in the high-altitude puna before returning to the city. The engineering is extraordinary: an incredible series of bridges, tunnels, switchbacks and loops built in the late 1920s and early 1930s that reach a maximum height of 4,220 m (13,770 ft) above sea level, making it the only train in the world that reaches that elevation without the use of racks. Even without racks, this is the planet's fourth highest line.

Passengers travel in clean and comfortable first-class carriages with reclining seats and video monitors. The train also includes a dining car, bar area, communications booth for phone calls, postal kiosk for postcards and letters, and infirmary

SHOPPING

Outside of Buenos Aires, Salta has the country's best selection of arts and craft shops, with dozens of outlets that specialize in traditional Argentine *artesanía* goods like silver, leather and weaving.

Shopkeeper Amelia Posadas runs **La Casa del Arte** ((387) 431-0050, Calle Buenos Aires 25, with loving care. Her selection of genuine antiques and sumptuous reproductions runs a broad gamut from religious icons and silver mirrors to alpaca knits and Indian blankets.

You'll find even more exquisite silver across the street at **Plateria de Horacio Beriero** ((387)

equipped with medical equipment including oxygen for anyone who's feeling the effects of high altitude. There are also English-speaking tour guides to answer questions about the train and about desert scenery.

The train once ran April to October only, but now operates on weekends year-round depending on the prevailing weather conditions. Departures are from **Estación Ferrocarril Belgrano** near the junction of Calle Mitre and Ameghino north of downtown Salta, but tickets should be purchased at least a day in advance from a local travel agency or **Trenes & Turismo** ((387) 431-4984 or (387) 431-4986 E-MAIL trenes&turismo@trenubes .com.ar, Calle Caseros 431. It's definitely a full-day junket: trips run from 7:10 AM to approximately 9:50 PM. The rates are US$99 (January to March) and US$105 (April to December) not including meals.

431-3585, Calle Buenos Aires 16, including silver picture frames, hand mirrors, gaucho belt buckles and *maté* mugs. Next door is **Ch'aska** ((387) 431-8185, Calle Buenos Aires 20, which specializes in modern designer leathers and knits made from the best Pampas and Andes materials.

A stone's throw away is another fine shop called **Sol Artesanía & Plateria** ((387) 431-7978 at the corner of Buenos Aires and Caseros. The prices can get a little steep, but the quality is unmistakable — antique and reproduction jewelry, picture frames and mirrors, plus gaucho spurs, whips and canes.

For low-priced regional souvenirs try **Anastasia** at Calle España 444 which hawks *panchos*, gaucho hats, sweaters and weavings at lower prices than the Calle Buenos Aires establishments. Another spot with an eclectic selection is **El Criollito** in the shopping arcade between Calle

Florida and the main plaza, where the selection includes pottery, picture frames and candlesticks. Inexpensive Indian arts and crafts dominate the shelves at **Artesanías Owet** ((387) 421-2364 at the corner of Caseros and Lopez where you can pick up wooden animal masks, clay figures and Andean flutes.

Salta's under-used and out-of-the-way **Mercado Artesanal** sits at the west end of Avenida San Martín beyond the railroad tracks. Open daily 9 AM to 9 PM. The selection is mostly cheap junk sold at rock-bottom prices.

WHERE TO STAY

Anywhere on the main square puts you in the heart of this thriving city in the northwestern part of the country.

Expensive

Salta's most indulgent hotel is the **Provincial** ((387) 432-2000 TOLL-FREE (800) 777-2582 FAX (387) 432-2002 E-MAIL reservas@hotelprovincial.com.ar WEB SITE www.hotelprovincial.com.ar, 786 Calle Caseros. Rooms are spacious and tastefully decorated in grays, blues and mauves. The restaurant is top notch while the Casino de los Nubes on the ground floor provides evening entertainment. Other amenities include swimming pool, gym and a rooftop deck that overlooks the central city.

The **Hotel Victoria Plaza** ((387) 431-8500 FAX (387) 431-0634 E-MAIL vplaza@arnet.com.ar WEB SITE www.usuarios.arnet.com.ar/vplaza, Calle Zuviría 16, has all the comforts you expect of a modern hotel. The 96 rooms range from suites to spacious doubles. A top-floor gym with modern workout equipment gives you a lovely view of the surrounding mountains and city. Relax in the sauna or the whirlpool after a workout. There is also snack bar that stays open 24 hours.

Moderate

Romantic ambience still reigns at the **Hotel Salta** ((387) 431-0740 FAX (387) 431-1918 E-MAIL hotelsalta @arnet.com.ar, Calle Buenos Aires 1, which dominates the southeast corner of the Plaza 9 de Julio. The rooms could do with renovation and the service is sometimes sluggish, but there's no place I would rather stay in the northwest. Constructed in the 1940s, the neocolonial design features solid wooden floors and staircases, blue-and-white Talavera tiles and balconies that look out onto an ancient cityscape reminiscent of Granada and Seville. The magnificent wood-beamed dining room is especially impressive, with frescoes by Ernesto Scotti. Out back, beyond the parking area, is a quiet garden with a swimming pool surrounded by bougainvillea.

Salta's best new hotel is the excellent little **El Portal de Salta** ((387) 431-3674 or (387) 431-7019 FAX (387) 432-1125 E-MAIL porsalta@satlink.com WEBSITE www.hotelnet.com.ar, Calle Alvarado 341, just three blocks from the main square. Rich wood floors and columns in the lobby area exude a colonial ambience. The 40 rooms are quiet and comfy with air-conditioning and central heating as well as private bathrooms, refrigerators and cable television. El Portal also has a swimming pool, restaurant and bar.

The 50-year-old **Hotel Colonial** ((387) 431-0805 or (387) 421-1470 FAX (387) 431-4249 E-MAIL hotelcolonialsalta@ish.com.ar, Calle Zuviría 6, has one of the best locations in the city, a busy corner of the main plaza where people lounge in sidewalk cafés and take in the scenery. The hotel's innate charm hasn't been affected by modern comforts. Don't let the dark hallways fool you. Inside, the rooms are spacious and have tubs, which is not always the case in other hotels in Argentina.

Located on the opposite corner is the **Regidor Hotel** ((387) 431-1305 FAX (387) 431-1305, Calle Buenos Aires 8, which could be Salta's best value for money. This rustic hotel is very well-maintained and the staff is extremely hospitable. Breakfast at the restaurant on the ground floor is also very affordable.

Inexpensive

The best thing about the **Hotel Italia** ((387) 421-4050, Peatonal Alberdi 231, is its location right on Salta's major pedestrian mall with lots historic buildings and museums nearby. There's no air-conditioning and television is optional, but there is a phone in most rooms. Also convenient is the restaurant next door, which serves Argentina's version of fast food.

If staying on a budget is your main priority, then the **Hotel Florida** ((387) 421-2133, Calle Urquiza 718, will suffice. The lobby is small and crowded but each room has a private bath. Another affordable option is the family-run **Residencial España** ((387) 421-7898, Calle España 319, where rooms come without air-conditioning or breakfast.

If you don't mind bunking up with total strangers, Salta has several low-priced youth hostels. The IYHF-affiliated **Backpackers Albergue Juvenil** (/FAX (87) 423-5910 E-MAIL hostalsalta @impsat1.com.ar, Calle Buenos Aires 930, has rooms for two and four people as well as dormitories. Facilities include laundry, communal kitchen, lockers and luggage storage room, free parking, Internet and e-mail service, video library and book exchange. There are mountain bikes for rent and tour discounts. IYHF cards accepted but not necessary.

Bolivian Indian dancers enliven the Corso parade during Salta's annual Carnival.

Another option is **Hostal Travellers** (/FAX (387) 421-4772 E-MAIL travellersalta@hotmail.com, Calle San Martín 104, which offers tidy rooms, hot showers, barbecue area, kitchen and laundry facilities. Tourist information and fax services available at the front desk.

WHERE TO EAT

Salta features an outstanding array of restaurants in every price category including eateries that serve delicious northwestern specialties like *tamales*, *humitas* and *locro*.

Expensive

The finest place to dine in all of northwest Argentina is the beguiling **El Solar del Convento** ((387) 421-5124, Calle Caseros 444. Despite the name, the building wasn't part of an old convent and really isn't all that old. But the decor reeks bygone charm, the mystical magical elements that make this region so appealing: a giant tapestry made from horse blankets, animal masks from local Indian festivals and huge wrought-iron chandeliers. The menu is typically beef-based but also daring, with dishes you'll find nowhere else: *lomo manhattan* is sirloin steak smothered in a ham and celery sauce, with hashed corn meal and asparagus tips on the side; *lomo Lloyd George* is sirloin cooked in a bittersweet apple and whisky sauce.

Carlos the guitarist may have never heard of this place, but **Santana** ((387) 432-0941, Calle Mendoza 208, is a class act. From the waiters in snappy white jackets to the impeccably restored colonial setting and wooden furniture, this is Salta's most elegant place to eat. The menu includes classic Argentine steak, pasta and fish dishes, which you can wash down with some of the region's best wines.

The upstairs dining room at the **Hotel Salta** ((387) 431-0740 boasts a well-seasoned appeal and big picture windows that look out onto the central plaza. The cuisine is also classic Argentine: *lomito a la parrilla* (grilled fillet of beef), *lomito a la pimienta* (black pepper steak) and *filet de trucha plateada* (grilled trout) among the finer selections.

One of the few places that serves up ample helpings of Argentine folklore is **Peñas Gauchos de Güemes** ((387) 421-0820, Calle Uruguay 750. The menu includes both international and regional cuisine.

Moderate

A place that always arouses my palate is **La Terraza de la Posta** ((387) 421-7091 in a huge warehouse-like space at Calle España 456. There's a great range of salads, from Hawaiian through Waldorf, which you can follow up with an eclectic selection of entrées like *arroz a la cubana* (with fried bananas, ham and egg), *lechon adobado* (barbecued pork),

trucha arco iris (rainbow trout) and *cabrito al asador* (baby goat). La Posta also features a great selection of regional wines including Etchart, Vasija and Domingo Hermanos. Eat indoors beneath the high wood-beam ceiling and the ocher-colored walls, or al fresco on the breezy terrace.

Locals flock to **Parrilla Don Martín** ((387) 421-3577, Calle Buenos Aires 61, for delicious, low-cost barbecue. The extensive menu includes old favorites like *lomo de frontera* (sirloin steak), *matambre a la portuguesa* (spicy beef flank) and *trucha a la vaca* (trout in a buttery garlic and parsley sauce). The chunky wooden chairs and tables and folk-art paintings give the place an earthy, Andes feel.

When I get hungry late at night I like to slip down to **El Palacio de Pizza** ((387) 421-4989, Calle Caseros 459, where they offer 30 different types of pie including the *tropical* (ham, pineapple and peaches), the *carinosa* (Roquefort and mozzarella cheese with pine nuts and cognac) and the savory *especial grande* which seems to have just about everything on it. They will also deliver to hotels in the central plaza area.

Inexpensive

One of cheaper places to eat on the Plaza 9 de Julio is the popular **Café Bahía** ((387) 431-9142 on the west side. The menu seems to run through several hundred items from pizzas and fresh pasta to *cabrito* (baby goat) and *lomito* (steak sandwich). Grab on outdoor table beneath the huge portico.

Try a wide variety of regional foods at **El Corredor de las Empanadas**, Calle Caseros 117.

As the name suggests, the house specialty is *empanadas*, but you can also sink your teeth into delicious *humitas*, *tamales* and *locro* soup. The café is situated in a lovely mission-style building with a leafy central patio.

Farther down the food chain are cozy inner-city snack shops like **La Tacita**, Calle Caseros 398 (opposite Iglesia San Francisco), which tenders inexpensive sandwiches, *empanadas*, coffee and other drinks. At the corner of Dean Funes and España is **La Granja**, a neighborhood deli with a good selection of sandwiches, pizza, pasta, *empanadas* and cold drinks. Down the block is another local hangout called **Café El Periodista** ((387) 421-0071, Calle Dean Funes 119, where you

bump and grind. There's similar music on Friday and Saturday nights at **Juanamanuela Pub** ((387) 422-4220, Calle Zuviría 172, where you can also pick up a late-night cup of tea or coffee. If you get bored with the music, the pub also offers access to the Internet.

HOW TO GET THERE

Salta is 1,616 km (1,000 miles) from Buenos Aires on Ruta 9 and Ruta 34 across the Pampas via Rosario and Tucumán; 1,308 km (813 miles) from Mendoza via Ruta 40 along the Andes; and 865 km (536 miles) from Corrientes via Ruta 16 across the Gran Chaco.

can buy breakfast for as little as US$1.50 and salads for as low as US$1.

Grab an ice cream cone from **Su Heladería** in the old red building at the corner of Calle Caseros and Peatonal Florida and munch it on one of the benches along the walking street.

NIGHTLIFE

One of Salta's most popular late-night hangouts is **Café Van Gogh** at the corner of Buenos Aires and España on the main plaza. The place rocks Wednesday through Saturday nights with live music that always kicks off around midnight. Indoor and outdoor seating; hot and cold drinks, plus light snacks.

A much younger crowd lingers at **Zero 2000** ((387) 431-0805, Calle Caseros 482, where DJs spin the latest Latin hits as the clientele does the

Most people take the two-hour flight from the federal capital to Salta's **Aeropuerto Internacional Güemes** ((387) 424-3115 on the city's southern outskirts. Local airlines offices include **Aerolíneas Argentinas** ((387) 431-1331 or (387) 424-1200, Calle Caseros 475; **Dinar** ((387) 431-0606 or (387) 431-0500, Calle Buenos Aires 46; and **LAPA** ((387) 431-7080, Calle Caseros 492. Many of the Buenos Aires services also stop in Tucumán.

Salta is also well served by long-distance buses from the **Terminal de Ómnibus** ((387) 431-5227 on Avenida Yrigoyen. Journey times are 22 hours to Buenos Aires, 12 hours to Córdoba, 15 hours to Rosario, 17 hours to Corrientes and 19 hours to Mendoza. Companies that offer long-distance service to other Argentine cities include **La Veloz**

OPPOSITE: Exotic spices aromatize Salta's Mercado Central. ABOVE: Salta offers some of the country's best buys in traditional souvenirs.

del Norte ((387) 423-0200, Avenida Tavella 54. Atahualpa((387) 421-4795 runs buses to La Quiaca on the Argentina–Bolivia border, but the 11-hour journey can be hot, dusty and frustrating.

JUJUY

Founded in 1593 as a garrison and trading post on the intra-Andes route between Bolivian mines and northern Argentina, San Salvador de Jujuy is one of the country's oldest cities.

Few relics of the past survive. Modern Jujuy is a rather somber city marked by dilapidated high-rise buildings in the downtown area and shantytowns around the periphery. Unlike other parts of Argentina, the economy hasn't prospered with the restoration of democracy and the city's many Indian inhabitants remain light years behind their fellow Argentines in terms of wealth, health and education.

The real glory of Jujuy Province lies farther north in the chromatic desert landscapes and quaint oasis towns that mark the Quebrada de Humahuaca and the sequestered salt lakes of the *altiplano* where wildlife gathers in abundance.

GENERAL INFORMATION

The dark and dank Secretaría de Turismo ((388) 422-1326 FAX (388) 422-1325, Calle Belgrano 690 in Jujuy, is pretty close to useless, with little in the way of maps or brochures on either the city or the province. Open Monday to Friday 7 AM to 9 PM, Saturday and Sunday 9 AM to 9 PM. If you're heading out to any of the national parks in the boondocks of Jujuy Province consult the Dirección General de Parques, at Calle Alvear 412, about road conditions and facilities.

Correo Argentino ((388) 423-7888 is at Calle Independencia 987. For international and long-distance calls, fax and Internet service try any of the downtown branches of Telecom including Calle Belgrano 730 ((388) 423-1066 or Calle Belgrano 696 ((388) 423-3033.

Change money at any number of downtown banks including Banco Río ((388) 422-7173, Calle Alvear 802; Banco Quilmes ((388) 423-3229 at the corner of Belgrano and Balcarce; or Banco Provincia de Jujuy ((388) 422-2988 at the corner of Alvear and Lamadrid, all of which have 24-hour ATMs.

For medical emergencies, Hospital Guardia ((388) 422-2025 is at Calle Güemes 1345. Fill prescriptions at Nueva Central Farmacia ((388) 422-2925 at the corner of Belgrano and Necochea.

WHAT TO SEE AND DO

Most of the city's historic buildings cluster around the Plaza Belgrano on the eastern edge of down-

town. Leering above the square is the Baroque façade of the Iglesia Catedral (1765) which features an even older gold-plated pulpit that's one of the finest of its kind in South America. On the square's north side is the Cabildo (1867), now the provincial police headquarters with a small museum dedicated to local law enforcement. Open Monday to Friday 8:30 AM to 1 PM and 3 PM to 9 PM, Saturday and Sunday 9 AM to noon and 6 PM to 8 PM. The plaza's other architectural landmark is the Casa de Gobierno (1921), an elaborate French neo-Baroque style palace where provincial authorities hold sway. Open to the public weekdays 8 AM to noon and 4 PM to 8 PM.

Two blocks west of the plaza is the Iglesia de San Francisco at the corner of Belgrano and Lavalle, completely rebuilt in the 1920s on the site of a seventeenth-century chapel. The lavish interior boasts its own intricate gilt pulpit and various other embellishments. The adjacent cloister museum is open Monday to Saturday 10 AM to 1 PM and 6:30 PM to 9:30 PM. Down the street is the Museo Histórico Provincial ((388) 422-1355, Calle Lavalle 250. The collection includes artifacts from the colonial and Republican periods and the wars of independence, displayed in a fine eighteenth-century mansion where revolutionary hero General Juan Lavalle once lived. Open Monday to Saturday 9 AM to 1 PM and 4 PM to 8 PM.

North of Jujuy, Ruta 9 crawls up the Río Grande Valley into increasingly arid desert country that culminates in the scenic Quebrada de Humahuaca with its picture-postcard Indian villages. One of the first stops along the route is sleepy little Tumbaya with its wonderful Franciscan mission church (1796) in the shadow of a hillside covered in *cardón* cactus.

Sixty-five kilometers (40 miles) north of Jujuy city and just off the main highway is Purmamarca, one of the region's most picturesque villages. An amazing multicolored cliff called the Cerro del los Siete Colores (Hill of the Seven Colors) hovers above the tiny town, especially brilliant at sunrise when the colors seem to vibrate with early morning light. The *cardón* cactus roof is the most impressive feature of Purmamarca's modest Santa Rosa de Lima chapel, which dates from 1648. The adjacent *algarrobo* tree is thought to be more than a thousand years old and is now a national monument. The village square is surrounded by shops and stalls selling Indian-made carpets, hats, blankets, vests and other trinkets at much lower prices than in the city.

Anchoring the southern end of the Quebrada de Humahuaca is the historic town of Tilcara, 84 km (52 miles) north of Jujuy. Besides an Inca-era stone fortress and numerous artisan shops, the village also boasts several good museums. The Museo Arqueológico Dr. Eduardo Casanova displays important artifacts from the pre-Hispanic era in a lovely Spanish colonial house. Across the plaza is another museum devoted to the paintings of **José Antonio Therry**. Tilcara's most important annual festival is Semana Santa (Holy Week).

At the valley's north end is **Humahuaca**, an oasis town and budget-travel Mecca famed for its adobe houses and cobblestone streets. Clustered around the plaza are several attractive buildings including the **Cabildo**, with its famous high-noon clock tower display of a mechanical San Francisco Solano blessing those on the plaza below, and the seventeenth-century **Iglesia la Candelaria**, the focus of the annual Virgen de Candelaria festival on February 1 and 2. The **Museo Arqueológico y el Folklórico Regional** presents a modest but interesting collection of regional arts, crafts and clothing including elaborate Carnival costumes.

Farther afield are several small but important reserves that safeguard the unusual flora and fauna of the northwest. **Monumento Natural Laguna de los Pozuelos** near La Quiaca centers around a high country lake where thousands of migratory birds flock each year including ducks, geese and three flamingo species. The grassy, windswept puna vegetation around the lakeshore is typical of the Andes above 3,400 m (11,100 ft). Tucked up along the Bolivian border is **Parque Nacional Baritú**, which protects a large tract of *yungas* cloud forest, found only on the eastern slopes of sub-Andean mountain ranges. The only reasonable way to access the park is down the Río Bermejo from Mezon, Bolivia. More accessible is **Parque Nacional Calilegua**, about 110 km (68 miles) northeast of Jujuy city, where a similar cloud forest environment is preserved.

WHERE TO STAY

Although it's hardly exceptional by Argentine standards, the 60-room **Jujuy Palace (** (388) 423-0433, Calle Belgrano 1060, is the city's best hotel. The rooms are relatively spacious, some with balconies offering views over downtown Jujuy. Other amenities include restaurant, bar, gym and sauna.

If you're looking for something a bit more posh, try the Spanish-colonial style **Altos de la Viña (** (388) 426-2626 or (388) 426-1666 E-MAIL lavina @imagine.com.ar, Avenida Pasquini Lopez 50, on the outskirts of town. This sprawling, modern resort hotel features very comfortable and well-appointed guestrooms in addition to a swimming pool, sauna, and miniature golf.

One of the better budget abodes is **Samana Wasi (** (388) 422-1191, Calle Balcarce 354 in downtown Jujuy. Set around a pleasant central patio where guests often gather in the morning and evening, the 16 rooms have a homey ambience. **Hotel Huaico (** (388) 423-5186 or (388) 422-8353,

Avenida Bolivia 3901, is another low-cost option. Despite its rock-bottom rates, all rooms have private bath. Other features include garden, snack bar, solarium and parking. Ten percent discount for ACA members.

Finding a good place to stay in the Quebrada de Humahuaca is problematic at best. The canyon's best choice is probably the **Hotel de Turismo (** (388) 742-1154, Calle Buenos Aires 650 in Humahuaca town. Rooms are best described as clean but Spartan.

One of Humahuaca's most distinctive inns is **Cabana El Cardón (** (3887) 156-29072 on the edge of the desert beyond the eastern bank of the Río Grande. The cabins, which sleep four or five

people, have private bathrooms with hot water and small kitchens. Bed linen is provided. Regional meals and snacks are served. Laundry facilities available.

Anybody with a hankering to sleep in the middle of the desert should check into **Hostal La Granja (** (388) 426-1766 or (388) 423-1067, in Huacalera village about halfway between Tilcara and Humahuaca. Rooms have private bathrooms and family plans are available. The hostel restaurant serves both regional and international dishes.

Of the many hostels and cheap hotels that cater to the backpack crowd, the **Albergue Juvenil (** (388) 742-1064, Calle Buenos Aires 447, Humahuaca, is the most popular. Affiliated with the international youth hostel association, it features communal kitchen, hot showers and local tourist

Purmamarca and other Indian villages draw visitors to the Quebrada de Humahuaca.

information. Similar atmosphere and amenities are offered at **Malka Hostel (** (388) 495-5197 FAX (388) 495-5200 E-MAIL malka@hostels.org.ar, Calle San Martin, Tilcara. Guests have access to barbecues, television, bike riding, guided trekking and archaeological tours in vans.

WHERE TO EAT

The best place in the town of Jujuy for *comidas regionales* is a cozy old café called **Ruta 9 (** (388) 423-0043, Calle Lavalle 287. Their delicious *locro criollo* soup is made with pumpkin, cheese, corn, beans and meat. Other house specialties include *lechoncito* (oven-baked pork), *mondongo* (tripe) and *chicharron* (pork rinds).

A woodsy Alpine atmosphere prevails at **La Ventana (** (388) 422-7962, tucked down in the basement of a lovely neoclassical building at Calle Belgrano 749. The menu harbors a broad range of Argentine favorites including steaks, pastas, trout, pork and chicken dishes.

For a light meal or a quick drink duck into **Café Bugatti (** (388) 422-6296, Calle Belgrano 836, which offers breakfast and a wide range of sandwiches in addition to gourmet and Irish coffee, fruit juices, cocktails and cold beer. They have outdoor and indoor seating, and live music around midnight on Friday and Saturday nights. Another pleasant place to while away an afternoon is the **Confitería La Royal (** (388) 422-6202, an outdoor café at Calle Belgrano 742.

Tía Katana at Calle Belgrano 678 sports a simple, blue-collar ambience. The food is also unpretentious: hamburgers, *empanadas*, pastas and meat dishes *pollo a la portuguesa* and *carne al horno*.

HOW TO GET THERE

San Salvador de Jujuy is 124 km (77 miles) north of Salta via speedy Ruta 34, and 92 km (57 miles) more via scenic but twisting Ruta 9. The Argentine-Bolivian border post at La Quiaca is 289 km (180 miles) north of the provincial capital via Ruta 9.

There is daily service between Buenos Aires and Jujuy's modest **Aeropuerto El Cadillal (** (388) 491-1101, plus weekly service to and from Tucumán and Córdoba. The only carriers that operate out of Jujuy are **Aerolíneas Argentinas/Austral (** (388) 422-5414, Calle San Martín 735; and **Dinar (** (388) 423-7100, Calle Senador Pérez 308.

Jujuy's **Terminal de Ómnibus (** (388) 422-6229 at the corner of Dorrego and Iguazú offers service to Buenos Aires (22 hours), Salta (two hours), Tucumán (five hours), Corrientes (17 hours) and the Bolivian frontier (seven tough hours). Local bus operators include **Panamericano (** (388) 423-7175, **Andesmar (** (388) 423-3293 and **La Veloz del Norte (** (388) 423-2366.

CAFAYATE

This sleepy little desert town in southern Salta Province makes an excellent base for exploring the picturesque Calchaquíes Valley and nearby attractions like the red-rock wilderness of the Quebrada de Cafayate, the ruins of Quilmes and the folk-art wonders of Amaichá del Valle.

Calchaquí Indians occupied this valley for hundreds of years before the Spanish arrived, and they fought hard against the Conquistadors to retain their fertile homeland. Their resistance didn't end until the late seventeenth century when they were forcibly relocated to Buenos Aires, where most of them subsequently died from disease and depression. Jesuit and Franciscan missions followed, paving the way for the modern town of Cafayate.

Today life still revolves around the leafy central plaza, enclosed by placid sidewalk cafés, eclectic craft shops and a well-preserved cathedral.

Cafayate itself is surrounded by lush vineyards, picture-postcard wine country that supports some of the country's most prestigious labels. Despite the fact that it makes a living off tourism, this ancient colonial outpost has lost none of its by-gone charm.

GENERAL INFORMATION

There's a municipal **tourist information kiosk** in the middle of the central plaza but don't expect it to be open too often. Cafayate is small enough to explore on your own without fear of getting lost. For information on the region, consult the provincial tourist offices in Salta and Tucumán.

Correo Argentino is two blocks north of the plaza at the corner of Avenida Guilmes (the main road into town from the north) and Calle Diego de Almagro. A small **Telefónica** office at the corner plaza's southeast corner offers long-distance service. **Banco de la Nación** at the plaza's south-west corner will change United States dollars, but not travelers' checks. There is no ATM.

If you need a guide — for a walk around town or excursions around the valley — try **Roberto Araoz Guanca** ((3868) 421120 or (3868) 156-39649. He can arrange anything from a short *bodega* (winery) visit to a day-long exploration of the Quebrada de Cafayate.

WHAT TO SEE AND DO

Other than shopping and an afternoon siesta, there really isn't much to do in Cafayate but just hang out and quaff some of the local plonk.

For those who have the inclination and the energy, there are two small museums within the city limits. The **Museo Arqueológico Rodolfo**

Founded around AD 1000, the fortress city of Quilmes withstood the Spanish invasion for nearly 200 years.

Bravo ((3868) 421054, at the corner of Colón and Calchaquí, showcases a private collection of pre-Hispanic and colonial artifacts including many fine Calchaquí Indian pottery pieces. Meanwhile, the region's wine-growing heritage is celebrated at the **Museo de la Vid y El Vino (** (3868) 421125 on Avenida Güemes two blocks south of the plaza. Both collections have erratic opening hours and both charge a modest entrance fee.

If you're really into wine, visit one of the local *bodegas* (wineries) for a tour and tasting. The valley's oldest vineyard is **Vasija Secreta (** (3868) 421503 E-MAIL labanda@infonoa.com.ar, on Ruta 68 near the Hostería ACA, whose production includes the famous Antigua Bodega la Banda. Open daily 9 AM to 1 PM and 3 PM to 7 PM. But the most famous is **Bodegas Etchart (** (3868) 421310 on Ruta 40 about three kilometers (two miles) south of town. Their white wine is especially tasty. Open Monday to Friday 8 AM to noon and 3 PM to 6 PM, Saturday 8 AM to noon.

The area's biggest attraction, and rightly so, is the **Quebrada de Cafayate**, a stunningly handsome red-rock canyon that stretches about 40 km (25 miles) along the Río de las Conchas between the villages of Los Medanos and Alemania. The scenery is strongly reminiscent of Arizona's Oak Creek Canyon and Sedona areas: a sparkling desert stream edged in thick riparian vegetation rising to hillsides smothered in *cardón* cactus and rising even higher to sheer sandstone cliffs that take on all sorts of peculiar shapes that people have named over the years — El Sapo (The Toad), Los Castillos (The Castles), El Anfiteatro (The Amphitheater) and the incomparable Garganta del Diablo (Devil's Throat) where you're surrounded by massive swirls of multicolored stone.

Ruta 68 between Cafayate and Salta runs right down the middle of the canyon, with signs that mark the major attractions. Besides the roadside snack and craft stalls in the village of **Santa Barbara**, the *quebrada* has no facilities of any kind. As long as you don't disturb the grazing cattle in the canyon bottom, you can simply strike out on your own for days at a time and camp wherever you like. Believe it or not, the canyon is not protected by national or provincial park status. Argentine authorities should make an effort to give it some sort of designation before this incredible resource is damaged.

The area's other great attraction is **Quilmes (** (3892) 421075, the ruins of a pre-Hispanic fortress and city that nestle against the side of a cactus-studded mountain about 50 km (31 miles) south of Cafayate off Ruta 40. Founded around AD 1000 by the Quilmes Indians, the stone bastion

The Quebrada de Cafayate is one of Argentina's most stunning natural attractions.

grew into the valley's most important urban center, with an estimated 5,000 residents at its height. Quilmes traded with the Inca and other more sophisticated groups and somehow managed to fend off the Spanish invaders for nearly 200 years after the rest of the region had been subdued. The Conquistadors finally breached the city's defenses in 1667. Near the entrance are a small museum with pottery fragments and a very large gift shop with regional arts and crafts. There's also a snack bar and hotel. Open daily sunrise to sunset. Admission is charged. For more information on the valley's pre-Hispanic heritage visit the ultra-modern **Complejo Cultural Pachamama** ((3892) 421004 in nearby Amaichá del Valle.

SHOPPING

It's hard to pass through Cafayate without browsing at least one of the many artisan shops. Prices are much lower than comparable goods in Buenos Aires or Salta, but that doesn't mean you don't have to bargain.

Regionales Amaichá on the plaza's north side sells all kinds of local arts and crafts from wooden masks and wall hangings to gourmet foods and T-shirts. Another good place to browse is the nameless little craft shop next to El Gordo restaurant.

The **Unión de Artesanos Juan Calchaquí** ((3868) 421293, Avenida Güemes 4487, is a regional cooperative where the artists and their families sell a wide range of local craft items including pottery, ponchos, woodcarving, fabulous wicker baskets and very original T-shirts.

If the local wine takes your fancy, pop into **Vinoteca** on the north side of the plaza where Vasija, Etchart and Michel Torino go for as little as US$1.70 a bottle or US$3.50 a jug.

WHERE TO STAY

Like a tranquil desert oasis, the family run **Hotel Gran Real** ((3868) 421016 or (3868) 421231, Avenida Güemes 128, offers a lush garden area with huge shade trees and Mexican palms set around a swimming pool. The rooms are pretty good too, featuring private baths with hot water and ceiling fans. Great location, just one block off the main plaza.

Next door is the colonial-style **Hotel Asturias** ((3868) 421328 FAX (3868) 421040, Avenida Güemes 154, where many of the package tours stay. Although they could do with some new carpet and furniture, the 70 rooms are clean and comfortable with private baths, hot water and ceiling fans. The lobby area is decorated with local woodcarvings and superb nature photos, and there are two places to relax outside: a pleasant central courtyard draped in bougainvillea and a garden with a kidney-shaped swimming pool.

The best of Cafayate's half a dozen shoestring places is **Hospedaje Familia Fernandez** ((156) 787142, Calle San Martín 162 about a block off the main plaza. This quiet family-run inn has five spacious rooms off a central courtyard, some with large, private baths with hot water.

Also recommended is the small but comfortable **Hospedaje Aurora** ((3868) 421342, on the west side of the plaza at Calle Nuestra Señora del Rosario 73 (near the church). Rooms are a little on the small side, but are clean and comfortable. Only one room has its own bathroom, but the communal bath has hot water.

WHERE TO EAT

La Carreta de Don Olegario ((3868) 421004 or 421208, Avenida Güemes 2 on the plaza, isn't nearly as humble — or mobile — as the name would suggest. The restaurant fills a huge, barn-like space with massive picture windows, wagon-wheel chandeliers and a fireplace at center stage. The menu is just as rustic, a delicious blend of regional favorites like *cabrito asado* (grilled baby goat), *cazuela de cabrito* (baby goat stew) and *trucha asado* (grilled trout) plus tasty *tamales*, *humitas* and *empanadas*. No matter what you order, the meal starts with a plate of *pallar* — white beans in garlic, olive oil and pimento sauce. The "carreta" (ox cart) of the title lounges in one corner.

Most of the other restaurants around the plaza feature similar cuisine, a blend of traditional *parrilla*

and regional items, including a snug little place called **El Rancho** in the southeast corner.

For a change of pace try **Confitería El Sol** at Avenida Güemes 48 on the plaza, which offers an eclectic range of inexpensive breakfast, sandwiches, burgers, sausages and steaks, which you can munch out front beneath the cool veranda.

How to Get There

Cafayate is 189 km (117 miles) south of Salta via Ruta 68 through the scenic Quebrada de Cafayate. You can also reach the town from Tucumán by Ruta 307 over the Abra del Infiernillo pass between Tafí del Valle and Amaichá del Valle, and then Ruta 40 north through the Calchaquíes Valley.

El Indio ((3868) 421002, Calle Belgrano 34, runs daily buses to and from Salta and several services each week to and from Tucumán.

TUCUMÁN

With more than 400,000 people, San Miguel de Tucumán (to use its full name) is the largest city in northwest Argentina. It's also one of the oldest, founded in 1565 as a way-station between the Pampas and the Bolivian *altiplano*. Surrounded by sugarcane fields and citrus orchards, the local economy is firmly based in agro-business. Unlike other urban areas in this region, the population is much less indigenous, and Tucumán has much more of a European feel. It comes across as a rather dreary, modern city that's really little more than a modern way-station for travelers headed to more interesting points to the north and west.

OPPOSITE: Río de las Conchas meanders through red-rock wilderness. ABOVE: The earth seems out of tilt inside the Garganta de Diablo (Devil's Throat).

GENERAL INFORMATION

The provincial **Secretaría de Estado de Turismo** ((381) 422-2199 TOLL-FREE (800) 555-8828 is right on the main plaza at 24 de Septiembre 484. They have lots of maps and fancy brochures but little in the way of practical information on where to stay, where to eat, etc. Open Monday to Friday 7 AM to 10 PM, Saturday and Sunday 9 AM to 9 PM.

The main branch of **Correo Argentino** sits at the corner of Córdoba and 25 de Mayo. **Telecom** has several branches for long-distance calls and fax service in downtown Tucumán including offices at Calle Maipú 360 and 762. Change cash or travelers' checks at **Maguitur**, Calle San Martín 765. For medical emergencies **Hospital Angel Padilla** ((381) 421-9139, Calle Alberdi 550, is probably your best bet.

Several local travel agencies run city tours and excursions to nearby areas like Tafí del Valle and the runs at Quilmes including **Duport Turismo** ((381) 422-0000 or (156) 047959, Calle Mendoza 720 in the Galería del Rosario shopping center; and **Turismo del Tucumán** ((381) 422-7636 or (156) 046967, Calle Crisóstomo Alvarez 435.

WHAT TO SEE AND DO

Argentina's declaration of independence from Spanish colonial rule was written on July 9, 1816 in the **Casa Histórica de la Independencia** ((381) 431-0826 at Calle Congreso 151. The original room where the document was signed is complemented by various museum exhibits and patriotic artwork. Open daily (except Tuesday) 9 AM to 1 PM and 3:30 PM to 7:30 PM. Admission is charged. Each evening at 8:30 PM the historic structure comes alive with a dramatic sound and light show that depicts the struggle for independence; Spanish only.

One block north of the casa is the **Plaza Independencia**, the heart and soul of modern Tucumán. Dominating the southeast corner if the neoclassical **Iglesia Catedral** (1852). On the square's western flank is the ornate French-style **Casa de Gobierno** (1910) where the provincial government sits. Right around the corner on Calle San Martín is the lovely **Iglesia San Francisco** (1891) which many consider to be Tucumán's finest church.

There are several small museums in the downtown area. The **Museo Histórico** at Calle Congreso 56 highlights the pre-Hispanic and colonial heritage of Tucumán city and province. Open Tuesday to Friday 8:30 AM to 1:30 PM and 3 PM to 7:30 PM; Saturday 8:30 AM to 1 PM. Admission is charged. The **Museo Folklórico** ((381) 421-8250, in the old colonial mansion at Calle 24 de Septiembre 565, is a rather eclectic display of indigenous arts and

crafts and gaucho gear. Open weekdays 9 AM to 12:30 PM and 5:30 PM to 8:30 PM; weekends 6 PM to 9 PM. Free.

WHERE TO STAY

Expensive

Until completion of the new Sheraton (still under construction as this guide went to press), the city's largest establishment is the hulking **Gran Hotel del Tucumán** ((381) 450-2250 FAX (381) 450-2222 E-MAIL ghotel@arnet.com.ar, Avenida Soldati 380, which attracts a fair amount of government and convention business. The hotel scores major points with comfort, but needs to do something about that dispassionate ambience. All 150 rooms are nicely furnished and well equipped. Facilities include an international restaurant, piano bar, gym, swimming pool, sauna and baby sitting service. Perhaps the most appealing thing about the Gran Hotel is the fact that the huge Parque 9 de Julio is right across the street.

European-style comfort and efficiency are the trademarks of the **Swiss Hotel Metropol** ((381) 431-1180 FAX (381) 431-0379 E-MAIL metropol @arnet.com.ar, Calle 24 Septiembre 524. This modern highrise boasts a rooftop swimming pool, solarium, room service, safe-deposit boxes, fax and e-mail service.

Moderate

It's difficult to find a really good mid-range hotel in Tucumán. An exception to the rule is the centrally located **Hotel Del Sol** ((381) 431-0393 or (381) 431-1755 FAX (381) 431-2010, Calle Laprida 35, which offers 100 modern rooms with cable television and mini bars, many of them overlooking the leafy main plaza. The hotel's tone is set by its granite floors and wood-paneled walls. Amenities include swimming pool, restaurant and bar.

Also recommended is the **Hotel Carlos V** ((381) 431-1666 FAX (381) 431-1566, Calle 25 de Mayo 330. The dark wood and thick carpets give the hotel a snug feel, and the sidewalk café on the ground floor is a great place for people watching. Both the main plaza and the financial district are within easy walking distance.

Bringing up the bottom end of this category is the quirky **Hotel Mediterráneo** ((381) 431-0025 or (381) 422-8351 FAX (381) 431-0080, Calle 24 de Septiembre 364. Only steps from the cathedral and the main plaza, it's hard to beat the location. But the guest rooms and public areas could use a good renovation and they must do something about those rock-hard bread rolls at breakfast.

Inexpensive

Several popular "traveling salesmen" hotels drift into the upper shoestring category, including the 55-room **Hotel Colonial** ((381) 431-1523

FAX (381) 431-1523, Calle San Martín 35, where the simple but clean rooms come with private baths, hot water, air-conditioning and cable television. Downstairs there's much more than you would expect of a budget hotel including gym, sauna, swimming pool, safety deposit boxes, restaurant and bar.

Down a notch is the **Hotel Bristol** ((381) 421-9321 FAX (381) 421-9321, Calle Laprida 150, where the rooms feature television, mini bar and air-conditioning. Similar features are found at the even cheaper **Hotel Francia** ((381) 431-0781, Calle Crisóstomo Alvarez near the historic Casa Independencia.

If you're really skint there are dozens of dank little *hospedajes* and *residenciales*, especially around Tucumán's train and bus terminals. Very few are recommendable. Two of the cleaner, brighter places are the **Residencial Independencia** ((381) 421-7038 at Calle Balcarce 50, and the **Residencial Florida** ((381) 422-6674, Calle 24 de Septiembre 610 near the main plaza. They even offer rooms with private bath.

WHERE TO EAT

Expensive
One of the city's few extravagant restaurants is the main dining room at the **Gran Hotel del Tucumán** ((381) 450-2250, Avenida Soldati 380, which features an enticing range of Argentine and international dishes including steaks, seafood, salads and freshly made pasta. After dinner take a stroll in the expansive park across the street.

Another posh place for steak is **Lenita** ((381) 422-9241, Calle 25 de Mayo 377, where well-healed Tucumán residents like to dine on Friday and Saturday nights.

Moderate
London meets Buenos Aires meets New York at **Sir Harris** ((381) 422-0500 at the corner of Laprida and Mendoza in downtown Tucumán. The eclectic menu runs a broad gamut from grilled trout and salmon and roast chicken to hamburgers, nachos, steaks and various pasta dishes. There are a couple of nice salad choices including the Waldorf, the Niçoise and the Oriental. Round everything off with a banana split. Sure the waiters have way too much attitude, but then again so do many of the local eaters.

One of Tucumán's best bets for barbecued meat is **El Parador** ((381) 435-4391, Avenida Maté de Luna 4305, where delicious *parrilla* and pasta dishes dominate the menu. You'll find a similar selection at **Parrilla del Centro** ((381) 422-6774, Calle San Martín 391 near the main plaza, where the house specials include *matambrito de cerdo* (barbecued pork), *parrillada mixta* (mixed grill), *trucha a la limón* (grilled trout with lemon sauce).

For a change of pace, dig into rich Middle Eastern cuisine at the **Restaurante Arabe** ((381) 421-4402, Calle Maipú 575, where Lebanese and Syrian dishes predominate.

Inexpensive
Bright lights and big pizzas rule the roost at **La Esquina Pizza la Piedra** ((381) 430-5514 or (381) 421-2682 at the corner of Laprida and Mendoza.

The downtown area boasts a couple of really good snack bars. **Confitería Nuevo Polo Norte** ((381) 422-5569, Calle Santiago 1046, offers sandwiches, pastries and freshly baked bread, in addition to chocolate delights. **Confitería Casapan** ((381) 421-7119, Calle 25 de Mayo 819, has fresh pasta, pizza and sandwiches.

A great place to try a selection of regional specialties like *humitas*, *tamales* and *locro* soup is **El Portal** ((381) 422-6024, Calle 24 de Septiembre 351.

One of Tucumán's best values for money is the *parrilla mixta* at **El Fogón**, Calle Marcos Paz 624, which includes *chorizo* sausages, *matambre* (rolled flank steak), *chinchulines* (small intestines) and *mollejas* (sweet breads) for an incredibly low price.

HOW TO GET THERE

Tucumán is 1,312 km (813 miles) north of Buenos Aires via Ruta 9 through Rosario and Córdoba, and 311 km (193 miles) south of Salta via Ruta 9 and 34.

Aeropuerto Benjamin Matienzo is served by daily flights from Buenos Aires, Córdoba, Salta and Jujuy. Local airlines offices include **Aerolíneas Argentinas** ((381) 431-1030, Calle 9 de Julio 112, and **LAPA** ((381) 430-2630, Calle Crisóstomo Alvarez 620.

Tucumán's fairly new **Estación de Ómnibus** at Calle Brigido Teran 350 is the largest in Argentina after the huge Retiro terminal in Buenos Aires. There is frequent service to Buenos Aires (16 hours), Corrientes (13 hours), Córdoba (eight hours), Cafayate (seven hours), Salta (four hours), Jujuy (five hours) and Mendoza (15 hours). Bus companies with Tucumán service include **Panamericano** ((381) 431-0544, **Aconquija** ((381) 433-0205, and **Veloz del Norte** ((381) 421-7860.

Anyone with loads of time on their hands can also catch a train out of Tucumán. The **El Tucumano** ((381) 430-7100, Calle Corrientes 1075, departs the city's Estación Ferrocarril Mitre three times each week on a southward bound journey that includes stops at Santiago del Estero, Rosario and Buenos Aires.

The Heartland

CÓRDOBA, THE SECOND LARGEST CITY IN ARGENTINA, lies between the Pampas and the Andes amid a series of small mountain ranges. Córdoba Province is one of the oldest settled regions in the country and one of the few to retain its colonial architecture. Rivers, lakes, forests, and mountain resorts attract thousands of tourists to the area during the summer; Córdoba rivals the Atlantic Coast as Argentina's most important vacation destination. Though national travelers tend to gravitate toward the province's resort areas, foreigners are happier exploring the city's many colonial-era buildings and public parks. Several tour companies offer day trips to the countryside, which are sufficient for most travelers. Though Córdoba's

It takes several days to explore even the most important regions in the province, as distances are vast and services somewhat limited.

CÓRDOBA

Córdoba is the second-largest city in Argentina and is the capital of Córdoba Province, the second most popular summer vacation destination for national tourists (after the beach), thanks to its location in the Sierras Chica and Sierras de Córdoba. The city is 400 m (1,312 ft) above sea level, and has a pleasant, temperate climate. About 1,200,000 residents live here year round and the population seems to double in summer, when

Sierras are beautiful, they dwindle in significance when compared with the Andes.

San Luis Province to the south also lies within the Sierra mountain ranges, and is treasured by adventurers and naturalists. Its dry red canyons, steep mountain peaks, and overall geological formations are stunning, and its parks nearly void of visitors. Villa de Merlo, the most important tourism center in the province, is a small colonial-era city surrounded by forests, and the province's Parque Nacional Sierras de las Quijadas is an important site for professional and amateur geologists and paleontologists.

Buses and planes link both areas with Buenos Aires, but it is far easier to visit Córdoba than San Luis. The tourist infrastructure in Córdoba's capital city is fairly well developed (though it helps immensely to speak Spanish). San Luis, on the other hand, is just starting to attract foreign travelers.

urbanites head for the region's lakes and mountain villages. Most treat the city as a secondary attraction they might consider visiting on a day trip from the countryside.

But Córdoba is interesting in its own right, especially for international visitors. The pace is far slower than that in Buenos Aires and the architecture more attuned to colonial times. While European belle époque palaces dominate Buenos Aires, modest convents and hacienda-style homes give Córdoba a less formal, more historic appearance. The presence of several universities lends a college-town feeling, as students burdened with backpacks stuffed with books rush about the streets and gather in casual cafés.

Porteños (residents of Buenos Aires) tend to denigrate Córdoba, calling it a second-rate city. It's not as sophisticated or frenetic as the nation's capital — which I find a major plus. Residents are quick to help foreigners with directions and advice. Police officers have walked me to my destination, and strangers have presented me with gifts of local bread and chocolate. Locals are extremely proud of their city and are eager to share its merits with strangers. Students are well versed in local history.

Córdoba is an important industrial center, and automobile factories are clustered on the outskirts of the city. Auto-repair and supply shops line the streets around the Fiat, Renault, and Volkswagen factories; mechanics from Córdoba are in great demand around the country. The city has been through rough economic times in the past decades, as the country's economy has faltered. Locals insist that the national government has long overlooked their city's needs. But the current President, Fernando de la Rúa, was born in Alta Gracia in Córdoba Province, and locals are hoping he takes up their cause in the nation's capital.

BACKGROUND

Explorer Jerónimo Luis de Cabrera is credited with founding Córdoba in 1573, before Juan de Garay founded Buenos Aires in 1580. Before they arrived, this region of mountains, rivers, and fertile valleys was sparsely populated by the Pampa, Sanavirones and Comechingones. As in most early settlements, the Spanish didn't have to battle the locals for long. Disease quickly achieved the same result as any instrument of war. Within a century the indigenous population fell from a few thousand to a few hundred.

Córdoba was an important center for Jesuit, Dominican, Carmelite, and Franciscan missionaries; several mission churches and convents still stand in the villages around the city. Its temperate climate and rich earth attracted settlers, who established large *estancias* in the valleys. Córdoba was a major political center for the early ranchers, and local leaders resisted orders and instructions from the politicians in Buenos Aires. Even during the battles for independence, Córdoba's elite questioned the wisdom of joining forces with Buenos Aires. But Buenos Aires had the port and the more powerful politicians. As the country grew stronger, Córdoba grew weaker and lost its influence over national politics.

Early on, however, Córdoba became famous as an intellectual hub. The Jesuits opened the nation's first university here in 1621. Now called the Universidad Nacional de Córdoba, it remains one of the most prestigious colleges in the country.

GENERAL INFORMATION

The main **Tourist Information Office** ((351) 433-1542 or (351) 433-2762, Avenida Independencia 30, is located in the historic Cabildo facing Plaza San

Martín. There is usually at least one English-speaking clerk on duty, and travelers can get assistance with setting up tours and reserving hotel rooms. The office distributes several valuable maps detailing touring circuits around the city. In addition, walking tours begin from this point. Most are in Spanish, but you can arrange for an English-speaking guide. The tours are well-worth joining, since each guide presents his or her version of the gossip, mysteries, and legends surrounding the city's history. There is a fee for these tours. There are also information booths at the airport and bus station. The provincial **Secretaría de Turismo** ((351) 423-3248 is at Avenida Tucumán 360.

There are several Internet access points in *locutorio* telephone offices around the main plaza, including one in the Cabildo at the Tourist Information Office. Dollars are not as commonly used in Córdoba as they are in Buenos Aires. It's best to exchange dollars or travelers' checks into pesos in Buenos Aires or at one of the *casas de cambio* around the main plaza.

Travelers may find the city to be disconcertingly quiet on Sundays, when locals evacuate en masse in search of country air. Most shops are closed, and the streets are virtually empty. Also, the city is not geared toward tourism. Museums have erratic hours at best; some are open only one day a week, or for just a few hours a few days each week. All are closed on Monday. Few have telephone numbers for information; the best source for current hours is the tourist office. Businesses close for four hours in the middle of the day during the summer, when temperatures reach 40°C (104°F). The city shuts down on July 6 for the celebration of its founding, and again on September 30, the feast day of San Gerónimo, Córdoba's patron saint.

TOURS

The municipal tourist office distributes several maps detailing walking tours of the historic district and La Cañada. The three brochures and tours overlap each other; I find it best to carry all three simultaneously. There are brief descriptions (translated into flowery, garbled English) of the most important sites. The walking tours provided by the city (see GENERAL INFORMATION, above) are delightful and far more personal than the bus tours provided by local tour companies.

Banana Tours ((351) 423-3299 run a Córdoba City Tour in a double-deck red bus which departs from the corner of 27 de Abril and Buenos Aires at the Plaza San Martín. Tours begin at 11 AM and 4 PM from Wednesday through Sunday. The buses don't run if there are fewer than four passengers. Several companies offer tours covering the nearby countryside; see CÓRDOBA ENVIRONS, page 179.

Córdoba's outdoor cafés provide a pleasant break from the office.

WHAT TO SEE AND DO

Most of the historic buildings in Córdoba are clustered around the main **Plaza San Martín**, bordered by Rivadavia, San Martín, 27 de Abril, and Dean Funes streets in the heart of the city. When the city was founded, the plaza was a dirt field used for bullfights, fiestas, and executions; now it is the geographic and social center of modern Córdoba. It is said that all streets in the province begin here, and all street names change at this point. As is the norm in most Argentine cities, the plaza contains a monument to General San Martín, the famed liberator of Argentina, Chile and Peru. Jacaranda and palm trees provide shade for those relaxing on park benches beside well-tended lawns.

Peatonal 9 de Julio north of the plaza is said to have been the first inner city pedestrian area in the country. It intersects the **Peatonal San Martín**. A few blocks of both streets are closed to vehicles; sections are covered with a wire trellis laden with scarlet bougainvillea. A tiled plaque mounted at the intersection, also called Jardín Florido, commemorates the memory of Fernando Bertapelle. In his later years, Bertapelle dressed in a top hat and dinner jacket and walked the pedestrian area as he flirted audaciously with all women walking down the street. Known as Córdoba's greatest *piropeador* (flirter), Bertapelle died in 1968. Even women who were little girls at the time remember his attentions, some with fondness, some with revulsion or fear. Other characters, including street performers, musicians, and artists, gravitate to these streets lined with shops and cafés.

Pedestrians also have free run of the **Peatonal Obispo Trejos** pedestrian walkway, also called Paseo de las Flores, which intersects 9 de Julio behind the cathedral. Men and boys (women are observers only) gather to play chess in the small park at Obispo Trejos and 27 de Abril. Blossoming jacarandas and vendors selling roses make this one of the prettiest little patches of nature in a city filled with similar surprises; you never know when you'll stumble upon a picturesque scene. There are several red enclosed phone booths here as well; it's one of the quietest places to make phone calls.

On the west side of Plaza San Martín is the **Cabildo**, or town hall, the center of civic activity in colonial times. Construction began in 1588, and the original Cabildo had only three rooms. It was renovated and expanded in 1789, and rooms continued to be added until 1906. The two-story structure is designed in classic Spanish hacienda style, with an interior courtyard and arched brick and lathe ceilings. The Cabildo was used as the mayor's offices, city hall, and police headquarters, and gradually fell into disrepair. The dilapidated structure was restored in 1949, and was fired upon during demonstrations against Peronism in 1955. You can still see bullet holes from the short-lived rebellion in the archways fronting the building. A second prolonged reconstruction lasted from 1990 to 1997. The Cabildo now houses the **Museo de la Ciudad (** (351) 433-1542, the city's cultural offices, and exhibition spaces. The museum includes the reconstructed presidential office, early maps of the city, and a fascinating collection of costumes from the early twentieth century, when high-society ladies and gentlemen favored elaborate European fashions. Rotating exhibits fill the other rooms.

Since Córdoba is a cultural center, the museum receives some high quality traveling shows, such as a recent exhibit of gold and stone artifacts from the Mexican ruins of Monte Albán. Concerts are held every Thursday night in the courtyard, and tango performances are presented every Friday night during the summer. On the right side of the main entrance a stairway leads down to the city's first prison; some sections date back to the sixteenth century. The museum is open daily; admission is free.

In contrast to the architecturally austere Cabildo, the **Catedral de la Señora de la Asunción** on San Martín at 27 de Abril, is rich in detail, with a unique blending of Baroque, neoclassic and indigenous influences. The first church built on the site in 1577 collapsed 20 years after its construction. Work began on the current cathedral in 1687 and ended in 1782 after a succession of architects, engineers, and priests influenced the design. Indigenous laborers also left their mark, giving Indian faces to the statues of angels and saints decorating the façade. The cathedral has a bell tower on each corner; according to legend it was designed in this manner so all parts of the city could hear the trumpets of the angels.

Even after the church was completed, subsequent pastors and congregations contributed to the ever-changing decor. A side altar of Bolivian silver was added in 1804; tiled floors were imported from Spain in 1895. In 1907, the cathedral was closed for seven years while Córdoba most famous artist, Emilio Caraffa, painted murals on the domed ceilings. The murals were such a hit that several other churches were subsequently similarly decorated.

Several important personages in Córdoba's history are buried here, including one of the province's first leaders and governors, General José Maria Paz. Fray Mamerto Esquiú, one of Argentina's first native-born priests and an important contributor to the country's constitution, is also buried here (though his heart is said to literally and figuratively rest in his birthplace in Catamarca). A side altar is dedicated to San Gerónimo, the city's patron saint, whose feast day on September 30 is a provincial holiday.

Pasaje Santa Catalina, a narrow brick passageway between the Cabildo and the cathedral, was used as a holding area for prisoners awaiting execution in the sixteenth century and as a cemetery. Today, it leads to **El Convento y Iglesia de Santa Catalina de Siena** on Riviera Indarte at Dean Funes. Built in 1613, the convent is still home to cloistered nuns who shun contact with the public. Santa Catalina is part of the larger **Monasterio de Carmelitas Descalzas de San José**, a complex of churches and cloisters used by the Carmelite nuns. **El Convento y Iglesia de las Teresas**, on Independencia one block south of the cathedral, is also part of the complex and an active cloister; it was built in 1628. Both cloisters are closed to the public.

Visitors can enter the complex at the **Museo de Arte Religioso Juan de Tejada** (4423-0175, at the corner of 27 de Abril and Independencia. The pink building, part of the overall complex, was donated to the nuns by Don Juan de Tejada in 1628. Don Juan and his wife, Doña Leonor de Tejada, were devout Catholics; some of their children became priests and nuns and the parents demonstrated their gratitude to God by supporting the cloisters. The museum building was the birthplace of Córdoba's first poet, Fray Luis de Tejada and houses a collection of religious art. Admission is charged, and the museum is supposed to be open from 9 AM to noon Wednesday through Saturday. I stopped by several times before finally finding the doors open, however.

Said to be the oldest church in Argentina, **La Iglesia de la Compañía de Jesús** on Obispo Trejo at Caseros was built by the Jesuits between 1640 and 1671. The ceiling is a construction wonder, made of imported cedar and shaped like an inverted ship hull. Adorning the main nave are portraits of the Apostles, painted by Córdoba artist Genaro Pérez. Next to La Compañía is **Capilla Doméstica**, also built by the Jesuits using a similar style of vaulted roof. The ceiling beams were held together by leather straps and then covered with painted cloth. The two churches are part of Córdoba's **Manzana de las Luces** (Street of Enlightenment). As in Buenos Aires, the *manzana* was the headquarters for the Jesuits in the region and a center for religion and education. The Seminario Convictorio de San Javier, built in 1613, evolved into the prestigious **Universidad Nacional de Córdoba**, Obispo Trejo 242. The university's library contains a collection of books from the eighteenth century. The **Colegio Nacional de Monserratt**, Obispo Trejo 294, was founded in 1695; its current building was constructed in 1782.

A stairway similar to a subway entrance leads to the **Cripta Jesuitica del Noviciado Viejo** under Avenida Colón at Calle Rivera Indarte. This extraordinary complex of three stone rooms was

discovered in 1989. Workers digging in the street found the underground rooms, and local historians quickly assembled to protect the historical site. The Municipality of Córdoba agreed to close the avenue and restore the crypts, which were constructed by the Jesuits in the 1700s and used as prayer rooms by Jesuit novices. The chilly, austere stone crypts are now used for art exhibits, plays, and dance performances. Admission is free, and the crypts are open from 9 AM to 1 PM and 4 PM to 8 PM Monday through Saturday.

Córdoba contains at least 30 historic churches. According to legend, Argentine President Sarmiento, who is credited with improving the nation's system of education, said Córdoba had more churches than houses. He instigated a program to build schools and educate locals in the sciences, thereby increasing Córdoba's status as a center for learning. But religious temples still dominate the city's landscape. The most impressive of all the churches, in my opinion, is **La Basílica de Santo Domingo** at the corner of Avenida General Paz and Calle Dean Funes. The blue tiles decorating its dome were a gift from General Justo

José de Urquiza, one of the authors of the nation's 1853 constitution. The main basilica dates back to 1861, though some parts of the building were constructed in the eighteenth century.

The basilica is as much a museum as a place of worship. Its silver altarpiece belonged to the Jesuits, who were expelled from the country in 1767. When the Jesuits departed, the altar disappeared (churches were looted and destroyed during this period). Many years later, a local family donated the altar to the church. Flags captured from the English soldier who invaded Buenos Aires in 1806 hang in a back chapel, as does a flag carried by General San Martín.

The most important relic in the basilica is the statue of the Virgen del Rosario del Milagro, which sits in a small chapel at the top of a stairway behind the main altar. The statue was supposed to be shipped from Spain to Córdoba in 1592, but the boat carrying it crashed near the shores of Peru. At the same time, a major earthquake drove thousands of Peruvians to the coast. The Peruvians discovered a box holding the saint; there was no trace of the shipwrecked boat or its crew. The Peruvians carried the statue via a relay of horseback riders to Córdoba; her existence and transport are considered a miracle. The Virgin's devotees climb the marble stairs to her statue on their knees, and leave gifts, flowers, and candles in her honor.

One of the more scandalous rumors in Córdoba's gossipy history involves a bishop from the church and the daughter of the house next door. The French manor, built in 1910, was home to the wealthy Doctor Genaro Pérez. The doctor, it is said, came home early one night and nearly caught his daughter in bed with the bishop, who leapt from a second-story window and escaped. Though this particular legend has never been illustrated, much of the rest of Córdoba's history is incorporated in the exhibits at the **Museo de Bellas Artes de Doctor Genaro Pérez**, Avenida General Paz 33.

The Pérez home was donated to the city and served as the provincial and municipal headquarters before being restored as a museum of fine arts. Paintings and sculptures by local artists fill the grand parlors and ballrooms. Emilio Caraffa, who painted the murals in the cathedral, created a mural of the Perez family on the ceiling in the largest room. Nineteenth and twentieth century portraits of the city's elite residents and paintings of the nearby countryside and *estancias* provide a tour of the province's history; modern works in the upstairs bedrooms demonstrate the city's ongoing devotion to the arts. There's another incentive for visiting the museum — its ground-floor Internet café. The museum is open from 10 AM to 8 PM Tuesday through Sunday. Admission is free.

What may well be the finest colonial home left in the city now houses the **Museo Histórico Pro-**

vincial **Casa del Virrey Marqués de Sobremonte** ((351) 433-1661, Calle Rosario de Santa Fé 218. The two-story building includes 26 rooms and five interior courtyards. Its esteemed collection of Indian and gaucho artifacts includes furnishings, costumes and household implements. Admission is charged, and the hours are maddeningly erratic. In summer the building may be open only one morning a week, while in winter, when school groups from throughout the province visit Córdoba on field trips, the museum is open from Tuesday through Saturday mornings.

La Cañada, an upscale district west of the historical center, lies along the banks of a tributary of the Río Suquía on Avenida Marcelo T. Alvear. The city's founders first settled along the river, until a massive flood in the sixteenth century drove them further east. The Spaniards built stone and lime walls to contain the river, but it continued flooding the city periodically. In the late nineteenth and early twentieth century the west banks of the river were called "El Otro Mundo" (The Other World), an unsavory neighborhood of gambling halls and whorehouses. A famous ghost, *la Pelada de la Cañada*, was said to inhabit the river, attacking anyone who tried to cross at night.

The neighborhood was literally washed away in a drastic flood in 1936, and steep walls were constructed to prevent future tragedies. Today, jacaranda and *palo borracho* trees line pedestrian pathways beside broad avenues above the river. Stone bridges arch over the river along Avenida Marcelo T. Alvear. The bridge along Calle 27 de Abril leads to the **Paseo Sobremonte**, a garden-like plaza designed in the late nineteenth century. The park once held the city's reservoir, a manmade lake with a loggia in the center. The lake has been replaced with a fountain, but many of the trees planted a century ago remain. Similar trees are the only remaining evidence of a turn-of-the-century neighborhood destroyed when the city constructed the austere **Plaza Municipal** at Avenida Alvear and Caseros in 1983. The plaza is used for city functions, and contains a statue commemorating the Malvinas War. The unremarkable **Palacio Municipal**, built in 1961, faces the plaza, as does the comber neoclassic-style **Palacio de Justicia**.

Fancy hotels, office buildings, and homes line the quiet, shady streets around La Cañada and the **Plaza Veléz Sarsfield**, a small circular park at the juncture of several major streets. Veléz Sarsfield, an attorney born in the Calamuchita Valley outside the city, is one of Córdoba's major heroes and the author of Argentina's civil code. His statue was sculpted by Giulio Tadolini in 1897. Catalan artist Alberto Barral is responsible for the lifelike polar bear sculpture in the same park.

The **Teatro San Martín**, Avenida Veléz Sarsfield 365, Argentina's oldest theater, faces the park. The French nouveau theater was constructed as an opera house, and has excellent acoustics. Nearby, a somewhat gaudy French palace from 1907 has been transformed into **Patio Olmos**, Avenida Veléz Sarsfield and Boulevard San Juan, the most popular shopping plaza in the city. Like Galerías Pacífico in Buenos Aires, Patio Olmos covers a full city block with several levels of shops, a movie theater complex, and a children's amusement area called Isla de Fantasia. The top floor is almost completely devoted to dining, with a wide array of takeout stands offering inexpensive meals.

Southeast of the city proper is a breath of fresh air, the large **Parque Sarmiento** along Avenida Poeta Lugones. Commissioned in 1911 and

Hotel rates rise in summer and fall considerably in winter. Hotels below are categorized by their highest rates. Most hotels offer complimentary Continental breakfast. Beware of telephone charges, which are usually exorbitantly high, even for local calls.

Expensive

Córdoba needed a modern hotel, but it got more than it bargained for with the **Sheraton Córdoba Hotel (** (351) 488-9000 TOLL-FREE IN THE UNITED STATES (800) 325-3535 FAX (351) 488-9150. Locals have dubbed it the "haircurler" for its ribbed glass towers rising above the skyline. It's nowhere near the historic center and is totally geared toward

designed by architect Carlos Thays, the park's attractions include a lake, a small zoo, and meandering pathways for bicyclists and rollerskaters. The Río Suquía curves along the northern edge of the city, providing a greenbelt along the river banks. The most significant park along the river is **Parque Costanera** which is closed to traffic between the Puente Avellaneda and Puente Eliseo Cantón bridges and overtaken by cyclists.

WHERE TO STAY

Like most Argentine cities, Córdoba has few modern hotels; instead, most hotels are located in older buildings that have been somewhat restored. Travelers are best off staying around Plaza San Martín within walking distance of most major attractions. However, some of the nicest hotels are located in the La Cañada district by the river.

business travelers. But the Sheraton does offer a level of service unheard of in this conservative city. A state-of-the-art business center, tennis courts, fitness center, and no-smoking rooms are all unexpected and welcome amenities. Rooms have safe-deposit boxes, satellite television, mini bars, and direct-dial long-distance phones. The modern Nuevocentro shopping mall is just across the driveway.

Moderate

Classy and elegant, the **Amerian Córdoba Park Hotel (** (351) 424-3586 FAX (351) 424-5267, Boulevard San Juan 165, is well situated by Plaza Vélez Sarsfield and La Cañada. Guests relax on the rooftop sundeck beside the pool and sauna. The large rooms have air-conditioning, cable television, and

Caramelized peanuts are a popular street snack.

enormous closets. The hotel has a business center and restaurant. I find this the best place to stay when you can splurge a bit on rooms. The **Panorama Hotel** ((351) 420-4000 FAX (351) 424-5248, Marcelo T. de Alvear 251, is another good upscale choice in La Cañada. As the name implies, the hotel's two towers have wonderful views of the surrounding mountains.

Ladies who lunch appear to have a fondness for the café at the **Windsor Hotel** (/FAX (351) 422-4012, Buenos Aires 214. Perhaps it's the piano bar that causes them to cluster in the restaurant, or the Club de Vida Spa with its heated swimming pool, workout room and sauna. The rooms are well suited to business travelers, and have fax and

modem lines on the phones, along with safe-deposit boxes and desks. National travelers gravitate to the **Gran Hotel Dora** ((351) 421-2031 FAX (351) 424-0167, Entre Ríos 70, but I don't find it a standout. Granted, the hotel was once part of a well-respected national chain. But the owners no longer operate the properties as a chain, and each one seems to be faltering. The Córdoba hotel has an air of faded grandeur, with worn carpets and furnishings. Still, the rooms are immaculately clean, and the location is excellent.

Inexpensive

Thanks to the accommodating staff, the **Felipe II** ((351) 425-5500, San Gerónimo 279, is my favorite budget hotel in Córdoba. Security is superb, and the front desk clerks quickly learn guests' names and preferences. Located just a couple of blocks from the Plaza San Martín, the hotel has plain

brown rooms with private bath. Air-conditioning is controlled by the front desk. Breakfast is served in the first-floor dining room, and light meals are available at the café and bar beside the lobby. Cleanliness is the main attribute of the **Hotel Cristal** ((351) 424-5000, Entre Ríos 58. Some of the tiny rooms have individual air-conditioning controls, along with ceiling fans. The same lobby is used by the **Hotel Argentino** ((351) 424-5000, Entre Ríos 60, which is a bit more bedraggled. International budget travelers gravitate to the **Dallas Hotel** ((351) 421-6091 FAX (351) 421-8024, Calle San Gerónimo 339. The room rates are rock bottom for a hotel with private baths, consistent hot water, and e-mail service for guests.

WHERE TO EAT

As a rule, restaurant meals are far less expensive in Córdoba than they are in Buenos Aires. Most serve Italian dishes and beef, beef, and more beef. There are a few good places for vegetarians, however. Credit cards are often not accepted.

Expensive

Guccio ((351) 422-5135, Avenida Hipólito Yrigoyen 81, is one of the fanciest restaurants in La Cañada, favored by business travelers on expense accounts. The leather and brass decor befits the undeclared dress code; suits are in style here. The menu ranges through France and Italy, offering sublime pâtés, crêpes, and pastas. Fancier than most *parrilla* restaurants, **La Yaya** ((351) 425-5010, Independencia 468, is one of my favorite restaurants in Córdoba. The large dining room covers the main floor of an older house with brick walls and brick and beam ceilings. Tables are spread far enough apart for peaceful conversation, and the waiters translate the menu with humorous patience. A fixed-price menu offers a selection of entrées (try the Roquefort steak) and a salad bar stocked with sausage, cheese, marinated tripe, and several prepared salads. Also included is a dessert display with sweet cakes and *dulce de leche*.

Moderate

Seafood is the specialty at **Las Rias de Galicia** ((351) 428-1333, Montevideo 271. Grilled trout, salmon and tuna are all good choices, as is the *cazuela de mariscos*, a seafood stew. The ambience is sedate, and the restaurant draws a big business lunch crowd. The executive lunch menu, offered on weekdays, includes an entrée, dessert, and drink at a reasonable price. Tourists in shorts are definitely frowned upon here. It seems every other restaurant features Italian cuisine; my favorite is **Il Gatto** ((351) 423-0334, Avenida Colón 628. Bright and airy, the large restaurant is packed at lunch time and again for late dinners. Tables are jammed so close together you can't avoid hearing other people's cell-phone conversations at lunch; it seems everyone is using Il Gatto as a temporary office. The menu lists several types of pastas diners can combine with a variety of sauces; naturally, you can also order a steak. There are several main course salads, a boon to those weighted down from too much pasta and beef. The extensive wine list includes several half-bottle selections.

Inexpensive

Even if you're not on a budget you may return frequently to dine at the food court in Patio Olmos (see WHAT TO SEE AND DO, page 177). Diners can choose from vegetable chop suey at **Wok**, pizza

and steak at **Metro**, salads at **Via Verde** and ice cream at **Freddo**. Best of all, you can eat any time you want, though it's best to avoid the weekday lunch rush from noon to 2 PM.

There is no shortage of cafés and *confiterías* in downtown Córdoba, yet it seems everyone eventually ends up at **El Ruedo (** (351) 422-4453, Obispo Trejo and 27 de Abril near the Santa Catalina Convent. Yellow umbrellas bearing the logo for Isenbeck beer shade the sidewalk tables, where advertising certainly seems to pay off. It seems nearly everyone is drinking a tall bottle of beer with their burgers, platters of meats and cheeses, or chicken milanesa lunches. Ruedo serves the best french fries I've ever had in Argentina, by the way. It's a good place to stop any time of day. It's also fun to hang out at **Café Sorocabana** across the Plaza San Martín. *Empanadas*, individuals pizzas, and sandwiches are incredibly inexpensive, and the

clientele is a fascinating mix of families and crusty old codgers who appear to be glued to their minuscule coffee cups and endless newspapers.

Gigantic fruit and vegetable salads are enough to make those tired of beef delight in finding **Sol y Luna (** (351) 425-1189, General Paz 278. Service is cafeteria style, with a long salad bar and several vegetarian dishes displayed. The fresh vegetables are typically overcooked, unfortunately, but sandwiches and soups are safe bets. Yellow tables and chair are set in a large atrium-style room in a renovated older building. The restaurant is fronted by a natural foods market where you can stock up on dried fruits, trail mix, granola, and herbal teas. Another good health-food restaurant, **Naranja & Verde (** (351) 425-8911, Rivadavia 50, serves my favorite breakfast — a plate of fresh fruit topped with yogurt and granola. They also have brewed decaffeinated coffee — nearly unheard on in Argentina — and do not allow smoking.

HOW TO GET THERE

Córdoba is located 710 km (441 miles) northwest of Buenos Aires. Aerolíneas Argentinas and Lapa Líneas Aereas fly into the **Aeropuerto Internacional (** (351) 481-0696, 11 km (seven miles) north of the city. There are precious few international flights into Córdoba, though airlines occasionally offer flights from Brazil and Chile. The airport underwent major upgrades in 1999, and may become more popular with international carriers.

The **Terminal de Ómnibus (** (351) 423-4704, Boulevard Presidente J.D. Perón 316, is a modern complex with restaurants and shops. Several lines operate from here, and there are direct, first-class buses to most cities in the Sierras. The trip between Buenos Aires and Córdoba takes about 10 hours. The bus terminal is conveniently located close to the historic center.

CÓRDOBA ENVIRONS

Tour companies offer day trips to several areas surrounding the city, stopping at Jesuit missions, mountain villages, lakes, and forests.

The **Valle de Punilla** circuit northwest of the city is one of the most interesting and covers several areas that are major tourism destinations for nationals. Ruta 20 in the Punilla Valley runs through two mountain ranges, the Sierra Chica and the Sierra Grande; the valley received its name because it resembles the puna landscape in the high Andes. Rivers and streams etch a landscape of forests and plains dotted with small towns. The first stop in the Punilla circuit is **La Calera**, a small

OPPOSITE: Colonial arches shade displays near the original city hall. ABOVE: Artists have contributed to the cathedral's grandeur for three centuries.

town named for its lime deposits and kilns. The town sits beside the Río Suquía, which provided the energy to run the mills that ground the lime. A small eighteenth-century chapel sits beside the river.

Traffic jams Ruta 20 on summer weekends when crowds head for **El Dique y Lago San Roque**, the largest lake in the region. The lake is actually formed by the San Roque Dam, an engineering marvel constructed in 1891 under the supervision of engineer Juan Biolet Massé, a student of Gustave Eiffel. A second dam was constructed over the first between 1939 and 1944, and most of the original walls are now underwater. Traffic literally comes to a halt near the dam, as drivers pull to the side every which way and pedestrians stroll along the pavement as if they were in a park. The lively beat of regional *cuarteto* music blares from boom boxes, and the air is redolent with the aroma of sizzling sausages. Vendors set up stands and barbecues along the roadside and sell grilled *chorizo* (fat, spicy sausages made in the region), along with regional cheese, salami, and *pan casero* (bread baked in wood burning ovens). Sightseers munch on *tutucas* (a puffed corn snack) and stock up on *maní dulce* (peanuts stirred in a hot sugar) and *alfajores* (cookies layered with *dulce de leche* or marmalade). Eating seems to be the main attraction here, though guides do lead groups around the edges of the dam, pointing out features of its construction.

The lake is the centerpiece of **Villa Carlos Paz**, the largest tourist resort in Córdoba Province. Founded by General Carlos Paz in 1915, the town was once a picturesque spot with chalet-style homes and hotels on hills overlooking the lake. Today, it is a somewhat peaceful spot with some 40,000 residents. The population swells tenfold in summer, however, as Argentines flee the cities and the blazing heat in the north and descend upon the low Sierras. Restaurants, discos, casinos, and hotels open for the season, and Villa Carlos Paz becomes as hectic and festive as Mar del Plata, Argentina's most popular coastal resort.

Absolutely everyone eventually climbs aboard on the **Teleférico Autosilla** on San Martín for the six-minute ride to the top of a hill overlooking the city and lake. Visitors must run the gauntlet through a mass of vendors to reach the ride, which costs US$10 per person. Naturally, there are plenty of photographers posted at the top to shoot instant family portraits. Similar vistas are available to those who climb **Cerro de la Cruz**, which rises 2,200 m (7,218 ft) above the city.

Since Carlos Paz is popular with vacationing families, amusement parks and manmade attractions abound. Boating, fishing, and windsurfing operations line parts of the lake. Mountain biking, horseback riding and hiking are all popular sports as well, and those on annual holidays find

plenty of distractions. Wealthy Argentines have not totally abandoned Carlos Paz as it has evolved into a mainstream destination. They just hole up in veritable family castles built in the early twentieth century, and play and dine at exclusive clubs.

Most foreign travelers are satisfied with a short tour of Carlos Paz, especially in its most crowded state. They prefer to continue on through the mountains to **La Falda**, a far more sedate resort town built around a dammed lake. Upscale travelers have been drawn to this mountain village since 1899, when the German immigrants built the magical **Hotel Eden** at the end of Avenida Eden. Now a crumbled ruin akin to a twentieth-century archeological ruin, the palatial hotel sits crumbling amid groves of eucalyptus trees, overgrown gardens, and worn statuary. At its peak, the Hotel Eden was like a small city. Visitors arrived in horse-drawn carriages and spent weeks in the 100 rooms, sharing 38 bathrooms. Grand dances and concerts were held in the ballroom, visible from the broken stairway leading to the entrance. The building is closed to the public, but plenty of holes in the walls provide glimpses of pillars and parquet wood floors.

In its glory days the hotel hosted Argentine presidents, Albert Einstein, writer Ruben Diario and countless famous personages. Some say even Adolf Hitler stayed here. During World War II, Nazi sympathizers (and Nazis on the run) made the hotel the center of Argentina's pro-Hitler society. During protests against the Nazi presence, demonstrators destroyed a large statue of an eagle holding a globe that was meant to represent Germany's control of the world. Similar Nazi symbols left no doubt who ruled this secluded enclave.

Stripped of all insignias and identifying markers, the hotel closed in 1957. It would take a considerable fortune to restore and reopen the property, which sits like a ghostly presence behind an iron gate. Visitors are allowed to wander the grounds when guards are present, usually from 9:30 AM to 12:30 PM and 3 PM to 5 PM.

Chalet-style hotels with window boxes and tidy flower gardens line Avenida Eden between the town center and the Hotel Eden. Visitors typically settle into the quiet local lifestyle, hiking and biking in the mountains (there are especially good views from atop Cerro de la Bandita, which rises 800 m/2,625 ft above the town). Golfing, fishing and boating on the lake, and shopping for regional woodcarvings and sweaters are the other major activities. In general, visitors come to enjoy the mountain air and relax.

Several small towns around Villa Carlos Paz and La Falda are worth checking out. The views along the mountain highways are soothing rather

The Colegio Nacional de Monserat was one of Córdoba's first universities.

than spectacular. The hills are rich in minerals and semiprecious stones; gold mining was once one of the region's main attractions. Ruta 38 leads north from La Falda to the mountain village of **La Cumbre**, known for its bountiful streams and valleys, gloriously clear air, and its golf courses. **Capilla del Monte**, at the northern end of the Punilla Valley, is favored by active travelers and naturalists, thanks to its orchards, waterfalls, springs, and hiking trails.

Pan de Azúcar towers over Ruta 38 south of La Falda near **Cosquín**, site of the country's largest folklore festival in January. A bustling, busy city, Cosquín was an important stop on the trail between Cusco and Córdoba even before the Spaniards arrived. The Inca are said to have traveled here from Cusco, and the city is named for the *cacique*, or chief, of the local tribe. The Conquistadors followed that same trail during in colonial times, and though modern highways have long bypassed the town, Cosquín remains an important cultural hub and the commercial center for the Punilla Valley.

Ruta 5 runs south of Córdoba city to the **Valle de Calamuchita**, another popular tour circuit. The most important stop of the route is **Alta Gracia**, birthplace of Argentina's current president, Fernando de la Rúa. The Jesuits established the **Iglesia Nuestra Señora de la Merced** here in 1643, and the town was the home of Viceroy Santiago Liniers, who led Argentina's resistance forces during the British invasion of Buenos Aires in 1806. His home is now a museum. A more modern revolutionary, Ernesto "Che" Guevara lived here during his youth. His family moved from Rosario to Alta Gracia in 1932, when Che was four years old, because doctors said the climate would help the boy's asthma. Best known for his role in Fidel Castro's invasion of Cuba in 1956, Guevara was a medical doctor devoted to populist causes from Guatemala to the Congo. He began his famed motorcycle trip around South America in Córdoba in 1951; the trip is detailed in *The Motorcycle Diaries*, a travelogue and interior monologue that follows the evolution of a revolutionary.

The Calamuchita circuit also covers **Villa General Belgrano**, a diehard German settlement 90 km (56 miles) southwest of Córdoba. German is far more common than Spanish in the town's restaurants and souvenir shops. Anyone hankering for Viennese pastries, homemade chocolates, or traditional German cooking will feel right at home. Normally low-key, Villa General Belgrano bursts to life for the October Fiesta Nacional de la Cerveza (The Beer festival or Oktoberfest).

The day trip circuit to these cities also includes a stop at the **Dique los Molinos**, a smaller and more picturesque dam than Dique San Roque. **Cerro Champaquí**, the highest peak in Córdoba's

Sierras, rises 2,800 m (9,186 ft) in the distance above the town of **La Cumbrecita**, another settlement of German émigrés and their descendants. Hiking trails lead into the mountain's cedar and cypress forests to rivers and waterfalls.

HOW TO GET THERE

Travelers typically visit these areas on tours from Córdoba or with a rental car. The Tourist Information office staff will willingly set up both for you, or you can arrange a tour on your own with **Agencia de Turismo Itati** ((351) 422-5020, 27 de Abril 220, or **Dalí Viajes** ((351) 424-6605, Chacabuco 321. Rental cars are available from **Avis** (351) 422-7384.

The best way to get around is by hiring a *remise* (private taxi) with a guide who speaks your language. Most hotels in Córdoba deal directly with *remise* companies and can set up a car for you. Be insistent about the language, however. I've hired English-speaking guides in Córdoba who don't have a very good command of the language. They've worked out fine, since we usually end up speaking a combination of English and Spanish. But if you don't speak Spanish you'll be lost. It may cost a bit extra to get a good guide through a tour or *remise* company, but their insights into the culture are worth every peso.

You can get to most of the towns on these circuits via public bus from Córdoba's main bus terminal.

SAN LUIS PROVINCE

Often overlooked by foreign tourists, San Luis Province is growing in popularity among national tourists, especially those seeking natural attractions. The province's eponymous capital city, **San Luis**, is located 450 km (280 m) southwest of Córdoba and 850 km (528 m) northwest of Buenos Aires. Alternately described as the doorway to the Cuyo District (around Mendoza) or the entryway to Nuevo Cuyo (which incorporates several outlying provinces), San Luis sits on the western side of the Sierras de Córdoba. The city has a population of about 150,000 residents and a few colonial-era buildings.

VILLA DE MERLO

Of more interest to tourists is Villa de Merlo, a colonial city in the Sierras de los Comechingones 180 km (112 m) northeast of San Luis. Etched by rivers and waterfalls, the region around Merlo is similar to that around Córdoba, with small mountain villages popular with summer vacationers. Merlo has long been considered a place of healing and is believed to have an unusual microclimate. Its mountainous location makes for cool, but not cold, temperatures and dry air. Believers say it is one of the few places in the world loaded with negative ions, said to reduce stress. Its ozone levels are high, and an abundance of nitrous oxide in the atmosphere is supposed to generate a feeling of well being. There is an abundance of uranium in the local mountains, which contributes to these atmospheric conditions. All these factors combined supposedly dilate the arteries and elevate the oxygen levels in the brain.

In addition to its atmospheric highlights, Merlo is surrounded by enough natural beauty to make anyone high on nature. Rivers, waterfalls, hot springs, and snowcapped mountain peaks surround the small town of some 7,000 inhabitants. The town's hotels and restaurants are clustered around Avenida del Sol near the **Plaza Marqués de Sobremonte**, bordered by Coronel Mercau, Presidente Juan D. Perón, Presbítero Mercau and Juan de Videla.

Hiking, horseback riding, bird watching, and rock climbing are all excellent, and the region is so sparsely populated that llamas, pumas, mountain lions, and foxes all thrive in the countryside. Dinosaurs may also have inhabited this remote region. In 1996, workers preparing roads for pavement in the Piedras Blancas district of Merlo discovered the carapace of a mammal dating to the Pliocene period; several other fossils have since been discovered. Visitors can reach the are via dirt road, or see some of the fossils at the small **Museo Lolma** at the west end of Avenida de las Incas in Piedras Blancas.

Few visitors make their way to the rugged red Sierras de Quijadas in the northwest corner of San Luis Province, though scientists find the region fascinating. Palaeontological digs are taking place at **El Parque Nacional Sierras de las Quijadas**, a remote 150,000-hectare (370,650-acre) national park. Dramatic ochre and gold sandstone cliffs and rock formations extend as far as the eye can see, and the air is dry and alternately hot and chilly. The park's greatest attractions are the dinosaur tracks and fossils dating back 150 million years uncovered by scientists from the National University of San Luis. Trails etch the canyons and casual hikers can follow a few well-marked paths. But serious hikers should check in with the rangers at the entrance to the park or hire a guide from one of the tour companies in Merlo. The park is 125 km (78 miles) from San Luis and 290 km (180 m) from Merlo off Ruta 147. The best tours for those interested in paleontology are offered by the **Grupo de Investigaciones Geológicas Aplicadas** at the Universidad Nacional de San Luis ((2652) 42-3789 extension 124, Chacabuco y Pedernera, San Luis. Scientists working in the park lead small groups to the fossil sites and explain the geology of the region. Reservations must be made in advance.

General Information

Merlo's **Tourist Information Office** ((2652) 476079 is located by the *rotunda* (traffic circle) at the intersection of Ruta 5 and Ruta 1. They can provide an excellent booklet on the region written in Spanish, along with information on accommodation and tours. The **Dirección de Turismo Municipal** ((2652) 47-6078 is located across from the Plaza Marqués de Sobremonte at Coronel Mercau 605. Spanish speakers can find extensive information at the WEB SITE www.merlo-online.com.ar.

A vehicle is essential for visiting the region around Merlo. Several tour companies offer transport in vans or four-wheel-drive vehicles. **Turismo Alternativo Merlo** (/FAX (2656) 47-6050 specialize in nature tours, bird watching, and hiking. **Turismo Fonseca** (/FAX (2656) 47-7165 is a full-service travel agency that can arrange accommodation, tours and airline tickets.

Where to Stay and Eat

Many of Merlo's hotels are open only during the summer tourist season, and fill up on weekends and holidays. One of the best resort-style hotels **Parque Hotel** ((2656) 475110 FAX (2656) 475659 E-MAIL nba@merlo-sl.com.ar is located close to the plaza. Many of the rooms have views of the forests and mountains, and the facilities include pools, tennis courts, massage services, and tours. Similar in style is the **Hotel Villa del Merlo** ((2656) 475335 FAX (2656) 475019, Pedernera at Avenida del Sol. Rates are moderate.

Yana Munay ((2656) 475055, Avenida de los Cesares at Rincón del Este, is an excellent choice for those on a budget. The hostel has several rooms with private baths, and a popular tea house.

Along with the typical meat and pastas dishes, restaurants in Merlo serve trout and other freshwater fish caught in the nearby rivers. **El Tonel** ((2656) 476597, Avenida del Deporte and Avenida de los Almendros, a chalet-style restaurant, specializes in fish, but also offers *parrilla* grilled meats. **El Ciprés del Tornado** ((2656) 475537 serves excellent roasted baby goat, another local specialty, along with crayfish, octopus, and mussels. Both are inexpensive to moderate. There are many small cafés and pizza parlors around the plaza and on Avenida del Sol. When you are traveling in the countryside keep an eye out for a *salón de té*. These tea houses serve lavish afternoon teas with homemade pastries and sandwiches.

How to Get There

Aerolíneas Argentina and Lapa Líneas Aereas serve the **Aeropuerto San Luis** ((2656) 423047 with flights from Buenos Aires and Córdoba. Local buses travel between San Luis and Merlo; long-range buses connect both cities with Buenos Aires (13 hours) and Córdoba (five hours).

Mendoza
and the
High
Andes

THE ROUGH AND RUGGED CUYO REGION IS ARGENTINA'S WILD WEST, a pair of neighboring provinces — San Luis and Mendoza — that span the transition zone from the High Andes to the Pampas. Aconcagua, the highest mountain in the western hemisphere at 6,959 m (22,834 ft), dominates the crest of the cordillera along the border with Chile. But the region boasts 19 other peaks over 6,000 m (19,680 ft).

Lying as they do in the rain shadow of the Andes, the area is extremely arid, with vast expanses of nothing but stone and sand. In fact, the name Cuyo stems from the local Indian word *cuyum* ("sandy ground").

Still, the glaciers and the snowy slopes of the Andes provide enough runoff to transform the sandy alluvial soil into some of the most fertile in all of South America. Irrigation has converted Cuyo into a veritable garden of delights, one of the nation's foremost fruit growing regions. The local specialty is grapes, stomped and pressed into wine in hundreds of wineries scattered around Mendoza. Nearly half of the region's cultivated land is devoted to grapes and more than 90% of Argentina's wine is made in Cuyo.

The dry climate, in combination with the mountains and rivers, makes Cuyo a nirvana of outdoor recreation. It goes without saying that this is one of the world's premier mountain climbing and trekking regions. Snow skiing is also prevalent. Other possibilities include kayaking and whitewater rafting, horseback riding and mule treks, fly-fishing and hang-gliding, as well as windsurfing and sailing on Andes-fed reservoirs.

MENDOZA

Fewer than 200 km (124 miles) from Santiago as the crow flies, Cuyo's major city was founded by Spanish settlers pushing up from the Pacific coast rather than the Atlantic. Named after an early Chilean governor-general, Mendoza sprang to life in 1561 as a military outpost, an Indian mission and a supply center for local cattle ranches and wineries.

Mendoza didn't come under Argentine sovereignty until the late 1700s and it didn't really prosper until the 1880s when the railroad arrived from Buenos Aires. Almost overnight, the city's population boomed with new immigrants from Europe — mostly Spaniards and Italians — who immediately infused the city with a distinct Mediterranean air.

Mendoza has grown into one of Argentina's largest cities, with more than 800,000 people in the metropolitan area and a solid economic foundation of wineries, petrochemical plants and small factories. The aquamarine waters of the Río Mendoza irrigate the city's myriad parks, plazas and gardens, as well as the leafy sycamore and poplar trees that line many of the avenues.

On sultry summer evenings, much of the population pours out onto the streets to promenade, watch buskers or lounge in the city's numerous sidewalk cafés. Mendoza is also an ideal place to organize climbing, treks and other ventures in the Central Andes.

Mendoza likes to fancy itself as the hometown of General José de San Martín, the liberator of Argentina, Chile and Peru. San Martín lived here for many years and left an indelible mark on the city — Mendoza's major avenue and park bare his name, as do many other local landmarks and institutions. But he was actually born at Yapeyú in far northern Argentina and is buried in Buenos Aires. Still, Mendoza is where the general's legacy seems to linger most decisively.

The city's biggest annual bash is the **Fiesta Nacional de la Vendimia** (National Wine Harvest Festival) which goes on an entire week in late February or early March during the height of the

harvest. Quaffing locally produced Cabernet and Merlot is the fiesta's primary aim, but there's plenty of special events including a parade, a beauty contest, concerts and gala balls. The festival also entails religious rites, with special ceremonies at the Calvario de la Carrodilla church in Godoy Cruz.

GENERAL INFORMATION

The best source of information in the city is the **tourist kiosk** at the corner of Garibaldi and San Martín ((261) 420-1333, run by the municipal government's Centro de Información y Asistencia al Turismo. This was the friendliest and most helpful tourist office I encountered in all of Argentina and it's generally staffed by an English-speaking clerk. The kiosk offers maps, brochures and handouts on hotels, restaurants and activities in both Mendoza city and province. Open daily 9 AM to 9 PM.

Staff at the Mendoza Province **Subsecretaría de Turismo** ((261) 420-2800 FAX (261) 420-2243, Avenida San Martín 1143, are equally cordial but not nearly as efficient. Open weekdays only, 7 AM to 9 PM.

Almost every travel agency in town offers city and local tours, but my own favorite is **Turismo Mendoza** ((261) 429-2013, Avenida Las Heras 543.

Among the better places to change money and travelers' checks are **Cambios Exprinter** ((261) 438-0333, Avenida San Martín 1198, and right across the street at **Cambio Santiago** ((261) 420-0277, Avenida San Martín 1199. If you require more complicated financial services try **Banco Mendoza** ((261) 449-1900 at the corner of San Martín and Gutiérrez.

Mendoza's **central post office** ((261) 429-0848 is situated at the corner of San Martín and Colón.

The Río Mendoza tumbles down from the Andes near the city that bears its name.

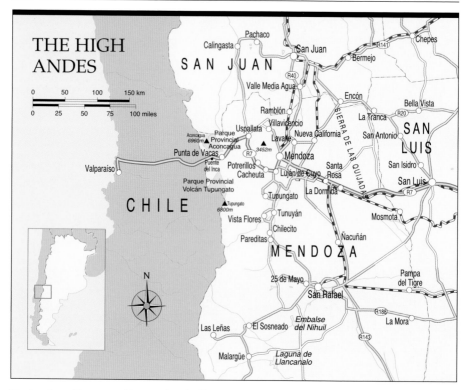

THE HIGH ANDES

0   50   100   150 km
0   25   50   75   100 miles

Valparaíso

CHILE

N

Pachaco
Calingasta   San Juan   R141   Chepes
SAN JUAN   Bermejo
R40
Valle Media Agua
Encón   Bella Vista
Ramblón   La Tranca   R20
Villavicencio   SAN
Aconcagua Parque Uspallata   Nueva California   San Antonio   LUIS
6960m Provincial   Lavalle
Aconcagua   3452m
Punta de Vacas   R7   Mendoza
Puente Potrerillos   Santa   San Isidro
del Inca Cacheuta Luján de Cuyo Rosa
Parque Provincial   San Luis
Volcán Tupungato   Tupungato   La Dormida   R7
Tupungato
6800m   Tunuyán   Mosmota
Vista Flores   Chilecito
Paretidas   Nacuñán
MENDOZA
25 de Mayo   Pampa
del Tigre
San Rafael
R188
Embalse   La Mora
Las Leñas   El Sosneado del Nihuil
R143
Malargüe   Laguna de
Llancanalo

SIERRA DE LAS QUIJADAS

To place long distance and international calls try **Telefónica** at Calle Chile 1584. A number of private outlets also offer long distance service including **Teléfonos Mendoza (** (261) 420-1704, at the corner of San Martín and Rivadavia, and **Fonobar (** (261) 429-2957, Peatonal Sarmiento 23. One of the city's few Internet cafés is **Calle Angosta (** (261) 423-4127 in the Pasaje San Martín which charges US$6 per hour for net surfing and US$2 per e-mail.

Medical treatment is available at **Hospital Central (** (261) 420-0600 or (261) 420-0063 at the corner of Moreno and Alem (near the bus station). **Farmacia del Puente (** (261) 425-8181, Avenida San Martín 1288, is open around the clock every day of the year.

WHAT TO SEE AND DO

At the heart of the city is the sprawling **Plaza Independencia** with its huge shade trees and gurgling fountains, daredevil skateboarders and legions of young lovers. On summer evenings the park transforms into an open-air stage for dozens of local artists and buskers who entertain the strolling crowds. On weekends the plaza hosts a sprawling arts and crafts fair. The plaza is also home to the **Museo Municipal de Arte Moderno (** (261) 425-7279 with its underground galleries (often opening after dark) and the **Teatro Julio**

Quintanilla with a year-round slate of drama, dance and music. Overlooking the square are a number of impressive buildings including the **Teatro Independencia** (1925) and the blue-and-white **Cámara de Diputados** (Mendoza provincial assembly).

Orbiting Plaza Independencia are four smaller squares, each of them two blocks away. The most interesting are **Plaza España** with its striking Don Quixote mural and **Plaza San Martín**, a glowing tribute to the city's favorite son that includes an equestrian statue and more than a hundred plaques from various organizations. At the corner of Necochea and España (opposite Plaza San Martín) is rose-colored **San Francisco Basilica**, the city's foremost church, which safeguards a sacred icon called the Virgin de Cuyo and the remains of many of General San Martin's relatives.

Like so much of the city, Mendoza's main streets are ripe for strolling. **Avenida San Martín** dissects the downtown area from north to south, flanked by banks, restaurants, souvenir shops and sidewalk cafés. The hustle-bustle runs from late morning until around midnight but is most active in the early evening, when thousands of people are prowling the sidewalks. There are a number of interesting structures including the art nouveau-style **Pasaje San Martín** and **Edificio Gomez**, modeled after the Empire State Building.

Running three blocks between Avenida San Martín and Plaza Independencia is the sycamore-lined **Peatonal Sarmiento** pedestrian mall with its many shops and cafés. At night, this is another popular hangout for roving musicians and magicians.

The downtown area's other busy street is **Avenida Las Heras**, which runs east–west from Avenida San Martín to the old train station. Las Heras has its own collection of cafés and coffee houses, as well as supermarkets and electronic stores. But its main attraction is one of the most peculiar "museums" in all of South America, the **Museo Popular Callejero**, nine display cases on the sidewalk outside the Theatre María Mazzarello that relate the history of the street from the 1830s through modern times. Dioramas and photos recall high points in local history including a 1935 visit by American actor Clark Gable and the 1885 inauguration of Mendoza's railroad depot by President Roca. The exhibits also show the evolution of transportation along the street from ox carts and wagons in the early nineteenth century to the introduction of horse-drawn trolleys in the 1890s to Model-T Fords in the 1920s.

History buffs also delight in the **Museo Histórico General San Martín** ((261) 425-7947, Remedios Escalada de San Martín 1843, housed in a modern building on the site where the general lived and planned the trans-Andes campaign. Exhibits include weapons, uniforms, paintings, flags and maps used by San Martín and his Army of the Andes, as well as household furnishings and clothing used by ordinary people in nineteenth-century Mendoza. Open weekdays only, 9 AM to noon.

A couple of blocks east of the San Martín Museum is yet another historical gem, the **Museo del Area Fundacional** ((261) 425-6927 on Plaza Pedro del Castillo, a shockingly modern structure with an eclectic collection that spans the origin of early man in the Cuyo region, the advent of local Spanish colonial culture and the foundation of Mendoza (hence the name). The museum's centerpiece is the ruined Cabildo, an exquisite Spanish building destroyed by the 1861 earthquake that razed much of colonial Mendoza. Open Tuesday to Saturday 8 AM to 2 PM and 4:30 PM to 8:30 PM; Sunday 3 PM to 10 PM. Scattered around the museum are other quake victims including the ruins of **San Francisco Monastery**, originally constructed in 1638 as a Jesuit compound and later seized by the Franciscans.

Dominating the western edge of Mendoza is yet another homage to the great liberator—**Parque General San Martín**. This is one of Argentina's finest urban parks, more than 50,000 trees set around an artificial lake and scattered across 420 hectares (1,038 acres) of green space. Other park attractions include the **Mendoza Zoo** (open Tuesday to Sunday 9 AM to 7 PM) and a lofty mount called **Cerro de la Gloria** crowned by a massive stone monument to San Martín's Army of the Andes. The park also boasts several **museums** including collections devoted to natural history and anthropology, geology, and local archaeology. If you don't feel like hoofing the 10 blocks from Plaza Independencia to the park, hop aboard bus number 110 on Calle Sarmiento at the west end of the plaza.

Mendoza's finest art collection is **Casa de Fader** (aka the Museo Provincial de Bellas Artes Emiliano Guinazú) ((261) 496-0224, about 40 minutes south of the city on a pleasant suburb called Luján de

Cuyo. The collection is dominated by Argentine painters and sculptors, but the historic residence is also worth checking out. If you don't have wheels, try bus number 200 from downtown Mendoza. Open Tuesday to Friday 9:30 AM to 1:30 PM and 3 PM to 7 PM; Saturday and Sunday 4:30 PM to 8:30 PM.

In nearby Godoy Cruz is the region's most revered church, **Calvario de la Carrodilla**, which shelters an eighteenth-century statue of the Virgin of Carrodilla, patron saint of grape growers and winemakers. The compound also offers a small museum of religious icons and artifacts, a very interesting modern mural, and a small but picturesque cloister. Across the street is a small restaurant that sells both souvenirs and delicious homemade *empanadas*.

More than 1,200 *bodegas* (wineries) lie within a two-hour drive of Mendoza.

Wineries

Mendoza is Argentina's Napa Valley, the fulcrum of a booming viticulture business that embraces more than 1,200 *bodegas* (wineries) within a 100-km (62-mile) radius of the city center. The climate and soil — in league with irrigation — make the area almost ideal for growing certain types of grapes. The main harvest takes place in February and March.

With a vehicle you can easily undertake a "winery hopping" tour of Mendoza's hinterland. Otherwise join a winery tour offered by one of the travel agencies in town. **Mendoza Tours (** (261) 429-2013 or (216) 420-1701, Las Heras 543, offers a half-day tour that includes visits to several prominent *bodegas* (wineries).

Although other wineries may produce better plonk, **Antigua Bodega Giol (** (261) 497-2592 or (261) 497-6777, Avenida Ozamis 1040 in Maipú, is the region's most famous. Founded in 1896 by Italian immigrants Juan Giol and Bautista Gargantini, it was once Latin America's largest winery and pioneered many gadgets and techniques used in wine production around the world. Giol went bankrupt in 1911 and the owners sold the property to the government for about 10% of its actual worth. Over the next 70 years, with provincial bureaucrats at the helm, quantity and quality plummeted. The downward spiral wasn't reversed until 1993 when the huge estate was finally transformed into a private cooperative.

The hour-long Bodega Giol winery tour includes a stroll through the original cellars, dominated by a giant French oak cask (with a capacity of 75,000 liters) declared a cultural monument by the provincial government. Giol's tasting room offers cabernet sauvignon, Riesling, Muscat and Chablis, as well as local gourmet food products like bottled olives and olive oil. A short distance from the winery is the **Museo Nacional del Vino (** (261) 497-5255, Avenida Ozamis 914, housed in the historic Casa de Giol.

For a glimpse of the modern side of the Mendoza wine industry drop into the **Bodega Fabre-Montmayou (** (261) 498-2330 FAX (261) 498-2511, Carral R. Sáenz Peña in Vistalba. This chic "boutique winery" uses traditional French techniques to produce a limited amount of high-quality Merlot, Malbec and Cabernet Sauvignon. The property was founded in 1988 by French immigrants, who decided that Mendoza's climate and soil were the very best in South America for growing red-wine grapes. Fabre churns out around 400,000 liters per year, with 80% slated for export to Europe and North America.

By contrast, **Bodega Chandon (** (261) 490-9966 FAX (261) 490-9925, Ruta 40 Km 29 in Agrelo, produces some of the region's best white wines, including Chardonnay, Riesling and

sparkling wine. **Bodega Rutini (** (800) 65999 on Avenida Montecaseros in Coquimbito, boasts a very good tasting room as well as its own wine-making museum.

Other visitor-friendly wineries in the Mendoza area include **Bodega Toso (** (261) 438-0244, Avenida J.B. Alberdi 808 in suburban Guaymallén; **Bodega Santa Ana (** (261) 421-1000 at the junction of Urquiza and Roca in Guaymallén; and **Bodega Escorihuela (** (261) 424-2744 or (261) 424-2282, Avenida Belgrano 1188 in Godoy Cruz.

SPORTS

Mendoza is an excellent place to arrange both summer and winter adventure sports outings into the nearby Andes and the Cuyo foothills.

Snow Skiing

The winter sports season runs from late May to early October depending on snow conditions. The closest place to ski is **Vallecitos (** (261) 431-1957 in the Cordon del Plata Mountains, 79 km (49 miles) northeast of Mendoza. It's pretty small by European or North American standards (just six runs) but the budget prices more than compensate. Most people ski Vallecitos as a day trip from Mendoza, but there's a modest *hostería* for those who want to spend the night.

Snuggled up in the High Andes near the base of Aconcagua is **Los Penitentes** ski resort **(** (261) 429-5500 or (261) 429-4868, which sits astride the Pan-American Highway route to Chile. It's much farther from Mendoza (160 km / 100 miles) and thus much harder to tackle as a day trip from the city. But Penitentes offers several accommodation options and it's a much larger ski area with multiple lifts and two dozen runs. Cross-country skiing and snowboarding are also available. Daily lift passes run around US$30.

Cuyo's top ski resort is **Las Leñas (** (2627) 471100 which requires an overnight stay because of its distance from the city. You can also duck through the trans-Andes highway tunnel to several ski resorts on the Chilean side of the border. To check the latest ski conditions at all of these resorts pop into **Esquí Mendoza Competición (** (261) 425-2801, Las Heras 583; **Rezagos de Ejército (** (261) 423-3791, Mitre 2002; or **Extreme (** (261) 429-0773, Colón 733. All three outlets rent out and sell winter clothing, skis, boots, etc.

Several local bus companies run daily coaches to Penitentes and Las Leñas during the ski season including **Autotransportes Mendoza (** (261) 431-4561 or (261) 431-4628 and **Expreso Uspallata (** (261) 425-7638 or (261) 438-1092 E-MAIL eusa@satlink.com WEBSITE www.turismouspallata.com, corner of Las Heras and Peru.

Mountain Climbing and Trekking

There are numerous challenging peaks in the nearby Andes. The most popular ascent is Aconcagua, the highest peak in South America and a "must climb" for anyone trying to scale the "Seven Sisters" — the highest mountains on all seven continents. Except for the extreme altitude, Aconcagua is actually considered a pretty easy climb compared to other Cuyo peaks. Permits are required for most climbs and treks, available at the **Dirección de Recursos Naturales Renovables** ((261) 425-2090 or (261) 425-7065, Parque General San Martín in Mendoza.

Anyone contemplating a climb or trek should consult the experts at **Club Andinista Mendoza** ((261) 431-9870, Calle Beltran 357. If you want someone else to organize your expedition try **Aymara Turismo y Aventura** ((261) 420-0607 or (261) 420-5304 E-MAIL aymara@satlink.com, Calle 9 de Julio 983, which can arrange instruction, equipment, supplies and transportation. An experienced local mountain guide is **Fernando Grajales** (/FAX (261) 429-3830.

Rafting and Kayaking

Every weekend you can spot dozens of kayakers and rafters running rugged waters of the Río Mendoza between Mendoza and Uspallata in the Andes foothills. Among the many local travel agencies that outfit whitewater rafting trips is **Betancourt Rafting** ((261) 439-0229 or (261) 439-1949 E-MAIL betancourt@lanet.com.ar, at the junction of the Pan-American Highway and Río Cuevas in Godoy Cruz. Trips vary from quick half-day jaunts to three-day camping expeditions.

Cycling

The rolling foothills to the west of Mendoza and the vast Pampas to the east present ideal terrain for cycling. Several local outfitters arrange guided mountain bike trips in the rugged terrain west of the city including the aforementioned Aymara and Betancourt.

SHOPPING

Mendoza's reputation as a shopping destination has improved greatly in recent years with the advent of new shops specializing in traditional Argentine arts and crafts or regional gourmet food items. Many of the better outlets are found within a few blocks of one another along Avenida Las Heras in the central city.

Las Vinas Centro Artesanal Argentino ((261) 425-1520 FAX (261) 438-0128, Avenida Las Heras 399, would seem to have something for everyone — gold and silver jewelry, leather goods, ceramics, T-shirts, and local wines. They'll also ship to anywhere in the world.

Similar merchandise is available at **Regional Los Andes** ((261) 425-6688, Avenida Las Heras 445, which also hawks local wines, sweets and textiles. The nearby **Galería Turistica Artesanal** ((261) 423-4102, Avenida Las Heras 351, offers up dried fruit and chocolates with its arts and crafts.

Sweet-tooths should also make a beeline to **Chocolates la Cabana** ((261) 430-6606, Avenida San Martín 2624. You can also visit their factory at Videla Correa 338.

Crafts with an aboriginal Indian flavor feature at **Neyu-Mapú** ((261) 425-3263 in the Piazza Centro Comercial shopping complex at the corner of San Martín and Amigorena. Although it's an awful long way south of the Río Grande,

Mexican arts and crafts are the specialty at **Tonala Tienda Mexicana** ((261) 420-4852, Peatonal Sarmiento 641.

Plaza Independencia transforms itself into a lively **mercado de las artes** every Friday, Saturday and Sunday. Prices tend to be lower than in the nearby shops. Another place to hunt for bargains are the stalls in the **Mercado Central** on Avenida Las Heras and **Mercado Artesanal** in the basement at Avenida San Martín 1133.

There are several general purpose shopping malls in the metro area including the **Palmares Open Mall** in suburban Godoy Cruz and **Mendoza Plaza** ((261) 449-0100. You can find a **Metro** supermarket at the corner of Mitre and General Paz in downtown Mendoza.

Automation has replaced foot stomping at this *bodega* in Maipú.

WHERE TO STAY

Expensive

Mendoza's only real luxury hotel is the **Reina Victoria (** (261) 425-9800 FAX (261) 425-9800, Calle San Juan 1127, in a lovely red-brick building with white trim that looks much older than it really is. The rooms are a tad bit on the prissy side for a masculine place like Mendoza, but they've got all the bells and whistles you could possibly want including mini bars, coffee makers, cable television, smoke alarms, safe-deposit boxes, and air-conditioning. If you've got time to relax, there's also an indoor heated pool and health club. Reservations are *strongly* advised — the Reina Victoria has just 20 rooms.

Visiting business people also flock to the **Hotel Aconcagua (** (261) 420-4499 FAX (261) 420-2083 WEB SITE www.hotelaconcagua.com.ar, Calle San Lorenzo 545, and to the **Grand Hotel Balbi (** (261) 423-3500 FAX (261) 438-0626 E-MAIL balbistarhotel @arnet.com.ar, at Avenida Las Heras 340 right in the middle of town. Both are efficient urban hotels with business services, 24-hour room service, swimming pool, parking and massage.

But they lack the bygone character and sense of history that one finds at the **Hotel Plaza** on Plaza Independencia, which is currently being renovated by the Hyatt Group, with reopening slated for 2001 — when it will be called the Park Hyatt Mendoza & Casino. Juan and Evita Perón are among the many celebrities and dignitaries who have slept here over the years and the long, empty hallways seem to echo with their ghosts. My room was rather small and shabby given the price, and service in the hotel restaurant was glacial at best. But the staff was friendly, the water hot and the beer always cold on the veranda overlooking the square. A large **Marriott Hotel** is also under construction in Mendoza as part of the city's headlong rush into the twenty-first century.

Moderate

It's always been difficult to find a good mid-range hotel in Mendoza, but this gap is slowly but surely being filled by new construction. One of the newer establishments is the **Gran Ariosto (** (261) 429-3051, Infanata Mercedes de San Martín 48. It boasts a bar and cafeteria-style restaurant, but the grape-colored carpets can get a little overwhelming at times.

Also fairly new is the **Crillon (** (261) 423-8963 or (216) 429-8494 FAX (261) 423-9658 E-MAIL h.crillon@satlink.com, Calle Perú 1065. Among its many features are safe-deposit boxes, laundry service and hair salon.

A pleasant place to bed down on the outskirts of town is **Cabañas Pacari Tampu (** (261) 444-4693 or (261) 444-6871, Calle las Delicias in El Challao,

which has genuine log cabins in a rural setting. The cabins are decorated with rustic furniture and modern conveniences like cable television, stove and refrigerator. Other amenities include hiking trails, horseback riding and mountain bikes.

Inexpensive

The **City Hotel (** (261) 425-1343, Calle General Paz 95, is one of the better places at the budget end of the spectrum. The rooms are rather small but include private baths, air-conditioning, cable television and telephones. There's also laundry, 24-hour beverage service and a car park. Credit cards accepted.

Another favorite with foreign tourists is the **Hotel America (** (261) 425-6514 or (261) 425-8284 FAX (261) 425-4022 E-MAIL visigiro@lanet .losandes.com.ar, Calle Juan B. Justo 812, with its reddish stone façade and whitewashed walls.

Other budget abodes include the **Imperial (** (261) 423-4671 FAX (261) 438-0000, Avenida Las Heras 88; the **San Remo (** (261) 423-4068, Calle Godoy Cruz 477; and the **Necochea (**/FAX (261) 425-3501, Calle Necochea 675.

Mendoza's **international youth hostel (** (261) 424-0018, Avenida España 343, is a low-cost alternative for those who don't mind sharing a room. Other hostels include **Veris Tempus (** (261) 426-3300 at Calle Tirasso 2170 in suburban Guaymallén; and **Campo Base (** (261) 429-0707, at Avenida Mitre 946.

Among the organized campgrounds in the Mendoza area are **Cirse (** (261) 425-0846 and **Churrasqueras del Parque (**/FAX (261) 428-0511 in the Parque General San Martín. The latter has its own open-air steak restaurant and is only open during the summer months (December to April).

WHERE TO EAT

One of Mendoza's most elegant restaurants is **Señor Cheff (** (261) 420-1303, Primitivo de la Reta 1075. Owned and operated by the Bodega Santa Ana winery, this traditional firewood *parrilla* features numerous meat and seafood dishes, as well as a salad bar and extensive wine list.

Other highly recommended *parrillas* are **Boccadoro (** (261) 425-5056, Avenida Mitre 1976, and **Sarmiento (** (261) 438-0824 under the red umbrellas at Peatonal Sarmiento 658.

With such a large Italian émigré population, Mendoza offers some of the country's finest Italian food. My favorite is **Il Tucco (** (261) 420-2565, Peatonal Sarmiento 68, with its sidewalk tables where you can sip delicious Mendoza wine and dig into a heaping plate of pasta while watching the strolling musicians, magicians and animal acts.

Other tasty Italian eateries in the downtown area include **La Marchigiana (** (261) 420-0212 or (261) 423-0751, Calle Patricias Mendocinas 1550;

Trevi ((261) 423-3195, Avenida Las Heras 70; and the veteran **Montecatini** ((261) 425-2111, Calle General Paz 370.

If you're cruising the Palmares Mall pop into **Señor Frogs** ((261) 439-9351 for a sandwich or a cup of tea.

HOW TO GET THERE

Mendoza is 1,100 km (680 miles) west of Buenos Aires via Argentina Ruta 7 and 400 km (250 miles) from Santiago, Chile, via the Redentor Tunnel through the Andes.

There is frequent bus service from Buenos Aires (14 hours) and Santiago (seven hours), as well as other destinations like Córdoba (eight hours), Salta (19 hours) and Neuquén (13 hours) at the northern end of Patagonia. Mendoza's modern **Terminal del Sol** bus depot ((261) 431-3001 is situated southeast of the downtown area

near the intersection of Avenida Acces Este and Avenida R. Videla.

For more information on intercity bus service contact **Transporte Chevallier** ((261) 431-0235, **Autotransportes Mendoza** ((261) 431-4561, **Expreso Uspallata** ((261) 425-7638, or **Empresa Jocoli** ((261) 423-0466.

The city is also served by daily flights from Buenos Aires, Santiago and a few other Argentine destinations including Córdoba and Neuquén. **Francisco Gabrielli International Airport** ((261) 448-7300 is located six kilometers (four miles) north of the city center. For information on flights contact **Aerolíneas Argentinas/Astral** ((261) 420-4100, Peatonal Sarmiento 82; **Dinar-TAC** ((261) 420-4520 or (261) 420-4521, Sarmiento 69; or **LAPA** ((261) 423-1000, Avenida España 1012.

Art deco fountains grace the tranquil Plaza España in downtown Mendoza.

USPALLATA PASS AND THE HIGH ANDES

Since the dawn of time, people have trekked across the Andes via the Uspallata Pass, the only natural break in the cordillera for a hundred miles in either direction. The aboriginal tribes who inhabited this region before the European conquest established a well-trodden trade route across the pass, bartering marine products from the Pacific coast for commodities more common to the Pampas. In the sixteenth century, Chilean-based pioneers and missionaries used Uspallata as their gateway to settling the Mendoza region. How ironic that General San Martín should utilize the pass as his main invasion route across the Andes in 1817, during a successful campaign to expel the Spanish from Chile and then Peru.

Naturalist Charles Darwin also trekked through the pass during a South American sojourn in 1835, during his landmark voyage around the world on the *Beagle*. Darwin was especially enamored with the panoramic views. On March 24 he wrote in his journal: "Early in the morning I climbed up a mountain on one side of the valley and enjoyed a far extended view over the Pampas… At first glance there was a strong resemblance to a distant view of the ocean. The most striking feature in the scene consisted of rivers, which, facing the rising sun, glittered like silver threads, till lost in the immensity of the distance."

Today the pass — with a little help from the Redentor Tunnel — serves as the primary land passage between Argentina and Chile. Anyone who drives the Pan-American Highway between Mendoza and Santiago will catch a glimpse of the vast mountainous landscape. But the area has so much fine scenery and so many historical quirks it deserves more than a passing glance.

Uspallata Pass is easily explored on a long day trip from Mendoza, either driving yourself or part of an organized tour offered by most Mendoza travel agencies. I recommend **Turismo Mendoza** ((261) 429-2013 or (251) 420-1701, Avenida Las Heras 543. Ask for guide Daniel Ortíz, who's a fountain of knowledge about the High Andes.

The Pan-American Highway heads west from Mendoza, following the sinuous course of the Río Mendoza as it dissects the Andes foothills. The first town of any size is **Cacheuta**, 42 km (26 miles) from Mendoza, once renowned for its hot springs but now a rather rundown resort. The Cacheuta area has many Arab immigrants, who have constructed a monument to Syrian independence (from the Ottoman Empire) in the Plazuela de Republic Syria.

Two historic **bridges** span the muddy Río Mendoza near Cacheuta: a funky little pedestrian suspension bridge ("Don't Rock the Bridge!" reads a sign near the entrance) and an old wooden railroad bridge that you can also cross on foot (but be very careful). The latter dates from the 1930s when two American brothers living in Chile built the Trans-Andino Railroad between Santiago and Mendoza. Unable to obtain construction funds from either government, the brothers secured investment from private British sources. The line ran for nearly 50 years before finally closing down in 1980. More remnants of the line — including rusty old tracks and snow sheds — litter the higher reaches of Uspallata Pass.

A further 16 km (10 miles) up the road is **Potrerillos**, another threadbare resort that's seen better days. There's little reason for lingering in

the town itself, but the surrounding area is a hub for outdoor sports. Birdwatchers flock to the Cordon del Plata mountains, while kayakers and rafters use the rocky beaches near Potrerillos as a staging point for runs along the Río Mendoza (there's even a kayak slalom course). Also nearby is the **Vallecitos** snow ski area.

Uspallata snuggles in the bottom of a broad valley of the same name at the base of the High Andes. The town is surrounded by pasture and flanked by the broad floodplain of the Río Mendoza. With a dozen roadside restaurants and some charming hotels, Uspallata is a good base if you're staying the in High Andes for several days. Along the riverbanks you might see some *bóvedas* — whitewashed adobe structures with conical

LEFT: High-altitude desert on the outskirts of Uspallata. ABOVE: The Andes mark an abrupt departure from the incessant flatness of the Pampas.

domes used as metal foundries during the silver and zinc rush of the nineteenth century. There's a small **museum** with displays on both metallurgy and San Martín's trans-Andes campaign.

The silver mines were situated near **Villavicencio**, about 40 km (25 miles) east of Uspallata, nowadays more famous for its hot springs and bottled mineral water. The serpentine road that ascends to Villavicencio is called the *Ruta del Año* (Route of the Year) because of its 365 curves and bends. Along the way is a viewpoint called **Cruz del Paramillo** which affords spectacular vistas of the Andes including Aconcagua and Tupungato volcano. From Villavicencio you can pick up a more direct route going back to Mendoza.

West of Uspallata, the Pan-American Highway scrambles across the desert-like floodplain and starts its steep climb into the Andes. The road roughly follows the route that General San Martín and 3,700 troops took in January of 1817 during their celebrated invasion of Chile. Accompanied by several thousand horses and mules — and hundreds of female volunteers responsible for preparing food, mending uniforms and aiding the sick or wounded — the Army of the Andes accomplished the difficult mountain traverse in 21 days. They defeated the Spanish at Chacabuco, captured Santiago and then turned back an enemy counterattack at Maipú on the southern outskirts of the capital to secure Chilean independence.

ABOVE: General San Martín marched his Army of the Andes up this riverbed nearly 200 years ago. RIGHT: A ruined health spa nestles beneath the Puente del Inca.

At **Punta de Vacas** is a small police station and international customs post (for cargo trucks) housed in stout brick buildings with red metal roofs. Just beyond, Tupungato volcano comes into view, one of the few places along the highway where you can see the Americas' fourth highest peak (6,800 m / 22,310 ft).

The next hamlet is **Los Penitentes**, renowned as both a winter ski resort and summer trekking base. It's named after a nearby rock formation which resembles a group of *penitentes* — hooded monks chained together and walking in single file as they atone for their sins. On the outskirts of town (opposite the mule stables) is the **Andinista Cemetery** where dozens of climbers and military scouts are buried, victims of climbing accidents and avalanches in the nearby mountains.

Another seven kilometers (five miles) up the road is **Puente del Inca**, a bustling little alpine village which also takes its name from a nearby rock formation — a massive natural bridge that leaps the Río Mendoza in a single span. The surrounding area bares a striking resemblance to the Himalayas and much of the movie *Seven Years in Tibet* (starring Brad Pitt) was filmed here rather than Asia.

Created by mineral secretions from underlying hot springs, the Puente del Inca arch is one of Argentina's most beloved natural wonders and is often crowded with tourists. You can walk across the top of the arch and underneath where you'll find the ruins of a spa hotel and thermal baths destroyed by a 1975 avalanche that killed 45 people. If you don't mind getting a little wet, explore beyond the ruins, a fantasyland of bright yellow sulfur secretions and stark white salt crystals. In winter, the underside is often hung with four to five meter long (13 to 16 ft) icicles. There's also a small grotto with statues of the Virgin of Lujo and Our Lady of Lourdes, where climbers come to pray before setting off into the High Andes.

Puente del Inca and Los Penitentes are the major staging points for climbing, trekking and horseback ventures into **Parque Provincial Aconcagua**. The park protects the world's highest area outside the Himalayas including numerous glaciers, whitewater streams and nine peaks over 5,000 m (16,400 ft). But the big challenge, of course, is reaching the 6,959-m (22,834-ft) summit of Cerro Aconcagua. First conquered by Swiss-Italian climber Mathias Zurbriggen in 1897, the peak was sacred to the ancient Inca who buried sacrificial victims on its upper slopes. A 1985 expedition discovered the mummified remains of a 10- to 15-year-old Indian child buried more than 400 years ago.

The popular route up the northwest face is not a difficult technical climb; altitude sickness is the major hurdle. The south face (aka the Polish route) should only be attempted by experienced

climbers in the company of a local alpine guide. Anyone attempting to reach the summit should set aside at least two weeks for the undertaking, including a week of altitude acclimatization in Puente del Inca or Los Penitentes. If you don't want to hump your own supplies up the mountain, you can hire mules in either village. Permits are required for all climbing and trekking expeditions into the park. They must be purchased in advance from the **Dirección de Recursos Naturales Renovables (** (261) 425-2090, Parque General San Martín in Mendoza. Rates vary according to activity, length of stay and time of year. Climbing is more expensive than trekking, summer more expensive than other seasons, etc. Foreigners can expect to pay about twice as much as Argentines for the same permit.

If you're traveling by car and interested in only a brief glimpse of Aconcagua or a short stroll through part of the park, the only access point is **Los Horcones** at 2,900 m (9,500 ft) on the outskirts of Puente del Inca. There's a small parking lot and a dirt road that leads to Laguna Horcones, a small alpine lake that's often bone dry. You can catch a fleeting view of the summit from this point, usually just after dawn before the clouds have started to form.

Puente del Inca is also the jumping off point for climbing and trekking in **Parque Provincial Volcán Tupungato** to the south. The routes up Tupungato are far less established and the slopes far more challenging than Aconcagua. Only experienced mountaineers should attempt an ascent of the smoldering, snow-covered volcano. Anyone planning a climb or trek in either park should consult the **Club Andinista Mendoza (** (261) 431-9870, Calle Beltran 357, for the latest on weather and trail conditions. One of the more experienced local guides is Mendoza-based Fernando Grajales (/FAX (261) 429-3830.

The Argentine **border post** is just beyond Los Horcones, but there's no reason to stop if you're not crossing the frontier into Chile. Continuing west along the Pan-American Highway you soon reach **Las Cuevas**, the last hamlet on the Argentine side and the country's highest settlement at 3,112 m (10,200 ft). Although Las Cuevas likes to fancy itself as a ski resort, there are no winter sports facilities. However, the village features several architectural oddities including a huge stone gateway that resembles a German medieval castle, and a small stone "igloo" used as a way-station by seventeenth- and eighteenth-century colonial travelers making their way across the Andes.

The stone gateway is the start of a gravel road called the "Antigua Ruta" that ascends to La Cumbre Pass and one of South America's most famous monuments — a statue of **Cristo Redentor** (Christ the Redeemer). Erected by the Argentine and Chilean governments in 1904 after

the successful resolution of a border dispute, the statue could not occupy a more spectacular site — a rocky, windswept ridge at 4,000 m (13,000 ft) with sweeping views of mountains all around. Before the tunnel, the Pan-American Highway used La Cumbre Pass to traverse the Andes. The first auto caravan between Santiago and Buenos Aires passed this way in 1929, shortly after the highway was completed. But these days you can no longer follow the old road down into Chile — ironically the roadway was blown up by the Chilean Army during a 1978 border dispute over the Beagle Channel islands. The old stone *refugio* on the Chilean side of the pass is now in ruins, many of the rooms filled with hard-packed snow even in summer. A café on the Argentine side hawks souvenirs, sandwiches and cognac-laced coffee.

Beyond Las Cuevas, the Pan-American Highway dives through the **Redentor Tunnel**, just over three kilometers (almost two miles) long and

198

finished in 1980. At the western end of the tunnel is a Chilean border post, which also features a small snack bar (the *empanadas* are about the only thing worth eating) and rather filthy public toilets.

WHERE TO STAY

Two veteran hotels provide mountain resort-type accommodation on the road between Mendoza and Uspallata. **Hotel Termas Cacheuta** ((2624) 482082, Ruta 7 Km. 38, offers standard rooms and apartments with kitchenettes for those who want to stay longer. Facilities include indoor and out-door thermal baths, hot tubs and massages. The once luxurious **Gran Hotel Potrerillos** ((2624) 482010 or (261) 423-3000 has rooms with full board.

Uspallata has the region's most charming ac-commodation, especially the riverside **Hotel Uspallata** ((2624) 420003 which still reeks of the 1940s. With tennis courts, swimming pool, gardens and bowling alley, this is an excellent place to hang for several days. Another bygone abode is the **Hotel Valle Andino** ((2624) 420033, which boasts a swimming pool, tennis courts, library and cable television. Those on a budget should try the **Hostería Los Condores** ((2624) 420002.

Los Penitentes really rocks during the winter season, but several places are open year-round including the popular **Hostería Ayelen** ((261) 425-9990, **Pequena Villa de San Jorge** ((261) 432-0440 E-MAIL emaccari@impsat1.com.ar, and **Lomas Blancas** ((261) 423-9329. Up the road is **Hostería Puente del Inca** ((261) 429-4124 or (261) 438-0480, long popular with climbers and trekkers. Great grub in the dining room complements the clean rooms and pleasant service.

A view from the Pan-American Highway as it begins its climb into the High Andes.

How to Get There

The Pan-American Highway (Ruta 7) connects Mendoza with the Chilean frontier via Uspallata, Los Penitentes and Puente del Inca. The highway is paved and generally in good repair, although rockslides can occur in summer and avalanches in winter. Anyone attempting to drive the highway in winter (June to October) should carry snow chains or cables and a shovel. For information on the latest road conditions, contact the **Auto Club de Argentine** (ACA) regional office in Mendoza ((261) 431-4100, corner of Gob. Videla and Reconquista.

to travelers. The right fork (Ruta 40) soon peters out into a gravel road as it continues south. At a dusty little oil town called **El Sosneado**, the pavement resumes for the drive down to Malargüe and the southern Mendoza Province ski resorts.

A winding dirt road (Ruta 220) follows the valley of the Río Atuel west from El Sosneado into the Andes. At the end of the road are the ruins of the Termas El Sosneado hot springs resort. In the high mountains beyond the hotel is Las Lagrimas Glacier where a charter plane carrying a Uruguayan youth rugby team crashed in the spring of 1972. Only 14 of the 45 passengers survived — largely by eating the flesh of their dead teammates — an episode that inspired the

More than a dozen long-distance bus companies ply the route between Mendoza and Santiago with stops along the Uspallata Pass. Tell the driver at the start of the journey where you want to be left off. Another alternative is taking a day-tour. Almost every Mendoza travel agency offers "High Mountain" tours that include Puente del Inca, Los Horcones and Cristo Redentor.

SOUTH FROM MENDOZA

Highway 40 shoots straight across the Pampas south of Mendoza, at first flanked by fruit trees and vineyards, and then sprawling plains and desert that seem to reach to the sky.

At **Pareditas** junction, 107 km (66 miles) south of Mendoza, the highway splits. The left fork (Ruta 143) shoots down to **San Rafael**, the largest city in this part of the province but of little interest

bestselling book *Alive* and a 1992 movie of the same name.

MALARGÜE

Over the last decade, this cheerful little outback town has become a hub for outdoor and adventure sports. Among the activities offered in the surrounding area are whitewater rafting, kayaking, windsurfing and spelunking. Nestled in the Andes foothills, it also makes an excellent base for skiing the slopes at Las Leñas.

Malargüe's **Dirección de Turismo** ((2627) 471659 sits at the north end of Avenida San Martín next to the regional museum. You can also get information on the area at the **Casa de Malargüe** ((261) 429-2515, Avenida España 1075 in downtown Mendoza. Adjacent to the tourist office is the **Dirección de los Bosques** (forest service) where you can purchase fishing licenses and get more information on nearby nature reserves.

There is little of interest in the town itself, other than a small **Museo Regional** in the Parque del Ayer, with exhibits on local human and natural history. But there are plenty of attractions within a short drive.

Among the many good nature parks in this region is the **Reserva Provincial Laguna La Payunia**, about 120 km (80 miles) south of Malargüe near a hamlet called Ranquil del Norte. This windswept *altiplano* area harbors the country's largest guanaco herd and is a place of uncommon beauty. Also worth a visit is the **Reserva Provincial Laguna de Llancanelo** in the

del **Nihuil** where water skiing, windsurfing and fishing are possible. There's a lakeshore campsite, as well as snack bar and general store.

WHERE TO STAY

The town's best hotel is the **Hotel de Turismo Malargüe** ((2627) 471042 or (2627) 471742, Avenida San Martín 224 on the west side of the Plaza San Martín. The whitewashed building sports a bright red roof and pine-scented garden. The hotel restaurant is probably the town's best bet for traditional Argentine food. Rates include breakfast.

Visitors with their own wheels can stay at the **Río Grand Hotel** ((2627) 471589, on Ruta 40

marshlands to the east of Malargüe, one of the foremost nesting spots of the Chilean flamingo. The best bird-watching is in spring (September to November).

Another popular natural attraction is the **Caverna de las Brujas** (Cave of the Witches), 70 km (43 miles) southwest of Malargüe. These extensive limestone caves are among the best in the region. Nearby is the fascinating petrified forest of **Llano Blanco** where 120-million-year-old Araucaria trees have fossilized into stone.

All three of these parks — La Payunia, Las Brujas and Llancanelo — can only be entered in the company of a locally licensed guide or as part of a guided tour. Ask the tourist office for recommendations.

Northwest of Malargüe is the impressive **Canon del Atuel**, a miniature version of the Grand Canyon, and a huge reservoir called the **Embalse**

in Cañada Colorada on the northern edge of town. Rooms here feature private bath, cable television, central heating and telephone. There is a restaurant and snack bar onsite. Rates include breakfast.

Also recommended is the **Reyen Hotel** ((2627) 470913, Avenida San Martín 938. Rooms look rather Spartan at first glance, but they're actually quite comfortable once you settle in. Most rooms feature telephone, cable television and private bath. German and some English are spoken at the front desk. There is a snack bar off the lobby and rates include breakfast.

Camping is offered at the **YPF gas station** ((2627) 471232 at Km. 327 on Ruta 40.

OPPOSITE: The famed statue of Cristo Redentor (Christ the Redeemer) at La Cumbre Pass. ABOVE: "Welcome to Chile" reads a sign on the western edge of La Cumbre.

WHERE TO EAT

Grilled meats and freshwater fish are the specialties at the **Turismo Malargüe** restaurant ((2627) 471042, Avenida San Martín 224, in the hotel of the same name. **Parrilla La Posta** ((2627) 471306, Avenida J.A. Roca 374, offers *chivito* (young goat) and other grilled meats, as well as trout.

HOW TO GET THERE

Malargüe is 277 km (170 miles) south of Mendoza via Ruta 40 and 182 km (112 miles) southwest of San Rafael via routes 144 and 40.

Several bus companies run daily services between Mendoza and Malargüe including **Expreso Uspallata** ((261) 425-7638 or (261) 438-1092. Most services stop at Tunuyán, San Rafael and El Sosneado.

LAS LEÑAS

Since its debut in 1983, Las Leñas ((2627) 471100 has evolved into Argentina's top winter sports resort and probably the best all-around ski area in South America. It's also one of the more expensive, although prices pale in comparison to some of the chic European and North American ski resorts.

Set in a picturesque valley surrounded by snowcapped peaks, Las Leñas sports 41 downhill runs spread across a massive area of 3,800 hectares (9,390 acres). Pistes range from easy to very difficult, with a maximum drop of 1,230 m (4,034 ft). There are 11 lifts, which operate daily between 9 AM and 5 PM. Las Leñas also features a pretty good ski school, comprehensive equipment rental facilities and four ski patrol stations up the mountain in case you get in trouble.

Lift tickets range from US$30 for a full-day adult pass in the low season to US$46 for a full-day adult pass in the high season. A one-week pass run from US$160 (low season) to US$220 (high season). There are special rates for children and seniors, and student promotions that include both lift ticket and ski school (US$170 for three days of downhill; US$184 for three days of snowboarding). Travel agencies in Buenos Aires and Mendoza and several hotels in Las Leñas offer packages that combine unlimited skiing with accommodation and meals.

The high season is the last two weeks of July (during Argentina's winter school vacation). The low season runs from late June to early July, and mid-September to mid-October. Weeks in between are the medium season.

The rugged mountains west of Uspallata offer almost infinite possibilities for adventure sport.

WHERE TO STAY

All accommodation in Las Leñas must be booked through a **central reservations office** ((2627) 471100.

Top of the line is the chic **Hotel Piscis**, which offers 107 rooms and suites, many with balconies and spectacular mountain views. All rooms have central heating, private baths (with showers) and direct-dial phones. There's plenty to keep you busy when you're not on the slopes, including a small casino, gourmet restaurant, heated pool and health club with Jacuzzi, sauna and massage.

Mid-range hotels include the 47-room **Escorpio**, which boasts an open-air terrace and solarium, and the 34-room **Géminis**, one of the few abodes in the Valle de Las Leñas that's open year-round.

Like any good ski resort, there are also a number of self-catering "apart hotels," including the **Esparta** (58 units), **Delphos** (34 units) and **Cirrus** (71 units). Rooms range from two beds with one bathroom to seven beds with two bathrooms. At the bottom end of the scale are "dormy houses" like **Payen** and **Milla** where you can cram as many as eight people into one room if you so desire.

WHERE TO EAT

Most of the restaurants are situated in hotels like **Il Legno** in the Hotel Piscis, which serves marvelous Italian cuisine in an elegant setting. Hotel Piscis boasts two other excellent eateries: the **Slalom Restaurant** with its eclectic international menu and the tasty **Schuzz**, which offers daily specials.

Non-hotel restaurants include **El Refugio** (French) and **Due** (international), both situated on La Pirámide, the resort's principle commercial street. At the base of the ski runs are the **Innsbruck** snack bar and a self-service restaurant called **El Brasero**. If your stomach starts to grumble up on the slopes, both the **Bacus** snack bar and **Elurra** restaurant offer all-day meal service.

HOW TO GET THERE

Las Leñas is about 300 km (200 miles) south of Mendoza via Ruta 40. The turnoff to the ski area (local route 222) is 20 km south of El Sosneado.

The closest airports are at San Rafael and Malargüe. There is no regular scheduled air service, but there are charter flights from Buenos Aires during the ski season.

Several Mendoza-based bus companies offer direct service to Las Leñas during the winter months including **Autotransportes Mendoza** ((261) 431-4561 or (261) 431-4628; and **Expreso Uspallata** ((261) 425-7638 or (261) 438-1092. During the ski season there are also direct buses from Buenos Aires, but it's a long, boring journey that takes 15 hours.

Patagonia

PATAGONIA — THE NAME ALONE IS ENOUGH TO SUM-
MON UP IMAGES OF FAR-OFF AND FORGOTTEN PLACES.
Argentina's "deep south" has long been a symbol
of untamed wilderness and the adventurous spirit
of the human soul, and over the last 500 years it
has attracted a steady stream of people searching
for solitude or exploring the enigmatic side of life
on this planet. The explorer Ferdinand Magellan,
pirate and patriot Francis Drake, naturalist Charles
Darwin, gunslingers Butch Cassidy and the
Sundance Kid, author Bruce Chatwin, and actor
Daniel Day-Lewis have all left their mark on
Patagonia's heritage, paving the way for the thousands of outdoor enthusiasts who venture to this
faraway-off shore today.

One hundred and fifty million years ago,
Patagonia was far different than it is today. It
was heavily forested and largely tropical, the
stomping ground of dinosaurs and other primordial creatures. Paleontologists have uncovered

thousands of fossils in Patagonia over the past
century, making it one of the world's greatest
depositories of dinosaur knowledge, along with
Mongolia and the Rocky Mountains. Recent
finds are among the most significant ever, including a 1998 dig that exposed a huge sauropod nesting site near Neuquén in northwest
Patagonia. The softball-sized eggs yielded both
embryo bones and the first embryo skin fragments
of any dinosaur — living DNA which theoreti-
cally could be cloned into a living sauropod à la
Jurassic Park.

Modern man arrived around 10,000 years ago:
scattered indigenous groups including the
Mapuche in the Lake District and Tehuelche on
the plains. They eked out a meager existence from
hunting and gathering, never developing a sophisticated civilization like the Inca and other Indian
groups in the north. Because there was no gold,
silver or other precious trinkets, the Conquistadors

withered and died, the victim of Patagonia's malicious environment and hostile natives.

Charles Darwin arrived in 1834 during his epic around-the-world voyage on the HMS *Beagle*, during which he ascertained the origin of our species and every other earthly life form. Although the Galápagos Islands are often given credit for stimulating Darwin's theory of evolution, there is little doubt that Patagonia also sparked his brain waves. In his epic travel book *Voyage of the Beagle*, Darwin waxes lyrical about his adventures in Patagonia, including his discovery of a prehistoric guanaco skeleton and an expedition up the Río Santa Cruz in whale boats to the Fitzroy Range.

Even after independence, the powers that be in Buenos Aires continued to ignore Patagonia in favor of settling much more hospitable areas in the north and west. Not until the War of the Triple Alliance (1865–1870) did Argentina start to think about securing its last frontier. There were worries about Chile making a grab for Patagonia, or perhaps a European power like Britain or Germany. In 1879, the government dispatched General Julio Argentino Roca to subdue the Indians and pave the way for white settlement of the region. What followed was an 11-year reign of terror that Argentines dubbed the "Conquista del Desierto" (Conquest of the Desert), a brutal and bloody military campaign that wiped out nearly all of Patagonia's indigenous population.

Even with Indians subdued, the government couldn't find enough Argentines who were willing to relocate to Patagonia and they were forced to recruit overseas for potential settlers. A handful of largely downtrodden Europeans took up the challenge—Welsh coal miners who pioneered the Chubut Valley, German and Swiss peasants who colonized the Lake District, English sheep farmers who staked claims around Río Gallegos and San Julián.

Still the region remained wild enough to attract a couple of American desperados on the run from the law. Butch Cassidy, the Sundance Kid and female companion Etta Place arrived in 1902, homesteading 4,800 hectares (12,000 acres) near Cholila in the upper Chubut Valley which they transformed into a sheep farm. But old habits die hard: within a couple of years they had reverted to bank robbery and life on the run. They sold the Cholila spread in 1907 and fled into the Andes, never to be (officially) seen again.

Two of the most endearing accounts of Patagonia are quite modern: Bruce Chatwin's 1977 classic *In Patagonia*, one of the best travel books of all time, and a quirky 1989 film called *Eversmile, New Jersey* in which Daniel Day-Lewis plays a young itinerant dentist who roams Patagonia by motorbike.

ignored the Patagonian nomads and the region remained largely untouched by European culture until the late nineteenth century.

The first "white men" to lay eyes upon Patagonia were Magellan and the sailors of a five-ship Spanish convoy that probed the coast in 1519–1520. One of their few landfalls was Bahía San Julián, where Magellan executed two of his captains who had organized a mutiny. Magellan also found time to quarrel with the local Tehuelche, who he dubbed the "Patagon" (Big Foot People) because of their height and huge moccasins.

The next notable visitor was Drake (1578), who seemed to follow a template set down by Magellan — the English sea dog beheaded a couple of mutineers and then clashed with the Tehuelche. By the end of the eighteenth century, the Spanish crown had dispatched several scientific and military expeditions to Patagonia and attempted to establish several colonies. Most of the attempts

Day hikes across Moreno Glacier are a popular activity in Parque Nacional Los Glaciares.

Modern Patagonia remains a sparsely populated place, dominated by huge *estancias* and nature preserves. There are no large cities and very few towns that muster more than a hundred people. Politically it's divided into four provinces south of the Río Colorado: tiny Neuquén Province which covers the upper part of the Lake District, Río Negro Province which harbors the popular resort town of Bariloche, Chubut Province which includes the Welsh enclaves of the Chubut Valley and a wildlife haven called the Valdés Peninsula, and Santa Cruz Province with its oil fields and glaciers.

The economy is still largely rooted in sheep and cattle farming, although the petroleum indus-

try — based in Comodoro Rivadavia and Río Gallegos — currently generates more hard cash. Real estate speculation is also on the rise, European and North American tycoons like Ted Turner, George Soros and Luciano Benetton have scooped up large tracts of wilderness and ranchland over the last few years.

Tourism has grown by leaps and bounds over the past decade and will probably dominate the economy within a few years. Although major destinations like El Calafate and Puerto Madryn can seem crowded during the peak summer months, they are barely more than specks on the giant Patagonian landscape. Vast areas remain beyond the pale of tourism. There are still hundreds of places "in Patagonia" where you can get as thoroughly lost as Bruce Chatwin did.

Bariloche's imposing Centro Cívico betrays the city's Germanic heritage.

BARILOCHE AND THE LAKE DISTRICT

Bariloche is the undisputed queen of the Patagonian Lake District, an incredibly picturesque town that snuggles in the shadow of the Andes along the south shore of Lago Nahuel Huapi. The skiing might be much better near Mendoza, but this is the country's top winter resort in terms of sheer number of people who come here to ski. It's also a popular summer retreat, with countless families and student groups tramping through town during the school holidays between December and March.

In many respects Bariloche is the spitting image of a European mountain retreat — a montage of A-frame chalets, wooden flower boxes, Saint Bernard dogs and just about every other Alpine cliche. A lot of this is pure pandering to the tourist trade, but it also reflects the culture of the Teutonic immigrants who founded the town in the late 1800s.

With so many hotels and houses — and hordes of camera-clicking tourists — it's hard to believe that Bariloche was wilderness barely more than a century ago. Mapuche and Tehuelche Indians lived around the lake, migrating back and forth across what is now the international divide between Chile and Argentina. The first Spaniards to explore the region arrived from the Pacific coast in the early seventeenth century, but Europeans didn't attempt the "tame" the inhabitants until 1720, when the Jesuits erected a small mission on the lakeshore and were promptly slaughtered by the locals.

Europeans didn't venture to the region for another 150 years, when several scientific expeditions — including an 1876 visit by the legendary Argentine naturalist Perito Moreno — began to probe the wonders of the Lake District. After General Roca wiped out most of the indigenous people in the early 1880s, pioneers were drawn to the region. German settlers were the first to arrive (1895) followed by Austrians, Scandinavians, Swiss, and northern Italians who founded Bariloche and other small towns along the south shore of Nahuel Huapi.

It didn't take them long to realize the area's tourism potential. Snow skiing and summer mountaineering were becoming popular back home in Europe. John Muir and Teddy Roosevelt were stoking the flames of nature-based tourism at places like Yosemite and Yellowstone in the United States. Bariloche offered similar scenery and many of the same distractions, and soon the elite of Buenos Aires were flocking to the Lake District. Tourism really took off when the railroad arrived in the 1930s and the boom has never really subsided.

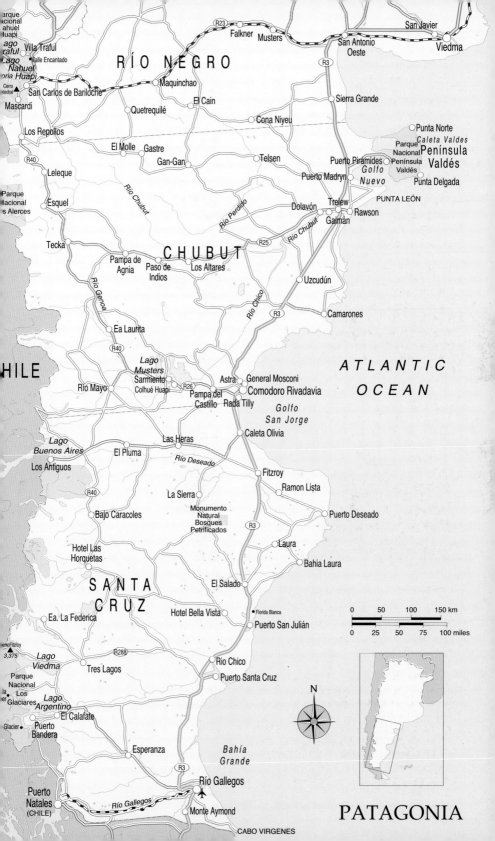

Bariloche is the sort of place you either love or hate. It's hard not to succumb to the lovely sunsets over Nahuel Huapi, but at the same time it's easy to loathe the bumper-to-bumper trekkers and lift lines that plague the resort during peak periods. Still, there's no denying its innate charm.

GENERAL INFORMATION

The dynamic **Secretaría Municipal de Turismo** ((2944) 423122 FAX (2944) 426784 E-MAIL securismo @bariloche.com.ar offers a blizzard of brochures, maps and other material, including a highly useful booklet called *Guía Busch* which is jam-packed with data about local activities, restaurants and hotels. Part of the city's gray-stone Civic Center complex, the tourist office is at the southwest corner of Plaza Roca opposite the Municipalidad. Open daily 8 AM to 9 PM. There are also tourist information desks at the airport (open 9 AM to 3 PM) and bus station (open 9 AM to 7 PM).

Information on Río Negro Province can be obtained from the **Secretaría de Estado de Turismo** ((2944) 423188 or (2944) 423189 FAX (2944) 426644, at Calle 12 de Octubre 605. Open Monday to Friday 9 AM to 2 PM.

Also in the Civic Center is the **Intendencia del Parques Nacionales** ((2944) 423111, Calle San Martín 24, a handy source of information on local national parks including places to camp, hike, climb and fish. Serious climbers and trekkers should also consult **Club Andino Bariloche** ((2944) 422266 FAX (2944) 424579, Calle 20 de Febrero 30, for the latest information on local peaks and trails. Open Monday to Friday 9 AM to noon and 3 PM to 8 PM. Both of these offices can issue the permits required for hiking and climbing in the parks.

If you are planning on traveling across the border to Chile and require a visa, the **Chilean Consulate** ((2944) 422842 is at Calle Rosas 187.

Money and travelers' checks can be cashed at a number of locations along Calle Mitre, including **Banco de la Nación** ((2944) 432905 at No. 180, **Scottia Bank Quilmes** ((2944) 421054 at No. 433, and **Bansud** ((2944) 424210 at No. 424. All three have 24-hour ATM machines.

The main branch of **Correo Argentino** is right next to the tourist office in the Civic Center. Numerous places offer long-distance calling service including **Unifon/Telefónica** with offices at Calle Quaglia 121 ((2944) 434445 near the Civic Center and Calle Onelli 400 ((2944) 421911 near the Hospital Zonal. **Cabiñas del Lago** ((2944) 430536 at the corner of Elflein and Morales offers overseas phone and fax service and Western Union money transfer.

Despite its remoteness, Bariloche is right on the "Internet superhighway" with a number of cybercafés that offer freshly ground coffee with their web connections, including **Net & Cappuccino** ((2944) 426128 WEB SITE www.capuccino.net, Calle Quaglia 220, and **Cyber M@C** ((15) 617195 E-MAIL cybercafe@infovia.com.ar, Unit 12, in the shopping complex at Calle Rolando 217.

For medical emergencies try the **Hospital Zonal Ramon Carillo** ((2944) 426119 at Calle Perito Moreno 601. Get your prescriptions filled at **Farmacia Nahuel** ((2944) 422490, Calle Perito Moreno 238.

A convenient and inexpensive way to reach many of the sights in Parque Nacional Nahuel Huapi is **Micro Ómnibus 3 de Mayo** ((2944) 425648 or (2944) 436241, Calle Perito Moreno 480, which runs frequent shuttles from Bariloche to the likes of Cerro Otto, Cerro Catedral, Llao Llao, Lago Gutiérrez, Villa Mascardi and El Manso.

WHAT TO SEE AND DO

The heart of Bariloche is the wonderfully romantic **Centro Cívico**, a combination town square and municipal government complex created by Argentine architect Alejandro Bustillo in 1940. The rustic style — sturdy gray-green stone, slate-gray roofs, timber gables and balconies — was christened "Bariloche Alpine" and seems a perfect match for the pristine mountain scenery. The equestrian statue in the middle of the square commemorates General Rosas and his controversial Conquista del Desierto (Conquest of the Desert), which "cleansed" the region of indigenous people. Photographers prowl the plaza searching for tourists who want to have their photo snapped with Saint Bernards or Siberian huskies.

Besides the municipal tourist office, the complex harbors several worthwhile sights including the excellent **Museo Perito F. Moreno** ((2944) 422309 in the northeast corner, a fascinating assemblage on Patagonian natural history, anthropology and settlement including great Indian displays and a revisionist exhibit on the Conquista del Desierto. The museum also offers an ongoing program of temporary exhibits, seminars and lectures that are open to the public. Next door is the **Biblioteca Sarmiento** ((2944) 422674 with a specialized collection of Patagonia and the Andes. Both museum and library are open Tuesday to Friday 10 AM to 12:30 PM and 2 PM to 7 PM; Saturday 10 AM to 1 PM.

Across Avenida Rosas from the Civic Center is a brand-new wharf area called **Puerto San Carlos**, which features restaurants, shops and lake ferries that run to Puerto Pañuelo, Isla Victoria, Los Arrayanes and Puerto Blest near the Chilean frontier (see below). Walking east from the port along the **Costanera** you eventually run into the city's modern **Templo Mejor** (cathedral), also designed by Bustillo and completed in 1946. Farther along is a rustic waterfront retreat called the **Club de Caza y Pesca** ((2944) 435963 where you can sip a cup of coffee or cold beer as you stare at the lake through big picture windows. The club's **Museo Icticola** offers a rare glimpse into the world of game fishing and freshwater marine biology. Open daily 2 PM to 8 PM.

Parque Nacional Nahuel Huapi

Of course, the main reason for venturing to Bariloche is to get *out* of town, tramping through the nearby woods, scaling the granite peaks, zipping down some snowy piste, or cruising deep blue Nahuel Huapi. The city is surrounded by Parque Nacional Nahuel Huapi, one of Argentina's

And for anyone who ventures up to the high peaks, there's always the possibility that you could spot a condor.

If you're staying in Bariloche, the closest place to "get back to nature" is **Cerro Otto**, a 1,400-m (4,600-ft) peak draped in native *lenga* trees that's only five kilometers (three miles) west of town. The popular mountain offers snow sports in winter and hiking, biking and parasailing in summer. There are two ways to reach the summit. The **Teleférico** ((2944) 441035 is a 1,200-m (3,930-ft) cable-car system that starts from Avenida Los Pioneros in Melipal village (US$15). You can also drive, hike or cycle to the top on a sinuous gravel road called **Camino al Cerro Otto** which runs off

largest and oldest (1934) national parks, which sprawls across 600,000 hectares (1,448,600 acres) of the Lake District. The park embraces all of the region's most important natural attractions including Nahuel Huapi, Traful and Mascardi lakes, Cathedral Mountain, Victoria Island and Tronador Volcano.

The park is a paradise for adventure sports and outdoor recreation (see below) including hiking, climbing, camping, fishing, sailing, cycling, horseback riding, kayaking, whitewater rafting, skiing and snowboarding. It's also a haven for nature: alpine meadows smothered in spring flowers and vast tracts of beech, cypress and pine forest that have never been logged. Among the animals that roam the park's woodlands are mountain lion, nutria and two rare deer species — the huemul and pudú. Inhabitants of the local lakes include rainbow trout, salmon and perch.

Avenida Los Pioneros about one kilometer (just over half a mile) west of town. A taxi from the Centro Cívico to the summit runs about US$20. There are numerous "attractions" at the crest of Cerro Otto: art gallery, playground, Siberian huskies and revolving restaurant called the **Confitería Giratoria** (one revolution every 40 minutes). But most people just come for the view, a stunning panorama of the lake and the Andes.

The park's other celebrated mountain is **Cerro Catedral**, 46 km (28 miles) west of Bariloche via Playa Bonita. The name derives from the craggy granite peaks that resemble the spires of a Gothic cathedral. By winter, this is the Lake District's largest and most popular winter sports area, with 32 lifts and 67 km (41 miles) of powdery trails, plus rental outlets, snack bars and ski schools.

Puerto San Carlos tenders ferries to the islands and distant ports around Lago Nahuel Huapi.

By summer, Catedral is ideal for day rock climbing and hiking, including a relaxed six-hour walk from the summit to the Club Andino's **Refugio Frey** — where you can soak your feet in a chilly alpine lake. Facilities at the 2,000-m (6,560-ft) summit include the **Punta Nevada** snack bar. The easiest way to reach the top is the **Cable Carrill**, a cable-car system that offers one of the most stunning views in the Argentine Andes (US$16).

The national park features two popular routes that can be taken by car, bus or even bicycle if you've got that kind of energy. The **Circuito Chico** (Small Circuit) follows Avenida Bustillo west from Bariloche along the southern shore of Lago Nahuel Huapi. The first stop is **Playa Bonita**, near the spot where the Jesuits founded their ill-fated mission. The beach affords wonderful views of Isla Huemul and the lake. Another 10 km (six miles) along the lakeshore is the parking lot for the chair lift (US$10) that ascends **Cerro Campanario** with its excellent vistas of the lakes and mountains. You can take a short detour onto the **Península San Pedro** or continue straight along Avenida Bustillo onto the incredibly beautiful **Llao Llao Peninsula** where there are hiking trails through thick stands of *coihues* trees.

Funky little **Puerto Pañuelo** is the peninsula's only real town, with a dock that offers ferry service to Isla Victoria, Los Arrayanes, Puerto Blest and Bariloche. Crowning a hillside near town is the spectacular **Llao Llao Hotel**, another Bariloche-Alpine masterpiece by architect Alejandro Bustillo. The nearby **San Eduardo Chapel** was also designed by Bustillo. The circuit continues across a bridge over Bahía Lopez and then doubles back along the south shore of Lago Perito Moreno, with detours to **Cerro Lopez** and a tiny hamlet called **Colonia Suiza**. Total distance is about 60 km (37 miles) roundtrip; allow at least half a day with all the stops.

A much more challenging drive is the **Circuito Grande** (Big Circuit), a giant loop through the national park's northern environs via Ruta 231 along the north shore of Lake Nahuel Huapi, Ruta 65 along the south shore of **Lake Traful**, and Ruta 237 through the **Valle Encantado** (Enchanted Valley). There are several hamlets along the way including **Villa La Angostura** and **Villa Traful** where you can eat lunch or buy fishing and camping supplies. The entire drive takes at least eight hours.

The islands of Lake Nahuel Huapi present other enticing destinations. **Isla Victoria** can be reached by boat (30 minutes) from either Puerto San Carlos in Bariloche or the dock at Puerto Pañuelo. After disembarking at the island's **Puerto Anchorena** you can walk numerous hiking trails through pristine forest or hop a chair lift (US$8) to the crest of **Belle Vista** peak, where the view lives up to the lofty name. Many of the boats also stop

at **Puerto Quetrihué** on the peninsula of the same name, where passengers can view the amazing cinnamon-colored trees of the **Bosque de Arrayanes**. The easiest way to reach Isla Victoria and Arrayanes in the same day is a halfway cruise on the catamaran **Modesta Victoria (** (2944) 426109, Calle Villegas 310, Bariloche. Rates are US$30 from Bariloche and US$22 from Puerto Pañuelo.

There are many other excursions you can make inside the park including the all-day boat trip from Puerto Pañuelo to **Puerto Blest** and **Laguna Frías**, the all-day drive to **Cerro Tronador** volcano and beautiful **Lake Mascardi**, and overnight trips to **El Bolsón** in the south or **San Martín de los Andes** in the north. In fact, you could easily spend two weeks in Parque Nacional Nahuel Huapi without exhausting your choices.

SPORTS

Trekking and Climbing

Permits are mandatory for all overnight backcountry trips and all mountain climbing expeditions, available from the **Club Andino Bariloche (** (2944) 422266 FAX (2944) 424579, Calle 20 de Febrero 30. Open Monday to Friday 9 AM to noon and 3 PM to 8 PM. The club is very happy to give advice on the trails, peaks and whatever else you need to know about the Nahuel Huapi wilderness. The **Intendencia del Parques Nacionales (** (2944) 423111, Calle San Martín 24, is also happy to dispense information on trekking and climbing.

Detailed topographic maps of park trails are hard to come by. A much better planning resource is *Trekking in the Patagonian Andes* by Lonely Planet publications, which you should buy before venturing to Argentina. If you require a guide for trekking or climbing consult the **Asociación Argentina de Guías de Montana (AAGM) (**/FAX (2944) 424818 or (2944) 428991, Calle Casilla de Correo in Bariloche. They can hook you up with an experienced professional.

Rafting and Kayaking

The Río Manso along the Chilean frontier throws up enough rapids and whirlpools for whitewater rafting and kayaking. The river is rated Class III–IV. Several Cerro Catedral-based outfitters offer summer trips including **Adventure World (** (2944) 41054 or (2944) 60164 FAX (2944) 22637, and **Extremo Sur (** (2944) 427301 E-MAIL info@ extremosur.com WEB SITE www.extremosur.com. A full-day trip including all equipment and guides costs US$98; a half-day trip runs US$68.

Fishing

Among the tasty game fish that prowl the park's countless lakes and rivers are rainbow and brown trout, Atlantic salmon, two different types of perch and Patagonian pejerrey. Fly-fishing and spinning are popular in backcountry streams while trolling from a boat is the preferred method on Nahuel Huapi and other lakes. Anglers must possess a valid fishing license, available at most tackle shops in Bariloche, the **Intendencia del Parques Nacionales** ((2944) 423111, Calle San Martín 24, or the **Direcciónes Provinciales de Pesca** ((2944) 425160, Calle Elflein 10. A weekly license is US$30. The fishing season runs from November 15 to April 15. Night fishing is not allowed.

Guided fishing trips are very popular. **Patagonia Fly Shop** ((2944) 441944 E-MAIL flyshop @bariloche.com.ar, Calle Quinchahuala 200 off

Buceo ((2944) 431040 E-MAIL arumcobuceo@ bariloche.com.ar WEB SITE www.bjs.com.ar/ arumco, Calle 20 de Febrero 680, and **ASAP Diving Center** ((2944) 427088 E-MAIL mazzolaj @bariloche.com.ar WEB SITE www.mercotour .com/mazzola, Calle Mitre 171 in the Galería Araucana.

Mountain Biking

An alternative way to explore the lakeshore and backcountry is thrashing along on a mountain bike. **Dirty Bikes** ((2944) 425616 E-MAIL dirtybikes @bariloche.com.ar, Calle V.A. O'Connor 681, and **Bikeway** ((2944) 424202 WEB SITE www.bikeway .com.ar, Calle V.A. O'Connor 867, both rent, sell

Avenida Bustillo in Melipal, offers both fishing equipment and fully guided trips with owner and expert angler Ricardo Ameijeiras. **Big Valley** ((2944) 420369, Calle John O'Connor 501, Bariloche, runs its own fly-fishing school.

Fishing & Company ((2944) 461768 can arrange guided lake boats and fishing equipment for up to eight people. Or you can rent your own boat at **Charlie Lake** ((2944) 448562, Avenida Bustillo Km. 16.6 near Cerro Campanario. Rental rates range from US$150 per hour to US$600 for a full dawn-to-dusk day.

Scuba Diving

Those who prefer to watch and photograph fish rather than fry them can scuba-dive the murky blue-green waters of Nahuel Huapi. Fully accredited PADI courses and diving excursions (including night dives) are offered by **Arum-Co**

and repair bikes. Rental rates vary from US$5 (one hour) to US$20 (one day).

At least a dozen outfitters in and around Bariloche organize guided mountain bike tours, including **La Bolsa del Deporte** ((2944) 423529, Calle Elflein 385, Bariloche and the aforementioned **Adventure World** ((2944) 41054 FAX (2944) 422637 at Cerro Catedral. Itineraries run the gamut from a half-day ride to the top of Cerro Otto to a marathon 10-day trip from Bariloche to El Bolsón.

Horseback Riding

Let another creature work up a sweat by taking a horseback ride through the countryside. Numerous stables around Bariloche offer hourly and half-day rides. **Tom Wesley** ((2944) 448193 E-MAIL tomwesley@bariloche.com.ar, offers saddle-back

The backcountry trails of Parque Nacional Nahuel Huapi are often crowded in summer.

tours from his base at Club Hípico Bariloche that range from a two-hour circuit around nearby Cerro Campanario to a six-day horseback camping trip along the upper reaches of the Río Chubut.

Aerosports

Aeroclub Bariloche ((2944) 426622 at the airport can arrange one-hour photographic flights for a single passenger in a single engine plane (US$120).

The only other way to get a bird's-eye view of the landscape is paragliding off one of the local peaks. **Escuela de Parapente Patagonia** ((2944) 442154 offers professional instruction and virgin flights from the crest of Cerro Otto and Cerro Catedral (US$70).

Golf

Only in Bariloche could golf be considered an adventure sport. But when you consider the altitude and the spectacular Andes scenery, putting a ball across a neatly manicured green takes on a whole new meaning. The 18-hole championship course at the **Hotel Llao Llao** ((2944) 448525 or (2944) 448544 is surely one of South America's more beautiful places to tee off. Other local links include the nine-hole **Pinares Golf Course** ((2944) 462416 overlooking the lakeshore west of Bariloche, and the nine-hole **Villa Arelauquen Golf Course** at Lago Gutiérrez.

Snow Skiing

Although it boasts the country's oldest piste, the **Piedras Blancas Ski Area** ((2944) 441035 or (2944) 425720 on the side of Cerro Otto isn't all that challenging for experienced skiers. However, with a small ski school and easy slopes, it's a good place to learn and is especially popular with families. Other amenities include equipment rental, snack bar and chair lifts. There's also 300 m (330 yards) of dedicated toboggan trails for youngsters.

Serious skiers head straight for **Gran Catedral** ((2944) 460051 or (2944) 460062 which features 67 km (41 miles) of ski trails spread across two different sky areas: Robles Catedral in the south and Alta Patagonia in the north. The resort has equipment rental, ski school and several food and beverage outlets.

It's cheaper to rent snow equipment and winter clothing in town at places like **Buenos Aires Ski** ((2944) 435366, Calle Perito Moreno 60, and **La Bolsa del Deporte** ((2944) 423529 E-MAIL bolsadep @bariloche.com.ar, Calle Elflein 385. For snowboarding gear try **Alligator Radical** ((2944) 433865, Calle Mitre 481, or **Xtornudo** ((2944) 432464 E-MAIL xtornudo@yahoo.com, Calle Mitre 340.

SHOPPING

Chocolate is the name of the game in Bariloche, another bequest of the German, Swiss and Scandinavian pioneers who first settled this place. A good place to start (and perhaps never leave) is **Abuela Goye Chocolate Factory** ((2944) 433861, Calle 24 de Septiembre 210. Abuela Goye also has a couple of sweet boutiques: at Calle Mitre 258 and Calle Quaglia 221 (the latter doubles as a quaint *Salón de té*). Chocoholics can also get their fix at **Mamuschka** ((2944) 423294, Calle Mitre 216, and **Dulcería Suiza** ((2944) 431872 with outlets at Calle Perito Moreno 14 and Calle Paso 130.

Ahumadero Familia Weiss ((2944) 423657, at the corner of Palacios and V.A. O'Connor, hawks a wide range of Patagonian gourmet food items including cheeses, jams, pâtés and acclaimed smoked fish and meats. Even more eclectic is **La Mexican de Bariloche** ((2944) 422505, Calle Mitre 288, where the selection runs from smoked salmon to gourmet chocolates and tasty fruit liqueurs.

Bariloche is a good place to find a broad range of traditional handicraft items from all around Argentina. Local artists and craftsmen sell their goods at a gallery supported by the **Asociación de Artesanos** ((2944) 442854 E-MAIL artesanos99 @hotmail.com, at Calle Elflein 38.

Cardón ((2944) 433908 E-MAIL cardon@sion .com, Calle Villages 216, offers an outstanding array of gaucho goods including *criollo* silver buckles and spurs, leather riding boots, saddle bags and other leather goods.

Another good source of gaucho silver is **El Establo Viejo** ((2944) 426208 at Calle Mitre 22, while the adjacent **Fitzroy** ((2944) 422335 at No. 18 specializes in ponchos, pullovers, woodwork and decorative deer antlers. Metalwork is the prevailing art form at **Tito Testone** ((2944) 421702 E-MAIL nelsi@bariloche.com.ar, Calle Quaglia 227.

The implements of summer and winter recreation are also easy to acquire in Bariloche. **Buenos Aires Ski** ((2944) 435366, Calle Perito Moreno 60, handles just about every sport that's possible in the area including ski gear, camping equipment, fishing tackle and golf clubs. Another good all-around shop is **La Bolsa del Deporte** ((2944) 423529 E-MAIL bolsadep@bariloche.com.ar, Calle Elflein 385, which carries skiing, trekking, kayaking, cycling and mountaineering equipment.

Alligator Radical ((2944) 433865, Calle Mitre 481, has a wide range of snowboards, inline skates, wakeboards and windsurfing equipment. **Xtornudo** ((2944) 432464 E-MAIL xtornudo@yahoo.com, Calle Mitre 340, handles gear for snow and skateboarding.

Fishing equipment and licenses are available at **Deportes Montana** at Calle Onelli 794. **Terra** ((2944) 433602 E-MAIL terra@bariloche.com.ar, Calle Palacios 669, makes and sells its own line of backpacks, fishing vests and other all-weather fabric items.

The place to stock up on food and other supplies for the backcountry is **La Victoria** supermarket ((2944) 430681 at Calle Alte. Brown 474.

WHERE TO STAY

Very Expensive

The wonderfully rustic **Llao Llao** ((2944) 448525 or (2944) 448530 FAX (2944) 448244 dominates a leafy ridge 25 km (15 miles) west of Bariloche. Built in 1938 from local wood, shingles and stone, this was one of architect Alejandro Bustillo's first creations and set the tone for many of his later masterpieces. The hotel underwent a long-overdue renovation in 1993 and is now recognized as a national historic landmark. Lakes, mountains and forests are all within walking distance of your room. Water sports and golf are available, as are tango and salsa lessons. The hotel also boasts a business center, indoor swimming pool, health club, and gourmet restaurant.

Nearby is another outstanding lodge: the **Tunquelen** ((2944) 448233 FAX IN BUENOS AIRES (11) 4394-9599. Its first-rate facilities including water sports, tennis courts and an indoor pool with a magnificent view of the lake. Eight hectares (20 acres) of woods and landscaped gardens add to the tranquil ambience.

The sleek, modern **Edelweiss** ((2944) 426165 or (2944) 426167 FAX (2944) 425655 E-MAIL reservas @edelweiss.com.ar WEB SITE www.edelweiss .com.ar, Avenida San Martín 202, is the most luxurious hotel in Bariloche city. Although the room decor isn't that different from most international

chains, the Edelweiss prides itself on personalized, attentive service. It's within walking distance of the Centro Cívico and the shopping district. Amenities include a tour desk, health club, indoor pool, beauty parlor, the El Patio piano bar and La Tavola restaurant.

Expensive

The Swiss Alps is the prevailing theme at **Hotel Nevada** ((2944) 422778 FAX (2944) 427914 E-MAIL hnevada@bariloche.com.ar WEB SITE www.nevada .com.ar, Calle Rolando 250. With a massive gabled roof flanked by twin towers, the building wouldn't look out of place in Zermatt or Gstaad. The 88 rooms are comfortable and well equipped (cable television, direct-dial phones), furnished in a rustic, mountain style. Meals and snacks are served in a combination café/bar on the ground floor and there's a gym and sauna for relaxation. The business center offers fax and Internet services.

If you crave a mid-city hotel with a little more action try the **Panamericano** ((2944) 425846 FAX (2944) 425850 E-MAIL hotel@panameri.com.ar, Avenida San Martín 536, which sports its own casino and nightclub. Just 300 m (330 yards) from the civic center, this magnificent modern hotel offers sweeping views of Lake Nahuel Huapi. Facilities include health club with heated pool, solarium, gym and beauty parlor, children's playroom, business center, and shopping mall.

One of the few places overlooking the lake in downtown Bariloche is the **Hotel Tres Reyes** ((2944) 426121 FAX (2944) 424230 E-MAIL consultas@ hoteltresreyes.com WEB SITE www.hoteltresreyes .com, Avenida 12 de Octubre 135, which has well-appointed rooms with telephones and cable television. Downstairs there's a cozy bar and a large private garden. Buffet breakfast is included in the rate.

Moderate

Like many of the city's mid-range abodes, the **Hotel Cristal** ((2944) 422442 or (2944) 426101 FAX (2944) 422002 E-MAIL htl_intl@risc6.infonet .com.py, Calle Mitre 355, makes up for an essential lack of character with solid service and good amenities. The 100 rooms are all equipped with minibar, safe, modem/fax connection and color television. For relaxation there's a swimming pool and solarium, sauna and gym. The food and beverage outlets are also comprehensive: an executive lobby bar, American snack bar, roof garden piano bar and sophisticated restaurant with an international menu.

Hotel Patagonia ((2944) 423515 FAX (2944) 429636 E-MAIL reservas@patagoniahotel.com.ar, Avenida Bustillo km 1.3. Overlooking the Nahuel Huapi lake, this 56-room "upside down" hotel is

German-style wooden clocks and other souvenirs grace a Bariloche shop window.

built on 10 levels cascading down to the lake. Rooms at this three-star establishment are large with magnificent views. There is room service, a restaurant and all-purpose common area.

One of the best values for money in central Bariloche is the **Hotel Pacífico (** (2944) 421532, Calle Perito Moreno 335, with well-appointed rooms and a great view of the lake. Rates include breakfast and dinner.

Anyone who's considering a week or more in Bariloche should consider a self-catering unit like **Les Petits Chalets (**/FAX (2944) 23628 E-MAIL frisch @bariloche.com.ar, at the corner of Piedras and Francia near the city center. Each spacious bungalow sleeps eight in three separate bedrooms, with two complete bathrooms, fully equipped kitchen, dining and living room with cable television. The adjacent tennis courts are open for guests during the summer.

There are a number of good hotels and hostels in the Playa Bonita area west of Bariloche, including the **Hostería Santa Rita (**/FAX (2944) 461028, Avenida Bustillo Km. 7.2, on the shores of Lago Nahuel Huapi. It offers 12 rooms with private bath and cable television, plus a game room, snack bar and restaurant. Tours of the park and airport transfers can be arranged. Both Playa Bonita and Cerro Catedral are nearby.

Another good place along the western shore is **Hostería Viejo Molino (** (2944) 441011 or (2944) 441024 E-MAIL viejomolino@bariloche.com.ar WEB SITE www.barilochepatagonia.com/vmolino, Avenida Bustillo Km. 6.4, which has a real home-away-from-home ambience. The tea room whips up wonderful homemade pastries and out back there's a wooden deck with a heated swimming pool. Room rates include breakfast, airport transfer and shuttle bus to Cerro Catedral. The hostel can also arrange skiing and fishing tours.

Tucked back into the *coihues* trees behind the lake are the **Pinotea Cabañas (**/FAX (2944) 461526, Avenida de los Pioneros Km. 8, a rustic refuge with comfortable A-frame cabins that sleep up to six. All units have private bath with hot water and kitchen/dining areas.

Even farther out in the woods is the **Hotel Tronador (** (2944) 468127 FAX (2944) 441062, on the shore of Lago Mascardi with a magnificent panoramic view of the lake and the surrounding mountains. There are 29 spacious guestrooms, three common sitting rooms, bar, video room, barbecue area and boat ramp. The twin dining rooms provide wonderful home-cooked meals.

Inexpensive

Serious climbers, trekkers and skiers often stay at the **Aldea Andina Club Hotel (** (2944) 441405 or (2944) 441930 E-MAIL aldea@bariloche.com.ar, on three hectares (over seven acres) of pure nature, minutes from Cerro Catedral. Simple clean and

comfortable cottages — with kitchenettes, cable television and telephone — sleep four to seven with full hotel service. The hotel plans activities and entertainment for the whole family, throughout the year. There's also a bar, restaurant and tennis courts.

Backpackers from around the globe flock to the **Alaska Youth Hostel (**/FAX (2944) 461564 E-MAIL alaska@bariloche.com.ar, Calle Lilinquen 328, about seven and a half kilometers (just over four and a half miles) west of downtown Bariloche. Sleeping choices include double and quadruple rooms, dormitories and bungalows that sleep six. The hotel offers individual lockers and storage room, cooking and laundry facilities, free parking, trekking information, mountain bike rental and maps. It also organizes horseback riding, whitewater rafting and ski trips, and offers discounts to IYHF and youth card holders. Open all year, but reservations are highly recommended in summer.

Another convenient hostel is **Albergue Mochilero's (** (2944) 431627 or (2944) 423187 E-MAIL cecilia@bariloche.com.ar WEB SITE www.nyn .patagonia.com/ar/amuncar, Calle San Martín 82 near the Civic Center. The small, clean dormitory rooms are complemented by hot-water showers, central heating, communal kitchen, storage facilities, restaurant and mini shop. Tourist information and adventure tours are available. **Ruca Hueney (** (2944) 433986 E-MAIL alec@bariloche .com.ar, Calle Elflein 396, is yet another city center youth hostel. Facilities include a communal kitchen, a barbecue area, showers with hot water, television, access to the Internet and views of the lake.

A great place to bed down in the southern part of the park is the **Lago Mascardi Hostel (** (2944) 490524 or in Buenos Aires (11) 4811-4105 E-MAIL hosteria@mascardi-patagonia.com.ar. It has rooms with or without private bath, as well as cottages sleeping up to six. There's also a 24-hour snack bar, restaurant, television and video room, plus sports activities and excursions.

Bariloche also boasts numerous *casas de familia* — ordinary houses and apartments that offer rooms to visitors. **Eduardo Calabresi (** (2944) 461648 E-MAIL eduardo_c@bariloche.com.ar, rents a single room with kitchen facilities in the Edificio Bariloche Center at the corner of San Martín and Pagano; it sleeps up to four people. **Irma Martínez (** (156) 32760 has rooms for up to five people. Located a block from the Civic Center, they come with bedding, private bathroom with hot water, central heating and kitchenette with refrigerator.

There are also multiple campsite options around the national park. **Camping Goye Bariloche (** (2944) 448627, in Colonia Suiza near the terminus of bus line 10 from Bariloche, offers electrical hookups, hot water, barbecues, picnic tables and a 24-hour snack bar. You'll find similar facilities at **Camping Arroyo Fresco** ((2944) 423918 or (2944) 424531 E-MAIL transita@bariloche.com.ar, on the north shore of Lago Mascardi, where horseback riding, kayaking, fishing and hiking are possible. Take Ruta 258 Km. 25 south from Bariloche.

WHERE TO EAT

Expensive

Some of Bariloche's most imaginative cuisine is created at **La Cave** ((2944) 461412, Calle Hua Huan 7831 near Avenida Bustillo 7800, including favorites like mozzarella roll filled with eggplant, sundried tomatoes and basil, sweet potato gnocchi with lamb stew, and chicken breast with prosciutto, sage and kidney bean salsa. For dessert try the pear and raspberry crème brûlée, oven-baked peaches with Amaretto or the traditional *dulce de leche* (caramelized condensed milk).

De La Granja ((2944) 435939, Calle Villegas 126, is a family owned and operated restaurant with a wonderful menu that includes smoked trout crêpes, cheese fondue, Granny's stewed rabbit and Gruyere cheese chicken.

Andes-Alpine cuisine is also the forte at intimate **La Marmite** ((2944) 423685, Calle Mitre 329, where the selection includes fondues that blend cheese and meats, *trucha* (fresh mountain trout), *jabalí* (wild boar) and *ciervo* (venison). The wine list here is also superb and the service is hard to top.

Moderate

Perhaps the best of Bariloche's many reasonably priced *parrillas* is an old favorite called **La Vizcacha** ((2944) 422109, Calle Rolando 279. Tasty choices include lamb chops and trout. And no, they don't have *vizcacha* (a type of wild rodent) on the menu.

Another good *parrilla* is **El Viejo Matias** ((2944) 434466, Calle Elflein 49, where the *tenedor libre* buffet includes various salads, barbecued meats and desserts. There's also an à la carte menu with regional favorites like trout, wild boar, venison and smoked salmon.

Bariloche is one of the few destinations that offers a respite from traditional Argentine beef. The Mexican owned and operated **Días de Zapata** ((2944) 423128, Calle Morales 362, churns out scrumptious tacos, enchiladas and fajitas as well as margaritas that'll knock your socks off. **Kandahar** ((2944) 424702, Calle 20 de Febrero 698, puts an exotic spin in local favorites like trout, wild boar, baby goat and loin steak. One of the owners is Argentine ski champ and Olympian Marta Peirono de Barber.

Relive your blurry recollections of Oktoberfest at **Viejo Munich** ((2944) 422336 at the corner of Mitre and Quaglia near the Civic Center. If the

Bavarian wood-beam decor isn't enough to jog your memory, the draft beer will certainly do the trick. The menu runs heavily toward German and Argentine-style meat dishes including steak, wurst and schnitzel.

Befitting an Alpine-Andes outpost, several Bariloche-area eateries offer magnificent views. **Confitería Giratoria** ((2944) 441035, a revolving restaurant at the summit of Cerro Otto, offers fairly good steaks, pasta and salads. But the view is the real reason to rise this high: a 1,400-m (4,600-ft) perch with sweeping views of the city, lake and mountains. The dining room makes a complete revolution every 40 minutes. You can reach Giratoria by taxi from the city center or via the

cable car that climbs from Avenida los Pioneros in Melipal. There's also a great view from windowside tables at **La Cima Restaurant** ((156) 03603, at the crest of Cerro Campanario on the drive out to Llao Llao.

One reason to venture up to Lago Traful on the north side of the national park is the excellent food at **Parrilla La Terraza** ((2944) 479077, Ruta 65 Km. 35.5, where the house specials include *chivito* (baby goat), *cerdo* (pork) and *cordero* (lamb). If you are there for lunch, ask for a table on the patio with its panoramic view of the water, trees and peaks.

Inexpensive

A great place for typical northwest Argentine food is **Simoca** ((2944) 426467, Calle Palacios 264, where

Andes-Alpine cuisine is the specialty at La Marmite and other Bariloche eateries.

you can sample a variety of *empanadas*, *humitas* and *tamales* and *locro* (hearty soup) from the Tucumán region.

Pin 9 ((2944) 442744, Avenida de Los Pioneros 4800 near the Teleférico station in Melipal, is a nice little family restaurant with indoor seating in a modern A-frame structure and al fresco dining in the garden. The menu is fairly simple but includes low-priced pasta, pizza, barbecued meats and regional dishes. There's a playground to keep the kids happy before and after the meal.

Variety is the spice of life at **El Mundo (** (2944) 423461, which boasts a hundred different types of pizza in addition to inexpensive chicken and veal dishes, salads, pasta and *empanadas*. **Don Pancho (** (2944) 425063, Calle Mitre 150, turns out excellent sandwiches and fresh fruit *licuados* (smoothies). If you're not looking for anything more elaborate than pizza and beer try **Friends (** (2944) 423700 at the corner or Mitre and Rolando.

NIGHTLIFE

A great place to grab a brew and watch the sunset is **Club de Caza y Pesca (** (2944) 435963, adjacent to the Museo Icticola at the corner of Avenida 12 de Octubre and Calle Onelli. The setting could not be more romantic: thick wood-beam ceiling, stag's head perched above a huge stone fireplace and picture windows that look out on Nahuel Huapi.

Quaffing large portions of German-style beer is the nightly routine at **Viejo Munich (** (2944) 422336, at Mitre and Quaglia. **Hola Nicolas (** (156) 10125 or (155) 57091, Calle Perito Moreno 10 just off Plaza Roca, is one of the few places in Bariloche that offers a variety of live music, stand-up comedy and dance acts.

Most of the local dance clubs blend Euro DJ tunes, American rap and Latin grooves. Among the happening spots are **Rocket (** (2944) 431940, Calle Rosas 424, and **ByPass Discotheque (** (2944) 420549, Calle Rolando 155.

HOW TO GET THERE

Bariloche and the Lake District are 1,600 km (990 miles) southwest of Buenos Aires and 900 km (560 miles) northwest of Puerto Madryn and the Península Valdés.

The most direct way to drive from Buenos Aires is Ruta 5 to Santa Rosa, Ruta 35 to General Acha, Ruta 20 to Ruta 151 and on to Neuquén and Ruta 237 to Bariloche. From Puerto Madryn take Ruta 3 south to Trelew, Ruta 25 west through the Chubut Valley to Tecka, then Ruta 40 and 258 north to Bariloche.

Aeropuerto Internacional Bariloche ((2944) 422555 is about 15 km (nine miles) east of town. Most airlines run their own shuttle bus service into town center, but you can also grab a taxi.

There are several daily flights between Buenos Aires and Bariloche, plus weekly service to Trelew, Comodoro Rivadavia and Neuquén. You can make reservations and purchase tickets at **Aerolíneas Argentinas/Austral (** (2944) 422425 or (2944) 423161 Calle Quaglia 238; **LADE (** (2944) 423562, Calle Quaglia 238; **LAPA (** (2944) 423714, Calle Villegas 121.

The city's **Terminal de Ómnibus (** (2944) 432860 occupies the old train station at Calle 12 de Octubre 2400 on the eastern edge of town. Various companies offer long-distance service to Buenos Aires (22 hours) and major destinations including Neuquén (seven hours), Mendoza (22 hours), Viedma (16 hours), Trelew (nine hours),

Puerto Madryn (10 hours), Comodoro Rivadavia (14 hours) and Río Gallegos (28 hours). Recommended services include **TAC (** (2944) 432521, Calle Villegas 147; **Mar Y Valle (** (2944) 432269, in the Terminal de Ómnibus; **Chevallier (** (2944) 423090, Calle Perito Moreno 107; and **Andesmar (** (2944) 422140, Calle Palacios 246.

TAS Choapa ((2944) 432521 or (2944) 422818 in the Terminal de Ómnibus is one of the few companies that offers service to Chile including buses to Puerto Montt and Santiago.

You can also arrive and depart Bariloche by rail, although the trip isn't nearly as romantic as Paul Theroux's Old Patagonian Express. **Servicio Ferrocarril Patagonia (** (2944) 423172 offers the region's last passenger service, a 14-hour marathon in antiquated carriages from Bariloche to Viedma on the Atlantic Coast. Onward service to Buenos Aires has been suspended.

Water transport is yet another option: a series of ferries and buses cross the Lake District to Puerto Montt on Chile's Pacific coast. You can buy individual sections or splurge on the water/road package offered by **Catedral Turismo** ((2944) 425443, which includes a ferry from Bariloche to Puerto Blest, a bus between Puerto Frías and Peulla in Chile, and a catamaran cruise across Lake Todos los Santos before a final bus trip along the south shore of Lake Llanquihue to Puerto Montt (US$105).

PUERTO MADRYN

Although it likes to fancy itself as a beach resort, the pleasant seaside city of Puerto Madryn is more renowned as the gateway to the wildlife wonderland of the Valdés Peninsula. The city has an easy atmosphere punctuated by a breezy promenade that stretches along the waterfront. Local residents don't seem to mind the mobs of tourists who migrate their way each summer.

Puerto Madryn was founded in 1886 during the first wave of Welsh migration to Patagonia, but unlike the nearby Chubut Valley the city has lost most of its Gaelic texture. There's the occasional Welsh teahouse or souvenir shop, but Puerto Madryn is really a late twentieth-century phenomenon and owes its boomtown atmosphere to a huge aluminum smelter (on the northern outskirts) and proximity to Patagonia's greatest concentration of wildlife.

GENERAL INFORMATION

Nearly everything a visitor craves can be found along Avenida Roca, the wide street that stretches along the waterfront — hotels, restaurants, bars, travel agencies, souvenir shops and rental car outlets.

The information desk at the municipal **Secretaría de Turismo** ((2965) 453504 or (2965) 452148 E-MAIL sectur@madryn.gov.ar WEB SITE www.madryn.gov.ar, Avenida Roca 223, is one of Argentina's best with English speaking staff and heaps of maps and brochures. Open daily 8 AM to 2 PM and 3 PM to 9 PM.

Correo Argentino ((2965) 451259 is at the junction of Belgrano and Gobernador Maíz. Long-distance and overseas calls can be placed at **Telefónica** on the Plaza San Martín. **Compulab** at Calle 25 de Mayo 95 offers Internet access.

There are a number of places to change money, access ATMs or arrange credit card advances including **Banco de la Nación** ((2965) 450465, Calle 9 de Julio 117; **Banco Almafuerte** ((2965) 451941 at the corner of 25 de Mayo and Roque Sáenz Peña; and **Banco del Chubut** ((2965) 471787 at Calle 25 de Mayo 154.

Medical emergencies can be handled at the **municipal hospital** ((2965) 451240 or (2965) 451010 at Calle Pujol 247 in the northern suburbs. Over-the-counter medicines are available at **Farmacia Libertad** ((2965) 456742, Avenida San Martín 568.

Puerto Madryn boasts dozens of travel agencies. Among the best bets for tours around the region (including excursions to Península Valdés) are **Argentina Vision** ((2965) 455888 FAX (2965) 451108 E-MAIL arvision@arvision.com.ar, Avenida Roca 536; **Factor Patagonia** ((2965) 454990 E-MAIL factorpm@infovia.com.ar, Calle 25 de Mayo 186; and **Tito Botazzi** ((2965) 474110 or (2965) 456900, Calle Mitre 80.

WHAT TO SEE AND DO

The best thing to do in Puerto Madryn is wander up and down the "costanera" waterfront, lounging on the fine white sands of **Playa Tomás Curti** or browsing the shops and boutiques along Avenida Roca.

A good introduction to Patagonia's natural and human history is the splendid **Museo Provincial Ciencias Naturales y Oceanográfico** ((2965) 451139 at the junction of Mosconi and Domecq García just north of downtown. Displays feature Welsh colonization, as well as local flora and fauna (including a special exhibit on whales). There's a terrific view from the museum's upper level, a panoramic view of the city and Golfo Nuevo. And there are regular audiovisual shows on local topics. Open daily (except Monday) 9 AM to noon and 4:30 PM to 8:30 PM.

Patagonia's rocks, gems and minerals are the stars at the **Museo del Viejo Minero** at Avenida 28 de Julio 293, a small collection that doubles as a jewelry store. Open Monday to Saturday 10 AM to 1 PM and 5 PM to 9 PM.

Seventeen kilometers (11 miles) south of Puerto Madryn is the **Reserva Faunística Punta Loma**, a seldom-visited wildlife sanctuary on the southern edge of Golfo Nuevo. Even farther out (80 km/ 50 miles) is **Reserva Faunística Punta León**, which straddles a narrow peninsula at the southern entrance to the gulf. Both parks harbor shorebirds and pinniped colonies but are difficult to reach without your own wheels. Argentina Vision (see above) is one of the few local travel agents that run regular guided tours to these isolated reserves.

The wildlife-rich waters of the Golfo Nuevo are a Mecca for scuba divers from around the globe. Former Argentine Navy diver Hugo Garcia runs an outfit called **Patagonia Buceo** ((2965) 452278 at the Balneario "Rayentray" on Boulevard Brown, which offers both scuba training and underwater safaris for experienced divers. Another highly

An entire culture has grown up around *maté*, an herbal tea that serves as Argentina's national drink.

recommended scuba outfit is **Hydro Sport** ((2965) 495065 FAX (2965) 495016 at Rayentray.

Sports fishing cruises in the South Atlantic can be arranged through **Raúl "Pelado" Diaz** ((2965) 450812, Calle Love Parry 343, or **Deport 2040** at Avenida Gales 2040, who also sell fishing equipment and can arrange trophy making. The sailing boat **Yhoshua** ((2965) 472808, Calle Albarracín 736, offers daily cruises in the Golfo Nuevo during the summer months to view right whales and other wildlife.

You can rent cycles by the hour or day at **XT Mountain Bike** ((2965) 472232, Avenida Roca 742. Experienced bikers with their own camping equipment, food and water can make a circuit around Península Valdés in about three days, but the roads are mostly gravel which makes for major cuts and bruises anytime you take a spill.

SHOPPING

This is one of the best places in Patagonia to pick up local souvenirs including wool sweaters, T-shirts, gourmet food, leather handicrafts and general knickknacks. There are dozens of shops along Avenida Roca and Avenida 28 de Julio in the heart of the city.

Establecimiento Artesanal del Chubut ((2965) 451311 or (2965) 473079, Avenida Roca 369, is a mouthful in more ways than one. Homemade chocolates, jellies and jams, Welsh and Christmas cakes, and *alfajores* filled with Patagonian jams and smothered in Italian meringue. You can stuff yourself in the tearoom or sneak some back to your hotel.

Similar sugary concoctions are sold at **Península Chocolates** ((2965) 454541, Avenida Roca 331, and **Conejo Blanco** at Calle 28 de Julio 62.

A good place to hunt for Patagonian arts and crafts is **Antilhue** ((2965) 452489, Avenida Roca 549, which hawks local pottery, wickerwork, wool basketry, sculptures and paintings. **Omelin** at 25 de Mayo 999 sells direct-from-the-factory leather jackets, pants and shirts.

WHERE TO STAY

Expensive

Dominating the Puerto Madryn waterfront is the nine-story **Hotel Península Valdés** ((2965) 451218 or (2965) 471292 FAX (2965) 452584 WEB SITE www.hotel-peninsula-valdes.com, Avenida Roca 155, which offers clean and comfortable (if rather Spartan) rooms, most with sea and/or beach views. The front desk staff speak English and they are most helpful with suggestions for local restaurants and shopping. There's secure parking in the basement. But the hotel restaurant could do with better food and service.

Moderate

Right along the waterfront is a charming 40-room hotel called the **Bahía Nueva** ((2965) 451677 or (2965) 450045, Avenida Roca 67. Many of the rooms have beach and bay views, and off the lobby is one of the city's best bars. Other amenities include a small library with books on local wildlife and plenty of parking.

Another good place to bunk down is the **Aguas Mansas** ((2965) 473103 or (2965) 456626, Calle José Hernández 51. This newcomer offers clean and comfortable rooms in quiet surroundings at the south end of town. The property also boasts a swimming pool and snack bar.

Open your window and listen to right whales sing at the **Southern Cross Inn** (/FAX (2965) 474087 or (2965) 472523 E-MAIL hotel@la-posada.com.ar WEB SITE www.la-posada.com.ar, near the beach at Calle Abraham Matthews 2951. The 24 double or triple rooms all come with private bath. There's a sunny breakfast room and sitting room.

The centrally located **Hotel Tolosa** ((2965) 471850 or (2965) 456122 FAX (2965) 451141 E-MAIL info@hoteltolosa.com.ar WEB SITE www.hoteltolosa.com.ar, Calle Roque Sáenz Peña 253 near the bus station, which tenders 80 rooms with buffet breakfast included in the rate.

For longer stays you might want to consider renting an apartment or house by the week or month. **Ruca Hue Bungalows** ((2965) 451267 FAX (2965) 471791 E-MAIL rucahue@cpsarg.com, at the corner of Matthews and Humphreys on the south side of town, offer handsome whitewashed cottages that sleep up to six people. Only two blocks from the seafront along Boulevard Brown, the bungalows are popular with visiting scuba and wildlife study groups. There are similar digs a couple of blocks away at **Cabañas Nueva León** ((2965) 472635 E-MAIL info@neuvaleon.com.ar, Calle Thomas 1750.

Inexpensive

Dozens of small hotels cater to Argentine sun-seekers on summer holidays, like the trim little **Hotel Costanera** ((2965) 453000 FAX (2965) 424400, Boulevard Brown 759 right across the street from the beach. The color schemes could be a bit more eye pleasing, but the rooms are clean and some offer impressive waterfront views. The ground floor snack bar has floor-to-ceiling windows that face the beach.

A couple of blocks back from the beach is **Hotel El Cid** (/FAX (2965) 471416 E-MAIL hotelcid@nfavia.com.ar WEB SITE www.advance.com.ar/usuarios/mapasa/Reservaeng, Calle 25 de Mayo 850. All 36 rooms have cable television, telephones and central heating. Deluxe rooms have fans, bathtubs and hairdryers.

Prices fall as you head away from the coast. **Hotel Tandil** (/FAX (2965) 456152 E-MAIL hoteltandil

@arnet.com.ar WEB SITE www. cpatagonia.com/pm/tandil, Calle Juan B Justo 762, has rooms with private bath, television and telephone. Other amenities include laundry service, breakfast, snack bar, room service and parking. But it's eight blocks to the beach. Nearby is the **Motel Mora** (/FAX (2965) 471424 WEB SITE www.cpatagonia.com/cp/mora/index.htm, which offers basic rooms with bath and television.

King of the local youth hostels is **Hostelling Internacional Puerto Madryn** ((2965) 474426 E-MAIL hi-pm@satlink.com.ar, Avenida 25 Mayo 1136. Dormitory-style accommodation with private baths sleeps three to four people. Other temptations include a full kitchen with a 'fridge, barbecue area, laundry room, free transfers from the bus terminal and a beautiful garden area for relaxation. Bungalow apartments are also available for two to four people, furnished with pots, pans and tableware. Another possibility is **Hostel Yanco** ((2965) 456411 or 471581, Avenida Roca 626.

There are three well-equipped campgrounds on the southern outskirts of Puerto Madryn: **Atlántico Sud** ((2965) 455640, **Camping ACA** ((2965) 452952, **El Golfito** ((2965) 454544. All sport great beachside locations as well as hot showers and snack bar.

WHERE TO EAT

Expensive

I make a point of having at least one meal at **Placido** ((2965) 455991, Avenida Roca 506, whenever I'm in Puerto Madryn. What's not to like about this waterfront eatery? The food is superb, a menu that ranges through fresh seafood, sumptuous steaks and delicious pasta. Start with something like spinach crêpes with Parmesan cheese or a lobster and mushroom omelet, then move onto main dishes like *pulpo a la gallega* (octopus) or grilled *abadejo* fish with cream and lemon sauce. The service has always been splendid and you simply can't beat the location: right on the beach. Ask for a table at the back near the big picture windows.

Moderate

El Barco ((2965) 451965 on the "Curva del Indio" seacoast south of town is probably the best place in Puerto Madryn for fresh seafood. Another stalwart of freshly caught and cooked seafood is **Cantina el Náutico** ((2965) 471404, Avenida Roca 790, one of the city's oldest (1970) and most popular restaurants.

New on the local scene is **Terraza** ((2965) 453291, Avenida Gales 32, which offers an enticing menu of Italian specialties and local seafood plates. Another new restaurant that's already become a hit with local diners is **Nola** ((2965) 456078, Avenida Roca 485.

Like most Argentine towns, Puerto Madryn has its fair share of tasty *parrillas* including **Estella** ((2965) 451573, at the corner of Mitre and Roque Sáenz Peña, which tenders tasty beef, lamb and fish dishes. Carnivores also flock to **Parrilla Don Jorge** ((2965) 450356 across the street.

Inexpensive

Puerto Madryn abounds with fast-food places, especially the stretch of Avenida Roca between the pier and Avenida Gales.

Pizzas La Casera ((2965) 456336 has two locations that serve up tasty pizza and pasta dishes: Avenida Gales 74 in the city center and Boulevard Brown 848 on the waterfront.

Al fresco dining and a typical pizza/pasta menu is the main attraction at **Adesso** ((2965) 453070, at the corner of 25 de Mayo and 9 de Julio in the middle of town.

La Cabildo ((2965) 456868, Avenida Yrigoyen 42, offers a slightly expanded menu that includes modest meat and seafood dishes as well as pasta, *empanadas*, and pizza. **La Criolla** ((2965) 450802, Calle 25 de Mayo 683, makes a good *empanada*.

NIGHTLIFE

One of the few places in Puerto Madryn to catch live music is **La Oveja Negra** (The Black Sheep), a smoky little pub at Avenida Yrigoyen 144, where cold beer and Patagonian rock and blues are the cornerstones of a rowdy night on the town.

HOW TO GET THERE

Puerto Madryn sits on the western edge of the Golfo Nuevo and the Península Valdés, 67 km (41 miles) north of Trelew and 616 km (382 miles) south of Bahía Blanca.

Anyone arriving by air must fly into the tiny **Aeropuerto Trelew** ((2965) 428021. The terminal is well stocked with rental-car agencies and there is a convenient minibus service that operates after every incoming flight, taking passengers directly from the air terminal to hotels in Puerto Madryn.

Local airline offices include **LAPA** ((2965) 451048 or (2965) 451773, Avenida Roca 303 and **LADE** ((2965) 451256, Avenida Roca 117 as well as **Aerolíneas Argentinas** ((2965) 420210 or (2965) 420170, Calle 25 de Mayo 33 in Trelew.

Puerto Madryn's busy little **bus terminal** lounges near the intersection of Yrigoyen (running up from the waterfront) and Zar. There is frequent service to Buenos Aires (18 hours), Trelew (one hour), Comodoro Rivadavia (six hours), Neuquén (12 hours) and Río Gallegos (18 hours).

Among the long-distance coach companies with offices at the Terminal de Ómnibus are **TAC** ((2965) 451537, **Andesmar** ((2965) 473764, and **El Pingüino** ((2965) 456256.

PENÍNSULA VALDÉS

The anvil-shaped Valdés Peninsula, flanked by Golfo San José and Golfo San Matías on the north and the Golfo Nuevo on the south, is South America's version of the Serengeti Plains. Nowhere else on the continent will you find so many large animals at such close proximity, seemingly oblivious to human presence. The *reserva faunística* and its adjacent maritime parks constitute Argentina's single most important wildlife area and a treasure of global ecology.

The scope of species is astounding: right whale, killer whale (orcas), sea lion, elephant seal, sea turtles, dolphin, shark, penguin, guanaco, rhea and flamingo. Not just present, but usually found in abundance — 43,000 elephant seals, more than 20,000 sea lions and the largest concentration of right whales (2,500) found anywhere on the planet.

The park's most spectacular animal, and in many respects its most elusive, is the killer whale. A pod of 20 to 30 orcas frequents the waters of Punta Norte between July and early December. Ranger Robert Bubas has observed their behavior for many years — including the brazen way in which they beach themselves at Punta Norte to catch sea lions.

Right whales (also called franca austral or franca del sur whales) also congregate around the peninsula between July and December, although you're likely to see some at the outer edges of the gulfs into early January. Their name comes from nineteenth-century American whalers who considered them the "right" or "correct" animal to harpoon, because their blubber was thicker than other species.

Like many marine species, right whales were hunted to the verge of extinction (from 60,000 worldwide in 1900 to fewer than 4,000 by the early 1970s) until a complete ban on hunting was imposed by the International Whaling Commission. Slowly but surely the right whale population has rebounded to around 7,000 animals today. The recovery has been especially significant off the Península Valdés, where the number of right whales has increased sevenfold (to 2,500) over the last 30 years.

The peninsula is the only place in the world where elephant seals can be observed in great numbers without traveling to a remote island. Valdés is their lone continental breeding site in the southern hemisphere. You can see them lazing along local beaches at any time of year, but peak season is between August and March.

These are huge animals: adult males can reach 3,000 kg (1,500 lbs) and five meters (15 ft) in length. Males have a large trunk-like nose, hence the name. Females are among the champion divers of the animal kingdom: they can plunge to depths of 1,500 m (4,500 ft) and remain underwater for as long as two hours. Look for dominant males (called "beachmasters") who gather together harems of a hundred or more females. Don't forget: elephant seals are quite aggressive — especially around their pups — and should never be approached on foot.

Elephant seals share their sandy domain with thousands of South American sea lions. They're only about a fifth the size of their humongous cousins, but just as aggressive towards people who wander too close. Unlike the well-known California sea lion with its slick black coat, males of the South American species sport shaggy manes similar to the African lion. They also have a loud bark. Sea lions gather on Valdés beaches year-round, but their numbers are greatest between mid-October and mid-January.

Cute little Magellanic penguins round out the "big five" of Valdés marine animals. Although not as large as the population at Punta Tombo, the colony at Caleta Valdés numbers thousands of birds. They spend the southern hemisphere winter at sea, fishing constantly and building up their bulk. Come early September they pour onto Patagonian beaches to breed and lay their eggs in shallow dugouts behind the beach. Around March, after the hatchlings are big enough to feed themselves, they head to sea again.

Although the whole of the Península Valdés is considered a wildlife viewing area, there are only three fully protected mainland areas: Punta Norte, Caleta Valdés and Punta Delgada. The bast bulk of the land area is taken up by sheep *estancias* that allow public access to the reserve areas. Remember to respect private property.

WHAT TO SEE AND DO

About an hour's drive from Puerto Madryn, the reserve **entrance station** sits on the Ameghino Isthmus, which connects the peninsula to mainland Patagonia. The gate is open from 7 AM to sunset; there's always a ranger on duty to collect the entrance fee. The visitor center includes a small museum with exhibits on Valdés wildlife and an observation tower with views across the peninsula and both gulfs.

Close to the entrance station (ask a ranger to point it out) is a dirt road that leads north to the Golfo San José, where right whales and other marine species breed during the summer. There's an offshore rock called the **Isla de los Pájaros**, haven for thousands of seabirds including cormorants, egrets, herons, gulls, terns and plovers. The island is off-limits to humans.

The peninsula's only town is a 20-minute drive beyond the entrance station. **Puerto Pirámide** owes its existence to the salt trade that flourished in the area during the late nineteenth and early twentieth centuries. Salt was collected from the surface of the dry lakes (*salinas*) in the middle of the peninsula, stored in caves in the cliffs around Puerto Pirámide and then shipped to Buenos Aires on clipper ships that use to drop anchor in the bay here.

The local economy is firmly grounded in tourism these days: whale-watching expeditions, scuba-diving adventures, beach camping and general outdoor pursuits. The permanent population is around 140, but the town can swell to several thousand during summer holidays. It's impossible to become lost because there are only three streets.

Several companies specialize in whale-watching cruises on the gulf. I prefer the smaller outfits like **Pinino Aquatours (** (2965) 495015 or (2965)

South of town is **Punta Pardeta**, one of the few places where you can get an expansive view of the Golfo Nuevo. It's not a bad place to view wildlife either: from the cliff tops I've seen right whale mothers and calves frolicking in the offshore waters. To reach the point by car you have to double back on the main road and follow a sandy track down to the shore. But it's a lovely, windswept spot for those who take the time to get there.

Beyond the turnoff to Puerto Pirámide is a big highway junction. The left fork (Ruta 3) heads north toward Punta Norte. The right fork (Ruta 2) heads east toward Punta Delgada. About halfway down the latter road you can see a couple of huge salt pans — **Salina Grande** and **Salina Chica** —

451954, because you can get closer to the whales in their little boats and you get much more personal service. One of Pinino's best skippers is Mariano de Franaeschi, a young Argentine who knows just about everything there is to know about right whales. Mariano lives in one of the old salt caves behind the beach and is more than willing to give you a tour of his eccentric home after the cruise. Pinino is on the right-hand side on the first street down to the beach (*primera bajada*).

Another reputable whale-watching firm is **Jorge Schmid (** (2965) 495012 or (2965) 495112 on the second road (*segunda bajada*) down to the beach. Jorge's been taking people out onto the gulf for more than a quarter century and knows the offshore waters like the back of his hand. Scuba diving trips and instruction are offered at both Pinino Aquatours and Jorge Schmid, as well as **Hydro Sport (** (2965) 495065 FAX (2965) 495016.

off to the left. Salina Grande lies 42 m (137 ft) below sea level, the lowest point in South America.

Punta Delgada is distinguished by an ancient red-and-white lighthouse that's now a popular ecotourism lodge called the Hotel Faro (see WHERE TO STAY, below). A private trail from the hotel leads down to the beach where elephant seals and sea lions gather in large numbers. Anyone who eats lunch or stays overnight at the hotel has access to the trail.

A marvelous coast road winds its way north from Punta Delgada to Punta Norte. There are lots of spots along the way to pull over and take in the coastal scenery. Every patch of sand has its only little colony of sea lions and elephant seals. But proceed with caution: the cliffs are several hundred feet high and you can easily lose your footing.

Patagonian foxes hang out around the Punta Norte ranger station.

At **Punta Cantor** is a small café run by a husband and wife team, and a nature trail that leads down to the beach. This is one of the best places on the peninsula to get an "up close and personal" glimpse of both seal species.

Continuing north, the cliffs gradually give way to a huge lagoon called the **Caleta Valdés**, which is flanked by sand dunes. One turnoff leads to a small a penguin colony. The birds dig their burrows right up the edge of the parking lot and are easily photographed. The northern edge of the lagoon is the wildest part of the entire peninsula, scrubby terrain and low rolling hills where I've seen guanaco herds and flocks of rhea.

Punta Norte marks the northern terminus of the coast road. Your first stop should be the small but excellent museum with extensive exhibits on local flora and fauna, including superb photos of the local killer whale pod. Head down to the beach for a close-up glimpse of elephant seals and sea lions. If the orcas are around you may get to see one of the most spectacular events in the natural world — killer whales beaching themselves to catch baby sea lions. Afterwards, duck into the little café for a sandwich and watch the resident armadillos and Patagonian foxes fight over your scraps.

From Punta Norte, the drive back to Puerto Pirámide is about one hour, and Puerto Madryn about two hours. There's a turnoff to isolated Punta Buenos Aires at the mouth of the Golfo San José, but very few people make that trip.

Regional handicrafts, T-shirts and photo supplies are available at **Puerto Palos (** (2965) 495043, opposite Hydro Sport on the first road down to the beach, and at **Casa Pirámides (** (2965) 494046, opposite the fire station on the main road.

WHERE TO STAY

The only bona fide hotel in town is the 12-room **Paradise (** (2965) 495030 or (2965) 495003. Don't expect high-tech amenities and world-class service, but the rooms are clean and front desk staff speak English. Just off the lobby there's a small restaurant with a seafood/steak menu and a bar with ice-cold beer — really all you need in a place as remote as the Península Valdés.

Farther out on the peninsula is the wildly romantic **Faro Punta Delgada (** (2965) 471910 FAX (2965) 451218 with accommodation in cozy rooms overlooking the South Atlantic. All have private bath with hot water. Full board (three meals per day) is available. A private trail leads down the cliffs at the back of the lodge to the sea lion and elephant seal colony at Punta Delgada.

The only peninsula ranch that throws its doors open to visitors is **La Elena Estancia (** (2965) 424400 E-MAIL alcamar@infovia.com.ar. Six "bunkhouse"

rooms feature private bath with Jacuzzi, plus hot water and electricity generated by solar panels. The ranch can organize transportation to various wildlife viewing areas around the peninsula and trekking across to Salina Grande.

Several establishments in Puerto Pirámide rent modest bungalows by the day, week or month including **Cabañas en el Mar (** (2965) 495049 E-MAIL cabanas@piramides.com WEB SITE www.piramides.com.

Pirámide's large **campground** spans the beach between the two streets that run down to the shore. The entrance is adjacent to the ACA service station on the main road.

WHERE TO EAT

Despite its strategic location on the Nuevo Golfo, seaside views are hard to come by in Puerto Pirámide. The only exception — other than organizing your own picnic on the beach — is **Punta Ballena (** (2965) 495012 or (2965) 495112 at the foot of the second road that runs down to the beach. Owned and operated by the same people who run Jorge Schmid whale-watching excursions, it offers seafood, sandwiches and other light meals. **Paradise Restaurant (** (2965) 495030 or (2965) 495003 in the hotel of the same name serves up pretty good seafood, barbecued beef, pizza and sandwiches. Also recommended is **La Posada del Mar (** (2965) 495055 — fresh seafood and pasta dishes and a low-price tourist menu. **Restaurant de los Cetaceos (** (2965) 495050 offers light snacks which you can munch on a sunny patio that overlooks the first road down to the beach.

Confitería El Salmon ((2965) 495065 on the main road is the best place for breakfast — cooked or Continental — including coffee that will kick-start your day. At other times of the day they offer a wide range of burgers, pizza, sandwiches, pasta and seafood.

HOW TO GET THERE

Península Valdés is 90 km (60 miles) northeast of Puerto Madryn. Follow Avenida Domecq García north from the city center, past the huge ALUAR aluminum smelter and out into the countryside (where it becomes Ruta 1). About 18 km (12 miles) north of town, Ruta 1 runs into another paved road called Ruta 2. Turn right onto Ruta 2 and drive due east to the reserve's entrance gate.

There is daily bus service from Puerto Madryn to Puerto Pirámide during the summer season, but most people either drive themselves or latch onto some sort of organized tour.

Nearly every travel agency in Puerto Madryn offers day tours of the peninsula including **Argentina Vision (** (2965) 455888 FAX (2965) 451108 E-MAIL arvision@arvision.com.ar, Avenida

Roca 536; **Factor Patagonia** ((2965) 454990 E-MAIL factorpm@infovia.com.ar, Calle 25 de Mayo 186; and **Tito Botazzi** ((2965) 474110 or (2965) 456900 E-MAIL bottazzipm@infovia .com.ar, Calle Mitre 80. Tours run around US$30 per person and include transportation, English-speaking guide and lunch (usually at the Hotel Faro).

CHUBUT VALLEY

The Chubut isn't the most handsome or fertile of the numerous valleys they dissect Patagonia, but it's certainly the most charming, the bequest of Welsh immigrants who settled here during the latter half of the nineteenth century.

small colony on the southern flank of the Valdés Peninsula and two years later the first shipload of 153 immigrants came ashore at Puerto Madryn.

Many were former coal miners without any agricultural experience, and even those who'd been farmers back in Wales were discouraged by the desolate Patagonian landscape. Frustrated by lack of fresh water and wretched soil, battered by the harsh winters, the colonists soon wandered south to the Chubut Valley, where they founded a string of agrarian communities based in irrigation. Each family was given 100 hectares (247 acres) to cultivate, while the chapel and the cooperative society became the twin pillars of Welsh society in the valley.

The Welsh migration resulted from a combination of English imperialism, Gaelic nationalism and Argentine expansionism. Angered by London's political and cultural domination of their homeland, Welsh nationalists, under the leadership of the Rev. Michael D. Jones, began lobbying for an overseas colony, a so-called "Little Wales beyond Wales," that would be free of English hegemony. They spent years raising funds, recruiting migrants and vetting locations around the globe.

This was around the same time that Argentina was vying with Chile for control of Patagonia. One of the best ways to lay claim to the land was establishing permanent settlements, but few Argentines were interested in migrating to the cold and lonely frontier. All of a sudden, the Welsh nationalists appeared on the scene, eager to create a new homeland. They brokered a deal with the Argentine government in 1863 to establish a

Eventually the farms began to prosper and some of the hamlets grew into bustling towns like Rawson (1865), Gaimán (1874) and Trelew (1886). By the turn of the century, thousands more Welsh had immigrated to the Chubut region from the British Isles and North America, and Welsh influence had pushed all the way up the Río Chubut to the foothills of the Andes.

The Patagonian settlers lost touch with Mother Wales during the early part of the twentieth century, a slow but inevitable assimilation into Argentine society brought about by better transportation links and communication with Buenos Aires. By the 1960s, the Welsh language was on its way to extinction in the Chubut Valley and many other Gaelic institutions were endangered.

Roadside restaurants are a rare treat on Patagonia's long and empty highways.

The centenary celebrations of 1965 changed everything, reviving many old customs and reestablishing long-lost links between Patagonia and Wales. Over the last quarter century, local children have begun to learn the Welsh language in school again (mostly from teachers visiting from Wales), traditional Welsh teahouses have appeared throughout the valley, and typical Welsh festivals have been revived.

Foremost of the traditional celebrations are the annual **Eisteddfod** folk festivals of Welsh poetry and music. Staged each spring in Trelew and Gaimán, dozens of local acts compete for the coveted grand awards — intricately carved wooden armchairs, a Welsh tradition that dates back to the sixteenth century. Another annual festival is the **Gwyl y Glaniad** (Day of Landing) on July 28, which commemorates the arrival of the first Welsh immigrants aboard the sailing ship *Mimosa*. Celebrations center on the valley's Welsh chapels where the flock gathers to sing religious hymns and drink tea in the vestry.

There are numerous books about the Welsh experience in the Chubut Valley, including Bruce Chatwin's classic *In Patagonia*.

GENERAL INFORMATION

The valley's best tourist office is the congenial **Dirección de Turismo de Trelew** ((2965) 420139, next to the city hall at Calle San Martín 171. Open weekdays 8 AM to 1 PM and 4:30 PM to 9:30 PM (summer only). Their airport branch seems to be open for most incoming flights; their bus station kiosk is open roughly the same hours as the main office. The **Dirección de Turismo de Rawson** ((2965) 496887 is adjacent to the waterfront Hotel Provincial at Playa Unión. Open daily 8 AM to 7 PM during summer.

Chubut Valley branches of **Correo Argentino** include the Trelew post office ((2965) 420809 on the Plaza Independencia and the Rawson post office overlooking Plaza Rawson. **Telefónica** ((2965) 422006 at Julio Roca and Fontana in Trelew provides long-distance telephone and fax service.

Trelew harbors a number of money changing outlets including **Banco del Chubut** ((2965) 420815 at the corner of Rivadavia and 25 de Mayo and **Banco de la Nación** ((2965) 435956 at the corner of Fontana and 25 de Mayo. Both have 24-hour ATM machines. **Sur Turismo** ((2965) 434081 at Calle Belgrano 326 will also change United States dollars, Chilean pesos and travelers' checks.

For medical emergencies try **Hospital Zonal** ((2965) 427543, Calle 28 de Julio 160.

A number of Trelew travel agencies offer guided tours of various Welsh sights in the valley or to the huge penguin colony at Punta Tombo including **Skau Op. Patagonicos** ((2965) 424390 E-MAIL skauop@infovia.com.ar, Calle La Rioja 388;

Nievemar Tours ((2965) 434114 E-MAIL nievemar @internet.siscotel.com, Calle Italia 20; and **Alcamar** ((2965) 424400 E-MAIL alcamar@infovia .com.ar, Calle San Martín 146.

WHAT TO SEE AND DO

Trelew

Most visitors make a beeline for the Welsh teahouses of Gaimán and Dolavón, but Trelew also has its fair share of Gaelic charms. The downtown area boasts many handsome buildings that date from the early Welsh period, including a tiny church called the **Capilla Tabernacl** on Avenida Belgrano between San Martín and 25 de Mayo. Built in 1889 shortly after the first Welsh immigrants arrived in the valley, the chapel is Trelew's oldest structure and one of the oldest in all of Patagonia. Sunday service is a must-see event, a combination of hard-boiled Spanish sermons and poignant Welsh hymns to a largely blond-haired, blue-eyed congregation that look as if they've just stepped off a steamship from Cardiff.

Half a block away is the **Salón San David**, a stout red-brick structure at the corner of Belgrano and San Martín that was erected in 1913 as the Welsh Community Center and is still an active cultural node. The lovely **Teatro Verdi** on Avenida San Martín is just a year younger (1914). Other historic buildings in the downtown area include the **Banco de la Nación** (1899) at the corner of 25 de Mayo and Fontana; the **Municipalidad** (1931) on the Plaza Independencia; and the **Salón de la Sociedad Española** (1920) on the opposite side of the plaza.

Chubut Valley history comes alive at the fascinating **Museo Regional Pueblo de Luis** ((2965) 426062 in the old railroad station (1889) near the intersection of 9 de Julio and Fontana. The eclectic displays include natural history (don't miss the huge stuffed condor), Tehuelche Indian artifacts, *estancia* life and early Welsh settlement including clothing, kitchenware and fascinating black-and-white photos. Behind the museum is a tiny locomotive (not much bigger than a minivan) manufactured in Germany in 1936 and once used on the Chubut Valley narrow-gauge line. Out front is a granite obelisk commemorating 100 years of Welsh colonization and a memorial to three local air force pilots who were killed in the Malvinas (Falklands) War. The museum is open weekdays 7 AM to 1 PM and 3 PM to 9 PM.

Trelew's most outstanding attraction and the finest of its kind in Latin America is the **Museo Paleontológico Egidio Feruglio (MEF)** ((2965) 432100 E-MAIL info@mef.org.ar, Avenida Fontana 140 on the western side of Trelew. Unveiled in June 1999, the high-tech museum takes full advantage of Patagonia's reputation as a dinosaur haven with displays on 30 different species that once roamed the area and more than 5,000 fossils in total. There are hands-on exhibits, multimedia shows and educational programs for children and adults. MEF also supports current dinosaur digs at several locations in Patagonia. Open daily 10 AM to 8 PM.

Rawson

Founded in 1865, Rawson is the oldest town in the Chubut Valley, but little of its past remains. Situated 20 km (12 miles) east of Trelew at the end of Ruta 25, Rawson boasts myriad government offices (it's the provincial capital) and an active South Atlantic fishing fleet. There are basically only two reasons for tourists to come here — the beach at Playa Unión and the penguins at Punta Tombo.

Lined with hotels, motels and seafood restaurants, **Playa Unión** is perhaps the only true beach resort in Patagonia. Argentines flock here during the summer months (December to February) to take advantage of the sea breezes and the blistering sand. Many Chubut Valley residents keep beach houses along the strand.

Nearby is the **Reserva Provincial Punta Tombo**, one of the best places along the entire Patagonian coast to watch penguins. More than a million Magellanic penguins gather here during the summer months, making this the largest mainland breeding colony outside Antarctica. The first birds arrive in late August and early September, a period of territorial fights and nest preparation. Egg laying takes place in October followed by an incubation period of 35 to 40 days. Chicks hatch in early November, after which both mothers and fathers take turns feeding and protecting the baby birds. By April, all of the birds have molted and headed back into the sea, leaving the beach completely empty. Reserve entrance is US$5.

Punta Tombo is 90 km (56 miles) south of Rawson via a gravel road marked Ruta 1, which is often impassible after rain showers. The only way to reach the reserve is by private vehicle, taxi (at least US$100 round trip to Trelew or Rawson) or guided tours.

Gaimán

Towns don't get any more charming than Gaimán, 17 km (11 miles) west of Trelew via Ruta 25. The pace of life seems to have changed little since it was founded in 1874, and Gaimán remains a stronghold of Welsh culture with an annual Eisteddfod poetry and song festival in October and a number of residents who still speak the mother tongue.

Traditional Welsh teahouses are the town's main attraction. **Plas y Coed** ((2965) 491133 at Calle Miguel D. Jones 123 is the oldest and most authentic. Octogenarian Marta Rees — whose grandfather was among the original group of Welsh who arrived aboard the *Mimosa* — tends both the kitchen and the immaculate flowerbeds outside the red-brick bungalow. Her delicious *"te gales"* spread includes hot tea as well as Welsh carrot-cake, homemade breads and jams, apricot sponge cake, biscuits with melted cheese, and my personal favorite — frozen raspberry-and-cream cake.

Another popular spot is **Ty Gwyn** ((2965) 491009, Calle 9 de Julio 147, where the late Princess Diana sipped tea during her visit to Gaimán. The whitewashed cottage looks much older than its 25 years, but the food is fairly authentic including tasty *torta negra* (fruitcake).

Gaimán is easily explored by foot, a circuit that takes you past numerous historic buildings including the **Capilla Bethel** (the largest Welsh church in Patagonia) and the **Museo Histórico de Gaimán** at the corner of Sarmiento and 28 de Julio. Photos, documents and other displays recount the struggle to survive during pioneer years and the settlers' ultimate triumph. The building used to be the Gaimán train depot.

Parque el Desafío on Calle Brown at the northern edge of town is a whole different trip — a fantasyland of pop art created by local eccentric Joaquín Alonso. Thousands of bottles and cans, miles of string and other junk recycled into statues, murals and thingamajigs of all shapes and sizes. Open whenever Joaquín feels like letting people in.

Wannabe fossil hunters should make haste for **Parque Paleontológico Bryn Gwyn** on Ruta 5, 11 km (seven miles) south of Gaimán. Administered by the highly regarded MEF in Trelew, this dig on the south bank of the Río Chubut is a journey back to the Tertiary period when saber-toothed tigers and woolly mammoths roamed the earth. Guided visits must be arranged before arrival by calling the MEF ((2965) 432100.

Dolavón

It's hard to believe there could be anywhere more laid-back than Gaimán, until you visit Dolavón, another authentic Welsh town 38 km (23 miles) west of Trelew along Ruta 25. There's a little Welsh chapel and a tiny city hall. The **Molino Harinero** at Calle Maipú 61 is a 1920s flourmill with a working water wheel.

Another 60 km (37 miles) up the Chubut Valley is the **Bosque Petrificado Ameghino**, a recently discovered petrified forest formed 58 million years ago when an earlier Patagonian landmass was flooded by rising seas.

WHERE TO STAY

Expensive

Overlooking the historic Capilla Tabernacl is the **Rayentray Hotel** ((2965) 434702 or (2965) 434703 FAX (2965) 435559 E-MAIL rcvtw@internet.ciscotel .com, Calle San Martín 101, Trelew, a favorite with

visiting tour groups and often booked solid during the summer high season. Amenities include swimming pool, sauna and restaurant, and nearly everything you'll want to see in Trelew is within walking distance.

Moderate

The five-story **Hotel Libertador** ((2965) 420220 E-MAIL hlibertado@infovia.com.ar, Calle Rivadavia 31, Trelew, is popular with business visitors but also makes for a good vacation stay. Although nothing fancy, the rooms are comfortable and feature private baths, cable television and direct-dial phones. Downstairs there's a restaurant, snack bar and plenty of parking.

Recent room renovations have made the **Centenario** ((2965) 420542 E-MAIL centernario@ infovia.com.ar, Calle San Martín 150, Trelew, into a much better hotel than it was a few years ago. Other advantages include a central location near the Plaza Independencia and an adjacent travel agency that can arrange Chubut Valley and Punta Tombo trips.

If you find yourself stuck overnight in Rawson try the old **Hotel Provincial** ((2965) 481400 or (2965) 481300, Calle Mitre 551, which features recently renovated rooms and a very nice restaurant on the ground floor.

There are a couple of good places at Playa Unión in Rawson for anyone who wants to stay near the beach. The brand new **Hotel Punta León** ((2965) 498041 or (2965) 498042 at the corner of José Hernández and Juan de la Piedra offers spiffy rooms in a two-story brick building two blocks from the strand. **Hotel Atlansur** ((2965) 496030 isn't as bright or clean but it's right on the beachfront at Avenida Rawson 399.

Inexpensive

Step back into the past at the slightly seedy but always charming **Touring Club** ((2965) 433997 E-MAIL htouring@internet.siscotel.com, Avenida Fontana 240, Trelew. The Chubut Railway Company founded the club as a restaurant for employees and patrons in 1907 and during the Roaring Twenties it evolved into Chubut's most luxurious hotel. Despite their age, rooms come with private baths, hot water and cable television.

Trelew's low-end hotels cluster around the Parque Centenario, including the backpacker-friendly **Residencial Argentino** ((2965) 436134, Calle Abraham Matthews 186, and the **Hostal Avenida** ((2965) 434172, Calle Lewis Jones 49. Both feature shared bathrooms and dingy rooms.

The only place to lay your weary head in Gaimán is the **Hostería Gwesty Tywi** (/FAX (2965) 491292 E-MAIL gwestywi@infovia.com.ar WEB SITE www.advance.com.ar/usuarios/gwestywi/cysyllt.html, Calle Miguel D. Jones 342, on a very typical street in a house dating back to the late nineteenth century. This cozy Welsh-style bed and breakfast offers airport transfers from Trelew and local tours as well as traditional Patagonian evenings with music and gaucho barbecues.

Despite its name, **Camping Mutual Gaimán** ((2965) 496819 is situated at Playa Unión in Rawson. Pitch your tent beneath a leafy tree on grounds that include shower blocks with hot water, barbecues and picnic tables and a *parrilla* restaurant. Unfortunately the campsite is four blocks from the beach.

WHERE TO EAT

One of Trelew's old standbys is **El Quijote** ((2965) 434564, Calle 25 de Mayo 90 near the Plaza Independencia, where the specialties include homemade pasta and seafood trucked in daily from the wharf at Rawson.

You can also find great *pastas caseras* and other Italian dishes at **Lo de Halda** ((2965) 430839, Calle Belgrano 455 near the Trelew casino. The city's best *parrilla* is probably **Don Pedro**, a popular place on the edge of town where junction of highways 25 and 3.

It's hard to beat the prices, food or atmosphere at the *confitería* in the old **Touring Club** ((2965) 433997, Avenida Fontana 240, Trelew, where the menu includes sandwiches and desserts. You can also find good value for money at **Churrasqueria Rancho Aparte** ((2965) 425090, Avenida Fontana 236, where the *tenedor libre* includes barbecued meats, pastas and salads.

Seafood doesn't come any fresher than **Cantina Marcelino** ((2965) 496960, Avenida Marcelino Gonzalez at the mouth of the Río Chubut in Playa Unión. A favorite with local residents for 30 years, the fish comes straight from the docks across the way. Barbecued fish, fowl and beef dishes dominate the menu at **Parrilla La Playa** ((2965) 496157, near the corner of Rifleros and Lista in Playa Unión. Finish off your seafood meal with an ice cream from **Michi** ((2965) 481700, Calle Yrigoyen 23 near the beach.

HOW TO GET THERE

The Chubut Valley towns of Trelew and Rawson are 1,450 km (900 miles) south of Buenos Aires, 67 km (41 miles) south of Puerto Madryn, and 400 km (248 miles) north of Comodoro Rivadavia.

Aeropuerto Trelew ((2965) 428021 isn't very big but given the tourist boom there are plenty of flights to Buenos Aires, Río Gallegos and Ushuaia, as well as weekly service to Bariloche, Neuquén and Comodoro Rivadavia. The terminal has a tourist information desk and several rental-car agencies.

Trelew airline offices include **Aerolíneas Argentinas** ((2965) 420210 or (2965) 420170, Calle 25 de Mayo 33; **LAPA** ((2965) 423438, Calle Belgrano 285; and **LADE** ((2965) 435740, Avenida Fontana 227.

Trelew's busy **Terminal de Ómnibus** ((2965) 420121 is at Calle Urquiza 150, on the east side of Plaza Centenario. There is frequent service to Buenos Aires (19 hours), Puerto Madryn (one hour), Comodoro Rivadavia (five hours), Neuquén (12 hours) and Río Gallegos (19 hours). Among the long-distance companies that service Trelew are **Andesmar** ((2965) 433535, **El Pingüino** ((2965) 427400, and **TAC** ((2965) 431452.

COMODORO RIVADAVIA

Comodoro is the Houston of Argentina, a hard-working city of 120,000 people on the Gulf of San Jorge, where the air is laced with petroleum fumes and giant fuel tanks glimmer in the noonday sun. About a third of Argentina's "black gold" derives from underground reserves in this region, and the city flaunts a boomtown atmosphere compared to the economically depressed towns you find along so much of the Patagonian coast.

Most travelers use Comodoro as a way-station on their journeys to more scenic Patagonian destinations. But for those who linger, the city has its own intriguing and rather peculiar sights.

GENERAL INFORMATION

The municipal **Dirección de Turismo** ((297) 446-2376 FAX (297) 447-4111 E-MAIL comodorodirectur @infovia.com.ar, sits near the corner of Rivadavia and Pellegrini in the heart of downtown Comodoro. Open weekdays 7 AM to 8 PM and weekends 1 PM to 8 PM (summer only). There's also an information kiosk at the Terminal de Ómnibus, but the opening hours seem to fluctuate wildly.

Correo Argentino is at the corner of San Martín and Moreno, a couple of blocks up from Parque Soberania and the waterfront. Change money at **Banco de la Nación** ((297) 447-2700, Avenida San Martín 102, or **Lloyds Bank** ((297) 447-4814, Avenida Rivadavia 266.

The **Hospital Regional** ((297) 442-2542 is at Avenida Hipólito Yrigoyen 950.

WHAT TO SEE AND DO

The city center has few attractions other than the **Cathedral of San Juan Bosco** and the rather modest **Museo Regional Patagonia** ((297) 443-1707, both situated in the leafy park that runs down the middle of Avenida Rivadavia. The museum features a variety of subjects including archeology, paleontology and natural history. Open weekdays 9 AM to 7 PM. Admission free.

Lichen is one of the few plant species that thrives in Patagonia's chilly clime.

Founded by the Yacimientos Petrolíferos Fiscales (YPF) oil company and now managed by the University of Patagonia, the superb **Museo de Petróleo** ((297) 455-9558 on Avenida Lavalle in suburban General Mosconi is one of Argentina's finest museums. Situated on the site of Comodoro's first oil well, the collection runs a broad gamut from Patagonia's geological history through the early days of the oil boom to the modern high-tech energy industry. The place is chock-full of scale models, historic photographs and antique drilling equipment, and there's an interesting video presentation. Open weekdays 9 AM to 2 PM and 4 PM to 9 PM; Saturday 4 PM to 9 PM.

The area's other outstanding attraction is the **Astra Museum** in Astra township 15 km (10 miles) north of Comodoro. Patagonian geology and paleontology are the fortes of this small but erudite collection, which also includes an open-air display of historic oil industry equipment. Open Tuesdays 11 AM to 1 PM, Wednesdays 2 PM to 4 PM and Sundays 3 PM to 6 PM.

Comodoro's waterfront is nice for a stroll, especially the stretch along Avenida Ingeniero Ducos, but serious beachcombers should head to **Rada Tilly**, about 12 km (seven miles) south of the city center. There's a starkly beautiful beach overlooking the Golfo San Jorge and several seaside restaurants and bars.

An interesting country town called **Sarmiento** lies 150 km (93 miles) due west via Ruta 26. Situated near the base of the Sierra de San Bernardo, this oasis town is flanked by two large lakes (Musters and Colhué Huapi) where migratory waterfowl gather. Also nearby are two small petrified forests.

WHERE TO STAY

Like so many of the Patagonian coastal towns, Comodoro Rivadavia doesn't offer a great choice of accommodation.

Best of the bunch is the 12-story **Comodoro Hotel** ((297) 447-2300 FAX (297) 447-3363 E-MAIL comhotel@satlink.com, at the junction of 9 de Julio and Rivadavia. Rooms are clean and comfortable, but lacking character. However, most offer sweeping views of the central city and the nearby gulf. Amenities include private baths with hot water, cable television, modem lines, safe-deposit boxes and access to tennis courts and a local golf course.

The same Argentine chain owns and operates the nearby **Austral Hotel** ((297) 447-2200 FAX (297) 447-2444 E-MAIL haustral@satlink.com, Avenida Rivadavia 190, which boasts similar atmosphere and amenities in addition to its own business center. Both hotels are often packed with oil executives and businessmen, so make reservations if you want to guarantee a room.

Down a notch is the centrally located **Hotel Azul** ((297) 443-4628, Avenida Sarmiento 724, two blocks from the cathedral. If you want personality try the ramshackle **Hotel Comercio** ((297) 443-2341, Avenida Rivadavia 341, with its funky old bar and restaurant. Slightly out of the downtown area is the **Hospedaje Belgrano** ((297) 442-4313, Avenida Belgrano 546 near the Plaza San Martín.

You can pitch your tent near the beach at the **ACA Campground** in Rada Tilly, 15 km (10 miles) south of Comodoro.

WHERE TO EAT

You don't expect to a find a truly elegant eatery in a hard-working town like Comodoro. Which makes the superb service and food at **Restaurante Tunet** ((297) 447-2200 in the Austral Hotel all the more surprising. The savory Mediterranean cuisine is prepared under the direction of executive chef Daniel Gomez, with fresh seafood trucked in daily from the docks at Rawson, Río Gallegos and Puerto Deseado. It's a big oil industry hangout and reservations are recommended on weekends.

As the name suggests **La Estancia** ((297) 447-4568, Calle Urquiza 863, is a typical *parrilla* restaurant, probably the best in Comodoro, but there's also plenty of pasta and salad dishes on the menu for anyone who isn't into exacting a pound of flesh. Another good steak house is **El Nazareno** ((297) 442-3725 at the corner of San Martín and España.

You're more likely to run into students than petro execs at **Pizzas La Casera** ((297) 444-2001, at the corner of Sarmiento and Francia, which offers both pizza and pasta at reasonable prices in a very relaxed atmosphere.

HOW TO GET THERE

Comodoro Rivadavia is 450 km (280 miles) south of Puerto Madryn and 945 km (585 miles) north of Río Gallegos via Ruta 3. The city is well situated for reaching just about any destination in Patagonia and serves as a hub for both plane and bus routes.

Aeropuerto General Mosconi ((297) 443-3355 is situated on the city's northern fringe, about 15 minutes by taxi or bus from downtown. There is frequent service to Buenos Aires and other Patagonian destinations like Río Gallegos, Trelew, Bariloche and Ushuaia. For reservations contact **Aerolíneas Argentinas/Austral** ((297) 442-4781, Avenida 9 de Julio 870; or **LADE** ((297) 447-0585 or (297) 447-6181, Avenida Rivadavia 360 between Pellegrini and 9 de Julio.

The city's **Terminal de Ómnibus** ((297) 442-7305 is at corner of 25 de Mayo and Ameghino. There is daily bus service to Buenos (24 hours),

Río Gallegos (11 hours), Trelew (six hours), Puerto Madryn (seven hours), Puerto Deseado (four hours), Perito Moreno (six hours). Long-distance bus companies with local offices include **El Pingüino** ((297) 442-2338 and **Transportes Patagonica** ((297) 447-0450.

Comodoro is also a jumping off spot for ventures to **Puerto Aisen** in southern Chile, which lies just 488 km (302 miles) to the west via Ruta 26 through the Andes. The border crossing at **Coihaique Alto** is usually low hassle.

PUERTO SAN JULIÁN

San Julián looks the sort of town you would expect to find in the Canadian arctic or along the Greenland coast: a cluster of prefab houses with brightly painted metal roofs (green, blue and red), wedged between an icy-blue bay and sparse plains that bear a striking resemblance to tundra. Rusty old American jalopies are jacked up on cinder blocks and flower gardens struggle to grow in the rocky soil.

Despite its bleak appearance, this town of 6,500 people has a rather vivid history and the destination of being the place where "Patagonia" was born.

Ferdinand Magellan's five-ship convoy sailed into Bahía San Julián in the winter of 1520, their first landfall in Argentina. The explorer promptly executed two of his own captains who had recently staged a mutiny. During subsequent weeks, Magellan's men collected firewood, food and freshwater to continue their circumnavigation of the globe. They also skirmished against warriors of the Tehuelche tribe. Soaring nearly two meters (six feet) and clad in heavy furs and straw-stuffed moccasins, the Spanish dubbed the local Indians "Patagon" (Big Foot People) and their land "Patagonia" (Land of the Big Foot).

A half century later (1578), Sir Francis Drake put into San Julián Bay during his around-the-world voyage. Drake had his own mutiny to deal with: the leader was promptly beheaded on an island near the mouth of the bay. Drake also sparred with the Tehuelche, losing two men in the process. Europeans ignored the bay for another two centuries. Then in 1780 the Spanish crown established a small colony called Floridablanca under the leadership of Antonio de Viedma. Plagued by food shortages and inhospitable weather, the settlement was abandoned after only 14 years. HMS *Beagle* dropped anchor in 1834 for eight days, enough time for naturalist Charles Darwin to examine the bay's geological strata and discover the bones of a giant prehistoric guanaco.

Modern San Julián began to take shape in the 1890s when British sheep farmers relocated from the Malvinas. They established huge *estancias*, which thrived well into the 1960s when synthetic fibers depressed the international wool market. Nowadays the residents make their living off fishing, government jobs and a bit of tourism.

GENERAL INFORMATION

A municipal tourist office called the **Centro de Información Turístico** ((2962) 454396 or (2962) 452871 is located at Avenida San Martín 1126 near the town center not far from the intersection of San Martín and Piedra Buena. Opening hours are sporadic and during winter the office is closed for days at a time.

Correo Argentino has its main branch at the corner of San Martín and Belgrano. The only places to change money are the **Banco Provincia de Santa Cruz** at San Martín and Moreno or the **Banco de la Nación** at Belgrano and Mitre (the latter has a 24-hour ATM machine). There is a small **hospital** on Avenida Magellanes near the municipal campground.

WHAT TO SEE AND DO

The attraction isn't the town itself but the surrounding region, with its abundant wildlife and wide-open spaces.

The history of the local sheep industry is recounted at the modest **Museo Regional y de Arte Marino** on Avenida Ameghino about a block north of San Martín. Open weekdays 10 AM to noon and 2 PM to 7 PM. For a different slant on local history, venture out to the ruins of **Florida Blanca** about 10 km (six miles) west of town off Ruta 25. Archeologists from the University of Buenos Aires are currently excavating the site.

Reserva Natural San Julián covers about 10,000 hectares (24,700 acres) of the Desengano Peninsula on the eastern side of the bay and several of the bay islands, where penguins and cormorants nest. Among animals that dwell in the reserve are terrestrial critters like guanaco and rhea and marine species like black-and-white Commerson's dolphins and seven-gilled sharks. Local boatmen offer nautical excursions in outboard Zodiacs from a pier at the foot of Avenida San Martín (near Club Náutico). The trips usually include the penguin colony on **Isla Cormorán** and historic **Isla de la Justicia**, where Magellan and Drake executed their respective mutineers.

Buenos Aires-based environmental group **Fundación Cethus** ((11) 4799-3698 FAX (11) 4823-9739 offer eight-day wildlife safaris around Bahía San Julián during the summer (January and February). Rates are US$360 for members and US$420 for nonmembers, including food and lodging. Reservations for these trips must be made well in advance.

One of the world's largest petrified forests is protected within the confines of the **Monumento**

Natural Bosques Petrificados about 220 km (136 miles) north of San Julián, in the middle of the vast Pampa de las Tres Hermanas. During the Jurassic era, a pine forest thrived on this site, some of the trees reaching more than 35 m (105 ft) in height. Volcanic eruptions toppled the trees and covered them in layers of fine ash which expedited the petrifaction process. One hundred and fifty million years later, the area is a natural wonderland, renowned as much for its stunning desert landscapes as the hundreds of petrified trees.

Modern ranch life and ancient art are the allures of **Estancia La María** ((2962) 452328 FAX (2962) 452269. This working sheep ranch, 150 km (100 miles) west of San Julián via Ruta 25, offers horseback and trekking trips to view 13,000-year-old rock paintings in the surroundings hills. Overnight and multi-day stays can be arranged.

WHERE TO STAY AND EAT

The 29-room **Hotel Bahía** ((2962) 454028 FAX (2962) 453145, Avenida San Martín 1075, is considered San Julián's best hotel, with modern amenities and comfortable rooms all with private bath. Not far behind is the **Hotel Municipal** ((2962) 452300, Calle 25 de Mayo 917, which offers some rooms with panoramic bay views. A third possibility is the somewhat shabby **Residencial Sada** ((2962) 452013 FAX (2962) 452458 at Avenida San Martín 1112. Out on Ruta 3 is a modest motel called **El Alamo** ((2962) 454092 with only seven rooms.

Some travelers might say that San Julián's best accommodation is **Autocamping Municipal** ((2962) 452160 along the shoreline near the junction of Avenida Magellanes and Calle Veils Sarsfield. Facilities include hot showers, laundry room and playground equipment.

Goods restaurants are even scarcer. **La Rural** at Calle Ameghino 811 offers a typical Argentine mix of steak, pasta and seafood. Grab a window table for a view of the costanera and the bay. Another good bet is **Restaurant Sportsman** at the corner of Mitre and 25 de Mayo. The restaurants in the **Hotel Municipal** and **Club Náutico** are also recommended.

HOW TO GET THERE

San Julián lies adjacent to Ruta 3, 413 km (256 miles) south of Comodoro Rivadavia and 342 km (212 miles) north of Río Gallegos.

There is a small airport with intermittent service to places like Río Gallegos, Puerto Deseado and Comodoro Rivadavia. Most people come by bus: five hours to Río Gallegos, six hours to Comodoro Rivadavia. San Julián's tiny **Terminal de Ómnibus** lies near the corner of San Martín and Pellegrini.

RÍO GALLEGOS

Río Gallegos sits astride a river of the same name near the southern tip of mainland South America, about 60 km (40 miles) from the Chilean frontier and the Strait of Magellan. Windswept, chilly and bleak — even during the height of summer — it would be difficult to find a more desolate city anywhere in Argentina. It's not an especially attractive place to stroll around and most of the 85,000 residents exude indifference or downright animosity toward visitors. I don't think it's anything personal, but rather their way of dealing with the harsh geography and climate.

It might also have something to do with the area's tortured history. Until 1885, when the city was founded, the region was largely inhabited by Patagonian Indian tribes. But soon English and Welsh immigrants flooded the hinterland, establishing huge sheep ranches. Around the turn of the twentieth century, large coal deposits were discovered at Río Turbio in the nearby Andes and Río Gallegos grew into a rather grim coal port and supply center for the mines. A spin-off from the coal rush was a thriving local banking industry, a fact that didn't escape a couple of exiled Americans — Butch Cassidy and the Sundance Kid — who allegedly robbed a Río Gallegos bank in 1905 after lunching with the branch manager.

In 1920–1921, the city found itself at the center of an anarchist rebellion led by Bolshevik Antonio Soto, who organized strikes by the local *estancia* hands and urban blue-collar workers. When the walkouts failed to bring the wealthy landowners and merchants to their knees, Soto launched his own revolution against private property with 500 armed men recruited from the strikers. Their uprising soon deteriorated into looting, drunkenness and general mayhem. The government in Buenos Aires dispatched a cavalry regiment to subdue the rebels. No match for the well-armed soldiers, most of the strikers surrendered without a shot... only to be mowed down by army firing squads. Hundreds were slaughtered, their bodies either burned or dumped into mass unmarked graves in a bloody campaign that foreshadowed the "Dirty War" that would hobble Argentina 50 years later.

Río Gallegos also played a major role in Argentina's ill-fated attempt to wrest the Malvinas (Falklands) from British control in 1982. Pilots from the local air force base flew hundreds of sorties over the islands, and many of them never returned.

The local economy is still based on energy extraction, only these days coal is overshadowed by petroleum pumped from offshore rigs in the Strait of Magellan and little "grasshopper" wells spread across the barren plains south of the river. Most travelers pass through Río Gallegos on their way to somewhere else, more enticing destinations like Parque Nacional Los Glaciares and Punta Arenas, so the city doesn't boast many hotels or restaurants that cater to the tourist trade.

GENERAL INFORMATION

Despite the city's rather somber tone, the people who run the **Dirección de Turismo** ((2966) 42159 could not be more cheerful or informative. The woman who runs the tiny tourist office at the bus station is especially helpful, someone who goes out of her way to find accommodation for people arriving in Río Gallegos. The main tourist office is near the intersection of Avenida San Martín and

matters—including ATM machines, money transfers and credit card advances—try any of the banks along Avenida Roca including **Banco de Santa Cruz** ((2966) 422281 at No. 812 and **Banco Tierra del Fuego** ((2966) 420936 at No. 831.

The main branch of **Correo Argentino** ((2966) 420046 is at the corner of Roca and San Martín. For long-distance calls and fax service try **Telefónica** at the corner of Roca and Chile. There are a number of independent telephone services including **Xpress** ((2966) 427183 at Avenida Roca 1084 and **Telefax** ((2966) 427169 at Avenida Roca 1328.

The city's primary healthcare facility is the **Hospital Regional** ((2966) 420025 or (2966) 425411 at the corner of 25 de Mayo and José Ingenieros.

Ruta 3 on the southern edge of the city; open weekdays 10 AM to 6 PM. But there are information kiosks at the airport and in the *carreton* at the busy Avenida Roca/San Martín intersection; open weekdays 10 AM to 6 PM and weekends (summer only) 10 AM to 1 PM and 5 PM to 8 PM.

The equally helpful **Subsecretaría de Turismo** (regional tourist office) ((2966) 422702 has offices at Avenida Roca 1551 and the airport. It offers maps and brochures of various attractions in Santa Cruz Province as well as reservations and transportation information. Open weekdays 9 AM to 8 PM; and weekends (summer only) 10 AM to 8 PM.

You can change your United States dollars and Chilean pesos at several independent money exchanges including **El Pingüino** ((2966) 422338, Calle Zapiola 469; and **Sur Cambio** ((2966) 422701, Avenida San Martín 565. Cash and travelers' checks accepted. For more complicated banking

Local travel agents can arrange fully guided tours to local attractions including Moreno Glacier and the penguin colony at Cabo Virgenes. **Interlagos/Escalatur** ((2966) 422466 or (2966) 422338, Avenida Roca 998, is reputedly one of the best, but I had to wait nearly half an hour for service and then the woman behind the desk was surly and unhelpful. You're better off trying one of the other agencies: **Tur Aike Turismo** ((2966) 424503 or (2966) 422436, Calle Zapiola 63; or **El Pingüino** ((2966) 425332 or (2966) 422169 with offices at the airport, bus terminal and Calle Zapiola 469.

WHAT TO SEE AND DO

There are few sights in the urban area that would interest the well-seasoned traveler.

Guanaco frequent the unpaved road between Río Gallegos and Cabo Virgenes.

If you're stuck with a couple of free hours between bus or plane connections, head for the **Museo Regional Padre Manuel Jesús Molina** ((2966) 423290 at the corner of San Martín and Ramon y Cajal, a rather grand name for a rather modest collect on local flora, fauna, geology, paleontology and history. The small exhibit on Tehuelche Indians is especially good. Open weekdays 10 AM to 6 PM, weekends 11 AM to 7 PM.

The hardships of early European immigrant life are detailed at the **Museo de los Pioneros** ((2966) 437763 at the corner of Alberdi and El Cano. Open daily 1 PM to 8 PM. The building itself is a genuine metal-clad pioneer home. The **Museo Malvinas Argentinas** at Calle Pasteur 74 recounts the country's maritime history, including the bloody Malvinas (Falklands) conflict. Open weekdays 8 AM to 1 PM.

Given its proximity role in the struggle to liberate the Falklands, Río Gallegos also sports a number of war memorials including the **Monumento a los Pilotos Caídos en Malvinas** along the banks of the Río Gallegos (near the foot of Avenida Chacabuco) and the **Monumento a los Caidos en Malvinas** overlooking the big roundabout at the intersection of Avenida San Martín and Ruta 3.

If you've more than a few hours in Río Gallegos, a journey to **Cabo Virgenes** makes a good daytrip. The two-hour drive via the rough and tumble Ruta 1 affords splendid views of the Patagonian countryside with the Strait of Magellan as a stunning backdrop. Wildlife is also plentiful including giant hares, rhea and guanaco.

At the end of the road is the **Reserva Provincial Cabo Virgenes**, where 80,000 Magellanic penguins gather to nest every year between October and April. After paying your entry fee and browsing displays in the A-frame range station, proceed to the beach. The nesting areas are in the bush-covered arroyo behind the beach, best explored on a short nature trail that takes you into the heart of the penguin colony.

The Argentine–Chilean frontier is just south of the reserve. You can't cross the border here (although there's no-one to really stop you), but you can easily spot offshore oil platforms in the Strait of Magellan and Tierra del Fuego in the hazy distance. Near the penguin colony are an imposing clifftop **lighthouse** and a small, sandy **cemetery** with the graves of local pioneers and bygone shipwreck victims.

The 100-year-old **Estancia Monte Dinero** (/FAX (2966) 426900 near Cabo Virgenes welcomes visitors for day tours and overnight stays. This sprawling property boasts more than 20,000 head of sheep, plus cattle and horses. Activities include horseback riding, sheepdog demonstrations, wildlife-spotting safaris in four-wheel-drive vehicles, and visits to the penguin colony. Transportation

to and from Río Gallegos is provided to overnight visitors, who sleep in a comfy pioneer cabin called the Casa Grande.

SHOPPING

Given the lack of overnight tourists, this isn't a great place for shopping. Still, if you browse around, you can find a good selection of Patagonian woolens, leatherwork and gourmet food items.

Most prominent among the local handicraft shops is **Artesanías Keoken** ((2966) 420335, Avenida San Martín 336 which dispenses spin-dyed woven goods like carpets, sweaters, gloves, caps and wall hangings, as well as potpourri and hand-painted hankies. All items are made with homespun Patagonia wool. There's another good handicraft shop called **Prepap** ((2966) 421910 at Avenida Perito Moreno 35 next to the provincial museum.

Pottery is the forté at **Taller Municipal de Cerámica** ((2966) 435527 at the junction of Maipú and Misiones, while homemade chocolates are one of the specialties at **Casa de Los Chicos** at Avenida Roca 1319.

Anyone stocking up for a camping or backpacking trip into the wilds of Patagonia will find plenty of selection in Río Gallegos, although the prices sometimes cause your heart to flutter. There are three branches of **La Anonima** supermarket including one at the corner of Roca and España, and three branches of **Alas** supermarket including one at the junction of Corrientes and Ruta 3 on the southern edge of town. **El Pionero** ((2966) 423173, Avenida Roca 638, hawks standard camping equipment, as does **Kau Camping** ((2966) 421023 at Avenida San Martín 555.

WHERE TO STAY

The oil business has driven local hotel prices into the stratosphere: you can easily pay more than US$100 for an absolute dump. That's assuming you can actually find a room that isn't occupied by an off-duty rig worker or equipment salesman.

Costa Río Apart Hotel ((2966) 423412 FAX (2966) 421108, Avenida San Martín 673, is undisputedly the best place in town, but it's often fully booked with the petrol crowd. The rooms feature modern private baths with constant hot water (a rarity in Río Gallegos), kitchenettes with little dining tables and a living room area with chairs and sofa.

My usual digs is the 47-room **Hotel Comercio** ((2966) 420209 or (2966) 422782 FAX (2966) 422172, Avenida Roca 1302. The rooms are small, drab and depressing, but the water in the showers is hot, the staff friendlier than most people who have anything to do with tourism in Río Gallegos, and the in-house restaurant is one of the city's best.

It's also in a prime location right in the middle of town and there's secure parking (behind a locked gate) in the back.

The **Hotel Santa Cruz** ((2966) 420601 FAX (2966) 420603 at the intersection of Roca and Rivadavia has similar rooms and amenities. It also boasts a very central location near the Plaza San Martín.

A notch down in both price and comfort are medium-range hotels like the **Covadonga** ((2966) 420190 FAX (2966) 421237, Avenida Roca 1244, which offers rooms with both private and shared bath (about half the cost); and the **Punta Arenas** ((2966) 422743, Federico Sphur 55, which has recently been remodeled (ask for a room in the new wing).

At the bottom end of the scale expect rooms without private baths, hot water or central heating (not the kind of places to spend a freezing Patagonian winter night!). Among the few recommendable hotels in this category are the dingy **Hotel Paris** ((2966) 420111 FAX (2966) 422432, Avenida Roca 1040; and the truly cheap **Hotel Nevada** ((2966) 425990 at Calle Zapiola 480.

Local campgrounds include **ATSA Polideportivo** ((2966) 442310, on Calle Asturias just south of Ruta 3; and **Pescazaike**, about 25 km (just over 15 miles) west of the city center on Ruta 3. The latter is adjacent to the Estancia Güer Aike.

Several ranches in the Río Gallegos area offer overnight accommodation, including the **Estancia Monte Dinero** (/FAX (2966) 426900 (see description above) and the **Estancia Güer Aike** (/FAX (in Buenos Aires) (11) 4394-3486. Like most Argentine ranches, the experience doesn't

come cheap: expect to pay at least US$150 per person, per day.

WHERE TO EAT

Río Gallegos doesn't offer much in the way of eats either. One of the truly good places is **Restaurant Comercio** ((2966) 422458 on the ground floor of the hotel of the same name at Avenida Roca 1302. Breakfast, lunch and dinner are all excellent and the prices moderate.

Other good bets are the **Bar Español El Horreo** ((2966) 420060 in the Sociedad Española building at Avenida Roca 862; and a modest little *parrilla* called the **Confitería Diaz** at Avenida Roca 1157.

Both the **Cosa Nostra** at Calle 9 de Julio 230 and **La Cantina** at Calle España 273 specialize in pasta and seafood dishes.

For an after-dinner snack pop into **Heladería Tito**, a marvelous ice cream parlor with two locations: the corner of Zapiola and Corrientes and the corner of Roca and San Martín right in the middle of town. Cold beer and bar snacks are the usual sustenance at **La Viola Pub** ((2966) 428954 at Calle Rawson 27, where you can groove to live bands on Friday and Saturday nights.

HOW TO GET THERE

Río Gallegos is 2,800 km (1,736 miles) south of Buenos Aires and 1,400 km (870 miles) south of Puerto Madryn via Ruta 3.

Patagonian post offices come in many shapes, sizes and colors.

Given the vast distances, most people choose to fly; there are regular services between Río Gallegos and Buenos Aires, Ushuaia, Comodoro Rivadavia, Bahía Blanca and Trelew. Flights can be booked through **Aerolíneas Argentinas/Austral (** (2966) 422020 or (2966) 422021, Avenida San Martín 545; **LAPA (** (2966) 430446, Calle Estrada 71; or **LADE (** (2966) 422316, Calle Fagnano 53. The city's tiny but efficient airport is five kilometers (three miles) west of town, just off Ruta 3.

Another popular option is bus service to and from Puerto Madryn (18 hours), Comodoro Rivadavia (11 hours), El Calafate/Parque Nacional Los Glaciares (five hours) and Punta Arenas, Chile (six hours). Among the companies

that offer long-distance coaches are **TAC (** (2966) 442042, at the corner of Sarsfield and Zapiola; **Andesmar (** (2966) 442195, at the Terminal de Ómnibus; **Transportes Patagonica (** (2966) 442160, at the Terminal de Ómnibus; and **El Pingüino (** (2966) 422338, Calle Zapiola 445. The **Terminal de Ómnibus** is on the western edge of town at the junction of Ruta 3 and Avenida Eva Perón.

The Argentina–Chile **border crossing** is at Monte Aymond, 65 km (40 miles) south of Río Gallegos. The guards are friendly and the frontier formalities quick and painless if your papers are in order. On the other side of the border, the highway continues to Punta Delgada (41 km/25 miles) where you turn off for the ferry to Tierra del Fuego and Punta Arenas (200 km/124 miles).

ABOVE: The mist-shrouded Fitzroy Range is one of South America's most challenging climbs. RIGHT: Springtime shimmers in the Patagonian uplands.

PARQUE NACIONAL LOS GLACIARES

Anchoring the southern end of the Argentine Andes is Parque Nacional Los Glaciares, one of the country's oldest and most beloved nature reserves. Founded in 1937 and selected as a UNESCO World Heritage Site in 1981, the park embraces more than 600,000 hectares (1,482,600 acres) of stone, ice and water. The park is divided into three areas: Zona Roca in the south, which receives the most day-trippers; Zona Centro in the middle which is largely deserted; and Zona Viedma in the north which is favored by long-distance backpackers and climbers.

Unless you arrive with tent and sleeping bag, there are limited accommodation options inside the park (a single hotel). Most visitor services are situated in the mountain resort town of El Calafate, 80 km (50 miles) east of Moreno Glacier, which offers dozens of hotels, restaurants and travel agencies.

Everywhere the scenery is extraordinary — sheer granite peaks that soar straight up into the clouds, dense forest wrapped around navy blue lakes, and the one of the earth's largest collections of subpolar glaciers—a mirror image of the famed Torres del Paine National Park in neighboring Chile. Outdoor activities are also diverse: backcountry trekking and camping, mountain climbing and glacier walking, fly-fishing and horseback riding. Or just plain sightseeing — sitting back against a rock and beholding the grandeur of nature in this part of the world.

The park's most celebrated attraction is Moreno Glacier, a 35-km (22-mile) tongue of ice that spills through a massive gap in the Andes and down into the aquamarine waters of Lago Argentino (the country's largest lake) where it forms a cotton-candy blue façade that measures five kilometers (three miles) across and 60 m (200 ft) high. Throughout the day huge chunks of the glacier "calve" into the lake with a thunderous crash, forming icebergs. The spectacle leaves you speechless — not just the frozen giant, but the whole setting: evergreen giants all around, snowy peaks behind and the most pristine sky you could ever imagine (look for condors gliding in the thermal updrafts above the glacier face).

You can observe the glacier from boat cruises on the Brazo Rico arm of Lago Argentino or a series of walkways that wind down from the parking lot at the western extreme of the Península Magallanes. Some people gaze for hours, transfixed by the ice. If you stare long and hard enough, all sorts of shapes arise — ice castles, goblins or great clipper ships sailing in the lee of the Andes. Despite its incredible beauty, Moreno is nothing to trifle with. Chunks of glacial ice can explode

like grenades when they hit the rocks below and the glass-like "shrapnel" is often deadly. Thirty-two people were killed by falling ice prior to 1988, when the park service decided to limit direct access to the façade.

The southern part of the Zona Roca wraps around the deep-blue Brazo Sur and can also be reached by road from El Calafate. Anyone with enough energy (and skill) to reach the summit of Cerro Cristal will be rewarded with a panoramic view of Torres del Paine across the border in Chile.

The secluded fjords and glaciers of the Zona Centro are best explored by boat. Daily sightseeing cruises (often combined with hiking) commence from Puerto Bandera, about 45 km (28 miles) west of El Calafate. The main attraction is Upsala Glacier, larger than Moreno and nearly as awesome.

Although the park's northern section is officially dubbed Zona Viedma, after a huge lake of the same name (which is almost as large as Lago Argentino), most of the climbers and trekkers who frequent this region call it the Fitzroy Area. Half a dozen trails radiate from the ranger station at El Chaltén including a breathtaking walk up the Río Fitzroy to the climbing base camp at Laguna Torre, from where you can see Cerro Torre, a 3,100-m (10,200-ft) granite needle that pokes straight up through the glacial ice.

GENERAL INFORMATION

The **national park service** maintains an information office ((2902) 491005 at Avenida Libertador 1302 in El Calafate. But other than passing out brochures and maps I've never found them very helpful and they will usually refer you to the municipal tourist office or park rangers for more detailed information. The Guarda Parque inside the reserve tend to be much more helpful, particularly at the Moreno Glacier ranger station. Gretel Muller is especially knowledgeable about glaciation.

Another great source of information is the extremely friendly and efficient **Secretaría de Turismo** ((2902) 491090 or (2902) 492884 E-MAIL secturelcalafate@cotecal.com.ar, in the Terminal de Ómnibus on Calle Julio Roca in downtown El Calafate. You can reach the bus station from Avenida Libertador via either of the two staircases that shoot up the hill.

The only place in the area to change travelers' checks or get a cash advance on your credit card is **Banco Provincia de Santa Cruz** ((2902) 491168 at the corner of Libertador and 1 de Mayo. Otherwise, try to change money to Río Gallegos.

Mail your glacier postcards at **Correo Argentino** at Avenida Libertador 1122 in El Calafate. **Telefónica** ((2902) 491000 at Calle Espora 194 offers international and long-distance calls, as

well as fax and Internet service. For medical emergencies try the **municipal hospital** ((2902) 491001 at Calle Julio Roca 1487, three blocks west of the bus terminal.

TOURS

Any of the town's two dozen travel agencies and adventure outfitters — or your hotel front desk — can arrange day trips to Moreno Glacier and other parts of Parque Nacional Los Glaciares. Prices can vary, so be sure to shop around.

A good general travel agency is **Los Glaciares** ((2902) 491159 E-MAIL losglaciares@cotecal.com.ar, Avenida Libertador 924, where you can sign up for a minibus tour of national park highlights including close views of Moreno Glacier.

For something more substantial try **Solo Patagonia** ((2902) 491298 FAX (2902) 491790, Avenida Libertador 963, which arranges glacier cruises

from Puerto Bandera, some of which include easy day-hikes inside the national park.

Patagonia Backpackers ((2902) 491234, in the Albergue del Glaciar on Calle Los Pioneros, offers "alternative" tours of Moreno Glacier as well as budget excursions to Torres del Paine and Puerto Natales in Chile.

WHAT TO SEE AND DO

There's only one reason to journey to Parque Nacional Los Glaciares — the great outdoors. An embarrassment of natural riches including glaciers, lakes, rivers, mountains, plains and forests.

There are so many things to do, such myriad choices, it's often hard to decide. Trekking the isolated foothills between Lago Viedma and Lago Argentino. Scaling some gnarly peak in the Fitzroy Range. Scrambling over the top of Moreno Glacier. Exploring the Península Magallanes by moun-

tain bike. Or riding roughshod of the ranchlands south of El Calafate.

Anybody with their own wheels can easily reach the park's top attraction: **Moreno Glacier** at the western tip of the Península Magallanes, about 80 km (50 miles) west of El Calafate via Ruta 11. Beyond the entrance station (where you are required to pay a US$5 entrance fee), the road hugs the shores of the beautiful **Brazo Rico**, cut off from the rest of Lago Argentino by the glacier. At the end of the road is a large parking lot, the start of a series of walkways that lead down to spectacular viewpoints. Rangers are usually around to answer questions about the glacier and other aspects of local natural history.

The only way to get a closer view of the glacier façade is on a "nautical safari" with **Hielo y Aventura** ((2902) 491053, which depart from the

A lone hiker drinks in the view from Laguna Azul in the Fitzroy Range.

small dock at Bahía Bajo de las Sombras near Los Notros hotel. The one-hour cruise (US$20) in a modern catamaran-type craft pulls to within a 100 m (325 ft) of the constantly creaking, groaning glacier. The same company offers an exciting glacier mini-trek (US$65), a two-hour adventure that includes a Zodiac ride across the lake and a guided hike around the southern end of Moreno and out onto the ice. For either excursion bring a warm jacket: even in summer, the chilly Andean winds can cut right through you.

Several hiking trails wind upwards from the lakeshore road to lofty spots on the Península Magallanes. **Sendero Cumbre del Cerro Cattle** takes you to a viewpoint overlooking Moreno Glacier, the Canal de los Témpanos and Brazo Rico, with the High Andes in the background. **Sendero Arroyo Cachorro** twists even higher, to a ridge that affords views of Torres del Paine

in Chile. You can pick up both trails behind the Los Notros hotel.

The southern extreme of the park around **Brazo Sur** can be reached via Ruta 15 from El Calafate. There's a ranger station with information and a primitive campground for those who wish to stay overnight. The main attraction of this area is walking: there are trails up into the mountains that divide Argentina from Chile, as well as a lakeshore trail that loops around to a couple of *refugios* on the western side of the fjord.

Unless you're willing to walk for miles, the only viable way to explore the glaciated wilderness of the park's central zone is by boat. **R.F. Campbell Navigation** ((2902) 491154 or (2902) 491155 offer several daily departures from **Puerto Bandera**, 45 km (28 miles) west of El Calafate. Their trips can also be booked at just about any travel agency in town. There are six different itineraries, most of them all-day trips that combine sailing and light hiking. One trip (US$107) takes in four different glaciers — Upsala, Onelli, Seco and Spegazzini. Another (US$60) combines a beautiful fjord cruise with three hours of trekking on Upsala Glacier.

The **Fitzroy area** in the north is easy to reach by road. Take Ruta 11 east and then gravel Ruta 40 north to the shores of Lago Viedma, and then dirt Ruta 23 west to the tiny hamlet of **El Chaltén** where there's a ranger station, campgrounds, snack bars and several modest hostels.

Climbers head straight for world-class peaks like **Cerro Fitzroy** and **Cerro Grande**. Long-distance trekkers usually prefer a circuit into the high and mighty **Fitzroy Range** north of El Chaltén. Lesser mortals can satisfy their wanderlust with long day-hikes from El Chaltén. One of the easier walks is straight up the Río Fitzroy to a stunning little alpine tarn called **Laguna Torre**, where there's a base camp for climbing Cerro Grande near the foot of Glaciar Grande. Total roundtrip time is about eight hours, including a couple of hours to languish by the lake. A much more rugged day hike is the trail to **Fitzroy Base Camp** that skirts the shores of Laguna Azul and Laguna Capri. Figure at least 10 hours for this roundtrip.

SPORTS

Hiking

Fitzroy Expeditions ((2962) 493017 FAX (2962) 49136 in El Chaltén is a full-service trekking and climbing outfitter that can organize just about any kind of trip you want in the Fitzroy Range. During the summer months they offer a daily guided hike from El Chaltén to Glaciar del Torre, with a chance to clamber up onto the ice. The eight-hour trek runs US$75 per person and can be combined with horseback riding.

Fishing

Parque Nacional Los Glaciares and the nearby pampa offer great lake and river fishing. **Fishing & Adventure** ((2902) 493050 or (2902) 493491, Calle Roca 2192, El Calafate, can arrange boat trips on Lago Argentino and Lago Viedma as well as fly-fishing expeditions along the Río Santa Cruz. Equipment and guides are included in the price.

Horseback Riding

Several companies offer horseback trips on the open plains around El Calafate, including the **Estancia El Galpón** ((2902) 492276 and **Cabalgata en Patagonia** ((2902) 493203.

Between December and March, **Fitzroy Expediciónes** ((2962) 493017 stages daily rides (US$45) out of El Chaltén to the picturesque Laguna Torre and the nearby Río Blanco valley. Views of the surrounding peaks are incredible.

Whitewater Rafting

The only company that currently organizes raft trips down the Río Santa Cruz is **Nonthue Aventura** ((2902) 491179, El Calafate. Devoid of rapids, whirlpools or anything else resembling whitewater, the voyage down the Santa Cruz (US$40) is really more an easy going float trip than a roller-coaster ride. But it's still a good way to get in touch with the local nature. During the summer months there are two trips per day: 8 AM and 3 PM; total time is about five and a half hours.

Hot-air Ballooning

Hostería Kau Yatun ((2902) 491059 can arrange hot-air balloon safaris (US$125 per person) with

a bird's-eye view of the Andes. The trips last about one hour and usually depart in the early morning in order to take advantage of calm winds.

Motorbiking

If the total peace and quite are driving you bonkers, call the folks at **Alquiler Cuatriciclos** ((2902) 492180, El Calafate, who can rent rugged dirt bikes by the hour or day.

SHOPPING

El Calafate is probably the best place to pick up souvenirs in the whole of southern Patagonia. Art and craft shops abound, many with similar merchandise.

OPPOSITE: El Chaltén village nestles at the base of the Fitzroy Range. ABOVE: An isolated farmhouse in the northern part of Parque Nacional Los Glaciares.

One of the more tasteful shops is **Posta Calafate** ((2902) 492388, Avenida Libertador 1058, which carries a wide range of typical Argentine handicrafts including ceramics, woodwork, *criollo* silver, leather goods and textiles as well as books, maps and postcards of the region.

An equally eclectic selection can be found at **Arte Rústico** ((2902) 491604, Avenida Libertador 1132, where you can buy anything from scented candles and cowboy boots to ceramic wall plaques and wooden utensils. If you're in the market for Inca hats or Andes flutes, browse through **Regionales Michay** ((2902) 492347, Calle Espora 48, which carries merchandize from Peru and Bolivia, as well as typical Argentine souvenirs.

La Rural ((2902) 492215, Avenida Libertador 1236, stocks gear for camping, fishing and trekking (including all-weather clothes), as well as regional books and maps.

WHERE TO STAY

Very Expensive
Somehow it just doesn't seem fair that the only accommodation that offers a panoramic view of Moreno Glacier should also be the most expensive — the exquisite **Hostería Los Notros** ((2902) 499510 FAX IN BUENOS AIRES (11) 4814-3934 E-MAIL notros@lastland.com WEB SITE www.lastland.com. Perched on a heavily wooded hillside inside the national park, nearly every guest room and most of the public areas offer sweeping vistas. If that isn't enough to keep you happy, the front desk can arrange plenty of other distractions including nature and glacier walks, nautical safaris, horseback riding and *estancia* visits. Although the hotel sells rooms by the night, most guests seem to purchase two- to four-night packages that include meals, nonalcoholic drinks, transfers from Río Gallegos, recreation equipment and all local excursions.

Fulfill your gaucho fantasies at **Hostería Kau Yatun** ((2902) 491059 or in Buenos Aires (11) 4443-9295 FAX (2902) 491260, on the Estancia 25 de Mayo, southeast of El Calafate. This old ranch house is a delightful place to stay. The rustic decor — rich wood and simple cotton textiles — is complemented by modern amenities that make your stay both capricious and comfortable. The stables can organize short rides across the pampa or longer treks into the Andes foothills with guides. La Brida restaurant is one of the area's best, with a menu that caters to both real and would-be *caballeros.*

Bygone ways also endure at the **Posada los Alamos** ((2902) 491146 FAX (2902) 491186 E-MAIL posadalosalamos@cotecal.com.ar, Calle Moyano 1355. This brick and timber edifice mimics the architectural style of a typical nineteenth-century *estancia* house. Both the public areas and guestrooms are decorated in lavish wood, leather and textiles. Los Alamos nestles in a copse about a block up from the shores of Lago Argentino. Sports facilities include tennis and paddleball courts.

Expensive
There's a huge decline in atmosphere and amenities from the luxury hotels to everything else in El Calafate. But the **Hotel El Quijote** ((2902) 491017 FAX (2902) 491103 E-MAIL elquijote@cotecal.com.ar, Calle Gregores 1155, is doing its best to fill the gap. This comfortable 80-room inn sports just about everything the modern traveler craves on the edge of the wilderness, including minibar, laundry and service, bilingual staff (English spoken) and a very good restaurant, El Molino.

A little bit farther from the town center is **Frai Toluca** ((2902) 491593 or (2902) 491773 FAX IN BUENOS AIRES (11) 4748-0119, Calle 6 No. 1016, which offers comfortable rooms, many with views of Lago Argentino and the distant Andes.

Moderate
One of El Calafate's best values for money is the **Michelangelo Hotel** ((2902) 491045 FAX (2902) 491058 E-MAIL info@patagonia-travel.com, at the corner of Moyano and Espora. Like so many Patagonian hotels, alpine A-frame is the prevailing design theme. But you can also expect a good deal of European-style service here, fast and efficient.

If wide open spaces are one of your primary considerations, try **Hotel Kalkén** ((2902) 491073 FAX (2902) 491036, Calle Valentín Feilberg 119, which offers 33 large rooms, all with private bath and hot water.

Down by the lakeshore is a pleasant little place called the **Hotel Bahía Redonda** ((2902) 491743 FAX (2902) 491314 E-MAIL hotelbahiaredonda @cotecal.com.ar, Calle 15 No. 148. There are just 10 rooms, but they're all cozy and well equipped.

El Chaltén's best hotel is the 18-room **Fitzroy Inn** ((2902) 491117 or (2962) 493062 FAX (2902) 492217, Avenida San Martín 520, which offers pleasant but rustic rooms with views of the nearby snowcapped peaks. All rooms have private bath. Another good option is the diminutive **Hotel El Pilar** ((2962) 493002 or in Buenos Aires (11) 4325-3102, which sits at the junction of Ruta 23 and Río Eléctrico.

Inexpensive

There are dozens of hostels, *hospedajes*, *residencias* and small hotels in the budget category that cater to the legions of backpackers that descend upon El Calafate each summer.

At the upper end is the quiet and comfortable **Hotel Upsala** ((2902) 491075 FAX (2902) 491166, Calle Espora 139. Like its Scandinavian namesake

Another excellent hostel is the **Albergue Lago Argentino** ((2902) 491423 FAX (2902) 491139 E-MAIL hostellagoargentino@cotecal.com.ar, Calle Campana del Desierto 1050. Besides all-day central heating and hot water, the hostel gives its guests access to both kitchen and laundry facilities.

Cabañas los Dos Piños ((2902) 491271, Calle 9 de Julio 358 on the north side of town, doubles as a youth hostel and campground. Rooms can fit up to six people.

The **municipal campground** ((2902) 491829 is in a grove of trees on the west bank of Arroyo Calafate. Sites include barbecues and picnic tables. The entrance is about 50 m (about 55 yards) up Calle José Pantín from Avenida Libertador.

(the Swedish university town) the place is tidy and tranquil, although a bit lacking in ambience. Right in the middle of town is the modest but laudable **Hotel Amado** ((2902) 491134 or (2902) 491023 FAX (2902) 491134, where rooms feature central heating and private baths with hot water. There's also a snack bar.

One of Argentina's best-run youth hostels is the **Albergue del Glaciar** (/FAX (2902) 491234 E-MAIL alberguedelglaciar@cotecal.com.ar WEBSITE www.glaciar.com, on Calle Los Pioneros in a quiet residential area east of Arroyo Calafate. It offers single and double rooms, as well as quads with bunk-beds, everything spacious and spanking clean. The showers have around-the-clock hot water and there's a good budget restaurant. Other services include Internet hookups, baggage storage, free transport to the airport and bus terminal, and minibus excursions to major sights.

The national park service maintains three drive-in campgrounds in **Parque Nacional Los Glaciares** ((2902) 491005, including two on the road between the main entrance station and Moreno Glacier and another at the end of Ruta 524 in the Zona Viedma (Northern) Sector.

Low-priced accommodation in El Chaltén includes the **Apart Hotel Al Aldea** ((2962) 493040 or (2966) 426099 FAX IN BUENOS AIRES (11) 4822-5639, on Avenida Güemes. Basic rooms come with four or six beds and all have private baths. Breakfast is an extra US$5. Cheaper still are the **Albergue Los Nires** ((2962) 493009 on Avenida Lago del Desierto and **Cabañas Cerro Torre**

PREVIOUS PAGES: Cerro Torre in the Fitzroys attracts world-class climbers. OPPOSITE: A quiet corner of Parque Nacional Los Glaciares. ABOVE: Ice castles sprout from Moreno Glacier.

((2962) 493061 or (2966) 421619 at the corner of Perito Moreno and Halvorsen.

WHERE TO EAT

Expensive

It's hard to argue with the conviction that **La Brida** at the Hostería Kau Yatun ((2902) 491059 is the region's most outstanding eatery. The menu runs a Patagonian gamut from enticing pasta dishes and beef steak to exotic venison and wild boar. Service is exemplary, just the right mix of efficiency and affability, while the bygone ambience makes you feel like you've been transported back in time to one of the grand *estancias* of the nineteenth century.

The restaurant at **Los Notros** ((2902) 499510 or (2902) 499511, inside the national park, is the only eatery in the area that offers a glacial panorama with breakfast, lunch or dinner. Like the hotel, it's a bit pricey and service can be a little lethargic at times. But everything I've tasted — from the *cordero de palo* (roast lamb) and grilled trout to the burgers and fries — has been thoroughly delicious.

Moderate

Given the Argentine emphasis on beef, it's always a pleasure to come across a restaurant like **Bordeaux** ((2902) 492118, in the little shopping mall at Avenida Libertador 1150, which offers reasonably priced French and Swiss dishes including wonderful cheese fondue. The dining room doubles as a tea salon in the afternoon.

Another treat is **Kau Kaleshen** ((9202) 491188, Calle Gregores 1256, a combination restaurant, coffee bar and tea salon that offers a wide range of atypical dishes including salads, cheese and cold meat platters and homemade pastries like *panes rellenos*.

Perhaps the best of the local *parrillas* is **La Tablita** ((2902) 491065, Calle Rosales 28 at the eastern end of the bridge. The menu runs usual meat and pasta range, but the sauces and flavors sometimes carry a certain regional tang.

Inexpensive

Anyone with an endless appetite should try the inexpensive *tenedor libre* at **El Lugar** ((2902) 493080, a favorite with mountain climbers and trekkers who've just come back from the Andes. The buffet spread includes 36 dishes ranging from pastas to barbecued meats, and dessert is included.

It's not gourmet cuisine, but it's hard to beat the prices at **El Témpano Errante** ((2902) 491234, the cozy little eatery at the Albergue del Glaciar youth hostel. **Black Pepper** ((2902) 492003, Avenida Libertador 1723, offers various types of fast food including sandwiches, burgers, hotdogs and

salads. If it's a nice day, eat outside on the sunny terrace.

If you get hungry on the drive to El Chaltén, pull off Ruta 40 into **Estancia Luz Divina**, where the cook will gladly rustle you up breakfast, lunch or dinner.

NIGHTLIFE

The blend of fresh mountain air and abundant of outdoor activity means that most people are in bed not long after dinner. But if you're a night owl, don't fret — El Calafate has a couple of places where you can hang after dark.

El Alambique Bar ((2902) 491059 at the Hostería Kau Yatun is a great place to snuggle up with a cold beer after a dusty day on the trail. A popular in-town watering hole is **El Gran Judas** ((2902) 491750 at the corner of Moyano and 25 de Mayo. Student and backpackers gather each night

at **La Guanaconauta Pub** ((2902) 491281, Avenida Libertador 351 on the east side of Arroyo Calafate, which seems to specialize in both cold beer and loud music.

The only place where you can really let your hair down and dance is **Night Club Champagne** ((9202) 493044, Avenida Libertador 1723, which rocks from 11 PM to 6 AM.

HOW TO GET THERE

El Calafate is 320 km (200 miles) northwest of Río Gallegos via long and lonely stretches of Ruta 40 and Ruta 11. The heart of Parque Nacional Los Glaciares — including Moreno Glacier — is another 45 km (28 miles) west along Ruta 11.

Half a dozen bus companies make the six-hour journey to Río Gallegos, including **Interlagos** ((2902) 492195, **El Pingüino** ((2902) 491273, **Quebek** ((2902) 491814 and **Cootra** ((2902) 491444.

Service is also available to El Chaltén, Río Turbio and Puerto Natales, Chile, with connections into Torres del Paine National Park. There are fewer departures in winter. The town's spiffy little **Terminal de Ómnibus** is located between Calle San Juan Bosco and Avenida Roca, one block south of Avenida Libertador.

Aeropuerto Lago Argentino is on the east side of Arroyo Calafate, but scheduled service to other Argentine destinations is limited. **LADE** ((2902) 491262 or (2902) 491705, Avenida Libertador 699 and **LAPA** ((2902) 491171, Avenida Libertador 1015, offer weekly service to Río Gallegos, Río Turbio, San Julián, Comodoro Rivadavia, Ushuaia and Perito Moreno in small, prop-drive planes. Most visitors to El Calafate and Moreno Glacier fly into Río Gallegos and transfer to ground transport (bus or rental car) for the onward journey.

Wind ripples the surface of Lago Viedma on the outskirts of El Chaltén.

Tierra del Fuego and the Falkland Islands
(Islas Malvinas)

EXPLORERS MIGHT NEVER HAVE VENTURED into the South Atlantic Ocean were it not for Cape Horn. But the cape was a mighty magnet for those seeking a passageway between the Atlantic and Pacific Oceans. The earliest navigators (Magellan among them) were searching for a route to Asia's famed Spice Islands when they passed by an isolated archipelago lit by hundreds of fires. The name Tierra del Fuego stuck to this cluster of islands, where nomadic Indians fed upon seals and guanaco.

These same early sailors discovered other islands as they searched the seas. Most bypassed the Falklands, now one of the most disputed pieces of island real estate in the world. The Falklands gained importance after Cape Horn became a well-known route for traders and settlers. By the early eighteenth century, several European nations claimed possession of this isolated archipelago. Great Britain claims to have won the early battle for possession of what it named the Falkland Islands (named the Islas Malvinas by Spain). But you'd better not speak such heresy in Argentina. As they say in Buenos Aires, "Las Islas Malvinas son Argentino" (The Malvinas Islands are Argentine).

Other islands are scattered about the South Atlantic near Cape Horn and Antarctica. Most are inaccessible except to cruise-ship passengers. Several cruise lines now ply the South Atlantic from December through March en route to the mighty Antarctic. Most include stops at Tierra del Fuego, the Falklands, and South Georgia. Independent travelers find it easy to reach Tierra del Fuego from Buenos Aires, but those wishing to visit the Falklands must travel via Great Britain or Chile. Still, it's worth the effort to explore as much of the South Atlantic as possible. Few places are as intriguing to explorers who favor exotic landscapes and quixotic societies.

TIERRA DEL FUEGO

Isolated, desolate, and battered by the South Atlantic, Tierra del Fuego sits at the end of the South American continent, separated from the mainland by the Strait of Magellan. It's nearly as close to the South Pole as it is to Buenos Aires, and feels like a country unto itself. Chile and Argentina share the 76,000-sq-km (29,344-sq-mile) archipelago; although Chile owns more land mass, the Argentine side is more populated and developed.

A sort of mystique attracts travelers to Tierra del Fuego. Those lacking the time or money required to visit Antarctica get a taste of South Atlantic wilderness, complete with brutally wet and chilly winds. The main island in the archipelago is called Isla Grande, whose southern area is mountainous and filled with rivers, lakes, streams, and inlets harboring a vast collection of rare seabirds and seals. Ushuaia, the Argentine capital on the shores of the Beagle Channel, is the largest city in the region with some 45,000 residents.

Until recently few people have actually chosen to live here. Convicts and political prisoners formed the base of the population in Ushuaia in the early twentieth century, and though the prison has since closed, certain personages are still banished to these frigid lands. In 1999, ex-general Lino Oviedo of Paraguay, who sought asylum in Argentina after being accused of masterminding a plot to assassinate Paraguay's vice president, was sent to Tierra del Fuego after offending Argentina's leaders. But most of today's residents are here because of economic opportunities. The population swelled in the 1970s, when Argentina granted international manufacturing companies generous financial packages for opening factories in Ushuaia. The plants have since closed, but many of the workers have remained and are now employed in the tourism industry.

Tierra del Fuego and the Falkland Islands (Islas Malvinas)

Ushuaia is Tierra del Fuego's most popular destination. Cruise ships fill the channel in the summer months as they depart for Antarctica, and tourism is highest at this time. A second wave of visitors arrives in winter, when snow covers the mountains and ski resorts open. Río Grande, Argentina's only other major settlement in Tierra del Fuego, is geared more toward the petroleum industry and holds little interest for tourists.

BACKGROUND

Most of the South Atlantic's famous explorers, from Magellan to Darwin, stopped by Tierra del Fuego during their journeys, though few saw any reason to hang around. The sight of snowcapped mountains and glistening glaciers so popular with today's travelers held little interest for settlers seeking warmth and fertile farmland.

The earliest inhabitants of Tierra del Fuego were the Ona, Yamana (later renamed Yahgan), Haush, and Alakaluf peoples, collectively known today as the Fuegians. Some traveled the land hunting guanaco; others fished the sea from bark canoes. Historians believe there were about 200,000 Yamana in Tierra del Fuego when white men arrived; within a century few remained. Most died from imported diseases; their systems could not handle even the common cold. The Yahgan are the best known of the early tribes, thanks to the writings of Thomas Bridges. One of the first settlers in Tierra del Fuego, Bridges learned to speak the Yahgan language and began compiling a Yahgan dictionary. His son Lucas, who was born in Ushuaia in 1874, described his family's life among the Yahgan in *The Uttermost Part of the Earth*, still one of the most fascinating chronicles of this remote region.

Horses are the preferred mode of transport in Tierra del Fuego's chilly rivers.

Tierra del Fuego and the Falkland Islands (Islas Malvinas)

TIERRA DEL FUEGO

Charles Darwin, who visited Tierra del Fuego in 1834, called the indigenous Fuegians "among the most abject and miserable creatures I ever saw." He retracted this statement later, after learning more about these remarkable peoples. Still, they must have been a disconcerting sight. Despite the cold climate, they wore little clothing except for capes made of sea lion or otter fur, and lived much of the time in their canoes. Fires were ever present, both in the canoes and on land. European explorers called the land Tierra del Fuego (Land of Fire) because of the many fires evident from the sea.

Magellan sailed through the Strait that now bears his name in 1520, but had little interest in exploring the land. In fact, most early sailors passed by Tierra del Fuego, deterred by fierce winds and narrow channels. European missionaries based in the Falklands made some attempts at converting the Fuegians; their forays into the area attracted the attention of the newly formed Argentine government. Chile expressed an interest in the region as well, inspiring Argentina to establish a base at Ushuaia in 1884.

Argentina's South Atlantic Expeditionary Division, commanded by Colonel Augusto Lasserre, hoisted the national flag in Tierra del Fuego on October 12, 1884, a date now celebrated as the birthday of Ushuaia. To this day Argentina and Chile dispute the boundaries between their parts of Tierra del Fuego; though a diplomatic settlement was established in 1984, Argentines still contest Chile's right to any part of the archipelago.

Argentina established a penal colony in Ushuaia in 1902, with convicts transported by ship from Buenos Aires. The prisoners built many of the town's early buildings and laid the electrical lines; photos of prison construction crews are on exhibit at the Maritime Museum.

The prison was closed in 1947, and the Navy took control of the prison camp and established an Argentine presence in Antarctica. At the time, Ushuaia had just over 2,000 residents. The population began to grow significantly after 1978, when the government introduced incentives for international industries to set up production plants in the area. Several companies, including Hitachi and Philco, opened manufacturing plants. Workers arrived from throughout Argentina; at the height of the manufacturing boom over 6,000 workers were employed by the factories. The industrial boom ended in the early 1990s when other countries provided even greater incentives to international conglomerates. But the residents stayed on, enjoying high wages in the tourism industry.

USHUAIA

Set at the edge of the Beagle Channel and backed by the snowy peaks of the Cordillera Darwin (part of the Andean chain), Ushuaia benefits from a striking natural setting. Mount Olivia rises 412 m (1,350 ft) above sea level north of town, while the Martial Glacier stands in frozen solidity to the southwest. But the town itself can hardly be called picturesque. A jumble of wooden homes and shops seems to tumble in utter disarray down the hillsides toward the waterfront. Some buildings boast bright yellow and red paint; others look as though they never recovered from the last earthquake (which shook Tierra del Fuego in 1949). The town's original houses, called *casa trineos*, were built on sled runners so they could be moved quickly from place to place. A sense of impermanence still prevails. At times, one gets the feeling that Ushuaia could easily become a Wild West ghost town.

Yet there is a certain charm here, and a pioneer sensibility that feels real and alive. Ushuaia's hardy residents seem quite happy and eager to share their beautiful surroundings with strangers. The friendliness of the town's residents is a pleasant surprise, especially after the aloof attitude one encounters in Buenos Aires. Perhaps the remote setting encourages conviviality.

Underneath the town's ramshackle appearance lies a wave of prosperity. Handsome tract houses with all the modern conveniences are rising in gated developments; new ski resorts are under construction; and the last remaining unpaved sections of the Pan-American Highway from Alaska are finally being covered with asphalt. Visitors from throughout Argentina spend thousands of pesos on imported goods; Tierra del Fuego is a duty-free zone favored by diehard shoppers.

A large percentage of Ushuaia's visitors arrive on cruise ships; over 120,000 came ashore in 1999.

But these travelers have little time to explore the surrounding wilderness. Those traveling on their own can easily spend three or four days hiking, mountain biking, and cruising around the Beagle Channel. Travel agencies are expanding their offerings to entice adventure travelers who find excellent hiking, fishing, and camping opportunities in the surrounding wilderness. Though tourism is highest in the summer months, Ushuaia is becoming more popular with winter sports fans tired of the crowded conditions at Argentina's ski resorts in Bariloche.

GENERAL INFORMATION

Ushuaia's **Subsecretaría de Turismo** ((2901) 432000 E-MAIL muniush@terradelfuego.org.ar, Avenida San Martín 674, operates an excellent information office, open Monday through Friday from 8 AM to 9 PM. There is usually an English-speaking clerk on duty, and any information you could possibly need is cheerfully granted. **Telecentro Ushuaia** ((2901) 432271, Avenida Rivadavia 163, offers long-distance phone service and computers for Internet and e-mail use, as does **Telefónica de Argentina** ((2901) 430973, Calle Lasserre 124.

It helps to have a car if you want to explore the area fully; expensive rental cars are available at the airport. Ushuaia has several excellent travel agencies that run tours to all the major attractions and wilderness areas; using their services is easier and sometimes less expensive than traveling about on your own. Taxis are available in town. They hover around the Tourist Pier on Avenida Maipú; drivers will wait for you at remote areas for a small fee.

Bring a waterproof jacket, gloves, and sturdy waterproof shoes even in summer; you never known when a chilly storm will blow through. Until recently travelers were advised to carry enough cash to cover their predicted expenses, but I found it easy to change travelers' checks and to use credit cards on my most recent visit.

TOURS

All Patagonia ((2901) 430725 FAX (2901) 430707 E-MAIL allpat@satlink.com is the best overall agency for booking transportation, accommodations and tours. All the conventional tours mentioned above are available, along with trekking, horseback riding, mountain biking, bird-watching and fishing trips. You can also arrange air tours over the channel, glacier and mountains. The agency can arrange for travelers to board Antarctica cruise ships in Ushuaia. **Rumbo Sur** ((2901) 422275 FAX (2901) 430699 E-MAIL rumbosur@satlink.com, Avenida San Martín 350, run boat trips to Isla de Los Lobos in the bay of Ushuaia. The comfortable

boats have bench seats and tables, heating, and food and beverage service. There's plenty of room on deck for those who would like to photograph the sea lions lumbering about the rocky island. The company also has land tours. **Canal Fun & Nature** ((2901) 437395 WEB SITE www.canalfun.com specialize in adventure tours including off-road vehicle tours, kayaking, and trekking. As their name suggests, **Fly Casting Ushuaia** ((2901) 435769 E-MAIL flycast@satlink.com, Avenida del Miche 667, offer intensive fishing trips including overnight camping, meals, and transport.

WHAT TO SEE AND DO

It takes little time to tour Ushuaia proper; the greatest attractions lie in the countryside. Most of the main sights in town are located along the waterfront Avenida Maipú or one block inland on Avenida San Martín. The waterfront area has been cleaned up and modernized in recent years, with benches and small parks, and a central plaza area lined with offices and stands for tour operators at the informally named **Muelle de Turística** (Tourist Pier), at Avenida Maipú and Calle Lassere.

The **Museo del Fin del Mundo** ((2901) 421863 FAX (2901) 431201 E-MAIL museo@tierradelfuego .org.ar WEB SITE tierradelfuego.org.ar/museo/ visita, Avenida Maipú 173, is the most accessible place to learn about Ushuaia's history. One of the city's oldest buildings (constructed in 1903) has been restored and contains several rooms of exhibits along with an excellent library and gift shop. The Yamana (Yahgan) people are well covered, and the exhibits on local animals and birds (including two enormous stuffed condors) include labels in the Yamana language. Photos of some of the most famous murderers held at the prison are exhibited on the walls alongside a yellow and black striped prisoner's uniform. Shipwrecks are also featured with displays of precious coins and glass bottles from sunken ships and the impressive carved figurehead from a ship called the *Duchess of Albany*. Admission is charged.

Ushuaia's original prison presidio now houses the **Museo Marítimo** ((2901) 437481, Avenida Gobierno Paz and Calle Yaganes. The life stories of some of the more famous prisoners are chronicled in posters on the cell walls; the prison was home to several politicians during times of upheaval. Other exhibits cover expeditions to Antarctica and Tierra del Fuego's history as a navigational hub. Admission is charged. The museum is located on the Navy base, and is sometimes closed without notice.

Shopping is immensely popular, with national tourists taking advantage of Ushuaia's duty-free status. Alcohol and cigarettes are astonishingly inexpensive; imported electronic goods, perfumes, and clothing also cost much less than in the rest of the country. **Atlántico Sur (** (2901) 423380 at Avenida San Martín 627 is one of the largest duty-free shops. Several stores cater to tourists, especially during the cruise season. The best place for books, maps, information on Antarctica, and local crafts is **World's End (** (2901) 434718 WEB SITE www.ushuaia.org, at Calle San Martín 788. The company has several shops in town, including one at the Museo Marítimo. **Tierra de Humos (** (2901) 433050, Avenida San Martín 861, has a lovely selection of handmade silver *matés* used for brewing tea. The selection of wood carvings, weavings, and silver jewelry is exceptional at **Patagon 1884 (** (2901) 435588, Avenida San Martín 809. Locally made candies and chocolates can be purchased at **Chocolates Cabaña Nevada (** (2901) 435904, Avenida San Martín 788.

Outside town the most popular attraction is the **Parque Nacional Tierra del Fuego**, located 12 km (seven and a half miles) west of Ushuaia on R3. The park is the final point on the Pan-American Highway from Alaska; in some areas it feels like it's at the end of the world. For maps and permits to camp in the park stop by the Park Administration Office **(** (2901) 431476 at Avenue San Martín 1395. The best way to visit the park, at least the first time around, is with a tour company (see TOURS, below).

The park covers 6,300 hectares (150,000 acres) and runs six kilometers (nearly four miles) along the Beagle Channel. It abuts the Chilean border in the southwestern corner of Tierra del Fuego, and encompasses mountains, rivers, lakes, rivers, and peat bogs. There are several marked trails; a rough map is available at the park. You can visit various areas by bus, boat, horseback, and even train; the Tren del Fin del Mundo ends its run here. I strongly suggest hiking with a guide to get a better sense of the unusual flora and fauna. Beavers, introduced for their fur, have wreaked havoc with park terrain, and enormous beaver dams block rivers beside hiking trails.

One of the best excursions in the park is a boat trip across Bahía Escondido to **Isla Rendonda**, a private nature reserve. The amiable Carlos Delorenzo maintains a cabin on the island where visitors warm their hands by a wood stove. With advance notice Delorenzo prepares a hearty lunch of crusty bread, red wine (or sodas) and *guiso*, a filling soup loaded with chorizo, carrots, macaroni, and potatoes. Bring your passport along to get a Tierra del Fuego stamp (totally useless for border crossings, but still a nice souvenir). Marked trails circle the island; there's a great view of the channel from atop a small hill. Book your tour through one of the agencies listed below.

There are a few small campgrounds in the park, and a small market and restaurant near Lago Roca. Contact the park office for camping information and campsite availability.

One of the best ways to visit the park is on **El Tren del Fin del Mundo (** (2901) 431600 FAX (2901) 437696 E-MAIL ush@trendelfindelmundo.com.ar WEB SITE www.trendelfindelmundo.com.ar, eight kilometers (five miles) west of Ushuaia on R3. The Train at the End of the World was built specifically for tourism, and follows a route taken by the prison crews sent to chop wood in the mountains. Trains depart from the Estación Fin del Mundo beside the Río Pipo, where passengers fuel up on steaming cups of coffee and hot chocolate. *Empanadas*, sandwiches, and pastries are sold at a small café; postcards and souvenirs are displayed in a small shop. Behind the main station a small building houses workshops and a great display of historical photographs.

The bright red, blue, and green train coaches are heated and have large windows. Steam locomotives travel along a narrow-gauge track up into the mountains as a guide describes the scenery. Travelers stretch their legs during a 10-minute stop at La Cascada la Macarena, a small waterfall. A replica of a Yamana home resembling a small teepee sits beside the waterfall. The one-way trip lasts approximately one hour and ends at the Estación del Parque (basically a hut by the tracks).

A short trail leads from the train depot to the ranger station at Bahía Lapatía where you can have your passport stamped with a Tierra del Fuego imprint. You may be able to hire a boat for a trip around the bay; it's best to arrange this ahead of time through a tour company. The train runs round-trip four times a day, so you can catch one of the later ones back to the highway. Purchase train tickets in advance at the station, the Tourist Pier, or your hotel.

Though not as impressive as Patagonia's Moreno Glacier, Ushuaia's **Martial Glaciar** is a must-see. The glacier is reached via a 15-minute ride on a ski lift from the **Glaciar Martial Ski Lodge (** (2901) 433712 at the end of Camino al Glaciar seven kilometers (four miles) from town. At the end of a lift a trail leads up to the glacier; plan on spending about two hours easy hiking each way. The views from this icy lookout are truly breathtaking. Be sure to bring a jacket, hiking shoes, and gloves even if it's warm in town. The chair lift is open from 10 AM to 4:30 PM. Consider staying longer to watch the sky glow against shimmering ice at sunset. Just be sure to start hiking down the ski trail to the lodge before dark. Also keep in mind that the sun doesn't set until 10 PM in summer.

Ushuaia's most famous personage, Thomas Bridges, built the **Estancia Harberton (** (2901) 422743, 80 km (50 miles) east of Ushuaia on R3. His son Lucas set much of his book *The Uttermost Part of the Earth* here, and the ranch is still owned by descendants of the Bridges family. The 20,200-hectare (50,000-acre) ranch covers coastal marshland and wooded hillsides along the north shore of the Beagle Channel. Most visitors arrive on full-day boat tours from Ushuaia, though you can also get there by car. Afternoon tea is served at the ranch's Casa de Té Mánacatush. The complex includes replicas of Yahgan dwellings, gardens, and a small museum.

Several companies (see TOURS, above) offer boat trips around the **Beagle Channel** to **Les Eclairears Lighthouse** and **Isla de los Lobos**, home to dozens of noisy sea lions. Other trips head to **Isla Martillo**, where Magellanic penguins build their burrows in the spring.

The highway (R3) east of town skirts the base of **Mount Olivia** and climbs the **Garibaldi Pass** at 430 m (1,411 ft), overlooking **Lago Escondido**

One of the more fascinating winter-sports attractions is **Altos del Valle** (/FAX (2901) 422234 E-MAIL gatocuruchet@hotmail.com, 19 km (12 miles) west of Ushuaia. This wildlife refuge is home to Siberian huskies and an Alaskan white wolf. Racing sleds are made by hand in the factory. Visitors can go dog sledding or skiing during the winter months, or mountain biking and horseback riding in summer.

WHERE TO STAY

Though Ushuaia has several hotels, rooms can be hard to come by in the summer season. Independent travelers hoping to join Antarctica cruises

and **Lago Fagnano**. The two lakes are popular fishing spots, and there are wonderful hiking trails around the mountain. It's best to hike with a guide, as the trails are nearly invisible to the uninitiated eye, and some areas can be covered with snow and ice even in summer. Fagnano Lake is the largest in Tierra del Fuego and attracts albatross and petrels. Tour companies offer bus, four-wheel-drive, and hiking trips in this area.

Ushuaia's reputation as a winter sports center is gaining, and new ski centers are under construction. Downhill and cross-country skiing are both popular, along with dog sledding. The main ski area is at the **Martial Winter Sports Center** (2901) 421423, seven kilometers (four miles) northwest of town on Avenida Martial. At **Valle de los Huskies** (2901) 431902, on Ruta 3, 20 km (12 miles) north of Ushuaia, you can travel along the snow on skis, snowshoes, snowmobiles, or dog sleds.

flock to town in January and February, and tour groups occasionally claim all the rooms in the best hotels. Make your reservations early, either through the hotel or a local travel agency. Rates are high for what you get, and inexpensive lodgings are hard to come by. Some residents rent out rooms in their homes; check with the tourist office for information.

Expensive
My choice for the best full-service hotel in the area is the **Las Hayas Resort Hotel** (/FAX (2901) 430710 E-MAIL lashayas@overnet.com.ar WEB SITE www .lashayas.com, at Avenida Martial 1650. The property has the feel of a mountain lodge, complete with blazing fire in the lobby lounge. The four-story white building with peaked roof sits against

Fly-fishing for trout in golden sunlight.

the mountain all by itself; views from the rooms are breathtaking. The 102 rooms have safe-deposit boxes, cable television, full baths with bidets, and warm floral furnishings; some have separate seating areas. Steam rises from the indoor lap pool and hot tub, and there's even a squash court. The Martial Restaurant is rather formal and pricey; less expensive meals are available in the coffee shop. The hotel offers frequent transport to town, and a full tour desk.

Moderate

Guests at the **Posada Fueguina (** (2901) 423467 E-MAIL pfueguina@tierradelfuego.org.ar, Avenida Lasserre 438, are treated as though they are stay-

daily transportation to the hotel's sister property in town, the **Hotel Albatros (** (2901) 430003 FAX (2901) 430666 E-MAIL hotalba@infovia.com.ar, at Avenida Maipú 505. The Albatros has an excellent location, right across the street from the tour boats, but it leaves much to be desired. Few rooms look out to the waterfront, and the facilities lack any sort of warmth or charm. The hotel is popular with tour groups, so book your room early. The restaurant does look out to the canal, and serves decent, unremarkable meals designed to please tourists. Those who prefer a mountain setting might enjoy the **Cabañas del Martial (** (2901) 433622 FAX (2901) 430707, Avenida Martial 2109. The cabins sleep four to six persons and have full

ing in a private home. The small inn sits atop a steep hill a few blocks up from the waterfront (walking back is a good way to work off your meals). A complimentary breakfast of ham, cheese, breads, and coffee is served in the main dining and living room area with a spectacular view of the channel. The 19 rooms are located in the main house and a separate wing, and are cozily furnished with comfortable beds, writing desks, and full bathrooms.

The **Hotel del Glaciar (** (2901) 430640 FAX (2901) 430636 E-MAIL glaciar@infovia.com.ar, Avenida Martial 2355, is one of the area's best hotels, although the property is somewhat rundown. The 124 rooms have carpeting, full baths, mini-bars, and queen or king beds; most have spectacular views down to the channel. Guests have use of a gym and sauna, and there is a restaurant on the property. It's located far from town, but there is

kitchens; packages including car rental and tours are available.

Inexpensive

One of the best low-cost choices is the **Cesar Hostal (** (2901) 421460 FAX (2901) 432721, Avenida San Martín 753, found in the center of town. The 28 rooms book up early; in fact, if you're planning to visit around the holidays, make your reservations six months in advance. The main reason for this popularity is the price. Though hardly a bargain, it's the cleanest, most accommodating place around with rooms less than US$100 a night. Breakfast is included in the rate, and all rooms have showers and toilets. The beds are comfortable, and the rooms are heated with radiators. The **Hotel Cabo de Hornos (**/FAX (2901) 401901 E-MAIL cabohornos @tierradelfuego.org.ar, on Avenida San Martín at Rosas, has 30 basic rooms and is popular with traveling salesmen. The rooms fill up quickly at the **Hotel Canal Beagle** ((2901) 421117 FAX (2901) 421120, Avenida Maipú 547, as well. The 56 rooms have private baths, heating, and televisions; try for one at the back away from street noise. The **Torre al Sur Youth Hostel** ((2901) 430745 E-MAIL torrealsur@impsatl.com.ar offers extremely inexpensive bed space in dormitory rooms; facilities include a kitchen and full bathrooms.

WHERE TO EAT

Restaurants in Ushuaia serve rather limited menus featuring local crab, mussels, trout, and hake. Prices are high even in informal restaurants; best bets for inexpensive meals are the pizzerias and cafés. Dinner is usually served earlier than in Buenos Aires; you can arrive at 7 PM and not feel gauche.

Moderate

Casually elegant, **Kaupé** ((2901) 422704, Calle Roca 470, sits atop a hill overlooking the town and channel. Local seafood is the specialty, and there is an impressive wine list. It seems everyone orders king crab (*centolla*) at **Tía Elvira** ((2901) 424725, Avenida Maipú 349. The preferred preparation is served as an appetizer and consists of cold crabmeat served in the shell. For a heartier meal try the rich crab baked with parmesan cheese, or the hake (a local fish) provençal with white wine, garlic, and tomato. The restaurant is a local institution and enormously popular; this is one place where it pays to dine unfashionably early. Crab is also the main attraction at **Alakush** ((2901) 435667, Avenida San Martín 140, a serene dining room with pale green walls and a gas fireplace. Meals begin with a complementary pisco sour; entrées include crab, grilled trout, cod, and hearty paella. Lamb and beef are grilled over an open fire at **La Estancia** ((2901) 421241, Avenida San Martín 253, the best place for big platters of grilled meats. Unlike most local restaurants (which tend to closed between meals) **Café Ideal** ((2901) 437860, Avenida San Martín 393, stays open all day. Light meals include pastas and pizza.

Inexpensive

Claim a window seat at **Café la Esquina** ((2901) 421446, Avenida San Martín 601, for a leisurely cup of coffee and a slice of outrageously sweet *torta dulce de leche* with thick caramelized cream spread between flaky layers of pastry. The café is the prettiest eatery in town, with lacquered wood tables, lace curtains, and plenty of windows. Pizzas and sandwiches are available for more filling meals. Steaks, pastas, and sandwiches are the fare at **Mi Abuela** ((2901) 436665, Avenida Roca 230, and reasonably priced pasta dishes are

served at **Café el Galeon** ((2901) 424415, Avenida San Martín 602.

Tucked in the mountainside on the way to Glacier Martial, **La Cabaña Casa de Té** ((2901) 469511 at the end of Avenida Martial is housed in a lovely wood cabin. Afternoon tea doesn't get any better, thanks to the steaming pots of the house blend served with a mouthwatering array of cakes, tarts, pies and toasted sandwiches.

HOW TO GET THERE

Aerolíneas Argentina has daily flights between Buenos Aires and Ushuaia; the flight takes about four hours.

THE FALKLAND ISLANDS (ISLAS MALVINAS)

About 2,200 hardy individualists inhabit the Falkland Islands, one of the loneliest and purest places on earth. Located 483 km (300 miles) east of Argentina, the Falklands cover an area roughly the size of Wales or Connecticut. Most residents are resourceful characters of indubitable fortitude and insight who consider their windy home to be paradise.

The air is incredibly clear here; since pollution is virtually nonexistent sunburns are common year round. In the summer months temperatures reach 20°C (68°F) and tulips bloom in front yards. The

OPPOSITE: Penguins outnumber people in remote areas of the South Atlantic. ABOVE: Islander Allan White points out the nests of Magellanic penguins in tussock grass.

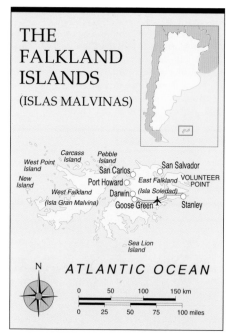

THE FALKLAND ISLANDS (ISLAS MALVINAS)

Carcass Island
West Point Island
New Island
West Falkland (Isla Gran Malvina)
Pebble Island
San Carlos
Port Howard
Darwin
Goose Green
San Salvador
East Falkland (Isla Soledad)
VOLUNTEER POINT
Stanley
Sea Lion Island

N

ATLANTIC OCEAN

| 0 | 50 | 100 | 150 km |
| 0 | 25 | 50 | 75 | 100 miles |

war over this collection of nearly 400 islands "counting knobs and rocks," as John Fowler, manager of the Falkland Islands Tourist Board, describes the isolated archipelago. We're not talking a tropical paradise here. Yet France, Spain, Argentina, and Great Britain have all claimed ownership of the Falklands, sometimes simultaneously. The British have had the most consistent presence, solidified by their victory over Argentina in the Falklands War of 1982. But Argentines still believe the Malvinas (as they call the archipelago) will always belong to Argentina; flags, banners, and maps all declare Argentine sovereignty over the islands. This desperate desire for ownership is partly due to the Falklands' geographical position near Cape Horn (once the only route between the Atlantic and Pacific Oceans), the rumored presence of undersea oil, and fierce national pride.

But the Falklands remain British to the core. Prince Philip, Duke of Edinburgh, has visited the islands twice, and contributed the following explanation to *The Falklands*, an excellent book by Tony Chater, who moved to the islands from England in 1972: "It may seem a bit odd to contemporary readers that the Falkland Islands should be a British dependency," the Duke writes. "At the furthest end of the Atlantic Ocean, with no significant natural resources, little attraction for tourists seeking the sun and not on the route to anywhere; they are a peculiarly British anomaly."

Most Falkland Islanders are descendants of British settlers; over 60% of the residents are native born and express a decided desire to be left alone by all outside powers. The vast majority live in the town of Stanley on East Falkland Island; the rest live in Camp — the local term for remote island outposts usually centered around sheep ranching. About 500 people live on the roughly 1,214,034 hectares (three million acres) of Camp. Most are remarkably content. "You've got everything you need to eat well, live well, and sleep well," says Allan White, a second-generation islander who works as a nature guide. "The relative isolation and perpetual hard work makes for some of the world's most wonderful characters."

The islands' residents are informally called Kelpers, though they don't harvest the abundance of giant kelp found around their homes. Instead, they herd bleating flocks of sheep. Until recently, wool exportation formed the base of the Falklands' economy; when the world market for natural fibers collapsed, the island lifestyle was sorely threatened. These days, the sale of commercial fishing licenses has more than made up for the declining demand for wool, and tourism is on the rise. Still, almost everyone living in Camp has a flock of sheep, along with cows and dogs. As might be expected, mutton is a big part of the

winters are milder than one would expect, given the South Atlantic's reputation for fierce storms. Temperatures rarely drop below 0°C (32°F) and snowstorms are rare. The winds can be brutal, however, as evidenced by trees bent in ghostly shapes by southwesterly gusts. Most visitors arrive in spring and summer, between October and April, when gorse-covered hillsides are striped with waves of yellow blossoms and snapdragons, daffodils, and poppies burst forth in window boxes and classic English gardens.

Spring also heralds the arrival of the islands' greatest attraction—huge colonies of nesting penguins. Comical rockhopper penguins, dubbed "punk rockers" by amused observers, bop about their nests on New Island as if traveling about on pogo sticks. Braying jackass or Magellanic penguins burrow in tussock grass on Carcass Island; striped gentoos wade onto sandy shores. King penguins, once slaughtered for their eggs and feathers, return to Volunteer Point to sit for months on their eggs. Hundreds and thousands of penguins nest all around the islands, sharing their turf with delicate cormorants and awesome black and brown albatross. Eager hikers sense their presence moments before spotting their prey; few aromas match the pervasive stench of a penguin colony. Over 25,000 human visitors arrive during spring and summer to witness this incomparable wildlife spectacle. The penguins alone make some wish to become full-time Kelpers, as Falkland Islanders are dubbed.

Despite the Falklands' wild natural beauty, it's hard to believe nations would actually wage

Tierra del Fuego and the Falkland Islands (Islas Malvinas)

Falklands diet. Sheep shearing is a major activity (and tourist attraction) in the spring, when professional shearers from New Zealand join local experts traveling a circuit through Camp ranches to shear hundreds of thousands of sheep.

The tangy aroma of peat fires settles over the islands most times of year; much of the terrain is composed of spongy peat bogs and peat cutting is as necessary an activity as sheep shearing. Though electricity and gas are available for cooking and heating, Kelpers seem to favor the earthy smell of burning peat (and the sensible use of free fuel). Horses were the original mode of transport in town and Camp; Land Rovers and other four-wheel-drive vehicles are now used to herd sheep and carry islanders on their errands. Even Camp settlements have telephones, computers, and televisions, though some residents shun such invasive inventions. "It's as remote as you want to be," says Chater, who lives on a private island far from Stanley. Travelers fortunate enough to visit this faraway outpost of British civility find that the Falklands remain vivid in their memories.

Background

The Yahgan Indians of Tierra del Fuego may have been the first humans to discover the Falkland Islands, though it's hard to imagine how they got there. The Yahgans traveled in flimsy beech bark canoes, and would have had to paddle 800 km (500 miles) northeast to reach the Falklands. There's no recorded evidence of this journey. Instead, speculation is fueled by the presence of the warrah, a land animal that had to have arrived with man.

Charles Darwin first pondered the presence of the warrah when he and Admiral Robert Fitzroy arrived in the Falklands on the HMS Beagle in 1833. The warrah, also known as the Falklands fox, was believed to have been domesticated by the Yahgan, who regularly carried pregnant bitches on their journeys. Darwin believed man brought the fox to the islands, and man would destroy it. Sure enough, the last warrah on the Falklands was shot in 1876, and the species is now extinct.

British Captain John Davis is usually credited with the discovery of the Falklands in 1592, though Dutch, Spanish, Italian, and French sailors are all rumored to have made early sightings. Captain Wood Rogers named the islands the Falklands in 1708, while the French named them the Îles Malouines after the port of Saint Malo in Brittany. The Spanish are believed to have changed that name to the Islas Malvinas, the designation that remains firm in the minds of Argentines. Thus begins the Falklands complicated history.

French explorer Louis Antoine de Bougainville established the islands' first settlement at Port Louis in 1764, then sold the port to the Spaniards, who renamed it Port Soledad in 1766. Purportedly unaware of the settlement, the British laid claim to sovereignty over the islands in 1766 as well, and soon the French and Spanish were established on East Falkland and the British on West Falkland. The Spanish, who were firmly entrenched in Buenos Aires, evicted the British in 1767, then readmitted them under threat of war. Three years later, the British abandoned the settlement but retained the claim of ownership by right of discovery, leaving a plaque declaring that their absence did not indicate withdrawal of British sovereignty.

When Argentina declared independence from Spain in 1810, the Spanish abandoned the Falklands and the Argentines claimed them as part of their conquest. Great Britain, however, never relinquished its claim over the islands. To this day, each side adamantly declares ownership of the islands in a dispute that seems insoluble despite repeated wars.

Louis Vernet, an entrepreneur of French birth and a naturalized resident of Buenos Aires, received a large parcel of land and the fishing and hunting rights on East Falkland from the Buenos Aires government in 1823, despite British protest. The United States of America entered the fray in 1831, when Vernet seized three American sealing vessels after prohibiting foreign vessels from capturing seals in the waters around the Falklands. At one point the Americans claimed that as a former colony of Great Britain, the United States had a right to work in the Falklands: after Vernet's seizure, United States Naval officer Silas Duncan led an attack that destroyed Vernet's settlement at Port Soledad.

As governments argued, the Falklands became ever more important to nineteenth-century shipping companies, thanks to the islands' strategic location near Cape Horn. The horn was the essential route between the Pacific and the Atlantic before the Panama Canal opened in 1914, and the islands' position in the South Atlantic near the Strait of Magellan and Cape Horn made them likely way-stations for explorers and traders following the treacherous route. The Falklands' maritime history is evident even today in Stanley Harbour, which serves as a watery graveyard for nineteenth-century sailing ships. Sailors, whalers, and traders formed a community in Stanley, where ship repairers earned a lucrative wage. Vessels beyond repair littered the harbor; many are still visible today.

British and Scottish pioneers began farming the islands after the British regained control in 1833; the first mission was established in 1863. By 1869, the Falkland Islands Company was established as a large landholder, with other portions of Camp divided among mostly English settlers. These early pioneers farmed the land and slaughtered the wild cattle left behind by early explorers. By the late

1800s, sheep ranching had become the primary industry for the settlers. In 1892, Great Britain granted colonial status to the Falklands.

The British government paid scant attention to the Falklands except during the world wars, when the islands became critical in establishing British supremacy over the South Atlantic. The population gradually increased, reaching its high point of 2,393 residents in 1931, and ranchers made a decent living by exporting wool. Argentina and Great Britain continued to debate their claims over the islands; by 1964 the United Nations was embroiled in the dispute. In 1966, a group of Argentine right-wing terrorists hijacked an Aerolíneas Argentina DC-4 and forced the pilot to land on the grass airstrip in Stanley. The hijackers claimed the Malvinas for Argentina, but their reign lasted less than 24 hours. They surrendered the next day, and returned home. The British Foreign & Commonwealth Office began to give Argentina a larger role in issues of transportation and commerce; some islanders felt the Brits were about to hand over the Falklands to Argentina.

Then, on April 2, 1982, Argentina invaded the Falkland Islands. At the time, Argentina had fallen into its bleakest era under the rule of a military junta led by General Leopoldo Galtieri. The Dirty War, with all its corruption and destruction, was in full swing, and the Argentine people were growing ever increasingly disgusted with Galtieri's government. Seeking a distraction and a way to rebuild his popularity, Galtieri dispatched the Argentine Navy who attacked the islands with thousands of troops. A small Royal Marine force on the islands attempted a defense, but were quickly routed. The marines and the Falklands' British governor were banished to Montevideo, Uruguay. On April 3, the Argentine Navy seized South Georgia Island, and Argentina General Mario Menéndez became the military governor of all the islands.

Galtieri's invasion proved wildly popular in Argentina, and the country was once again united and proud. But Galtieri had underestimated Prime Minister Margaret Thatcher's response (and her need for a public relations coup of her own). On April 3 the United Nations called for the withdrawal of the Argentine troops from the Falklands. On May 1, 1982, British harrier planes attacked Stanley.

The 1982 war was short and horridly violent. The conflict lasted 74 days in all; nearly 1,000 people died. The poorly equipped Argentine military bore the brunt of the casualties, and 252 British sailors and soldiers and three civilians died.

The Falklanders suffered greatly during the war, though their highly developed sense of irony and self-reliance remained firmly intact. Some Kelpers were subjected to severe interrogations

by Argentine officers, experienced torturers in Galtieri's Dirty War. When the schools were closed teachers visited their students at home. Residents whose farms had been overtaken by the military moved into dormitories in town. Argentine forces took over Goose Green and confined the residents to the community hall for over a month. Port Howard was seized by 1,000 Argentine troops. And though Stanley was never attacked in full, some homes were bombed.

John Fowler, the current manager of the Falkland Islands Tourist Board, was away when his Stanley home was bombed. Three women who had sought refuge in the well-fortified structure were killed. With typical Kelper understatement Fowler describes the war as "not among the most pleasant lifetime experiences."

On June 14, 1982, the Argentine Commanding Officer Mario Menéndez signed the official surrender; dispirited Argentine troops descended upon Stanley chanting "Viva Argentina." A lengthy cleanup and recovery process began. To this day, unexploded mines litter fields around Stanley. British and Argentine military cemeteries are now part of the tourist circuit, as are battlefields and worn-down bunkers.

As might be expected, Falkland Islanders have little interest in restoring relations with Argentina, while the Argentines still insist the Malvinas are rightly theirs. The prevailing sentiment on the islands seems to be "I was born here; I think the Falklands belong to us." The British now keep a force of 2,000 soldiers near Stanley and use the Falklands as a training camp. Argentine citizens whose relatives are buried on the Falklands are allowed to visit the islands, where locals express profound sympathy for the opposition troops who fought under miserable conditions.

Sheep ranching remains a critical part of Camp life, though the wool market has slumped and profits are way down. But the Falklands sit in the midst of one of the world's richest fisheries, and the sale of fishing licenses to Asian and European fleets has become the Falkland's greatest source of revenue.

GENERAL INFORMATION

The best source of information on the islands is the **Falkland Islands Tourist Board** (22215 FAX 22619 E-MAIL manager@tourism.org.fk WEB SITE www.tourism.org.fk. Information is also available from **Falkland House** ((020) 7222-2542 FAX (020) 7222-2375, 14 Broadway, London, SW1H OBH.

You can book hotel rooms and tours through the tourist board or with travel agencies in Stanley, including **International Tours & Travel Ltd.** (22041 FAX 22042 E-MAIL int.travel@horizon.co.fk and **Stanley Services Travel** (22622 FAX 22623 E-MAIL ssl.cab@horizon.co.fk.

In the United States, LADATCO Tours ((305) 854-8422 TOLL-FREE (800) 327-6162 FAX (305) 285-0504 E-MAIL tailor@ladatco.com WEB SITE www .ladatco.com, offers full-service Falklands tours include air, accommodations, and Camp stays. The agents have spent considerable time in the islands and offer valuable advice.

Once you are in Stanley, stop by the Tourist Board's aqua and white tourist information trailer on the Public Jetty at the east end of Ross Road. Shelves are stocked with a good supply of brochures for restaurants, hotels, Camp lodges, and tours. The office sells several fine booklets on nature and history, and the clerks have an solution for nearly every quandary.

papers. The rise of the Internet has made communication much easier, and computers and modems are common even in the most remote parts of Camp. The **Hard Disk Internet Café** (22589 is in the Atlantic House on Fitzroy Road.

Avoid visiting the Falklands in winter, when chill winds make navigation a dicey prospect. Snow falls infrequently, but when it does Stanley becomes a fantasyland of dripping icicles and snow-covered eaves. The best months for visitors are from October to April, when the weather is similar to spring and summer in Southern England. Be sure to bring a windbreaker or other waterproof jacket and sturdy hiking shoes. Rubber boots or wellies come in handy for boat landings.

Valid passports are necessary for all visitors; visas are also required for travelers from many Latin American and Asian countries. There are restrictions on travelers carrying passports from Argentina, though arrangements are easily made for those visiting the graves of deceased relatives on the islands. Contact the Tourist Board for further specifics.

The telephone country code for the Falklands is 500. The Falkland pound equals one pound sterling, and British currency circulates freely. Travelers' checks and credit cards are readily accepted; there are no automated teller machines on the islands. The emergency number for police, fire, and ambulance is 999.

The Falklands has its own radio station, which broadcasts such essential information as daily birthdays, birth announcements, and upcoming flight schedules. There are two weekly news-

Those interested in the islands' natural attributes may want to visit the offices of **Falklands Conservation** (22247 FAX 22623 in the Beauchene Shopping Complex on John Street. The nonprofit organization carries out research projects and owns a few offshore nature preserves; books, clothing, souvenirs and abundant information are available at the office.

Visitors hiking outside Stanley and in Camp should pay special attention to signs posted around minefields. One of the unfortunate reminders of the 1982 war is the unexploded charges littering certain areas. Minefields are fenced off with barbed wire and labeled with red metal triangular signs which read "DANGER/MINES." Minefield maps are available at the Explosive Ordinance Disposal Office on Ross Road (22229.

Fields of yellow gorse announce the arrival of spring on the islands.

GETTING AROUND

There are precious few roads on the islands, and you don't need a car while staying in Stanley. **Falkland Islands Tours and Travels** (21775 offers transport to and from the airport. **Ben's Taxi** (21437 and **Lowe's Taxis** (21381 also provide airport transfers and transport within Stanley. If you get the urge to explore the backcountry, four-wheel-drive vehicles are available for rent from the **Falkland Islands Company** (27600 FAX 27603 and **Robert's Vehicle Hire** (22529 FAX 22450. Drive on the left.

Most of the lodges in Camp provide marine transport. **Byron Marine** (22245 operates an interisland cargo ferry with limited room for passengers. Schedules are established a few weeks in advance; call ahead for reservations. The **Falkland Islands Government Air Service** (27219 operates eight-passenger aircraft and offers flights to the other islands. Scheduled flights are announced on the radio; the planes fly only when there are several paying customers.

Visitors can easily explore all points of interest in Stanley on their own; maps and a walking tour brochure are available at the tourist information booth on the Public Jetty. **Tenacres Tours** (21155 FAX 21950 E-MAIL tenacres@horizon.co.fk offers overland tours into the Camp, historical tours to the British and Argentine military cemeteries. Trips to several of the 1982 battlefields are available from **Tony Smith** (21027; **South Atlantic Marine Services** (21145 offers boat trips around Stanley Harbour.

WHAT TO SEE AND DO

Stanley is the Falkland's largest town and has served as the islands' capital since 1845. About 2,050 residents live on its neatly ordered streets, arranged in even grids between Stanley Harbour and endless peat bogs. You can easily explore the town in a couple of hours, though time passes by quickly if you chat with locals in shops and on the street. A well-marked **Maritime History Trail** runs along the harbor; the visitor information center sells a self-guided tour brochure.

Ross Road is the main waterfront thoroughfare running along Stanley Harbour. Begin your walk at the intersection of Ross Road and Philomel Street at the Tourist Information trailer at the end of the Public Jetty. From here you can see the rusted hulks of several ships destroyed while trying to sail around Cape Horn. The two gray wooden hulls with rusted anchor chains are from the Charles Cooper and Actaeon, two nineteenth-century cargo ships. A plaque on the jetty commemorates the visit of Prince Alfred, Duke of Edinburgh, in 1871, and the subsequent visit by Prince Philip,

Duke of Edinburgh, in 1991. Up the first block of Philomel Street sits the yellow and green **Philomel Store** (21123, a classic general store, which opened in the 1950s. Des Peck, the original proprietor, was known as the Falkland Poet Laureate; his verses on island life and the ignominy of the war of 1982 hang about the shop. News of the latest merchandise is broadcast over the radio, and customers can find everything from musical instruments to Princess Di memorabilia to stuffed penguins. Stop by and hang around the aisles for a while. You're sure to soak in a bit of local lore.

Head west on Ross Road to **Christ Church Cathedral** (21100, between Philomel and Dean Streets. Red bricks frame arched windows in the gray stone church, consecrated in 1892 as the Anglican base of the Diocese of South America. Rather humble by European standards, the cathedral is the largest and most important building in Stanley, and is fronted by an immense arch made from the jawbones of two blue whales. The church is open daily from 8 AM to 5 PM, and is often used for community events. Across the street is **South Atlantic Marine Services** (21145 FAX 22647 E-MAIL sams@horizon.co.fk, which offers dive trips for the foolhardy fascinated by underwater shipwrecks.

Four cannons from Port Louis, the first British settlement on the Falklands, sit on the lawns of the Victory Green running between the Public and Government jetties across from the Upland Goose Hotel. The nineteenth-century cannons are fired during holiday celebrations and to salute certain incoming ships. Government services are clustered in the block between Villiers and Barrack Streets by the Government Jetty. The jetty and adjacent dockyards are in the oldest part of town, where the first storehouses, jail, and guardhouse were located. The Canadian vessel Margaret lies party submerged at the end of the jetty, where it came to rest in 1850. Be sure to stop by the **post office** (27180, where you can purchase intriguing stamps portraying penguins and shipwrecks, along with trout fishing licenses, amateur radio licenses, and commemorative coins. A poster in front of the building states what may well be the Kelpers' motto: "The Falkland Islands, Where Nature is Still in Charge." **Saint Mary's Roman Catholic Church** (21204, 12 Ross Road (across from the post office) is an early timber-framed building constructed in 1899; behind it is a long green-roofed building constructed in the 1840s as Marine Barracks. Many of the buildings in this area were constructed in the 1840s. The **Liberation Monument** between Cable Street and Reservoir Road, commemorates the islanders who gave their lives in the 1982 war.

The islanders' current pride and joy, the Falkland Islands Community School, opened in 1992 on a broad green at Ross and Reservoir Roads, at a cost of 14 million pounds. School is mandatory and free for children between the ages of 5 and 16; children in Camp attend small settlement schools or are educated at home. Teachers travel through Camp to check on students' progress, visiting individual settlements about once every six weeks. Those who wish to go on to college usually attend school in Great Britain; substantial government grants are available, and many of the graduates return to raise their families on the islands. The **Sports Center (** 21291 next door houses the island's first swimming pool, constructed in 1990, along with a gym, squash courts, and football field.

Gorse hedges surround **Government House**, which sits on a slight rise overlooking West Ross

was held in 1867; the annual Horticultural Show, held in February or March, is a lavish affair drawing competitors from the most remote parts of Camp.

The **Falkland Islands Museum and National Trust (** 27428, Holdfast Road just off Ross Road West, contains a fascinating hodgepodge of artifacts and exhibits covering the history of the Falklands Islands. Stuffed fur seals, guanacos, and sea lions dominate the nature collection, and the recreation of a Camp dental station complete with a drill powered by a foot treadle is enough to send shivers up your spine. Naturally, considerable space is devoted to the Falklands War, with exhibits including a reconstruction of an Argentine

Road. The house was originally constructed in 1845 under the direction of then-governor Richard Moody, whose simple vision of a stone governor's home has been altered many times over by successive residents. Several green-roofed buildings now sit in the compound, which also contains what is believed to be the oldest kitchen garden on the islands and the largest and loveliest conservatories (which are, unfortunately, closed to the public).

Islanders take great pride in their gardens; nearly every house in town has a front-yard bed of bright blossoms and a backyard plot of carrots, cabbages, and leeks. Roses, hollyhocks, California poppies, marigolds, and chrysanthemums burst forth in a riot of color throughout the more temperate months, and African violets and other houseplants provide a bit of green indoors year round. The Falkland's first vegetable competition

bunker complete with military rations and weapons. Other dioramas and collections cover the whaling industry, sheep farming in Camp, shipwrecks, and geology. The staff is forever adding items from the museum's considerable collection, and staff members are veritable fonts of facts and folklore.

Stanley's back streets are lined with homes and shops. The aptly named **Pink Shop (**/FAX 21399, 33 Fitzroy Road, is also known as "The Harrods of the Falklands." Travelers seeking souvenirs find everything they need here, including books, T-shirts, jewelry, homemade diddle-dee jam, and Tony Chater's books, calendars, and prints. **Home Industries (** 22750, 31 Fitzroy Road, is the best place to purchase locally made wool sweaters with penguin designs; **Falkland Farmers (** 21276 on

Adventurers hike through peat bogs, mud, and sharp rocks to reach penguin nesting grounds.

Davis Street East is stocked with waterproof clothing and rubber boots—essential supplies for those planning to trudge about Camp.

Once you've completed your Stanley tour you're pretty much finished with civilization. From here on out **wildlife** is the main attraction. Most visitors are particularly keen on spotting penguins, though there are plenty of other species worth discovering. Birders are entranced with the islands' preponderance of black-brown albatross; researchers believe over 680,000 breeding pairs build their nests of guano, mud, grass, and seaweed on the islands. Upland geese (which make regular appearances on dinner menus), peregrine falcons, caracaras, kelp geese, Falklands flightless steamer

particularly good at throwing darts, you may want to contact the **Darts Club** (21199 for information on the numerous darts tournaments.

Outside Stanley, East Falkland Island has several outlying settlements accessible by road or boat. **Goose Green**, a 40-minute drive west of Mount Pleasant Airport, was at the heart of the ground war in 1982, and is the site of the Argentine military cemetery. Nearby **Darwin** is on a narrow inlet linking East Falkland and the Lafonia Peninsula. Bodie Creek bridge, which some claim to be the southernmost suspension bridge in the world, connects Darwin and Goose Green. Continuing along the island's northwest shore on a dirt track one reaches **San Carlos**, where British forces first

ducks, red-backed buzzards, and Magellanic oystercatchers are all easy to spot. Six species of dolphin swim beside tour boats; fur seals, sea lions, and elephant seals bask in the sun on beaches and rocks.

Opportunities for **hiking** abound all around the islands. Hikers should wear sturdy hiking boots; knee-high rubber boots come in handy for wet landings on rocky shores and for hiking through swampy peat bogs. There are no national parks on the islands, and much of Camp is private land. For the most part ranch owners tolerate hikers, as long as they're well behaved. If you pass through fences and gates, be sure to close and lock them—no-one wants to race about herding wayward sheep.

Trout fishing is popular at Murrell River, within walking distance of Stanley; permits are available at the post office. If you happen to be

landed in 1982. The British military cemetery and a small museum are located here. On the north shore, **Salvador** sits near the mouth Port Salvador. The island's oldest sheep farm is located here, and five species of penguins have colonies nearby. **Volunteer Beach** on the northeast coast has the Falkland's largest king penguin colony; **Volunteer Point** has a large colony of southern fur seals. Tour operators in Stanley run trips through this region, which makes a good launching point for hikes to areas with macaroni, Magellanic, and gentoo penguin colonies.

West Falkland is nearly as large as East Falkland and is filled with touring possibilities. Lakes, ponds, mountains, and bogs provide endless opportunities for hardy trekkers. **Port Howard**, West Falkland's oldest farm and settlement, is home to about 40 residents. Most work at the 80,900-hectare (200,000-acre) farm where over

4,000 sheep and 800 cattle graze under the Hornby Mountains. Visitors learn everything they ever cared to know about sheep while touring the farm; the summer sheep shearing is a major event. A small museum contains paraphernalia from the 1982 war. Trout fishing is excellent here, and hikers who reach the top of 658-m-high (2,158-ft) **Mount Maria** are rewarded with superb views. A nine-hole golf course delights frustrated duffers. Sheep far outnumber humans on **Pebble Island** as well. A small settlement sits by a beach occasionally used as a landing strip; airplane remains from the 1982 war still litter the airstrip. Several small mountains dot the 39-km-long (24-mile) island, where wetlands attract breeding sea birds.

Elephant seals visit the appropriately named **Sea Lion Island** every spring to breed on sandy beaches, joining an abundant population of birds and animals. The island's farmers took particular care to preserve wildlife habitats from grazing livestock and other encroachments. Native tussock grass, which once covered most if the islands, still grows wild over one-fifth of the island, providing shelter for over 47 species of birds. Penguins, cormorants, and petrels are easily sighted, and killer whales swim offshore eyeing an abundance of food in the form of sea lions and leopard seals. Cruise ships and tour boats regularly stop at Sea Lion, the most southernmost inhabited island in the Falklands.

Lucky passengers on some cruise ships have the opportunity to wander about **West Point Island**, a haven for rockhopper and Magellanic penguins. Roddy and Lilly Napier, descendants

of the family who first purchased the island in the 1879, serve a lavish tea for tour groups. A similar spread greets visitors to **Carcass Island**, owned by Rob McGill. Penguins abound on Carcass, and McGill's farmhouse sits on a lovely spread surrounded by flowers and New Zealand palm trees.

Tony Chater, the author and photographer of *The Falklands*, moved from Great Britain to the Falklands in 1972 after answering a help-wanted ad for sheep ranchers. He has since become the islands' greatest chronicler and a co-owner of **New Island**. His neighbor, Ian Strange, is the author of *A Field Guide to the Wildlife of the Falkland Islands and South Georgia*. The most westerly of the Falklands, New Island is a breeding site for fur seals along with several species of penguins. In addition, cottontail rabbits introduced by New England sailors in the eighteenth century hop about the tussock grass. An old whaling station sits by the shore, inspiring Chater to write:

"…time has turned the slaughter, sweat and stench of the station to a romantic memory. The rusting bedsteads, lathes and boilers are now overgrown with yellow-flowered sea cabbage. Sheep graze amongst giant skulls, bits of baleen and bleached and crumbling vertebrae, and the whalemens' graves lie untended and undermined by rabbits and petrels."

WHERE TO STAY AND EAT

Travelers have a surprising array of accommodations to choose from when visiting the Falklands. There are about 150 beds in hotels, guesthouses, and lodges combined in Stanley and in Camp; some landowners will also allow visitors to pitch tents on their property. The **Falkland Islands Tourist Board (** 22215 FAX 22619 E-MAIL manager @tourism.org.fk WEB SITE www.tourism.org.fk, Shackleton House, Stanley, handles reservations at many places and can suggest alternatives when it seems all rooms are claimed.

Stanley has the most formal hotels and guesthouses and is the most practical base for short-term visits. The oldest hostelry is the **Upland Goose Hotel (** 21455 FAX 21520, 20-22 Ross Road, which has undergone several incarnations since it first opened in the mid-nineteenth century. Snapdragons and pansies bloom outside the bright white building, which houses 16 rooms, all but six with en-suite baths. The rooms have televisions, radios, tea and coffee makers and telephones, and are cozily furnished. Rates are in the moderate range and credit cards are accepted. The hotel's restaurant is the most formal in town, with green walls and velvet-covered chairs; the menu posted over the bar features pan-fried plaice (a local fish), chicken stir fry, mullet, mutton, and, as

Rubber boots are essential for wet landings on the pebble beaches of the islands.

might be expected, roasted upland goose. The hotel also offers a full afternoon tea with sandwiches, scones and tarts.

Another historic property, the **Malvina House Hotel** (21355 FAX 21357 E-MAIL malvina@horizon .co.fk, 3 Ross Road, first opened in the 1890s. The current hotel opened in 1983 and has undergone several improvements and expansions. All 18 rooms have private bathrooms, hairdryers, phones, and coffeemakers; some have televisions. A session in the hotel's hot tub and sauna cures most aches from cold, damp hikes. The hotel has a full restaurant and bar. Rates are in the moderate range.

Diners peer between lace curtains on the sun porch dining room at **Emma's Guesthouse and Restaurant** (21056 FAX 21573 E-MAIL emmas@ horizon.co.fk, 36 Ross Road, which overlooks the harbor. The eight rooms all have central heating and bathrooms with showers. The restaurant is open to guests only at breakfast and to the public at lunch and dinner. Rates are inexpensive. **Tenacres Tours** (21155 FAX 21950 E-MAIL tenacres @horizon.co.fk offers two centrally heated rooms with shared bath about a five-minute walk from Stanley. Several homeowners have guestrooms for rent as well; reservations are available through the tourist board.

A few non-hotel restaurants offer inexpensive homestyle cooking. As a rule, the food is hearty and tasty, though hardly of gourmet quality. Mutton and lamb are sold everywhere in ever-inventive preparations — mutton burgers are surprisingly tasty. Sea trout and mullet are also common; beef is a bit pricey. Vegetables come from kitchen gardens and Stanley's relatively new hydroponic garden, which provides islanders with salad greens and tomatoes throughout the year. Between meals, locals stop their work for "smoko," otherwise known as morning or afternoon tea — coffee or tea are taken with cakes and biscuits. **Shorty's Diner** (22855 on Davis Street serves beef and chicken burgers, hotdogs, curries, and pastas at lunch and dinner; beer and wine are available with meals. The restaurant is closed on Wednesdays. Fish and chips are the specialty of the **Woodbine Café** (21002 on Fitzroy Road; closed Mondays. The fragrance of freshly baked bread from **Stanley Bakery, Ltd.** (22692 on Philomel Street is nearly irresistible, especially after a long walk along the waterfront. Hot meat pies and burgers satisfy sudden hunger pangs.

A half-dozen pubs serve as the social hubs for islanders and guests. The gaily painted green, red, and white **Globe Tavern** (22703 on Crozier Place a block up from the Public Jetty serves sausage rolls and other snacks along with Guinness and even heartier drinks; locals bask in the summer sun in the outdoor beer garden. The Falkland's oldest pub is **The Rose** (21067 on Brisbane Road;

pool and darts provide competition at **The Victory Bar** (21199 on Philomel Street.

Travelers intent on fully experiencing the Falklands must spend at least a few nights in Camp. There are several lodges in Camp, some in quite remote areas where penguins and birds abound. Rates are usually in the moderate range; some lodges provide transportation while other will arrange boat trips and flights for an additional cost. Meals are sometimes included. If not, kitchen facilities are available; guests must bring in groceries from Stanley. Reservations for all the lodges can be made through the Tourist Board and travel agencies listed above; if you're on a tight budget ask if anyone is renting out rooms or cottages.

East Falkland has the Camp's best road system, infrastructure, and hotel selection. The **Blue Beach Lodge** (32205 FAX 32202 in San Carlos is accessible by road from Mount Pleasant Airport. The six rooms all have central heating; bathrooms are shared. Owners William and Lynda Anderson have perfected the art of Camp hospitality. William, a native islander, is a font of local lore. Lynda, who comes from Manchester, England, prepares bountiful meals. New in 2000, the six-room **Darwin House** (/FAX 32255 sits by Choiseul Sound on a narrow isthmus. Rooms are available in the main house, where the restaurant and bar are located. Two three-bedroom cottages have kitchen facilities. A paved road runs 56 km (35 miles) from the airport to the hotel, making it an easily accessible outpost.

On West Falkland, a farm manager's house has been converted into the **Port Howard Lodge**

(/FAX 42187 E-MAIL rlee@horizon.co.fk. Some rooms have private baths and central heating; meals are provided. Guests can take advantage of nearby fishing spots, go horseback riding in the mountains, and join boat and four-wheel-drive tours to wildlife areas. **Pebble Island Hotel** (/FAX 41093, on Pebble Island off the north shore of West Falkland, faces a white-sand beach and offers full board with its comfortable rooms. Six twin rooms have en-suite bathrooms; the two single rooms share a bath. All have central heating and tea and coffee-making setups. Tours are available. There are a few cottages available for rent as well, though you must bring in all food and supplies.

FAX 32003 can easily walk the length and width of the island to reach penguin rookeries and marvel at the sounds of breeding sea lions on the beaches. Most rooms have private baths and central heating.

HOW TO GET THERE

There are precious few flights to the Falklands' **Mount Pleasant Airport**, 56 km (35 miles) southwest of Stanley. Lan Chile operates one flight a week from Santiago and Puerto Montt, Chile; make reservations through the tour companies listed above (see GENERAL INFORMATION, above). The Royal Air Force provides passenger services

Several private islands offer accommodations for travelers. There are two self-catering cottages and a separate stone cottage available for rent on **Saunders Island** (41298 FAX 41296 E-MAIL davidpe @horizon.co.fk. A small store provides some necessities, but guests are advised to bring fresh bread and produce from Stanley. Diehard isolationists may prefer the island's primitive cabin located 16 km (10 miles) from the airstrip, though bathroom facilities are minimal (no shower, no hot water). The owners of **Weddell Island** (42398 FAX 42399 have a five-bedroom house and a three-bedroom cottage for rent to individuals or groups. Both have kitchen facilities, hot-water baths, and central heating. The McGill family at **Carcass Island** (41106 FAX 41107 has two cottages for rent.

Small and remote Sea Lion Island offers extraordinary opportunities for wildlife sightings. Guests at the **Sea Lion Lodge** (32004

on twice-weekly flights between the Brize Norton Air Base near Burford, England, and Stanley. For information and reservations contact the Falkland House in London or the Falkland Islands Tourist Board in Stanley (see GENERAL INFORMATION, above). At press time there were no flights between Argentina and the Falklands. Travelers are best off crossing to Punta Arenas, where flights depart at least once weekly for the Falklands.

The majority of visitors arrive via cruise ship; most ship itineraries include tours to penguin colonies in Camp and a few hours' stay in Stanley. See TAKING A TOUR, page 45 in YOUR CHOICE, for information on South Atlantic cruises.

The Clipper *Adventurer* sails along the shores of New Island beneath a whale-bone arch.

Travelers' Tips

GETTING THERE

The main airport for Argentina is **Aeropuerto Internacional Ezeiza** ((11) 4480-6111 in Buenos Aires, which receives flights from throughout the world. Some flights from other South American countries arrive at the smaller **Aeroparque Jorge Newberry** ((11) 4514-1515, by the waterfront in Buenos Aires. Several city airports around the country have international status, but receive precious few international flights. Flights to Santiago, Chile, do depart from Mendoza. Travel to Argentina is quite costly from outside South America; fares are lowest during the country's winter season.

Ask about ticket packages that include flights within the country. Aerolíneas Argentina, for example, offers an air pass with reduced fares for regional flights; the pass must be purchased in conjunction with your international ticket. Aerolíneas now works in partnership with American Airlines, passengers on either line can take advantage of the pass. Flights from the United States and Europe are often routed through Miami or New York, then on to Buenos Aires, sometimes with a detour to Santiago or Lima. Flying time from New York is about 12 hours, eight hours from Miami. Airlines serving Argentina include:

Aerolíneas Argentina ((11) 4340-3777 TOLL-FREE IN ARGENTINA (800) 2228-6527; in the United States TOLL-FREE (800) 333-0276; in the United Kingdom ((020) 7494-1001.

Air France in Buenos Aires ((11) 4317-4747.

All Nippon in Buenos Aires ((11) 4314-1600; in Japan ((03) 5435-0333.

Alitalia in Buenos Aires ((11) 4310-9999; in Italy (01) 4786-5642.

American in Buenos Aires ((11) 4318-1111; in the United States TOLL-FREE (800) 223-5436.

United Airlines in Buenos Aires ((11) 4316-0777; elsewhere in Argentina TOLL-FREE (800) 222-0777; in the United States TOLL-FREE (800) 241-6522.
Varig in Buenos Aires ((11) 4329-9211; in Brazil TOLL-FREE (800) 997000.

BORDER CROSSINGS

There are several border crossings between Argentina and Chile. Most involve crossing the Andes. The most popular is located near Mendoza at Libertadores; buses and *colectivo* taxis travel between Mendoza and Santiago, Chile, daily. Boats travel between the two countries in the Lake District at San Martín de los Andes and Bariloche. Obtain your Chilean visas and tourist cards at the embassy in Buenos Aires. The crossing between Tierra del Fuego and Punta Arenas is also popular. Travelers wishing to visit the Falkland Islands (Malvinas) while in the south are best off crossing to Punta Arenas, where flights depart at least once weekly for the Falklands.

Travelers frequently cross into Brazil at the Puerto Iguazú/Foz do Iguaçu crossing. Border crossings between Bolivia and Argentina are located in Salta and Jujuy. Ferries and hydrofoils cross the Río de la Plata from Buenos Aires to Colonia, Uruguay, where you can catch a bus to Montevideo. Paraguay can be reached by bus and/or river launch.

ARRIVING AND LEAVING

In most airports, a private company handles shuttle transportation—usually the cheapest way to get into the city. Shuttles in Buenos Aires stop at a main office; passengers are then transported in smaller vans to their hotels. Private taxis are lined up outside the airports. You can also rent a *remise*, or private car and driver, at desks in the airport.

Expect long lines when departing, even for regional flights. Be at the airport 90 minutes before a regional flight, and two and a half hours before an international one. Keep your passport accessible to show to airline clerks and customs officials.

Austral in Buenos Aires ((11) 4317-3605.
Avianca in Buenos Aires ((11) 4394-5990; in Colombia ((91) 410-1011.
British Airways in Buenos Aires ((11) 4320-6600; in Britain ((0345) 222-111.
Canadian Airlines in Buenos Aires ((11) 4322-3632; in Canada TOLL-FREE (800) 426-7000.
Iberia in Buenos Aires ((11) 4327-2739; in Spain (902) 400500.
KLM in Buenos Aires ((11) 4312-2660; in the Netherlands (20) 474-7747.
Lan Chile in Buenos Aires ((11) 4312-8161; in Chile 661-3651; in the United States TOLL-FREE (800) 735-5526.
LAPA in Buenos Aires ((11) 4812-1008.
Lufthansa in Buenos Aires ((11) 4319-0600.
Qantas in Buenos Aires ((11) 4515-4730; in Australia (131313.
Swissair in Buenos Aires ((11) 4319-0000; in Switzerland (0848) 800 7000.

VISA AND TRAVEL DOCUMENTS

All foreign visitors are required to carry a valid passport; citizens of the United States, the United Kingdom and Canada do not need a visa for stays of up to 90 days. Check with your consulate at home to see whether or not you will be required to obtain a visa before entering Argentina.

A honey-colored sunset tinges the façade of Cerro Torre in the Fitzroy Range.

CUSTOMS

Upon entering Argentina, those traveling directly by air or by ship will usually have smooth sailing through customs. Bus travelers can expect to open their luggage for custom officials. The international airports have recently introduced a "nothing to declare" system, allowing for a quicker venture through customs. Personal clothing and belongings are duty-free, including your computer and camera equipment, as long as they have been used. You may also bring in two liters of alcohol, 400 cigarettes, and 50 cigars, duty-free. After picking up your luggage, you'll be required to push a button beside a machine similar to a traffic light. If you get a green light, you'll be allowed to leave customs without having your luggage checked. Get a red light and you'll be opening your bags.

United States citizens who have been in Argentina for more than 48 hours and are returning to the States may bring with them US$400 worth of foreign merchandise without paying a duty. If you are over 21 you may bring back one liter of alcohol. Anyone may bring 200 cigarettes and 100 non-Cuban cigars. It is also allowable to mail home packages, up to US$200 worth of goods, with a limit of one shipment per address, per day. Make sure that you keep your receipts while shopping so that you can prove the worth of your goods when clearing customs.

EMBASSIES AND CONSULATES

ARGENTINE AUTHORITIES ABROAD

Australia ((02) 6282-4555/5855, MLC Tower, Suite 102, Woden, ACT 2606.
Canada ((613) 236-2351, 90 Sparks Street, Suite 620, Ottawa KIP 5B4.
France ((01) 4553-3300, Rue Cimarosa, 75016 Paris.
Germany ((496) 923-1050, Wiesenhuettenplatz 26, Eighth Floor, 6000 Frankfurt.
Italy ((06) 4201-0879, Via Veneto 7, Second floor, Rome.
Japan ((03) 5420-7107, 2-14-14, Moto-Azabu, Minato-Ku, Tokyo, Japan.
Netherlands ((02) 023-2723, Herengracht 94, 1015 BS, Amsterdam.
New Zealand ((04) 472-8330, Sovereign Assurance Building, Level 14, 142 Lambton Quay, Wellington.
Spain ((01) 442-4500, Paseo de la Castellana 53, Madrid 1, Madrid.
United Kingdom ((020) 7318-1340, 27 Three Kings Yard, London, W1Y 1FL.
United States ((212) 603-0400, 12 West 56th Street, New York, New York 10019.

Iguazú Falls marks the watery margin between Argentina and Brazil.

FOREIGN EMBASSIES IN ARGENTINA

Foreign embassies or consulates in Argentina, all in Buenos Aires, are:
Australia ((11) 4777-6580, Villanueva 1400.
Canada ((11) 4805-3032, Tagle 2828.
France ((11) 4312-2409, Avenue Santa Fe 846, Floors 3 and 4.
Germany ((11) 4778-2500, Villanueva 1055.
Israel ((11) 4342-1465, Avenue de Mayo 701.
Italy ((11) 4802-0071, Marcelo T de Alvear 1125.
Japan ((11) 4318-8200, Bouchard 547.
Mexico ((11) 4821-7172, Larrea 1230.
New Zealand ((11) 4328-0747, Carlos Pellegrine 1427.
Spain ((11) 4802-6031, Mariscal Ramón Castila 2720.
United Kingdom ((11) 4803-7070, Calle Luis Agote 2412.
United States ((11) 4777-4533, Calle Columbia 4300.

TOURIST INFORMATION

There are tourist information booths in most bus terminals, airports, and train stations. Most can provide a map and help arrange accommodations. General information on the entire country is available from the **Secretaría de Turismo de la Nación** ((11) 4312-2232 or (11) 4312-5550 TOLL FREE IN ARGENTINA (0800) 555-0016 FAX (11) 4313-6834 WEB SITE turismo.gov.ar, Avenida Santa Fe 883 in Buenos Aires. The office distributes a good country map and some general information brochures in Spanish and English.

Nearly every province in Argentina has a tourist information office in the provincial capital, and most tourist-oriented cities have information offices as well. Much of the information provided is in Spanish. Offices in the most popular tourist areas such as Ushuaia and Iguazú Falls employ English-speaking clerks, though their proficiency may be limited.

Many provinces also have information offices in Buenos Aires, and most are extremely helpful (though you can wait in line interminably to speak with a clerk). Most offer maps and brochures. Some also display and sell regional crafts; others will book hotel rooms for you. If you plan on traveling around the country plan to devote a day to visiting these offices while you're in Buenos Aires. You can usually pick up much of the same materials available in the local offices, and prepare for your visit during long bus and plane trips. Important regional offices in Buenos Aires include:
Buenos Aires ((11) 4371-3587, Avenida Callao 237.
Catamarca ((11) 4374-6891, Avenida Córdoba 2080.

Córdoba ((11) 4371-1668 FAX (11) 4476-2615, Avenida Callao 332.
Corrientes ((11) 4394-0859, Avenida San Martín 333, Fourth Floor.
Chaco ((11) 4476-0961 FAX (11) 4375-1640, Avenida Callao 322.
Chubut ((11) 4382-8126, Avenida Sarmiento 1172.
Entre Ríos ((11) 4328-9327, Calle Suipacha 844.
La Pampa (/FAX (11) 4326-0511, Calle Suipacha 346.
La Rioja (/FAX (11) 4815-1929, Avenida Callao 745.
Mar del Plata (/FAX (11) 4811-4466, Paseo la Plaza, Avenida Corrientes 1660.
Mendoza (/FAX (11) 4371-7301, Avenida Callao 445.
Misiones ((11) 4322-1671, Avenida Callao 445.

Río Negro ((11) 4371-7066 FAX (11) 4476-2128, Calle Tucumán 1916.
Salta ((11) 4326-2456, Avenida Peña 933.
San Luis (/FAX (11) 4822-3641, Calle Azcuenaga 1083.
Tierra del Fuego (/FAX (11) 322-8855, Avenida Santa Fe 919.

GETTING AROUND

BY AIR

Given the vast distance between destinations in Argentina, flying is often the most efficient way to get around the country, particularly if you are short on time. **Aerolíneas Argentina (** (11) 4340-3777 in Buenos Aires offers the most flights within the country, along with international flights. **Austral (** (11) 4317-3605 in Buenos Aires, and **LAPA (** (11) 4912-1008 in Buenos Aires offer flights to domestic destinations. Smaller regional lines come and go, and provide valuable links when up and running. One major drawback with regional flights is the lack of connections. You usually end up flying through Buenos Aires to get from one place to another.

Aerolíneas Argentina offers a Visit Argentina pass for internal flights on Aerolíneas and Aus-

tral. Flights must be booked and the pass purchased outside Argentina. A package of four tickets costs around US$500. Each ticket is good for one flight segment; if you are traveling between Córdoba and Ushuaia, for example, you will use two tickets as you must change flights in Buenos Aires.

Be sure to arrive at the airport at least 90 minutes before your flight, as the lines can be extraordinarily long and you may be required to queue up at several desks before finishing the check-in process. There is a departure tax for domestic flights.

BY BUS

Argentina has some of the finest buses and safest drivers I've ever seen in Latin America. Perhaps it's because bus travel is so popular and the most well-traveled routes are so very long. A travel agent once told me to purchase the most expensive bus seat I could afford; I now follow his advice religiously. The best buses are double-tiered, with seats on top and the luggage compartment and driver's seat in the bottom. They have reclining upholstered seats, clean toilets, and coffee and refreshment service. Movies are often shown on screens mounted above the front seats. Sit towards the back (but not close to the toilet) if you're bothered by noise. It's best to carry along snacks, water, and a sweater (the air-conditioning can be quite chilly). Buses usually make a 15-minute stop every six hours or so.

Hardy travelers often use the buses as hotel rooms, traveling at night and sleeping en route to their next destination. If you plan to sleep bring ear plugs and an eye mask — the movies often run through the night.

Purchase your tickets a day or two before you travel. If you're departing from Buenos Aires allow time to navigate the enormous terminal. Multiple bus lines serve the same routes and offer a baffling array of fares, which will surprise those accustomed to bus travel in other South American countries. It can cost almost US$100 to travel from Buenos Aires to Bariloche, for example. Still, it's far cheaper and easier to travel by bus than to rent a car.

BY CAR

Driving in Argentina is an adventure. Drivers seem to be puzzled by designated lanes, and prefer to straddle the line rather than commit to one lane. They switch back and forth as if no-one else were on the road, and treat red lights and stop signs as if they were suggestions rather than commands.

Toll highways are becoming more common between major destinations. Tolls are high; you can spend US$20 or more between Buenos Aires and Mar del Plata, for example. But you can save hours and even days by using them to follow the straightest, fastest route. Speeds are high (130 km per hour/80 mph in some places) in open country; again, local drivers consider posted speed limits to be mere suggestions. Speeding is common, but so are speed traps.

No matter how fast Argentines drive on the open road (usually in excess of 160 km/h or 100 mph), slower speeds are advised for anyone not used to these conditions. Never pass unless it's absolutely safe and be on the lookout for drivers coming in the opposite direction who are passing on a blind curve or other dangerous situations. If the vehicle in front of you

an annoyance than a threat. Young, attractive women or anyone else who can provide an interesting distraction may endure lengthy inspections.

Modern service stations are plentiful along all major routes. Many feature cafés or snack counters, convenience stores, long-distance telephone kiosks and sparkling clean restrooms. They're almost always full service, which means someone to pump the gas, check the oil and clean your windshield at no extra cost. Regular gasoline is called *nafta* or *común*; diesel is called *gas-oil*. Gas prices are roughly the same — about US$2 per liter for *nafta* — throughout Argentina. The only exceptions are cities near the Brazilian and Paraguayan frontiers, where low-priced competition

flashes its left-turn signal or indicator, it doesn't necessarily mean the driver is going to turn left — more likely it's a friendly signal that passing is safe.

Don't argue with traffic and highway police; uniforms hold great weight in Argentina. As a rule, the police inspire fear in those accustomed to military rule. Don't try to bribe the officer unless you're utterly convinced you're being taken for a ride. Even then, do so very discreetly by asking if you can pay the fee on the spot. It's better to say you'll be contacting your embassy or consulate for advice. The threat and hassle alone may discourage further extortion.

Police and military checkpoints are common at the borders between provinces. You may be asked to show your passport and rental car agreement or vehicle registration, and an officer may check your trunk. These stops are usually more

across the border drives Argentine gas prices down as much as 25%.

Don't drive at night, especially on rural roads. Street lights are virtually nonexistent, and some drivers prefer to conserve their headlights by not using them too often. Buses and trucks travel at extraordinary speeds in the dark, passing slower cars as if they were bugs on the road. Head-on collisions are common. Wandering cows are a concern day and night. Keep an eye out for *lomadas* (speed bumps) and *pozos* or *baches* (potholes).

As in many South American cities, driving in Buenos Aires can be a bewildering experience to the uninitiated. Drivers tend to be aggressive and unyielding. Also, private vehicles are banned in the financial district of downtown (bounded by

OPPOSITE: Young *porteños* share a joke at a Buenos Aires pub. ABOVE: Sidewalk cafés provide the perfect perspective on street scenes.

Leandro N. Alem, Avenida de Mayo, 9 de Julio and Corrientes Avenues) on weekdays from 7 AM to 9 PM. Only taxis, buses and cars with a special permit are allowed in these areas. My advice is to use public transport as much as possible while touring in the capital. If you do drive in a private car, wearing your seatbelt is mandatory.

Foreign licenses are valid in the capital and the province of Buenos Aires. Legally, you need an international license to drive in the rest of the country, though I've never seen a rental-car company or police officer ask for an international license. The **Automóvil Club Argentino** (ACA) ((11) 4802-6061, Avenue Libertador 1850, 1112 Capital Federal, can be a great asset to those

driving around the country extensively. If you plan to spend a month or more doing so, you may want to sign up for a membership (about US$30) which entitles you to good maps, free road service and towing, and discounts on accommodations. The ACA has offices all over the country, and decent hotels with reduced room rates at most major destinations.

Car Rental

Driving a rental car in Argentina is an expensive and time-consuming proposition. Car rental is available in all major cities and tourist destinations. Prices are relatively high compared to many countries: US$80 to US$100 per day in Buenos Aires and up to US$150 per day in Patagonia for a standard no-frills sedan. One way to save substantial money is pre-booking your car before arrival. Liability insurance is mandatory and will prob-

ably add about US$20 a day to the cost of your rental. Check with your credit card company to see if free insurance is included with car rentals in foreign countries.

Gas and tolls are both high. But distance is the most important factor in deciding whether to drive about the country. A stalwart tolerance for monotony is absolutely essential if you're driving through the pampas or Patagonia. I think the best way to get around the country is to use public transportation between major destinations and rentals cars within specific regions.

The following is a list of national car rental agencies in Buenos Aires:

Avis ((11) 4300-8201 TOLL-FREE (800) 331-1212 WEB SITE www.avis.com.

Budget ((11) 4311-9870 TOLL-FREE (808) 527-0700 WEB SITE www.budget.com.

Dollar ((11) 4393-5454 TOLL-FREE (800) 342-7398 WEB SITE www.dollar.com.

Hertz ((11) 4312-1317 TOLL-FREE (800) 654-3131 WEB SITE www.hertz.com.

Thrifty ((11) 4315-0777 TOLL-FREE (800) 367-5238 WEB SITE www.thrifty.com.

As a general rule, Avis seems to offer the best service.

ACCOMMODATION

I'm not impressed with the overall quality and selection of accommodations in Argentina; many travelers echo my sentiment. Few hotels in any price range stand out in one's memory; mostly they are serviceable, relatively comfortable, and unremarkable. Room rates are high in the big cities and major destinations, especially from November through February at the peak of national summer vacations. Rates are by far the highest in Buenos Aires, where a mid-range double room with a few frills such as direct-dial phones and cable television can cost upwards of $150 per night. Rooms are significantly cheaper in remote areas.

Almost all hotels offer complimentary Continental breakfast of some sort included in the room rate. Most private baths have a bidet. Some hotel operators are so fond of background music they pipe it into the rooms; others control the air-conditioning and heat from the front desk. The room tax (IVA) is a whopping 21%, sometimes included in the room rate. Ask in advance to avoid shocks.

More and more private ranches or *estancias* are opening their doors to overnight guests, with mixed results. Some are run as well as the standard European bed and breakfast; others offer little more than a bedroom in the family home. Since *estancias* are usually working or former ranch headquarters, they're often located far from the cities and towns. Transportation can be an expensive consideration. National tourists rely on them for weekend getaways, combining a drive in the country with peaceful lodgings and activities including horseback riding, hiking, and bird watching. Meals are usually included in the room rate.

Several organizations represent *estancias* around the country. It's important to gather as much information as possible before splurging on an overnight stay. Ask specific questions about meals, house rules, and available activities — all areas ripe for disappointment. Reservations are essential for all *estancias*; some require a deposit. Ask for specific directions to the ranch when making reservations, as most are located on remote rural roads.

Estancias Argentinas WEB SITE www.argentina-ranches.com.ar handles most of the *estancias* in San Antonio de Areco (one of the best places to experience the gaucho lifestyle) and several others around the country. Owner Patricia Acuña matches client's expectations with the appropriate lodgings remarkably well, and has a keen eye for properties with overinflated rates or inattentive service. **Comarcas** ((11) 4826-1130 E-MAIL comarcas@tournet.com.ar, Laprida 1380, Buenos Aires, represents several accessible and remote *estancias* in Buenos Aires Province. **Eco Aventura Travel** ((11) 4794-8200 FAX (11) 4794-8964, J.M. Estrada 3608, Buenos Aires, specializes in ranches that offer fishing, trekking, horseback riding, and other nature-oriented experiences.

Rates used in this book for a double room in high season are as follows:

Very Expensive	more than US$300
Expensive	US$200 to US$300
Moderate	US$100 to US$200
Inexpensive	less than US$100

EATING OUT

Argentina has the full gamut of restaurants. Fast-food franchises abound, especially in Buenos Aires, where it seems there's McDonald's on every corner. Beef in all its forms is ubiquitous; the national meal appears to be a steak (the larger the better) with salad and french fries. Thanks to the large population of Italian immigrants, pastas are nearly as prevalent. The abundance of Italian restaurants is a boon to vegetarians and those unaccustomed to eating meat at every meal. Actual vegetarian or health-food restaurants are harder to find, especially outside the main cities.

Certain restaurateurs in Buenos Aires are enamored with French and Continental cuisine, but precious few offer anything new and exciting. Regional Argentine dishes are given short shrift, except in the northern provinces. For a description of regional dishes see GALLOPING GOURMET, page 38 in YOUR CHOICE.

Breakfast is typically a light meal of coffee, juice, and *medias lunas*, pastries similar to croissants. During the week, lunch lasts just an hour or so

but can consist of a full meal with wine. On weekends, particularly Sundays, families linger over the midday meal for hours. The afternoon tea or coffee break is the most important part of the day.

Restaurants don't even open their door for dinner until 8 PM or 9 PM, and then diners consume enormous meals followed by coffee and dessert. Those accustomed to dining earlier can order sandwiches at a *confitería* or café.

Our restaurant prices are based on the average cost of a three-course meal per person, not including drinks.

Expensive	more than US$20
Moderate	US$10 to US$20
Inexpensive	less than US$10

BASICS

TIME

Argentina is three hours behind Greenwich Mean Time, one hour behind New York, and four hours later than Los Angeles.

MONEY

The currency in Argentina is the peso, with one peso roughly equal to an United States dollar. There are 100 centavos in a peso, with peso denominations of 100, 50, 20, 10, 5, and 2. Taxi drivers and shopkeepers sometimes study bills closely and refuse to accept any that might be counterfeit.

OPPOSITE: Elaborate murals cover the walls at the Galerías Pacífico in Buenos Aires. ABOVE: Catholicism is the main religion in Argentina.

Most businesses in Buenos Aires accept United States dollars; some take travelers' checks. Make sure that any dollars you want to spend are clean and not ripped, as damaged bills may not be accepted.

United States dollars will be less readily accepted in the more rural areas, so be sure to obtain some pesos either at your hotel, a bank, or a *casa de cambio* (money changer) before you leave the city.

Credit cards are accepted at all but the least expensive hotels in Buenos Aires and most major destinations. Most better restaurants also accept credit cards, but it's a good idea to ask before running up a large tab. Some businesses attach a *recargo* or additional fee for using a credit card.

ATMs or automatic cash machines are available in most major cities and tourist destinations. Many are located in a locked room that you can open by swiping your card through a slot in the doorway.

TIPPING

When it comes to tipping, waiters, bartenders, and tour operators all expect between 10% and 15%. Bellhops at mid-range to luxury accommodation expect US$1 to US$2 a bag and valets US$1 to US$2 whenever your car is delivered to you. Taxi drivers need not be tipped, although those who work primarily near the more luxury hotels seem to expect a tip.

TAXES

Argentina has a whopping 21% tax on all goods (except medicine and some foods) and services. This tax applies to gifts, medical services, hotel rooms, clothing, rental cars, and all other goods and services.

ELECTRICITY

The electric current in Argentina is 220 volts, 50 cycles alternating current (AC). An adapter and converter are necessary for American-made products. Wall outlets vary. Some accept plugs with two round prongs; others require a plug with one round prong and two slanted ones. Carry a collection of adapters.

WEIGHTS AND MEASURES

Argentina uses the metric system. For those unfamiliar with this system, here are some conversions to help you along:

Distance and Length
1 inch = 2.54 centimeters
1 foot = 0.305 meters
1 mile = 1.6 kilometers

Weight
1 ounce = 28.35 grams
1 pound = 0.45 kilograms

Volume
1 gallon = 3.78 liters

Temperature
To convert Fahrenheit to centigrade, subtract 32 and multiply by $\frac{5}{9}$.
To convert centigrade to Fahrenheit, multiply by 1.8 and add 32.

COMMUNICATION AND MEDIA

TELEPHONES

The country code for Argentina is 54. The phone system throughout the country was changed in 1999, creating massive confusion. All phone numbers received an additional digit; the number 4 now precedes all local calls. For example, the number for the Buenos Aires Tourist Information office was changed from 371-4045 to 4371-4045. In addition, the area code for Buenos Aires was changed from 1 to 11.

Similar changes occurred throughout the country, though the changes often do not appear in tourist information and brochures. The regions north of Buenos Aires now have a 3 at the beginning of their existing area codes; those to the south have a 2. The area codes for major destinations in Argentina are:

Buenos Aires   11
Bariloche   2944
Córdoba   351
Mendoza   261
Mar del Plata   223
Tierra del Fuego   2901
Iguazú Falls   3757
Jujuy   3882
Cafayate   3868
La Rioja   3822
Esquel   3945
Salta   287
Humahuaca   3877
Tucumán   281

Telephone calls are extraordinarily expensive in Argentina, and calls from most hotels are prohibitive. One hotel I stayed at in Buenos Aires charged 15 cents per minute for a local call; an-

other charged US$5 just to make a long-distance connection. Locals are as horrified by phone charges as visitors, and telephone boycotts occur every so often. The least expensive way to make a call is by purchasing a Telefónica card, sold in values of 10, 20, 30, and 50 pesos. Except in the most remote areas, you can usually find a public phone that accepts the card. The phone display will show you how much time you have left on your card after your call.

Telephone offices (*locutorios*) are common all around the country, and are frequented by locals who don't have phones in their homes or who wish to avoid the additional charges involved in calling from home. The operators at these offices are usually quite friendly and helpful; their services

OPPOSITE: The red-rock wilderness of Quebrada de Cafayate. ABOVE: Musicians of all ages perform in the streets of San Telmo.

come in handy when you can't figure out the changes in local numbers and area codes. The offices are extremely busy at lunch time and in the evenings; rates are lowest from 10 PM to 8 AM. You usually cannot make collect or credit card calls from the phone offices.

Access codes for the major phone card companies are:

AT&T   001-800-200-1111
MCI   001-800-333-111
Sprint   001-800-777-1111

To reach an international operator dial 000. To dial to another area code within the country, dial 0 first.

MAIL

Typically a letter takes one to two weeks to travel from Argentina to the United States, 10 to 15 days to the United Kingdom. An international airmail costs US$1. For UPS service in Buenos Aires, call ℂ (11) 4314-5321; for Federal Express, dial ℂ (11) 4325-6551.

INTERNET

Cybercafés are nearly as abundant as McDonald's in Buenos Aires, and many telephone offices have one or two computers hooked up to the net as well. Rates range from US$4 to US$8 per hour. The demand is heaviest at lunchtime and early evening. In more remote locales check at a *locutorio* for info on net availability; there's usually a computer or two somewhere.

MASS MEDIA

Newspapers

The *Buenos Aires Herald* WEB SITE www.buenos airesherald.com is Argentina's international newspaper, written in English. The printed version was founded in 1876. It reports on Argentina and the world, seven days per week, and can be found newsstands all over Buenos Aires. The *Herald* may arrive a day late in rural areas, but you can find a recent issue in most cities. The Sunday "Food & Wine" page and Friday "Get Out!" sections are particularly useful for travelers.

Clarín, published in Buenos Aires, claims the largest daily Spanish-language circulation. *La Nación* WEB SITE www.lanacion.com.ar, founded in 1870, is highly respected in Argentina, as well as by the international press.

Radio and Television

Local and national radio stations broadcast a lively mix of rock, easy listening, jazz, and tango music; many include English-language hits in their play lists. Television viewers can usually

get the Spanish-language edition of CNN and ESPN; English-language news is less common except in high-end hotels. Precious few have English-language movies. In most areas you can find an all-tango station, broadcasting film clips of great dancers from the past and listings of tango events.

HEALTH

There are no special inoculations required to enter Argentina and no special health hazards to be forewarned about. Your most serious threat will probably be diarrhea, a condition often accompanied by travel to a new and different country. The water, except in the most remote locales, is safe to drink. I have no problem drinking tap water in Argentina, and only need bottled water when the local stuff has an unpleasant taste. But queasy stomachs are no fun, especially when you're on

vacation. You may want to stick with bottled water in remote regions.

Altitude sickness, called *soroche* is a very real problem for anyone traveling from coastal Buenos Aires to the Andes. One can easily experience dramatic shifts in altitude frequently when traveling about the country; those most affected by such changes should shape their itineraries accordingly.

Drink plenty of water and little alcohol when in the mountains, where the altitude exacerbates the effects of liquor and the resultant hangovers. Take it slow the first day or two, and get plenty of rest. Try not to smoke. Hikers and climbers should pace themselves and ascend no more than 300 m (1,000 ft) per day when above 1,800 m (6,000 ft), and only 150 m (500 ft) per day when over 3,650 m (12,000 ft). If the symptoms are severe, get back to sea level and you should recover quickly.

EMERGENCIES

In a medical emergency dial (107 for help. To summon the police, dial (101, and if your emergency is a fire, call (100.

SECURITY

Porteños say Buenos Aires has become a dangerous city. It is certainly safer than it was during the Dirty War, when military officers and the police were virtual terrorists. But street crime has risen. Locals and tourists are both susceptible to pickpockets, especially the clever ones who squirt mustard or some other foul liquid on your clothing and offer to clean it off. They usually have a partner who deftly swipes your wallet, camera, and other valuables while you're distracted.

Argentina's Palacio del Congreso was designed to resemble the capitol building in Washington, DC.

I met a Dutch traveler in Buenos Aires who lost absolutely everything important — passport, travelers' checks, credit cards, cash—when she dashed to a McDonald's for a bite right after checking into her hotel. She hadn't locked up her valuables before running this quick errand and was carrying everything in her purse. I always keep my passport, plane ticket, credit cards and the bulk of my cash locked up in my hotel, and carry only a copy of my passport and the money I need for the day. When traveling about I keep most valuables and the passport copy in a money belt and my official passport in my purse readily available for officials. Hotel clerks have advised me to use a *remise* or private radio cab when traveling to the airport late at night; I always follow their advice.

WHEN TO GO

Argentina's climate is as variable as its terrain, with hot, muggy jungles and snowcapped mountains. The northern section is subtropical with rain throughout the year, while Tierra del Fuego in the south has a subarctic climate. The main central area is temperate, but can be hot and humid during the summer months (November to February) and cool in winter. The average daily temperature here is between 25°C (76°F) to 32°C (85°F) in summer and between 0°C (32°F) to 10°C (50°F) during the winter.

It's a bad idea to try to travel about the country in the height of summer (December through the end of January), as schools are closed and summer holidays are in full swing. The beach and mountain resorts are absolutely packed, and plane seats and hotel rooms are hard to come by. The summer heat is utterly miserable in Buenos Aires and in subtropical Misiones Province.

Nature lovers have the best chance of spotting whales and penguins in October and November, which is also a good time to visit Iguazú Falls. October, November, and late February and early March are the best months for traipsing about the entire country. School and work are in session, yet tourist facilities are open and the overall climate is pleasant.

WHAT TO TAKE

Buenos Aires is a cosmopolitan city and you should plan to wear casual, yet clean and neat clothes. Argentines tend to be spiffy dressers and don't usually wear shorts in the city except in the height of summer. Business suits are common for men and women. If you plan to dine in expensive restaurants or party in the flashier nightclubs bring at least one stylish outfit. For the most part, however, jeans, khakis, and simple dresses and skirts will suffice.

Though travel gear, clothing and books are available in Argentina, you're better off bringing these things with you. Pack lightweight, comfortable long pants, shorts, skirts, and shirts, and one warm jacket or sweater and thermal underwear for the higher elevations. A waterproof, breathable rain poncho is essential most times of the year for the subtropical rainforests of the lowlands. A small umbrella may come in handy as well, and you will need two pairs of sturdy walking shoes and lots of socks. Throw in a knee-high pair to wear under rubber boots, which you may need if you plan on visiting Tierra del Fuego or the Falklands.

Photography supplies are not overly expensive in Argentina, but it's still a good idea to bring all the film and batteries you might need. Disposable, waterproof cameras are convenient for boat and jungle trips.

Adventures in Argentina will probably include bug bites, as well as a scratch or two; your first-aid kit should include strong bug repellent (DEET), lotion for itches and stings, an antiseptic such as Bactine and gauze or bandages for covering wounds.

Foreign-language books are expensive, and used-book exchanges are hard to find.

LANGUAGE BASICS

The Spanish spoken in Argentina is unlike any other you've ever heard. Even fluent Spanish speakers have trouble understanding the Argentine accent, and slang, at first. Argentines proudly proclaim that they speak Castellano, with the "ll" pronounced as *zh* rather than *y* as is common in other Latin American countries. Argentines also use the pronoun *vos* rather than *tu*. Their style of speech seems almost Italian with flamboyant emphasis, plenty of hand gestures, and extraordinary speed. Still, travelers should attempt to speak Spanish as often as possible. Locals may have as much trouble understanding your accent as you have with theirs, but they do appreciate the effort.

English is Argentina's second language, and many *porteños* speak it fluently. English is less common outside the capital, though many tourist-oriented businesses employ a few workers with at least rudimentary knowledge of the language.

Below are some common Argentine words and phrases and general Spanish useful for travelers.

KEY WORDS AND PHRASES

beautiful   *bello(a)*, *hermoso(a)*
big   *grande*
can/may I...?   *¿puedo...?*
cheap   *barato(a)*
closed   *cerrado(a)*

cold *frío(a)*
do you have...? *¿tiene...? ¿hay...?*
do you speak English? *¿Habla usted inglés?*
excuse me *con permiso, desculpe, perdon*
expensive *caro(a)*
far *lejos*
get in line *haga fila*
good afternoon *buenas tardes*
good morning *buenos días*
good evening/night *buenas noches*
goodbye *adios / chau*
he/she/it is/you are *está*
hello *alo, hola*
here *aquí*
hot *caliente*

open *abierto(a)*
please *por favor*
right (direction) *derecha*
right there *allí*
see you later *hasta luego*
see you soon *hasta pronto*
small *pequeño(a) chico(a)*
straight on *derecho*
thank you (very much) *(muchas) gracias*
that *ese(a)*
there *allá*
there is/there are *hay*
this/this one *éste(a)*
welcome *bienvenidos*
well/good *bien/bueno*

how? *¿cómo?*
how are you? *¿cómo está?*
how many? *¿cuánto(a)s?*
how much is it? *¿cuánto vale? ¿cuánto es?*
I don't know *no sé*
I don't speak Spanish *no hablo castellano*
I don't understand *no entiendo*
I understand *entiendo*
I would like *quisiera*
I'm sorry *desculpe, lo siento*
Left (direction) *izquierda*
Money *dinero*
much, very, a lot (of) *mucho/a*
near *cerca*
new *nuevo(a)*
no *no*
none *ningun(o)*
OK/fine/I agree *está bien*
old *viejo(a)*

what? *¿qué? ¿como?*
where is? *¿dónde está?*
who? *¿quién?*
why? *¿por qué?*
Yes *sí*
you're welcome *de nada*

PLACES AND THINGS

airport *aeropuerto*
beach *playa*
bookshop *librería*
bribe *coima*
bridge *puente*
bus station *terminal de ómnibus*
bus stop *parada*
ATM *cajero automático*

Petrified "souvenirs" on sale at Puente del Inca
in the Andes.

cathedral   *catedral*
church   *iglesia*
cigarette   *cigarrillo*
cigar   *puro*
city   *ciudad*
complaint   *queja*
dam   *dique*
harbor, port   *puerto*
highway   *autopista, autovia*
highway, rural   *ruta*
lane or alley   *callejón*
market   *mercado*
mountain   *montaña*
mountain range   *cordillera*
museum   *museo*
nightclub   *peña*
pedestrian walkway   *peatonal*
person of mixed indigenous and Spanish blood   *criollo*
police station   *delegación*
post office   *oficina de correo*
river   *río*
road   *jirón*
street   *calle*
tax   *IVA*
tip   *propina*
tourist office   *oficina de turismo*
travelers' checks   *cheques de viajeros*
train   *tren*
viewpoint   *mirador*
weekly market   *feria*

FOOD AND RESTAURANTS

appetizers   *tapas*
avocado   *palta*
baked   *al horno*
bakery, cake shop   *panadería, pastelería*
barbecue   *asado*
beans   *frijoles*
beef   *carne de res*
beefsteak   *bistek, lomo*
beer   *cerveza*
beer, draft   *chopp*
bill, check   *cuenta*
blood sausage   *morcilla*
boiled   *hervido*
bread   *pan*
breakfast   *desayuno*
butter   *manteca*
cake   *torta*
carbonated water   *agua con gas*
charcoal grilled   *a la parrilla*
cheese   *queso*
chicken   *pollo*
chicken, boneless   *pollo deshuesado*
chicken, breast   *suprema*
cocktail   *trago*
coffee with milk   *café con leche*
cold cuts   *fiambres*

corn   *choclo*
crêpe   *panqueque*
dessert   *postre*
dinner   *cena*
eggs   *huevos*
fish   *pescado*
fixed-price menu   *menú ejecutivo*
fruit   *fruta*
fruit juice   *jugo de fruta*
garlic   *ajo*
glass   *vaso*
goat   *cabra*
goat, young   *chivito*
green salad   *ensalada verde*
grilled   *a la plancha*
grilled meat platter   *parrillada*
ham   *jamón*
hot sauce   *aji*
ice   *hielo*
ice cream   *helado*
kidneys   *riñones*
lamb   *cordero*
lobster   *langosta*
lunch   *almuerzo*
meat   *carne*
medium   *tres cuartos*
menu   *menú*
milk   *leche*
mineral water   *agua mineral*
mushroom   *champiñón/hongo*
octopus   *pulpo*
olives   *aceitunas*
onion   *cebolla*
orange   *naranja*
pepper   *pimienta*
pineapple   *ananá*
pork sausage   *chorizo or salchicha*
potatoes   *papas*
rare   *jugoso or rojo*
red wine   *vino tinto*
restaurant   *restaurante*
rice   *arroz*
rosé wine   *vino rosa*
salad   *ensalada*
salt   *sal*
sandwich   *sandwich*
sea bass   *corvina*
shrimp   *camarones*
soda   *gaseosa*
soup   *chupe*
spicy, hot   *picante*
squid   *calamar*
steak   *bife*
steak, flank   *churrasquito de entraña*
steak, short rib roast   *asado de tira*
steak, rump   *currasco de cuadril*
steak, sirloin   *bife do lomo*
steak, T-bone   *bife de costilla*
steak, thick cut   *bife de chorizo*
stewed   *estofado/a*

still water   *agua natural*
strawberry   *fresa*
sugar   *azúcar*
supermarket   *supermercado*
sweetbreads   *mollejas*
tea   *té*
trout   *trucha*
tuna   *atún*
udder   *ubre*
veal tripe or intestines   *chinchulin de ternera*
vegetables   *verduras*
watermelon   *sandía*
well done   *cocido*
white wine   *vino blanco*
wine list   *lista de vinos*

IN THE HOTEL

double room   *habitación doble*
room   *habitación, cuarto*
key   *llave*
laundry   *lavandería*
shower   *ducha*
single room   *habitación sencilla*
soap   *jabón*
toilet paper   *papel higiénico*
towel   *toalla*
with a bathroom   *con baño*
with a double bed   *con cama matrimonial*
without a bathroom   *sin baño*

ON THE ROAD

accident   *accidente*
brakes   *frenos*
bus   *autobus, ómnibus*
diesel   *diesel*
fill it up   *lleno*
gas   *gasolina, nafta*
lights   *luces*
oil   *aceite*
parking lot   *playa*
petrol station   *grifo*
pothole   *poszos, bache*
road   *calle*
tire   *llanta*
toll   *cuenta*
water   *agua*

Road Signs
detour   *desvio*
slow down   *despacio*
stop   *pare*

IN THE POST OFFICE

air mail   *por avión*
general delivery   *poste restante*
letter   *carta*
parcel   *paquete*

postcard   *tarjeta postal*
stamp   *sello, estampilla*

IN EMERGENCIES

altitude sickness   *soroche, apunarse*
clinic   *clínica*
cough   *tos*
diarrhea   *diarrea*
doctor   *médico(a), doctor*
fever   *fiebre*
flu   *gripe*
headcold   *resfriado*
healer   *curandera/o*
help   *ayuda*
hospital   *hospital*
I am allergic to   *tengo alergia a*
I am diabetic   *soy diabética*
I have a toothache   *tengo dolor de muela, me duelen
   los dientes*
It hurts   *duele*
nurse   *enfermera*
pain, ache   *dolor*
pharmacy   *farmacia*
sick, ill   *enfermo(a)*
stomach ache   *dolor de estomago*
sunburn   *quemadura del sol*

NUMBERS

1   *uno*
2   *dos*
3   *tres*
4   *cuatro*
5   *cinco*
6   *seis*
7   *siete*
8   *ocho*
9   *nueve*
10   *diez*
11   *once*
12   *doce*
13   *trece*
14   *catorce*
15   *quince*
16   *dieciséis*
17   *diecisiete*
18   *dieciocho*
19   *diecinueve*
20   *veinte*
21   *veintiuno*
30   *treinta*
40   *cuarenta*
50   *cincuenta*
60   *sesenta*
70   *setenta*
80   *ochenta*
90   *noventa*
100   *cien*
200   *doscientos*

500 *quinientos*	month *mes*
1,000 *mil*	year *año*
2,000 *dos mil*	
100,000 *cien mil*	
1,000,000 *millón*	
2,000,000 *dos millones*	

TIME

morning *mañana*
noon *mediodía*
afternoon/evening *tarde*
night *noche*
today *hoy*
yesterday *ayer*
tomorrow *mañana*
what time is it? *¿Qué hora es? ¿Qué horas son?*
now *ahora, ahorita*
later *más tarde*

CALENDAR

Monday *lunes*
Tuesday *martes*
Wednesday *miércoles*
Thursday *jueves*
Friday *viernes*
Saturday *sábado*

Sunday *domingo*
January *enero*
February *febrero*
March *marzo*
April *abril*
May *mayo*
June *junio*
July *julio*
August *agosto*
September *septiembre*
October *octubre*
November *noviembre*
December *diciembre*
spring *primavera*
summer *verano*
autumn *otoño*
winter *invierno*
day *día*
week *semana*

WEB SITES

Considerable information on Argentina is available on the web, though much of it is in Spanish. The sites are not necessarily accurate, however. The most extensive site is **www.turismo.gov.ar/g/menu.htm** provided by the Secretaría de Turismo. The site includes a wealth of information about the country, with listings for towns, tourist sites, activities, and suggested day trips. Text is available in English, French, Portuguese, Italian, German, Spanish. Other sites to visit are: **www.info.gov.ar** The web site for the Undersecretary of Public Administration of Argentina is for those interested in the Argentine government. There is good information here, with links to the government web sites for the provinces and municipalities.

www.**surdelsur**.com/ Maintained under the auspices of the National Department of Culture for Argentina, this site is available in both English and Spanish and provides information on the geography, history and art of the country.

http://**grippo**.com/**index**.htm Argentina's search engine with categories for the arts, business, health and tourism, as well as search capabilities for the Argentine Internet.

www.**buenosairesherald**.com Argentina's English-language newspaper site is updated every Monday.

www.**travel**.state.gov/**argentina**.html The United States government's fact sheet for Argentina

FRANCE, MIRANDA. *Bad Times in Buenos Aires*. London: Weidenfeld & Nicholson, 1998.

GREENE, GRAHAM. *The Honorary Consul*. New York: Simon & Schuster, 2000.

GUEVARA, ERNESTO CHE. *The Motorcycle Diaries*. London: Verso, 1995.

HUDSON, W.H. *Idle Days in Patagonia*. New York: AMS Press, 1968.

MARTÍNEZ, TOMÁS ELOY. *Santa Evita*. New York: Knopf, 1996.

PERÓN, EVA. *In My Own Words*. New Press, 1996.

PUIG, MANUEL. *Kiss of the Spider Woman*. New York: Knopf, 1979.

SHAW, EDWARD. *At Home in Buenos Aires*. Abbeville Press, 1999.

includes entry requirements, warnings, and health information.

Recommended Reading

AIRA, CESAR et al. *Argentina: The Great Estancias*. Rizzoli, 1995.

BORGES, JORGE LUIS. *Labyrinths: Selected Stories & Other Writings*. New York: New Directions, 1964.

CHATER, TONY. *The Falklands*. St. Albans: The Penna Press, 1993.

CHATWIN, BRUCE. *In Patagonia*. New York: Penguin, 1988.

CORTAZAR, JULIO. *The Winners*. New York: Pantheon, 1965.

DARWIN, CHARLES. *Voyage of the Beagle*. New American Library, 1996.

FIETLOWITZ, MARGUERITE. *A Lexicon of Terror*. Oxford University Press, 1998.

STRANGE, IAN. *A Field Guide to Wildlife of the Falkland Islands and South Georgia*. New York: HarperCollins, 1992.

THEROUX, PAUL. *The Old Patagonian Express*. London: Hamish Hamilton, 1979.

THORNTON, LAWRENCE. *Imagining Argentina*. New York: Bantam, 1991.

TIMMERMAN, JACOBO. *Prisoner Without a Name, Cell Without a Number*. New York: Vintage, 1988.

WILSON, JASON. *Buenos Aires: A Cultural and Literary Company*. New York: Interlink Books, 2000.

OPPOSITE: A tapir strikes a noble pose at the Complejo Ecológico in Roque Sáenz Peña.
ABOVE: Patrons are apt to ask, "What's the beef?" in Salta's central market.

Quick Reference A–Z Guide
to Places and Topics of Interest with
Listed Accommodation, Restaurants and
Useful Telephone Numbers

The symbols Ⓕ FAX, Ⓣ TOLL-FREE, Ⓔ E-MAIL, Ⓦ WEB-SITE refer to additional contact information found in the chapter listings.

Photo Credits

All pictures were taken by Robert Holmes except for those by:

Brian McGilloway: Page 248 and 266. **Markham Johnson:** Page 249, 251 and 255. **Maribeth Mellin:** Pages 257, 261, 263, 264 and 267.